Contemporary Irish Social Policy

Social policy in Ireland

Other titles published by UCD Press:

Irish Social Policy in Context
edited by GABRIEL KIELY, ANNE O'DONNELL,
PATRICIA KENNEDY and SUZANNE QUIN

Disability and Social Policy in Ireland
edited by SUZANNE QUIN and BAIRBRE REDMOND

Theorising Irish Social Policy
edited by BRYAN FANNING, PATRICIA KENNEDY,
GABRIEL KIELY and SUZANNE QUIN

Mental Health and Social Policy in Ireland
edited by SUZANNE QUIN and BAIRBRE REDMOND
(forthcoming, 2005)

Contemporary Irish Social Policy

edited by
Suzanne Quin
Patricia Kennedy
Anne Matthews
Gabriel Kiely

University College Dublin Press

Preas Choláiste Ollscoile
Bhaile Átha Cliath

First published 1999
Second edition 2005
University College Dublin Press
Newman House
86 St Stephen's Green
Dublin 2
Ireland

www.ucdpress.ie

ISBN 1-904558-30-5

Cataloguing in Publication data
available from the British Library

Typeset in Ireland in
Adobe Garamond and Trade Gothic by
Elaine Shiels, Bantry, Co. Cork
Text design by Lyn Davies
Index by Jane Rogers
Printed on acid-free paper in England
by Creative Print & Design Ltd

Contents

Health Boards

Important note
Since January 2005, the administration of the health services
has been taken over by the Health Services Executive and the
term 'health board' is no longer in use.

Contributors to this volume

PATRICK CLANCY is an Associate Professor of Sociology and Dean of the Faculty of Human Sciences at University College Dublin. He was a member of the Secretariat of the National Education Convention and served on a variety of advisory boards and education policy committees. He is a graduate of St Patrick's College, Drumcondra, University College Dublin and the University of Toronto.

ANTHONY COTTER is an assistant principal probation and welfare officer and is currently responsible for probation and welfare services in Dublin. He also has responsibility for the development of policy for the management of sex offenders in the community. He is a member of the Social Work Qualifications Board, holds a Master's degree in Social Science from University College Dublin and has been an associate lecturer on the Crime, Order and Social Control Course at the Open University.

NIALL CROWLEY is chief executive of the Equality Authority. He previously worked in the non-governmental sector with Pavee Point and the Community Workers' Co-operative. He has been a member of the National Economic and Social Forum and the National Economic and Social Council.

EITHNE FITZGERALD has taught social policy in University College Dublin and Trinity College, Dublin. She was Minister of State for Finance and Minister of State for Labour Affairs and is now senior research officer at the National Disability Authority.

PATRICIA KENNEDY is a senior lecturer in Social Policy in the Department of Social Policy and Social Work, University College Dublin. She co-founded the Irish Social Policy Association in 1997. Her books include *Maternity in Ireland: A Woman-Centred Perspective* (2002) and *Motherhood in Ireland: Creation and Context* (2004).

ELIZABETH (LIZ) KIELY is a lecturer in Social Policy in the Department of Applied Social Studies in University College Cork. Her main teaching and research interests are in youth policy, research methodology and women's studies. She was awarded her PhD by the National University of Ireland.

GABRIEL KIELY is Professor of Social Policy and Social Work at University College Dublin and Jean Monnet Professor of European Family Policy. He was the Irish member of the European Observatory on the Social Situation,

Demography and the Family until 2003. He is a contributor to the *International Encyclopedia of Marriage and Family*. He has also served on numerous national and international committees dealing with social work, social policy and family policy.

HILDA LOUGHRAN is a lecturer in the Department of Social Policy and Social Work, University College Dublin. She worked for many years in the alcohol services in the Dublin area. Her areas of interest include alcohol and drugs policy, social work education and research. She is a member of the Irish Association of Alcohol and Addiction Counsellors, Irish Association of Social Workers, and the International Motivational Interviewers Network Trainers (MINT).

ANNE MATTHEWS is a lecturer in Nursing and Health Policy at the School of Nursing, Dublin City University. Her research interests are in the areas of health policy, childbirth and midwifery.

FRANK MILLS is a Director of Social Inclusion, Mental Health Services, for the Health Service Executive, South Western Area. He is a social policy analyst with a particular interest in income maintenance, who has lectured part-time on social policy in University College Dublin and the Institute of Public Administration.

JOE MORAN worked with refugees and asylum seekers in the public and voluntary sector for almost ten years. He currently teaches social policy at the Waterford Institute of Technology and at the Institute of Technology, Carlow – Wexford Campus. He studied at University College Cork, Trinity College, Dublin, University of Liverpool and the Institute of Public Administration.

ANNE O'LOUGHLIN is principal social worker in St Mary's Hospital, Phoenix Park, Dublin. Her social work career has been in the geriatric medicine service of North Dublin City and County. Her main area of interest is in elder abuse. She is working on a PhD thesis on elder abuse in long-term care. She was formerly President of the Irish Association of Social Workers.

SUZANNE QUIN is a senior lecturer in Social Policy and Social Work and Director of the PhD in Social Work Structured Programme, University College Dublin. She has worked in St Vincent's Hospital, the Eastern Health Board and as Head of the Social Work Department in the National Rehabilitation Hospital. She has also lectured in social policy at Trinity College, Dublin and the Institute of Public Administration.

BAIRBRE REDMOND is a lecturer in Social Policy and Social Work and Associate Dean of Teaching and Learning, Faculty of Human Sciences at University College Dublin. She is Chair of the Complaints Committee of the Advertising Standards Association of Ireland and she is also a member of Private Residential Tenancies Board of Ireland. She was awarded her PhD by the National University of Ireland.

PADRAIG REHILL is employed by the Health Service Executive. He worked as a community welfare officer in Dublin city centre and as a superintendent social welfare officer in the Asylum Seekers Unit. In 2001 he was appointed social inclusion manager in the South Western Area Health Board for the Dublin West Area. He holds an MA in Adult and Community Education from St Patrick's College, Maynooth.

VALERIE RICHARDSON is a senior lecturer in the Department of Social Policy and Social Work, University College Dublin. She is the Irish expert on the European Observatory on the Social Situation, Demography and the Family. A graduate of the University of Wales, she undertook her postgraduate professional training in social work in the University of Edinburgh, and was awarded her PhD by the National University of Ireland.

DAVID SILKE works in the National Economic and Social Forum as a policy analyst. His particular areas of interest are equality and social inclusion, housing and issues regarding older people. He worked as a research officer in the Combat Poverty Agency and as a senior research officer in the Analytical Services Division of the Department of Social Security (UK). He is a graduate of University College Dublin and of the London School of Economics.

Abbreviations

ADM	Area Development Management
AG	Attorney General
ASTI	Association of Secondary Teachers of Ireland
CAB	Criminal Assets Bureau
CADs	Community Actions Against Drugs
CAO	Central Applications Office
CE	Community employment
CMRS	Conference of Major Religious Superiors
CORI	Conference of Religious in Ireland
CPI	Consumer Price Index
CSO	Central Statistics Office
DASS	Directorate for Asylum Support Services
DICP	Dublin Inner City Partnerships
DIT	Dublin Institute of Technology
DJELR	Department of Justice, Equality and Law Reform
DPP	Director of Public Prosecutions
ESF	European Social Fund
ESLI	Early School Leaver Initiative
EMCDDA	European Monitoring Centre for Drugs and Drug Addiction
ESRI	Economic and Social Research Institute
EU	European Union
FÁS	Foras Áiseanna Saothar
FETAC	Further Education and Training Awards Council
FLAC	Free Legal Advice Centre
GAIE	Gross Average Industrial Earnings
GMS	Traveller chapter
GNP	Gross National Product
HCSL	Home–School–Community–Liaison Scheme
HEA	Higher Education Authority
HMSO	Her Majesty's Stationery Office
HRB	Health Research Board
IBEC	Irish Business and Employers Confederation
ICCL	Irish Council for Civil Liberties
ICON	Inner City Organisations Network
ICT	Information and Communication technologies
ICTU	Irish Congress of Trade Unions
IFA	Irish Farmers Association
IFUT	Irish Federation of University Teachers

IILT	Integrate Ireland Language and Training
ILO	International Labour Office
INOU	Irish National Organisation of the Unemployed
INTO	Irish National Teachers Organisation
IOT	Institute of Technology
IPA	Institute of Public Administration
IRB	Irish Republican Brotherhood
IRCHSS	Irish Council for the Humanities and the Social Sciences
IRCSET	Irish Research Council for Science, Engineering and Technology
ISPCC	Irish Society for the Prevention of Cruelty to Children
ISME	Irish Small and Medium Enterprises Association
IWA	Irish Wheelchair Association
LCA	Leaving Certificate Applied
LES	Local Employment Service
LR	Live Register
NAPS	National Anti-Poverty Strategy
NCCA	National Educational and Psychological Services
NCEA	National Council for Educational Awards
NCO	National Children's Office
NCUA	National Council for Vocational Awards
NDA	National Disability Authority
NESC	National Economic and Social Council
NESF	National Economic and Social Forum
NFYC	National Federation of Youth Clubs
NIHE	National Institute of Higher Education
NPC	National Parents' Council
NQAI	National Qualifications Authority of Ireland
NRB	National Rehabilitation Board
NSPCC	National Society for the Prevention of Cruelty to Children
NUI	National University of Ireland
NYCI	National Youth Council of Ireland
NYF	National Youth Federation
NYP	Neighbourhood Youth Projects
OECD	Organisation for Economic Co-operation and Development
PAYE	Pay As You Earn
PES	Principal Economic Status
PESP	Programme for Economic and Social Progress
PLC	Post Leaving Certificate
PRSI	Pay Related Social Insurance
PRTLI	Programme for Research in Third-Level Institutions
QNHS	Quarterly National Household Survey
RIA	Reception and Integration Agency

RTC	Regional Training College
SIPTU	Services Industrial Professional Technical Union
SMI	Strategic Management Initiative
SSI	Social Services Inspectorate
SSRI	Stay in Schools Retention Initiative
STIAC	Science, Technology and Innovation Advisory Council
SWA	Supplementary Welfare Allowance
TCD	Trinity College, Dublin
TUI	Teachers Union of Ireland
UCC	University College Cork
UCD	University College Dublin
VEC	Vocational Education Committee
VHI	Voluntary health Insurance Board
VLTU	Very Long-term Unemployed Programme
VTOS	Vocational Training Opportunities Scheme
WHO	World Health Organisation
YEP	Youth Encounter Projects
YMCA	Young Men's Christian Association

Chapter 1

Introduction: social policy in contemporary Ireland

The first edition of *Contemporary Irish Social Policy* and its companion volume *Irish Social Policy in Context* were published in the last year of the old millennium, a time associated with rapid social change and unprecedented economic growth that earned Ireland the nickname of the 'Celtic Tiger'. Anyone who might be under the illusion that social policy is a static phenomenon will be surprised by the changes that have taken place in the different areas addressed in the chapters in this volume over a relatively short timeframe from the first to the second edition of this volume. In putting together this revised edition, the editors approached each of the original contributors to request an update of their chapters. It was very fortunate for us that all but two of the original contributors were in a position to do so and the remaining two chapters were updated in collaboration with the original author. This meant a level of continuity between the two editions so that those interested in the development of policy in a particular area can read the relevant chapters in each edition for an even fuller understanding of the evolution of policy over time and the impact of the social and economic circumstances in which it occurs.

The period of rapid economic growth provided the opportunity for the creation and development of social policies which contributed to the quality of life of all citizens and ensured that each sector of society benefited. That this does not happen automatically becomes evident from the different chapters. Fitzgerald in chapter 6 quotes Lemass's assumption that a rising tide will raise all boats. That this is not so is illustrated by Fitzgerald in relation to the long-term unemployed, Silke (chapter 4) on those who are homeless or at the lowest end of the housing market and Crowley (chapter 11) in relation to Travellers. The last provides a graphic account of deprivation in the midst of relative plenty, while Silke shows how substantial economic growth can even result in a deterioration of conditions for those caught at the lowest end of the housing sector.

The early years of this century have seen a slowing down of the high levels of economic growth achieved in Ireland in the latter part of the 1990s. Associated with this has been the gradual reduction in migration and a slowing down in the numbers of refugee and asylum seekers coming to Ireland. Overall, this has presented the opportunity for consolidation and policy development that can be difficult in periods of rapid change. Whether or not this window of opportunity has been used has varied from one policy area to another, as is apparent in the individual chapters. In regard to income maintenance, for example, Rehill and Mills (chapter 2) point to a real increase of 58 per cent in expenditure on income maintenance in the decade from 1993 to 2002 which was three times greater than the rate of increase in the consumer price index. Unlike previous decades, this increase was not accounted for by rising rates of unemployment but rather reflected an overall increased rates of benefit and the easing of qualification criteria in benefits such as those for carers.

An important change to be noted also is the declining power, influence and service capacity of the Roman Catholic Church which, in most of the last century, had played a major role directly and indirectly in many areas of social policy in Ireland but particularly in the fields of educational provision (see Clancy, chapter 5), childcare (see Richardson, chapter 8), youth policy (see Kiely and Kennedy, chapter 9) and health care (see Quin, chapter 3). Over the decades of the twentieth century, it had acted as a conservative, tradition-alist force, as a service provider, a service innovator while, at times, also acting as a critical voice in regard to service provision for vulnerable groups such as the homeless.

An overriding theme of social policy in Ireland over the past decade has been the development of the Strategic Management Initiative (SMI) in the public sector overall. This has resulted in a shift from reactive responses to social issues as they arose to a focus on the development of policy strategies in each of the policy areas. In contrast to the previous decades, a substantive number of policy documents now exists, ranging from those that are broad in focus setting out the thrust and parameters of policy (such as the National Children's Strategy, 2000) to those which address specific aspects within it. In the sphere of education (chapter 5), for example, the White Paper 1995 which set out the future directions of education policy was followed by policy documents on different aspects of education policy such as early childhood education, adult education, access to third-level education and the future of the third-level sector. In relation to health policy (chapter 3), the two broad strategy documents of 1994 and 2001 have been followed by policy documents on aspects of health care such as women's health, cancer services, palliative care, the health of Travellers and health promotion.

However, the creation of policy documents does not guarantee that they will result in changes in actual provision of services in line with the recom-mendations and even commitments contained within them. The lack of translation between policy and the development of services is reflected in a number of chapters such as Kiely and Kennedy's (chapter 9) in relation to youth services and Cotter's (chapter 13) regarding development of alternatives to custodial sentences in the criminal justice system. Crowley in chapter 11 on social policy and Travellers makes the point that a decade of widespread and innovative policy thinking and policy making in relation to this group is not reflected in the level of change in their social situation and experiences.

The shift from a monocultural to a multicultural society is no longer a new phenomenon in Irish society. However, time has not necessarily resulted in greater acceptance of ethnic minorities and the development of services to facilitate integration. On the contrary, Moran in chapter 12 argues that policy has shifted from a relatively benign approach, albeit with few services in place, to a policy characterised by containment, restriction and emotional distance for those seeking a new beginning in a country which, as Moran points out, might be expected to be a great deal more welcoming given its own history of emigration.

Along with the change to a multicultural society, other social and demographic changes in Irish society have reflected overall international trends. The growing participation of women in the workforce (Fitzgerald, chapter 6) has implications for the provision of childcare (see Richardson, chapter 8), for those with physical dependency arising from disability or those with a serious learning disability (see Quin and Redmond, chapter 7) and for older people in need of care (see O'Loughlin, chapter 10). This has consequences for the policy of community-based care in health and personal social services which has been based on the assumption of availability and willingness on the part of one sector of society to forgo gainful employment in order to provide largely unsupported care. The policy also makes assumptions for those on the receiving end, as O'Loughlin (chapter 10) points out, that older people prefer family care.

The assumption of altruism in the face of social and economic change is a good example of how social policies can be based on principles, expectations and assumptions about what is appropriate and desirable. In some aspects of social policy there has been seemingly wide acceptance of what are appropriate and desirable goals. Silke's chapter on housing (chapter 4) illustrates this in regard to home ownership. He shows the extent to which pursuance of this policy has resulted in significant attainment of the desired goal, but at a high cost to consumers in a time of rapidly increasing house prices and in costs to the exchequer in subsidies given and income foregone. The greatest costs, however, have been borne by those unable to enter the housing market either into home ownership or the relatively small and heavily subsidised public sector. Further examples of the focus on accepted 'givens' is the continuing public/private mix in the education sector (see Clancy, chapter 5) and the health sector (see Quin, chapter 3) in spite of the clear inequalities created and perpetuated by this dual approach.

The impact of changing demography is of significance for the provision and development of hitherto relatively neglected areas of Irish social policy.

Clancy (chapter 5) refers to the decline in numbers of those enrolled in primary and secondary level education as an opportunity to develop second chance education to a much greater extent than exists at present. He points to the marked achievement of education policy in recent years in that around 50 per cent of those leaving second level now go on to some form of third-level course. At the same time, overall levels of adult literacy is a cause for concern with the OECD finding that 25 per cent of the Irish population are operating at the minimum level of literacy. This clearly shows the importance of developing second chance education for the broad reasons of social citizenship and participation along with increasing employment chances in the context of an employment market where there are few opportunities for the non-literate and unskilled worker (see Fitzgerald, chapter 6). Indeed, as Fitzgerald points out, the direct relationship between educational achievement and the probability of employment means that measures to prevent early school leaving offers high economic as well as social returns.

As in other countries, older people in Ireland constitute a growing sector of the population, albeit to a lesser extent than in other EU countries such as Germany, France and the UK. The disproportional increase in the 'old elderly' is likely to place increased demands on health and, even more particularly, on personal social services for this group as described by O'Loughlin (chapter 10). Furthermore, she highlights growing concern about the abuse of older people in both domestic and alternative care contexts, a topic which, she states, is slowly making its way onto the political agenda. The issue of abuse has long been a focus of services at the other end of the age spectrum. Richardson (chapter 8) charts the development of services for children based on changing recognition of the needs of children and the different forms that abuse and neglect can take. Neglect of the social needs of young people, especially those in deprived urban and underdeveloped rural areas, are highlighted in the chapter on youth policy by Kiely and Kennedy (chapter 9). The costs of not recognising and not responding to such needs is demonstrated by Cotter (chapter 13) in relation to criminal behaviour and its consequences and Loughran (chapter 14) in respect to drug abuse.

Changes in thinking and attitudes can lead to the redefinition of a social issue and its solution on the part of those concerned. This is evident in chapter 7 by Quin and Redmond in relation to disability. The growth of a consumer voice with its emphasis on rights to services has so far failed to be translated into rights-based legislative provision for this group. The shift in focus from a medical model of service provision to a social model of disability is clear. So too is the evidence that the media plays an increasingly important role in both putting and maintaining a social issue on the policy agenda. Loughran (chapter 14) refers to the power of the media to serve as a catalyst for marshalling public opinion and to create pressure for particular action.

This impact is not always positive in its effects. For example, as Loughran points out, certain events can be sensationalised and create an environment where there is pressure to respond to specific cases rather than to overall patterns. On the positive side, the impact of the Special Olympics demonstrated the value of combating negative stereotypes with positive images of achievement and inclusion (see Quin and Redmond, chapter 7).

The continuing challenge is to use such opportunities to secure the commitment and resources needed to create a multidimensional range of services informed by the voice of consumers. This is also evident in the development of services for children and families. Richardson (chapter 8) describes the beginning of the twenty-first century as being characterised by increasing commitment on the part of professionals and the state to listen to children, to involve them and their families in decisions regarding their welfare and to move towards a children's rights perspective in policy and practice. The involvement of a number of government departments and other statutory and non-governmental agencies is essential in developing comprehensive services for vulnerable children.

It is the very interrelationship between different aspects of social policy which makes a multidimensional approach to the solution of social issues so important. Examples of the connectedness between different areas identified in this book are the relationship between early school leaving (Clancy, chapter 5) and the subsequent risk of long-term unemployment (Fitzgerald, chapter 6). Another is the effect of homelessness or of poor quality housing (Silke, chapter 4) linked to poverty (Rehill and Mills, chapter 2), criminal behaviour (Cotter, chapter 13) and poor health (Quin, chapter 3), and the link between poverty (Rehill), youth (Kiely and Kennedy, chapter 9), criminal behaviour (Cotter) and drug abuse (Loughran, chapter 14). Each of the chapters reflects the importance of recognising this interrelationship as expressed in Cotter's comment that the changes needed to address crime effectively must happen both within and beyond the criminal justice system. Recognition of the importance of a multisectoral approach to addressing social problems is reflected in the partnership models developed between different elements of state provision and non-government agencies (for example, in the area of family support described by Richardson (chapter 8) and the National Drugs Strategy 2001–8 discussed by Loughran, chapter 14), in the National Anti-Poverty Strategy first launched in 1997, revised in 2002 which is referred to in a number of the chapters, as well as the EU requirement that each member state must draw up a national action plan against poverty and social exclusion every two years.

Readers who are interested in pursuing the contextual influences which have impacted on the development of the many areas of social policy contained in this book are referred to its companion text *Irish Social Policy in*

Context. The factors which have shaped current policy – the impact of the EU on policy development, the changing social climate and the growing participation of service users – are considered at length in that volume. A further volume in this series recently published is *Theorising Irish Social Policy* (edited by Fanning, Kennedy, Kiely and Quin). Taken separately and together, these three texts offer the reader a reference point for understanding current Irish social policy, the elements which have forged its creation and development, and the challenges facing it in the early decades of this century.

Chapter 2

Income maintenance

Padraig Rehill
Frank Mills

Introduction

This chapter traces the historical development of income maintenance services in Ireland and examines some of the factors that influenced this development. The distinctive features of the Irish system are outlined and the growth in expenditure and the reasons for this growth are explored. The criteria for evaluating the system employed by the Commission on Social Welfare (1986) are examined. Some current problems with the system are outlined. These include problems of take-up, unemployment traps and poverty traps. The factors contributing to unemployment and poverty traps are described and recent changes introduced to tackle these problems are enumerated. Some recent developments including contributions to wider policy issues and changes to the Supplementary Welfare Allowance Scheme are examined. Finally, a radical alternative to the present system i.e. a Basic Income System is described including the contribution of the 2002 Government Green Paper to that debate.

Historical background

Until the middle of the nineteenth century, no state income maintenance system existed in Ireland. Under the Brehon Law, local rulers provided hospitable facilities for the sick and homeless. However, with the coming of Christianity and the subsequent development of a network of monasteries, a system of care for the destitute, sick and homeless was provided throughout the country. Following the Reformation this system was no longer available, and over the following centuries a combination of plantations and penal laws by the second quarter of the nineteenth century resulted in a population that was dispossessed, poverty-stricken and with no recourse to relief other than begging and charity.

In England the Poor Relief Act of 1601 was introduced to deal with the problem of pauperism and begging. Its provisions did not, however, apply to Ireland. This Act allowed for the provision of work, the establishment of workhouses and the levying of local rates to pay for these provisions. In the eighteenth century a small number of workhouses were established in Ireland – Dublin (1703), Cork (1735) and Belfast (1774). Under the legislation, beggars and vagrants were rounded up and effectively forced to work within the workhouses. In Dublin and Cork these workhouses also catered for abandoned children.

Throughout most of the eighteenth century and the earlier part of the nineteenth century, relief was provided in Britain mainly outside the workhouse. This was changed by the Act of 1834 which provided for relief to be given only within the workhouses. It also introduced the infamous 'workhouse test', which stipulated that the condition of inmates should be less tolerable than that of the lowest labourer outside. The provisions of this Act were applied to Ireland under the Poor Relief (Ireland) Act 1838, but with the lowest labourers themselves below subsistence level, enforcing the workhouse test in Ireland was problematic.

The Irish were unwilling inmates of the workhouse until the failure of the potato crop in 1846 and the ensuing famine. The workhouses were then overwhelmed with the numbers seeking entry, forcing the government of the day to introduce the Poor Relief (Ireland) Act 1847. This introduced the concept of outdoor relief for the first time in Ireland, albeit in a very limited form.

The development of income maintenance services in Ireland

The form of outdoor relief introduced under the 1847 Act remained the only form of state income maintenance until the Workmen's Compensation Act of 1897, which required employers to pay compensation when an accident at work led to the injury or death of an employee. The Old Age Pension Act, 1908, introduced a strictly means-tested pension for people over seventy years old. The concept of social insurance was introduced with the National Insurance Act, 1911. This provided for the payment of Unemployment Benefit and Sickness Benefit to insured persons. However, it was not until 1933 that the means-tested Unemployment Assistance was introduced.

Statutory provisions for blind persons were introduced in 1920, but those for widows and orphans did not come into effect until 1935. While these and other categories were awaiting designated state schemes, claimants had recourse only to the provisions of the Poor Law, which had been renamed Home Assistance in 1923. Children's Allowances were introduced in 1944 for families with three or more children. The war years saw the introduction of Cheap Fuel and the Cheap Footwear schemes.

There were no developments of income maintenance schemes during the 1950s. The 1960s, however, saw the introduction of the Contributory Old Age Pension (1961), and Occupational Injuries Benefit (1966), Free Travel and Free Electricity (1967). In the 1970s a wide range of new schemes were introduced: Retirement Pension, Invalidity Pension and Deserted Wife's Allowance (1970); Deserted Wife's Benefit and Unmarried Mother's Allowance (1973); Prisoner's Wife's Allowance, Single Woman's Allowance and Pay-related Benefit (1974) and, most significantly, the Supplementary Welfare Allowance Act (1977), which, in the words of the late Frank Cluskey, removed 'the last vestiges of the Poor Law'.

The 1980s saw the introduction of the National Fuel Scheme (1980), Family Income Supplement (1984) and Lone Parent's Allowance (1989). The 1990s commenced with the introduction of the Carer's Allowance and the Back to School Clothing Scheme (1990), followed by Survivor's Pension, Health and Safety Benefit and Adoptive Benefit (1994), Disability Allowance (1996) the One Parent Family Payment (1997) and Carer's Benefit (2000).

While all of the above schemes are under the control of the Minister for Social and Family Affairs, it is important to note that over the years a number of income maintenance schemes were introduced by the Department of Health. These included the Infectious Diseases Maintenance Allowance (1947), the Disabled Person's Maintenance Allowance (1954) and the Domiciliary Care Allowance (1973). The Supplementary Welfare Allowance Scheme is unusual in that it is funded by and under the control of the Department of Social and Family Affairs, yet it is administered by the health boards, which come under the control of the Department of Health and Children.

Factors influencing the development of income maintenance
At the outset it must be said that income maintenance services in Ireland developed in a fairly ad hoc and piecemeal manner. There is no evidence of any coherent plan or consistent ideology underlying their development. However, at various stages a number of factors can be seen to have influenced the type and the timing of income maintenance schemes. Indeed, as Cousins (1995: 10) points out, it could be argued that 'the social welfare system is a reflection of the economic, political, ideological and cultural structures and conflicts in Irish society'.

The UK influence
Clearly, in the period prior to independence, developments in Ireland followed on from developments in the UK, albeit with a time lag. However, the introduction of workmen's compensation, old-age pensions and national insurance coincided with their introduction in the UK, with the notable exception that medical care was not covered by national insurance in Ireland.

Ireland did not adopt the Beveridge model of the welfare state introduced in the UK in 1948. Indeed, for several decades following it lagged far behind income maintenance services in the UK. Ireland did not, however, experience the retrenchment of services that occurred in the UK in the 1980s. In many cases schemes were introduced in Ireland after they had been tried and tested in the UK. A recent example would be Family Income Supplement.

During the early decades of the welfare state, commentators frequently pointed out the meagreness of the income maintenance provisions in Ireland compared with their more generous counterparts in the UK. It is arguable that the situation has been reversed since the 1990s in that many mainstream schemes in Ireland are now more generous than their UK equivalents.

Economic developments
The economic state of the country at any point in time had an important influence on income maintenance services. In times of economic depression expenditure on income maintenance tended to rise, because of increased levels of unemployment, while at the same time developments came to a standstill. A good example is the 1950s where, at a time of economic depression, no developments took place. However, in the economic boom of the sixties and early seventies a lot of important developments were introduced. The late 1970s and 1980s saw rapid increases in expenditure on income maintenance, mainly due to the dramatic increase in unemployment. This in turn led to attempts to control, and in some cases cut, income maintenance services.

The role of the Catholic Church
While the Catholic Church has played a major role in many aspects of social policy in Ireland, notably in the areas of health and education, its role in income maintenance is less clear cut. In 1911, when social insurance was being introduced, the Catholic Church and the medical profession both opposed the extension of social insurance to cover medical costs. However, in 1945, the bishop of Clonfert, Dr Dignam, was ahead of the government of the day when he published a paper calling for the increased coverage and expansion of social insurance. In more recent times the Conference of Religious of Ireland (CORI) has played a major role in providing a critique of the existing social welfare system and in suggesting radical alternatives.

In the early part of the century the Catholic Church would have been opposed on the principle of subsidiarity to excessive intervention by the state in income maintenance, though the state at that time was not in a position for economic reasons to provide improved services. It is interesting that in recent years the Catholic Church has been calling for increased action by the state to combat poverty and social exclusion.

Special interest groups

Special interest groups have always played a role in lobbying for change in the income maintenance system. The First Commission on the Status of Women, which reported in 1972, led to the development of a number of income maintenance schemes targeted specifically at women. The trade union movement through its involvement in national agreements has been an important voice in calling for and securing improvements in income maintenance schemes. In more recent times, community and voluntary groups and groups representing the socially excluded have played an important role and have been given a voice in the development of services through involvement in the National Economic and Social Forum (NESF).

Role of the European Union (EU)

The EU Directive on the equal treatment of men and women in matters of social security (Council Directive 19.12.1978, 79/7/EC) was a very important development for income maintenance services in Ireland. Prior to the implementation of the directive, married women received lower rates of social welfare payments and in some instances were paid for a shorter period than men. Likewise, married women were in most cases excluded from claiming unemployment assistance. The Government did not introduce the requisite legislation to give effect to the Directive until two years after the operative date, leading to successful claims for arrears by the women affected. It also changed the means test in relation to unemployment assistance to ensure that households were no better off if the wife claimed unemployment assistance or remained as a dependant of her husband (See Doyle 1999 and Langford 1999 for further discussion of the role of the EU in Irish social policy) .

Distinctive features of the Irish income maintenance system

Contingency-based

Entitlement to income maintenance is based on the contingency experienced by a claimant (e.g. unemployment, old age, illness). The one exception is the Supplementary Welfare Allowance Scheme, which is based on need. The contingency can determine not only the category of payment but also the amount of payment. Thus two households of similar size and similar need may receive different amounts of income maintenance depending on the category of payment they receive. While efforts have been made in recent years to equalise the rates of payment between the different categories, the difference between the lowest rate of payment for a single person (Supplementary Welfare Allowance) and the highest rate payable to that person (Contributory Old Age Pension) is 19 per cent (2004 rates).

Social insurance payments

Payments based on contributions to the Social Insurance Fund by both employees and employers are an important feature of the Irish income maintenance system. Deductions are a percentage of pay up to a ceiling, hence the term pay-related social insurance (PRSI). The policy over the years has been to increase the number of people paying PRSI and thus increase the numbers in receipt of social insurance payments. In general, claimants must have paid a defined number of contributions in order to qualify for payment. If they meet this condition, the prescribed rate of payment is made irrespective of any other income the claimant or their adult dependant may have. Some social insurance schemes are of a fixed duration (e.g. unemployment benefit is payable for a period of 15 months). Over the years, the contributions made into the Fund have been insufficient to cover payments made and the shortfall has been met out of general taxation. Recently, however, the Fund has shown a surplus because to the increased level of employment.

Social assistance payments

The essential difference between social insurance and social assistance payments is that in the case of the latter a means test is applied to determine eligibility. There are different means tests for different schemes. This can lead to a situation in which people recently unemployed could find themselves applying within the space of a week for unemployment assistance, Supplementary Welfare Allowance, a medical card, Back-to-School clothing scheme, and undergoing a separate means test for each scheme. The main items taken into account in a means test are cash income, the value of investments, the income of a spouse or cohabitee and, in some instances, the value accruing from the enjoyment of free board and lodgings. The manner in which these factors are taken into account varies between the schemes. The situation is extremely complex and can at times lead to perverse results, for example applying a value to free board and lodgings to a single person living at home can result in their being asked to leave. They would then be paid their full entitlement and if they moved into private rented accommodation they might also qualify for a rent allowance. The eventual cost to the state wwould be greater than if they had paid the full entitlement to the person while they were residing at home. Some minimal changes have been made to the means test in recent years and from 2004 the rate relating to board and lodgings will not apply to those aged 27 years and older.

Cash *vs* Kind

The majority of income maintenance payments are in cash rather than in kind, although over the years a number of payments were made in kind. The Cheap Footwear Scheme and the Cheap Fuel Scheme are examples of goods or vouchers being supplied to claimants. Other examples of payments in kind are free electricity, free travel and free telephone rental. It was also the practice over the years under the Home Assistance Scheme, and more recently the Supplementary Welfare Allowance scheme, to provide applicants for exceptional needs payments with goods rather than cash. It has been argued that in many instances the provision of goods or vouchers is demeaning and paternalistic. Payments under the national fuel scheme and the Back-to-School clothing scheme are now made in cash and, similarly, most payments under the Supplementary Welfare Allowance scheme are made in cash.

Entitlement *vs* discretion

Virtually all the main income maintenance schemes are entitlement based, that is they are prescribed by rules and regulations governing entitlement and if individuals fulfil the conditions for entitlement they receive the payment. If they fail to meet the conditions they receive no payment, subject to a right to appeal against the decision. In effect the administrator has virtually no discretion in the matter. This system has the merit of being transparent and impartial. It can lead, however, to situations in which an individual is disallowed on a minor technicality.

The Supplementary Welfare Allowance scheme has by contrast large elements of discretion, especially in relation to exceptional need payments, one-off payments designed to meet unplanned need. The sole criterion for eligibility is need. The scheme recognises that no two individuals' needs are ever totally identical, and allows payments to be tailored to suit individual circumstances. The downside of this is that the impression can be given that decisions are arbitrary and are based on the particular prejudices of the administrator. The fact that internal guidelines were not published added to this impression. This situation was rectified in October 1998 when the Freedom of Information legislation was applied to the scheme. It is clearly not possible for entitlement-based schemes to anticipate and cater for all the possible current or future needs of individuals. A scheme with large elements of discretion is therefore an important safety net for all the schemes of income maintenance.

Expenditure

The total expenditure of the Department of Social and Family Affairs in 2002 was €9520m. The following table shows the expenditure over a ten-year period to 2002.

The 1995 to 2002 total expenditure figures include expenditure on the Redundancy and Insolvency Schemes which are administered by the Department of Enterprise, Trade and Employment. As this expenditure

Table 2.1 **Social Welfare Expenditure 1993–2002**

	Total Expenditure (€m)	Index of Expenditure	Consumer Price Index	As % of net Government Expenditure	As % of GNP
1993	4,607	100.0	100.0	34.5	11.9
1994	4,775	103.6	102.4	33.7	11.4
1995	5,332	115.7	104.9	34.7	11.4
1996	5,558	120.6	106.6	34.5	10.8
1997	5,744	124.7	108.3	32.3	9.7
1998	6,046	131.2	110.8	33.1	8.9
1999	6,283	136.4	112.7	31.9	8.3
2000	6,713	145.7	119.0	32.3	7.7
2001	7,842	170.2	124.7	38.4	8.1
2002	9,520	206.6	130.5	40.8	9.1

Source: Department of Social and Family Affairs (2002a)

accounts for a minute portion of the total expenditure: 0.3% in 2000, 0.4% in 2001 and 0.6% in 2002, its distorting influence is minimal.

Table 2.1 shows a year-on-year increase in the levels of social welfare expenditure during the ten years 1993 to 2002. In nominal money values the increase was the order of 106.6% for the ten years, while in CPI adjusted real money values, the increase yielded a gain of 58%. This level of increase is of significantly greater order of magnitude than that which occurred in previous decades, i.e. in the ten years 1987 to 1996 the nominal increase was of the order of 68%, while the CPI adjusted figure was of the order of 33%. For the decade to 2002, the rate of growth of social welfare expenditure was three times the rate of increase in the consumer price index.

Unlike previous years, the increased expenditure during this period was not the result of demand pressures such as those which occur in periods of high unemployment (the seasonally adjusted rate of unemployment fell from 15.6% in 1993 to 4.3% in 2002), or measures to offset high inflation rates, but was due to increases in the level of payments and easing of qualification criteria for a number of schemes, such as changes to the qualifying conditions for carers' payments and the introduction of Carer's Benefit.

The increase in expenditure was not spread evenly across the various schemes; old age pensions and child benefit payments gained most. Of the €1,678 million increase in expenditure between 2001 and 2002, child related payments amounted to €521 million or 31% while old age pension increases accounted for another 18.4%.

The growth of the economy during these years along with the influence of social partnership and high tax receipts facilitated the significant increases in social welfare payments. However, given the more modest current economic growth rates it is unlikely that this recent history can be maintained in the near future.

Commission on social welfare

The system of income maintenance in Ireland had developed in a piecemeal and ad hoc manner from the mid-nineteenth century. By the early 1980s it was clear that a review was badly needed. In 1983 the Minister for Social Welfare established the Commission on Social Welfare. The brief of the Commission was to review and report on the entire social welfare system and related social services. The Commission reported in 1986 with 65 major recommendations. Most importantly, the Commission listed five principles to guide the operation of the system and be used in its evaluation, which are discussed below.

1 Adequacy
Payments should prevent poverty and be adequate in relation to prevailing living standards. The Commission adopted a relative definition of poverty (i.e. people are poor when they are excluded from ordinary living patterns, customs and activities). In addressing adequacy, differences in family size have to be taken into account with appropriate payments for adult dependants and children. There should also be in place a method of altering the amount of payments in line with evolving prices and incomes.

The Commission found that there were no links in the existing structure to any standard of adequacy, that different categories received different levels of payment and that adult dependants and child dependants were treated differently under the schemes. Indeed, it found that there were 36 different child dependant rates in the system. It recommended a standard basic rate of payment be made to all recipients which in 1985 figures was in the order of €63.50–€76.20 per week. By 1999, these figures €71.40–€85.70, when uprated by the Consumer Price Index, had been attained for all social welfare rates.

2 Redistribution
The Commission noted that social welfare payments were an important part of the redistributive process. They could not, however, be considered in isolation from the tax system that finances them. They concluded that in terms of redistributing resources from the better off to the less well off the social welfare system was more effective than the tax system.

3 Comprehensiveness

The Commission pointed out that in assessing the comprehensiveness of the social welfare system, an important dimension is the extent to which individuals are covered, as of right, to benefits under social insurance. There is a perceived stigma attached to applying for social assistance schemes, because of the means test, which might deter some people from applying. In addition, because schemes are categorical in nature, people who do not fit into the defined categories are excluded and have to rely on Supplementary Welfare Allowance, the lowest rate of payment in the system. Comprehensiveness also implies that the process of application and the method of delivery of services should respect the dignity of the individual.

4 Consistency

It is important that the system be consistent both internally and with other aspects of social policy. The Commission found large levels of inconsistency between levels of payments for different categories and also between the various means tests applied to social assistance payments. It also found inconsistencies between social welfare and other Government agencies (e.g. between social welfare recipients residing in private rented accommodation receiving a rent allowance and people with similar incomes and family size residing in local authority accommodation).

5 Simplicity

The Commission found a system that was extremely and unnecessarily complex, with a plethora of different schemes covering different contingencies, a range of means tests and a large variation in the manner in which applications were processed and decisions made. This complexity made it very difficult for applicants to understand their entitlements, resulting in low take-up or unnecessary appeals and also greatly added to the cost of administering the system.

Some current issues

Take-up of benefits

Very little research has taken place in Ireland to indicate the level of take-up of various income maintenance schemes. Two surveys conducted in Dublin in recent years produced some interesting results. The first was conducted by Free Legal Advice Centres (FLAC) in a housing suburb in west Dublin (Cousins and Charleton, 1991). The second was conducted by the Dublin Inner City Partnership (DICP) amongst inner city communities (DICP, 1994). Both surveys showed remarkable similarities.

FLAC interviewed 103 households, of whom 85% were not claiming their full entitlement, and DICP interviewed 101 households, of whom 87% were not claiming full entitlements. FLAC identified 305 possible claims of which 42% referred to the exceptional needs provisions of Supplementary Welfare Allowance. A claim was made by applicants in respect of just 32% of these claims. At the conclusion of the survey 44% were successful in their claim, 27% were refused and 29% were still pending a decision. DICP identified 211 possible claims of which 49% referred to the exceptional need provision of Supplementary Welfare Allowance.

In this survey a claim was made in respect of two thirds of those eligible. At the conclusion of the survey 38% were successful in their claim, 41% were refused and 21% were still pending a decision. The surveys indicate the importance of information in relation to benefit take-up. However, there are clearly other factors operating given the number who still did not apply after they had been given information about their possible entitlements. The following emerged as the main reasons why people did not apply:

- Lack of information as to what is required in relation to particular applications e.g. what back-up documentation is required.
- Fear of bureaucracy generally. The complexity of the system and the form filling.
- The stigma attached to the means test.
- The costs associated with applying, relative to the actual benefit.
- Specifically in relation to Supplementary Welfare Allowance – the queues, the discretionary nature of the scheme, the lack of trust in the appeals system.

Unemployment traps
This term refers to a situation in which, because of the combined impact of the tax and social welfare system, an unemployed person could find that accepting paid employment produced little or no increase in net disposable income. It is therefore argued that some unemployed people have no incentive to move into employment.

The relative severity, though not the actual extent of unemployment traps, is measured by means of replacement ratios, i.e. the ratio of income when unemployed to the net income if employed. These show, for given levels of gross earnings, the disposable income of an unemployed person in relation to the disposable income gained from employment. They take into account cash and non-cash benefits and costs associated with the withdrawal of medical cards, rent allowance reductions, travel costs etc.

Unemployment traps tend to increase at a time when social welfare rates are rising faster than increases in general wage rates and when there is a high tax burden on the low paid. The following table shows the real changes in the value of both net income for a married couple with two children on the average industrial wage, and unemployment assistance for the same family size, over an 18-year period:

Table 2.2 **Index of growth in net income and unemployment assistance, 1977–94**

Year	Net income	Unemployment assistance
1977	100	100
1978	110	101
1979	121	101
1980	113	111
1981	106	111
1982	101	116
1983	97	116
1984	98	121
1985	100	123
1986	102	122
1987	104	120
1988	106	128
1989	108	133
1990	109	139
1991	110	143
1992	112	145
1993	114	147
1994	118	148

Source: Expert Working Group on the Integration of Tax and Social Welfare (1996)

As can be seen from table 2.2, in the period 1977–80 wages grew at a faster rate in real terms than unemployment assistance. However, from the mid-1980s onwards the increase in unemployment assistance greatly outpaced wages. This was due to an explicit decision to target extra increases at the long-term unemployed and the high tax rates faced by people on relatively low incomes. It must also be borne in mind that in 1977 unemployment assistance was starting from a very low base.

Table 2.3 shows the replacement ratios for the same hypothetical family, consisting of a couple with two children. In the case of the unemployed person it takes into account the value of the medical card, free fuel allowance, differential rent and back-to-school clothing allowance. In the case of the employed person it takes into account tax and PRSI and it assumes take-up of Family Income Supplement. This is a social welfare payment made to people in employment with dependent children. The amount paid depends on family size and level of earnings.

Table 2.3 **Replacement ratios: couple with two children**

Gross earnings €	Net weekly wages (€)	Replacement ratio %
6,348.69	180.30	88
7,618.43	186.65	85
8,888.17	194.27	82
10,157.90	193.00	83
11,427.64	191.73	83
12,697.38	186.65	85
13,967.12	189.19	84
15,236.86	200.62	79
16,506.60	210.78	75
17,776.33	223.47	71
19,046.07	237.44	67

Source: Expert Working Group on the Integration of Tax and Social Welfare (1996).
Table has been converted from IR£ to €

Table 2.3 shows that this family faced high replacement ratios at low wage rates. Clearly, there was not a huge incentive to take up employment at wages up to €13,967.12 gross. However, as the wage approached the average industrial wage of approximately €19,046.07, the incentives increased. The bigger the family size, the higher the replacement ratios (as social welfare payments increase with family size) and therefore, the greater the disincentive. In this context it must be borne in mind that large families constitute a small proportion of the unemployed with single people comprising 62% of the live register. Employment also has many positive psychological impacts and people may seek employment even if the monetary gain is slight.

Poverty traps
The poverty trap refers to the position of people in employment, on particular incomes, who are faced with a reduction in net income as their gross income increases. This arises because as income increases taxation comes into play and means-tested benefits (such as Family Income Supplement) decrease or are withdrawn. Table 2.3 above gives a good illustration of the poverty trap.

Between a gross income of €8,888.17 and €13,967.12, net income decreased so that the person on €13,967.12 was actually worse off than the person on €8,888.17.

Factors contributing to unemployment and poverty traps

In 1996 the Report of the Expert Working Group on the Integration of the Tax and Social Welfare Systems outlined a number of factors, which at that stage were contributing to unemployment and poverty traps. These included the following:

Adult Dependant allowances
This is an additional allowance paid to a social welfare recipient who has a spouse/partner. It is valued at approximately 65% of the basic rate. No allowance is made for an adult dependant in respect of people in employment. It thus adds to the unemployment trap. However, it also creates a severe poverty trap if the adult dependant has earnings. If the earnings are less than €88.88 the full social welfare rate for that family is paid, but more than that amount results in a reduced payment.

Child Dependant allowances
These are paid to social welfare recipients at the rate of €16.80 per week (2004 figures) for each dependant child. Clearly these increase the unemployment trap for large families.

Family Income Supplement
This was introduced to combat the unemployment trap by compensating people with children who lose their child dependant allowances on taking up employment. However, since its inception it has had a low take-up and was calculated on gross income. Perversely, it also contributes to the poverty trap as it has a sharp withdrawal rate when income increases.

Rent and mortgage supplements
Under the Supplementary Welfare Allowance Scheme, people on social welfare payments can receive assistance with their rent (if in private rented accommodation) or their mortgage. The amounts payable can go from €50 per week for a single person to over €260 per week for families. The allowance is not payable to people in full-time employment (defined as more than 30 hours per week). It can therefore contribute greatly to the unemployment trap. Similarly, it can act as a disincentive to spouses/partners taking up part-time work, as all earnings are assessable.

Medical cards

Because of the fairly severe means test attaching to medical cards, people in employment with relatively low incomes can be disqualified from entitlements. Clearly, the extent to which this would act as a disincentive depends on the value one places on the card. Families with children are likely to value this more than single people.

Tax rates and tax bands

The rates of income tax have always contributed to poverty traps as people entered the tax system on relatively low incomes well below the average industrial wage.

Recent changes aimed at reducing unemployment and poverty traps

In recent years explicit measures were introduced to deal with unemployment and poverty traps. The principal measures are:

- If the earnings of an adult exceed €88.88, the recipient of the social welfare payment does not immediately lose the adult dependant rate. It is now phased out between earnings of €88.88 and €210.00 and withdrawn completely when earnings exceed €210.00.
- Child dependant allowances have not increased since 1994. Increases in respect of children have been concentrated on Child Benefit which benefits equally those in work and those out of work. Significant increases have been made in recent years with the rate for a single child being €131.60 (2004 figures). The government has explained this policy as one of not creating a disincentive to take up employment, which happens when child dependant allowances are lost.
- The most important change in relation to Family Income Supplement is that it is now assessed on net income. Also the number of hours worked per week to qualify has been reduced to 19 and it is now paid after three months of employment instead of six.
- Medical cards can be retained for a period of three years after obtaining employment.
- Other employment supports have been introduced which allow people to work, become self-employed or obtain work experience. Participants on most of these schemes are allowed to earn up to €317.43 per week, which in some cases includes their social welfare payments and may also retain their rent or mortgage payments which are known as secondary benefits.

Included in those schemes are the following:

- The Back to Work Allowance Scheme allows long-term unemployed to take up paid employment or become self-employed. Participants retain 75% of their social welfare payment in the first year and this reduces to 50% and 25% in the second and third years.
- The Community Employment Scheme is part time at 39 hours per fortnight with rent or mortgage payments retained for the first three years on a tapered basis.
- Revenue Job Assist is a scheme of extra tax credits over three years for certain social welfare recipients who have been unemployed for at least 12 months and return to work.
- Jobs Initiative is a scheme for people who have not had regular employment in the previous five years. It is administered by FÁS, the Training and Employment Authority.
- The Very Long-term Unemployed Programme (VLTU) is aimed at people who are at least five years on the live register or on training schemes. It involves a training component and participants progress to the Back-to-Work Scheme.

The above are examples of some of the employment initiatives that are tailored to meet different categories of unemployed. All include retention of secondary benefits including rent or mortgage supplements which are reduced on a tapered basis with 75% payable in the first year, 50% in the second and 25% in the third and fourth years. In the case of the Community Employment Scheme payments are retained for up to three years.

The standard rate of income tax has been reduced to 20% over a number of budgets up to 2003. This has resulted in 90% of those on the minimum wage becoming exempt from income tax.

Incremental change vs radical reform

In many ways the changes to the system in recent years have had little real impact. They have had a slight effect on unemployment and poverty traps but hardly at all on take-up problems. It could be argued they have shifted the timing of the traps rather than eliminating them. Thus after three years when the medical card is withdrawn and after two years when the rent/mortgage is withdrawn the poverty trap will reassert itself. Likewise, the withdrawal, as income increases, of the now more generous Family Income Supplement will lead to a further poverty trap. Reducing unemployment traps may in the short term reduce disincentives and encourage people to take up employment.

However, people would then face sharp poverty traps after a few years of employment. The government of the day might then be forced to either extend the ameliorating measures or introduce some other cushion, thus complicating the system even further.

This raises the question of whether incremental reform will ever really tackle the fundamental problems and has led some commentators to suggest a more radical approach. One such approach, known as the Basic Income Approach, has gained currency in recent times in Ireland and is considered below.

Basic Income
A Basic Income can take several forms, although each type of Basic Income system has the following characteristics:

- Every individual (man, woman and child) would receive an income from the state.
- The Basic Income would not be taxed.
- All other income over and above the Basic Income would be subject to a standard rate of tax.
- The Basic Income would replace the entire social welfare system.
- It would be paid automatically to every citizen without the need to apply.
- There would be no means test or work test attached to it, thus reducing stigma.
- It would treat men and women equally and the concept of adult dependency would be abolished.
- It would be age-related with children receiving a lesser amount than adults.
- It would be administered by a single agency.

The advantages of such a scheme can be summarised as follows:

- It eliminates unemployment traps and poverty traps. There would be no withdrawal of benefit as people move from unemployment to employment or as income increases.
- It provides a comprehensive and automatic safety net. There is no stigma attached as people are paid automatically.
- It would provide an independent income for all, including those who do not participate in the labour force, such as people who work in the home.
- It would be simple to administer with no need for form-filling, means-testing etc. It could be paid automatically into a person's bank account.

In 1994 the Economic and Social Research Institute (ESRI) published an analysis of the various Basic Income options (Callan et al., 1994). The biggest drawback it identified was the high tax rate required to finance such a scheme.

A tax rate of 69% would be necessary if everyone were to get a Basic Income that was not less than the current rate of Unemployment Assistance. For many people this made the concept politically unacceptable.

In the same year, Sean Ward (1994) put forward a proposal that could be achieved at a tax rate of 50%. However, this involved giving people in the age group 21–64 a Basic Income less than the current lowest social welfare payment. This age group constituted over half the population of the country. It also envisaged giving everyone under the age of 21 an income of €25.39 per week. The problem with this proposal was that virtually everyone between the ages of 18 and 64 not in employment would require a top-up. They would, though, be subject to a means test thus creating a new layer of bureaucracy and adding to the problems of stigma and low take-up.

Since 1994, however, there have been significant changes in the Irish economy. Growth has remained at an exceptionally high level and is forecast to remain so over the coming years; unemployment has decreased and the numbers at work have greatly increased thus increasing tax buoyancy. This changed environment led Clark and Healy (1997) to revisit the debate. They suggested that a basic income scheme which would give everyone over the age of 21 a Basic Income of at least €88.88 per week (1997 figures) could be achieved with a tax rate of 48%. The proposal envisaged the establishment of a Social Solidarity Fund, which would be a replacement for and an enhancement of the existing Supplementary Welfare Allowance Scheme. This would provide a top-up to those requiring it. Employers would pay a Social Responsibility Tax instead of PRSI at a reduced rate of 8%. The disadvantage of this proposal is that it still leaves people in the age group 18–20 requiring a means test to determine if they require a top-up.

The debate on Basic Income moved a step further when a Steering Group was established by the government in 2000. This included the social partners and relevant government departments. The Group examined the implications of introducing a Basic Income payment for all citizens and took into account previous work such as that of the ESRI, Clarke and Healy (1997) and international research. The report of the Steering Group formed the basis for a Government Green Paper in 2002, which concluded that attempting to predict the effects of introducing a Basic Income was difficult and uncertain. It pointed out that such a system has perceived advantages of transparency and simplicity and could eliminate poverty and unemployment traps. On the other hand the ESRI has suggested that a tax rate of 48% could lead to a fall in employment and have a negative effect on productivity and possible higher tax rate over time. The Green Paper says that apart from considering costs, the impact it could have on certain groups will need to be considered. It might for example, be a disincentive for married women with children to take up paid employment. On the other hand there could be greater choice regarding the balance between paid employment and the caring role. Other possible effects could be the facilitating of increased innovation and entrepreneurship, which would have a positive effect on economic activity and participation in the labour market. The Green Paper also noted that some features of Basic Income were already being incorporated into the Child Benefit Programme and the Supplementary Welfare Allowance Scheme.

It concluded that more debate was needed on Basic Income and this should also include the implementation of a tax welfare policy that would increase the benefits and minimise less desirable effects.

Other issues that will also require consideration in that debate are:

- What happens if the economy takes a downturn? Will tax rates have to be increased to the levels suggested by the ESRI in 1994 or will Basic Income have to be reduced?
- How are Basic Income rates to be adjusted each year? Would it be in line with inflation or at a higher level? Could Basic Income itself fuel inflation?
- What would be the impact on wages? Would employers take Basic Income into account and seek to reduce wages?
- Could we have an influx of immigrants seeking to enjoy Basic Income?
- How would we make the transition from the present system to the Basic Income system?

The above are just some of the questions that need to be addressed in the absence of firm evidence, as Basic Income has not been introduced in its complete form in any other country. It remains to be seen where the debate will go from here, whether elements of the Basic Income will be further incorporated into future policy or changes become more radical.

Recent developments affecting those on low incomes

National Anti-Poverty Strategy (NAPS)
In 1997 a National Anti-Poverty Strategy was introduced which was designed to put a policy focus on the needs of the poor and socially excluded. One of its strategic actions was income adequacy. While it is revised periodically, the central strategy of NAPS is to ensure that government policies impact on income levels in such a way as to provide sufficient income for a person to move out of poverty. This policy has underpinned the significant social welfare increases in recent years. One of the key NAPS targets is to achieve a rate of €150 per week in 2002 terms for the lowest rates of social welfare by 2007 and that combined child support payments be set at 33%–35% of the minimum adult social welfare payment. Another key target is to maintain

people in employment and, in line with this, income tax rates have been reduced significantly in recent budgets with the target of 80% of all earners paying at a standard rate and those on low pay not subject to income tax. In addition the National Minimum wage has been increased to €7 per hour from February 2004.

The overall implementation of NAPS is overseen by the National Office for Social Inclusion, which is located in the Department of Social and Family Affairs. In 2001 the government's *National Action Plan Against Poverty and Social Inclusion 2003–5* was published (Department of the Taoiseach, 2001a). This was prepared to meet the requirements of the EU Commission which had asked each member state to prepare an action plan against poverty and social exclusion for 2001–3. Following a consultative review of the first NAPS, *Building an Inclusive Society: National Anti-Poverty/Social Inclusion Strategy* was published in February 2002. This builds on the first NAPS, setting out a new Action Plan for 2002–2007 (Department of the Taoiseach, 2002). Systems are in place for continuing monitoring and evaluation of the strategy.

Benchmarking and indexation of social welfare payments

Following the achievement by 1999 of the Commission on Social Welfare recommended minimum rate for all social welfare payments, the National Economic and Social Council (NESC) recommended that payments be linked to improvements in the general standard of living. In order to progress this recommendation, the Social Welfare Benchmarking and Indexation Working Group was established in 2000. This comprised representatives of the social partners and relevant government departments.

The terms of reference of the Group required it to:

(i) examine the issues involved in developing a benchmark for adequacy of adult and child social welfare payments, including the implications of adopting a specific approach to the ongoing uprating or indexation of payments, having regard to their long-term economic, budgetary, PRSI contribution distributive and incentive implications, in the light of trends in economic, demographic and labour market patterns; and
(ii) examine issues of the relative income poverty.
(Department of Social, Community and Family Affairs, 2001)

The Final Report of the Group in 2001 concluded that there was no one universally agreed rate of adequacy and that any definition was as much a reflection of prevailing political and economic circumstances as any objective view of what level of income would be sufficient.

The majority view of the Group, with government and employee representatives dissenting, was that the lowest adult rate should be 27% of Gross

Average Industrial Earnings (GAIE) by 2007 and the level of child income support should be set at 33%–35% of the minimum adult payment rate, the latter category having the same target rate under the National Anti-Poverty Strategy.

On the issue of indexation, where the real value of payments would be protected against inflation, the Group was less prescriptive and saw potential practical difficulties in adopting a suitable index that would be reasonably well understood and would not fluctuate from year to year. It is worth noting here that the ESRI, in their analysis of the 2004 budget (Callan et. al., 2003), concluded that the welfare increases were approximately €265m above what was required for indexation.

Individualisation of social welfare payments

Individualisation of social welfare payments has been on the policy agenda for a number of years. The historical model, which is largely based on an employed male earning and supporting a dependent spouse and family, is no longer seen as appropriate. Therefore individualisation, where each partner would receive their own payment rather than one being an adult dependant, is considered important for the social welfare system and a key issue in addressing both poverty and equality for women. Government policy over a number of years has been directed at the accumulation of individual rights and wider social insurance coverage. In line with that a Working Group of the Social Partners and the Government was established in 2002 to examine the issue. While it was not able to agree on a method by which individual payments should be made, it did agree that individualisation would be introduced on a phased basis over time. Some progress has been made and from 2002 new applicants for Contributory Old Age Pensions can request that their spouse or partner receive their portion of payment directly and this facility will be extended to other categories over time.

Supplementary Welfare Allowance

Changes to the Supplementary Welfare Allowance (SWA) scheme introduced in 2004 have caused considerable anxiety for those dependent on SWA payments to meet particular needs. Under the changes introduced, a rent supplement will not be paid unless a person has been renting for six months. While some exceptions are made such as in the case of homelessness, it is possible that this will cause considerable hardship and force people into homelessness who would otherwise claim a rent allowance and meet their own housing needs.

In addition, payment of diet supplements has been restricted and crèche supplements are to be discontinued. Diet supplements are paid to people with certain illnesses who need more expensive food, which they may not be able to afford. Crèche supplements have been paid to parents where it is recommended for social reasons that they make use of a crèche or pre-school option for their child. These changes are in stark contrast to other policy developments in the social welfare area and are of concern to both claimants and those who work with people on low income.

Asylum seekers

Over recent years the number of people coming to Ireland seeking asylum has grown with figures increasing sharply since 1999. In response to the perception that our welfare system is part of the attraction of Ireland as a country of destination, the government introduced in 2000 a system of direct provision. Under this system, asylum seekers are provided with accommodation and food and a reduced weekly supplementary welfare allowance payment of €19.10 for adults and €9.60 for each child. Apart from the inhumane nature of aspects of this policy, it could also be regarded as an inappropriate use of the Supplementary Welfare Allowance scheme.

Conclusion

The present system of income maintenance may have served us well over the years. Recent changes to that system have been highlighted. Judged by the principles set down by the Commission on Social Welfare the present system is still found wanting. It is extremely complex, it lacks consistency and comprehensiveness, and in its interaction with the tax system the welfare system creates unemployment and poverty traps. The complexity of the system and the means testing act as a deterrent to people. Recent income tax reductions and welfare increases do not address fundamentally the weaknesses. It is therefore of interest that while the government is addressing low income in the context of an anti-poverty strategy and the benchmarking and indexation of social welfare payments, it is also prepared to examine Basic Income as a more radical alternative. It is timely that the Government is prepared to examine radical alternatives to the present tax and welfare systems, which have to some extent created a dependency culture. It would be more appropriate to move in the direction of a culture in which people are encouraged to participate fully as citizens in society.

Table 2.4 **Table of policy developments**

Nineteenth century	Workhouses established
1838	Poor Relief (Ireland) Act
1847	Workmen's Compensation Act
1908	Old Age Pension Act
1911	National Insurance Act
1920	Provision for Blind Persons introduced
1923	Poor Law renamed Housing Assistance
1933	Unemployment Assistance introduced
1935	Provision for Widows and Orphans
1944	Children's Allowances introduced
1947	Infectious Diseases Maintenance Allowance
1954	Disabled Person's Maintenance Allowance
1961	Contributory Old Age Pension introduced
1966	Occupational Injuries Benefit
1967	Free travel and electricity introduced
1970	Retirement Pension, Invalidity Pension and Deserted Wife's Allowance
1973	Deserted Wife's Benefit and Unmarried Mother's Allowance
1974	Prisoner's Wife's Allowance, Single Woman's Allowance and Pay-Related Benefit
1977	Supplementary Welfare Allowance Act
1980	National Fuel Scheme
1981	Maternity Benefit introduced
1984	Family Income Supplement
1989	Lone Parent's Allowance
1990	Carer's Allowance and Back to School Clothing Scheme
1994	Survivor's Pension, Health and Safety Benefit and Adoptive Benefit
1996	Disability Allowance
1997	One Parent Family Allowance
1999	Farm Assist
2000	Carer's Benefit
	Direct Provision for Assylum Seekers

Recommended reading

Commission on Social Welfare (1986) *Report*. Dublin: Stationery Office.

Department of the Taoiseach (2001) *National Action Plan against Poverty and Social Exclusion 2003–2005*. Dublin: Stationery Office.

Department of the Taoiseach (2002) *Building an Inclusive Society: National Anti-Poverty/Social Inclusion Strategy*. Dublin: Stationery Office.

Expert Group on the Integration of the Tax and Social Welfare System (1996) *Report*. Dublin: Stationery Office.

Government of Ireland (2002b) *Basic Income – A Green Paper*. Dublin: Stationery Office.

Chapter 3

Health policy

Suzanne Quin

Introduction

Spending on public health care represents a substantial portion (almost 23 per cent) of overall public spending in Ireland (Commission on Financial Management and Control Systems in the Health Service, 2003). Public spending on health care has increased significantly in recent years amounting to over €9 billion in 2003 (Prospectus Report, 2003). This does not even take account of ongoing capital expenditure on building and updating facilities that rapidly become outdated in size and design. Health is one area of government spending which impinges on the vast majority of the population. It is certainly an area of public provision which excites a great deal of attention and is one of the few which generates public protest when cutbacks are proposed or are introduced, such as the reduction in hospital beds in the latter part of the 1980s (Curry, 2003).

There is a long tradition of providing health care in Ireland. In the Brehon Laws there is reference to the proper conditions for a hospital which, in many respects, would be in keeping with good medical care as we know it today. These stated that the hospital 'should be free from dirt, have four doors that the sick man may be seen from every side and there should be a stream of water running through the middle of the floor' (Robins, 1960: 145). The monasteries of mediaeval Ireland offered refuge and care to the sick and dying. Later the Poor Law system developed institutionally based care for the indigent sick along with other categories of those without the most basic resources. A system of voluntary hospital care also grew from the individual and group efforts of various philanthropists who established institutions such as the Adelaide and Meath Hospitals in Dublin. After Catholic Emancipation, the Roman Catholic Church also began to set up hospitals for those too poor to pay for any medical care such as the Mater Misericordiae and St Vincent's Hospital in Dublin (Robins, 1960). Apart from such institutions, there was no attempt to provide generalised coverage in the form of a general hospital system (Hensey, 1988: 3). The Medical Charities Act 1851 required the Poor Law Commissioners to provide dispensaries and appoint medical officers. The geographical boundaries of the dispensary system remained until the Health Act 1970.

The perceived responsibility of the state to provide health care for the population as a whole is very much a twentieth-century characteristic. Barrington (1987) points out that, at the beginning of the twentieth century, government responsibility was limited to controlling outbreaks of serious epidemics and providing the poorest people with the most basic general practitioner and infirmary services which originated from the Poor Law. By 1970, the government had accepted responsibility for providing a high standard of health care for all the population at no cost or at a very subsidised cost to the recipient of services. By 1991, entitlement to free public hospital care was a basic right of everyone (1991 Health (Amendment) Act).

There are many factors which influence the provision of health care in a country. These include the prevailing disease patterns, the demographic profile and the way in which the health services are structured and funded. It is the unique blend of these features in tandem with historical, cultural and ideological influences, economic conditions, contemporary knowledge about health and disease and the relative power positions of the various protagonists involved in providing health care which have determined the shape and thrust of current services in Ireland.

Changing disease patterns

At the beginning of the twentieth century, the most common causes of disease and death in Ireland were infectious diseases arising from poverty, malnutrition, poor and unsanitary housing conditions, lack of clean water and ignorance about the mechanisms by which disease will spread. In many respects, the conditions then are similar to the ones facing many in the so-called developing countries where famine and disease are constant twin hazards. By the beginning of the twenty-first century, Ireland's disease patterns (morbidity) and death statistics (mortality) mirrored those of other relatively affluent countries. In terms of maternal mortality, Ireland achieved an average of less than two per 100,000 live births per year. This was far lower than the World Health Organisation target of less than 15 per 100,000 for every country by the year 2000. However, in other respects health statistics show that Ireland has somewhere to go yet in furthering the nation's health.

With regard to lowering premature mortality (death before 65 years), for example, Ireland trails behind other EU Member States (European Commission, 2003). When one looks at the causes of death in this category, it can be seen that many of these deaths are regarded as potentially preventable, since strokes, heart disease and many forms of cancer are linked to a greater or lesser extent with aspects of lifestyle such as diet, smoking, lack of exercise, alcohol consumption and stress – the hazards of affluence. A target of current health policy, therefore, is to reduce the numbers who die before the age of 65 to the level of or, better still, lower than, the EU average (Department of Health and Children, 2001c).

There has been recognition for some time that tackling premature mortality involves strategies other than just the provision of curative services. The Department of Health Report (*Health: The Wider Dimensions*, 1986), followed by the World Health Organisation's document, *Health for All by the Year 2000* (WHO, 1993), emphasised the need for health promotion programmes to reduce levels of morbidity and early mortality by giving people the knowledge and sense of responsibility to maximise their health potential for as long as possible. This approach was further endorsed in the health strategy documents, *Shaping a Healthier Future* (Department of Health, 1994) and *Quality and Fairness: A Health System for You* (Department of Health and Children, 2001c) which emphasised the importance of health gain (improvements in health status) and social gain (quality of life changes resulting from improved health status). In 1995 the Department of Health issued its proposals for improving the health promotion aspect of health services in *Making a Healthier Choice the Easier Choice* (Department of Health, 1995e), which established goals and targets for a national strategy for health promotion. This was followed by a second policy document, *The National Health Promotion Strategy, 2000–2005* (Department of Health and Children, 2000a), which set out further goals for the improvement of the population's health status.

Demographic characteristics

Ireland's demographic profile is changing in common with other countries in the EU and this has implications for health care demands and provision. Yet the link between demographic change and resulting adjustments in health services is not always as direct and immediate as might be expected. Falling birth rates, for example, do not necessarily mean the automatic closure of maternity hospitals or wards, as other factors also influence provision, such as the geographical spread of facilities, public pressure, tradition and employment. Nevertheless, the proportion of those aged over 65 years in the population is considered to have particular implications for health care services.

While the proportion of those over 65 relative to others in Ireland is increasing, in comparison with most other European countries, it is not a significant feature of demographic trends in Ireland (Fahey, 1998b). Estimates of the proportional size of this group by the year 2006 are projected to be 11.8 per cent of the population, thereafter to rise gradually to 17 per cent of the population by 2026 (Fahey, 1998b). Within the older population, while the greatest overall increase will be in the younger age group, the greatest relative increase will be the very old population with the numbers of 85+ year olds expected to increase by 120 per cent (Fahey, 1998b). The increase in the proportion of the population over 65 and, in particular, the growth in the older population has implications for the provision of health care. Those over 65 make more than twice the number of visits to their GP compared to the average for the population as a whole and, when admitted to hospital, they spend a longer time on average as in-patients (Department of Health and Children, 2002c). Increasing frailty and poor health generate the need for community-based services which are provided by health services – public health nurses, physiotherapy, occupational therapy, home help, meals-on-wheels and day care. Some of these are provided directly by the health services and others are provided by voluntary organisations subvented by public funding. Deficits in the availability of primary care such as these are likely to lead to increased demand for the more expensive secondary (acute hospital) and tertiary (long-term care) services.

Eligibility for health services

Entitlement to publicly funded health services is determined by a person's income from whatever sources. All Irish residents belong either to Category 1 or Category 2 eligibility. Those in Category 1 hold what is known as a medical card. This is subject to a means test, the amount allowed being reviewed on a yearly basis. In circumstances where the need for medical services may be greater than the average, those whose income exceeds the guidelines may be given a medical card if they are considered to be unable to provide necessary medical services for themselves and their family (Department of Health, 1994: 3).

The decision to grant or withhold a medical card is at the discretion of the health board (now restructured into four regional areas of the Health Service Executive). Thirty-one per cent of the population hold medical cards (Commission on Financial Management and Control Systems in the Health Service, 2003). Within this overall percentage, the statistics reveal considerable variations between different counties and whether these variations are entirely due to income differences is subject to question. Since 2001, those aged over 70 years of age are entitled to a medical card without a means test. This added over 80,000 to those eligible for a medical card by 2003 and is set to rise further with the increasing numbers of older people in the population (Tormey, 2003: 42). For those under 70 who must qualify on income grounds, the low threshold is a particular issue for those on low but not the lowest incomes. Wren (2003: 204) points out that in 2002, one visit to a GP would cost one third of the weekly income of those just above the income threshold for eligibility.

Equity in regard to medical card eligibility is of particular importance given the range of medical care to which the holder is entitled. This includes free general practitioner service with a choice of doctor, provided the practitioner is listed to take medical card patients and has not exceeded the maximum number of such patients he/she is allowed. Prescribed medicines and drugs are also available free of charge. The holder is also entitled to free dental, ophthalmic and aural services and appliances, although actual provision in these areas is in reality limited. All public hospital out-patient and in-patient services in a public ward, including consultant services, are free of charge.

Category 2 comprises the rest of the population who, on grounds of income, are not entitled to medical cards. Category 2, therefore, comprises just over 64 per cent of the population. This group shares with Category 1 entitlement to public hospital out-patient and in-patient services in a public ward, including free consultant services in both instances. Category 2 patients, however, must pay for every visit to their general practitioner. They are also liable for a nominal charge per day for all public hospital accommodation up to a maximum in any twelve-month period for all public in-patient treatment. These charges do not apply to maternity services, services for prescribed infectious diseases, children referred from school health assessment and health clinics for children who are receiving treatment for certain conditions such as cystic fibrosis. In addition, there is a fee for use of a hospital's accident and emergency department without a referral note from a general practitioner, a charge which can be waived in situations of hardship.

Drugs and medicines are available free of charge to any person suffering from certain conditions, that is those drugs necessary for the treatment and control of their specific illness. These are: learning disability; mental illness (for those under 16); phenylketonuria; cystic fibrosis; spina bifida; hydrocephalus; diabetes mellitus; diabetes insipidus; haemophilia; cerebral palsy; epilepsy; multiple sclerosis; muscular dystrophies; Parkinson's disease and acute leukaemia. Those eligible are given a Long-Term Illness Book which lists the drugs and medicines for the treatment of that condition which they are entitled to receive free of charge.

Apart from those conditions listed above, individuals in Category 2 must pay for all prescription costs. However, a drug refund scheme operates in which any cumulative expenditure by a person and/or that person's dependants which exceeds the limit in a specified one-month period is refunded. In addition, there is a drug cost subsidisation scheme available to those who do not hold a medical card or a Long-Term Illness Book, but who are certified as having a long-term medical condition requiring regular, continuing medical case and drug prescriptions. In these circumstances, the person makes direct payment to their pharmacist which covers all prescriptions relating to the condition for that period.

As Curry (2003) points out, it has never been government policy to aim to provide a free health care service for all the population. The aim has been to ensure that no one goes without appropriate and necessary care for themselves or their dependants on account of lack of means. This was first explicitly stated in the 1966 White Paper, *The Health Services and Their Future Development* (Department of Health, 1966), and has formed the basis for developments in health entitlement to date. While entitlement to public hospital care has been extended to all, those without medical cards must pay for their general practitioner services, prescriptions and hospital charges as described above. The Report of the Commission on Health Funding (Commission on Health Funding, 1989) did not favour the provision of free primary care (i.e., general practitioner) to all. An argument could be made that free general practitioner care for all would encourage those whose incomes exceeded the medical card guidelines to seek care at an early stage of their illness, thus reducing demand for the more expensive and invasive secondary services provided by acute hospitals. The Labour Party policy document *Curing Our Ills* (Labour Party, 2001) set out proposals for a new system of health cover based on a social insurance model. An important aspect of this model was that primary care (i.e. general practitioner services) would be available to all of the population free at point of usage.

However, as it stands, general practitioner services have to be paid for by over two-thirds of the population. Wren (2003) explains that the initial point of access to health services, the GP, is not free for the majority of the population. While free general practitioner care for the whole population is not envisaged, the plan to increase the brief of general practice through the development of primary care is laid out in the policy document *Primary Care: A New Direction* (Department of Health and Children, 2001b). The importance of primary care is emphasised in both the promotion of good health and early intervention in ill health. General practitioners, rather than being separate structurally and spatially from other health professionals as has been the case, will now play a pivotal role in the new multidisciplinary primary care team. This team will act as a single point of entry to all (other than A & E) health services, providing a comprehensive range of care on a geographical basis.

Financing health care

Barrington describes Irish health services as an 'extraordinary symbiosis of public and private medicine' (1987: 285). Indeed, Ireland can be truly described as having a public/private mix of health care in terms of both funding and delivery. By public is meant those services which are financed and/or delivered by public funds, while private services have been defined by Tussing (1985: 81) as 'that part in which fees or charges are imposed and where patients may not avail of the services unless they pay for them.' The Report of the Commission on Health Funding (Commission on Health Funding, 1989) emphasises that the distinction between public and private applies both to funding and delivery systems in that public funding can be compatible with private delivery systems, and vice versa. Nolan (1991: 19) argues that a four-fold classification system is necessary in order to separate out the different strands of the public/private interweave. These are:

1   services which are publicly financed and delivered such as hospital services for those with a medical card;
2   services which are publicly financed and privately delivered such as GP services for those with a medical card;
3   services which are privately financed and publicly delivered such as the element of direct payment for public acute hospital facilities for those in Category 2;
4   services which are privately financed and privately delivered such as GP services for Category 2 patients and use of private hospital services.

The Report of the Commission on Health Funding (Commission on Health Funding, 1989) considered that there was a consensus among the population as a whole that health needs were matters of priority and public justice. It did not regard the public/ private mix in provision as being incompatible with these. This view was endorsed in the strategy document (Department of Health, 1994), which cited the public/private mix as being a compatible arrangement which it regarded as one of the strengths of the Irish health services. This fits with O'Shea's (1992: 238) view that 'private practice has been quite deliberately retained and encouraged at all levels in the medical services – primary care, secondary care and tertiary care'. It can be argued that such a policy which enables those who can afford it to access alternative paths to what they see as being a more comprehensive, superior quality and faster service is hard to justify on grounds of social justice. Tormey (1992: 381) argues that 'fundamental change bringing real equity in access to services will only come when there is the political will to change the state's well-entrenched policy direction. There is little cause to believe that such change is likely.'

This view put forward over a decade ago still holds true for health care in 2004. The most recent strategy document *Quality and Fairness: A Health System for You* (Department of Health and Children, 2001c), while acknowledging the importance of providing high quality services in the public system, does not indicate any change in the view that the public/private mix is both complementary and desirable. This approach has been reinforced by the OECD Report (2003) that considered Ireland was getting good value overall in health care spending as a result of the mixture of public and private financing.

Payment for private services is largely through the insurance mechanism. Until the mid-1990s, the Voluntary Health Insurance Board (VHI) held a monopoly position in providing health insurance. VHI was established in 1957, at a time when approximately 15 per cent of the population were not covered for acute public hospital care. It was required to provide cover at what is termed 'community rating' which is a standard charge for all members regardless of age and health status. At the outset, therefore, it was created to cater for the relatively affluent minority who were at the time excluded from access to public provision. In reality, far more joined than needed cover for basic care and, when entitlement to public hospital care was extended to the whole population in 1991, it had little effect on VHI membership. In a study of VHI membership, Nolan (1991: 132) estimated that, in 1989, 34 per cent of the population had VHI cover. Furthermore, he found that, even when premiums were increased substantially, it had little effect on the membership size. Clearly, those who take out cover must consider it worth the costs incurred. According to Nolan and Wiley (2001), the most important reasons why people take out private health insurance are the sense of security it engenders as well as speed of access and perceived quality of care. A further incentive has been the tax relief on premia which was of greatest advantage to those in the highest tax bands. The Report of the Commission on Health Funding (Commission on Health Funding, 1989) recommended that this tax relief should be eliminated on the grounds that those who opted for cover for private care should not be subsidised by tax remits. However, this recommendation was only taken in part when the tax relief was reduced to the standard rate in 1994.

The Third Directive on Non-Life Insurance for the European Union resulted in the VHI losing its monopoly position and, since the Health Insurance Act 1994, any company is entitled to offer cover for medical care provided it operates the community rating system. So far, the major alternative to the VHI has been BUPA, a company which had been offering health insurance in Britain for many years before entering the Irish market.

Health care can be funded using one or more of three basic mechanisms: general taxation, social insurance or private insurance schemes. Most countries have one predominant means which is supplemented by one or both of the other two. The main determining factor is the historical development of health cover that can vary from country to country. In Germany, for example, health care schemes developed from employment-related benefits; the National Health Service in the UK is primarily funded by general taxation, while the US is based on private insurance with a state funded system for those who cannot cover themselves on account of age or low income. Ireland's public system is paid for through general taxation. There is some cover via social insurance and the private system and aspects of the public system are funded through private insurance for those who can afford to pay.

The amount spent on health care is determined by a number of factors such as the relative wealth of a country, the amount paid in taxes, the value placed on health care services vis à vis competing demands from other welfare sectors, the age and health status of the population and the way in which health care is funded. Given the demands that an ageing population will make on health care, as discussed earlier, it might reasonably be assumed that the larger the propor- tion of those over 65 in a population, the more will be spent on health care. Fahey (1995), in a comparison of spending across countries, argued that this factor can be overridden by a more important one – that of the relative wealth of the country. He found that the higher the Gross Domestic Product, the greater the proportion of overall spending devoted to health care. This does not necessarily mean that the more that is spent on health care, the better the quality and cover for health care. Depending on the funding mechanisms used and the system of delivery of health care, a country may get relatively good or poor value for the amount spent.

Within overall spending, a further concern is the amount that is appor- tioned to the different sectors of health care. Since the costs of health care are constantly rising, and potential demand is virtually limitless, difficult decisions must be made about the allocation of funds for prevention, cure and ongoing care. Within these categories, there will also be competition for scarce resources and choices may revolve around the conflicting demands for development of services for life-threatening conditions against those which are not life-saving but life-enhancing, such as the expansion of organ replacement procedures or increasing the number of hip replacement operations. At present, just under one half of total state spending on health goes on the acute hospital sector (Department of Health and Children, 2002c). This is similar to the proportion in other EU countries where the labour intensive and high-tech facilities of this sector consume a similar proportion of spending, and there is no indication that the needs of this sector will diminish. While much attention has been given to the importance of health promotion and illness prevention, spending in this area has not matched aspirations. Spending on community-based services accounts for just 16 per cent of total expenditure. Curry (2003: 132) comments that 'despite the increased emphasis on the value and importance of community care and some rationalisation of hospital services, this pattern of expenditure has not altered significantly over the past two decades'. The large proportion of overall spending which is taken up by the acute hospital sector has made this area a particular, and unsuccessful, target for cost containment.

Waiting periods for so called elective procedures have been a persistent problem within the public, acute hospital sector. Emergency admissions via Accident and Emergency along with staff and bed shortages have contributed to long waiting times for routine hospital admissions, with some specialist areas being particularly problematic. In 2001, the National Treatment Purchase

Scheme was established to offer patients who had been on a waiting list for more than one year the option of being treated in the private sector or going abroad for treatment. In 2003, this fund had the capacity to pay for 600 patients per month, 400 in Ireland and 200 in Britain (Tormey, 2003: 65). However, in spite of this development, waiting lists continue to be an issue in health care.

One aspect of the acute hospital which has changed radically in recent years is the average length of stay per patient. Changes in treatment processes arising from increased knowledge and treatment options as well as alterations in funding hospital care have all contributed to this phenomenon. Increasing numbers of patients are being treated as day cases. In 1994, Department of Health figures put the total number at just over 193,000; by 1996 this figure had risen to over 200,000 and had reached almost 350,000 by the end of the decade. Attendance for day cases is at a prearranged time for a planned procedure following from an out-patient visit. The Audit Commission (1995: 298) in Britain identified three main factors which have influenced the growth in day surgery:

1 changes in clinical practice which have contributed to the decline in the number of days a patient will spend in hospital;
2 technological developments which have radically changed a range of procedures on account of less invasive techniques and improved analgesic/anaesthetic drugs;
3 financial pressures resulting in a reduction of in-patient beds.

Writing about the United States, Duffy and Farley (1995: 675) describe the shift to day care as 'swift and far-reaching'. They comment that 'many interventions that could have been performed for years safely and effectively on an out-patient basis remained in-patient procedures. It was not until new reimbursement policies encouraged treatment in out-patient settings that a significant shift occurred' (1995: 675–6). In Ireland, overnight admission to hospital for those with private insurance was, in the past, encouraged by the policy of VHI of not paying for other than in-patient treatment for its members. In the public sector, there was pressure to maintain full usage of existing hospital beds even at a time when, by the standards of other European countries, such beds were over-supplied relative to the size and demographic profile of the population.

Financial considerations would therefore seem to play a significant role in the direction and speed of change in the functioning of the acute hospital sector. The cost-saving potential of increased day care include a reduction of staff needed for overnight and weekend shifts, patient 'hotel' costs are reduced substantially and throughput can be maximised. In this instance, financial expediency may not clash with good patient care. There is plenty of evidence that day admission may be both appropriate and in line with most patients' wishes concerning the nature of their hospital care. Kelly (1994), in a study of day case patients in Ulster, found that compliance among patients of post-discharge instructions was good and that the patients reported little post-operative pain, though many reported various side-effects. In Kelly's study, few had recourse to their GP immediately following discharge. However, there is conflicting evidence as to whether or not the advent of day surgery has increased the demand for GP services in the immediate aftermath of discharge which is likely to involve evening or night-time calls. This illustrates that a change in policy in one aspect of health care may have implications for another.

Structures for providing health care

Given the escalating costs of providing health services, it is not surprising that attention has increasingly focused on value for money. An important aspect of this is to ensure that structures for providing services are as efficient and cost-effective as possible. This was emphasised in the Department of Health's (1994) health strategy which regarded the framework for service provision as one of three dimensions needing reorientation to take cognisance of the changing demands of health care into the new millennium. The last major change had taken place over twenty years before, following the 1970 Health Act. This had created a structure of eight regional health boards with responsibility for the provision of services in their area within the budget allocated to each by the Department of Health. The health boards differed substantially from each other both in terms of size of population and the geographical area. In terms of population size, by far the largest was the Eastern Health Board (EHB), which, encompassing the counties of Dublin, Kildare and Wicklow, covered approx-imately one third of the total population of the country. The management structures of the health boards when they were established followed the recom-mendations of the McKinsey Report (1968). Services provided by each board were divided into three areas: general hospital care, special hospital care and community care. The board in each instance was made up of a majority of elected representatives from local corporations/councils, professionals involved in the provision of health care, and some nominees of the Minister for Health.

While each health board was given responsibility for general hospitals, this referred only to the hospitals directly run by the board and did not include the acute voluntary hospitals within the geographical area which continued to receive direct funding from the Department of Health. Over time, this emerged as one of a number of structural difficulties which hindered efficiency and effectiveness of service delivery. The community care structure, as conceived, did not develop to its full potential as the range and numbers of professionals providing community-based services were insufficient to meet existing and emerging needs. The fact that the GP service remains outside the system meant that a pivotal primary care service operated independently from other primary care services. Voluntary organisations which were engaged in the provision of services similar or ancillary to those required of a board could be funded by a grant under Section 65 of the Health Act 1953, but there was no built-in mechanism of accountability for funding given or received. The division into three programmes (some of the boards only operated two in effect, on account of the limited number of hospitals in the area under their jurisdiction) led to problems of continuity of care for patients across programmes, because of separate funding and management structures. Moreover, there were tensions between the individual health boards and the Department of Health concerning issues of funding and accountability.

Problems relating to the control of expenditure and provision of services in all areas of the publicly provided health services intensified in the economic recession of the mid to late 1980s. The Department of Health document, *Health: The Wider Dimensions* (Department of Health, 1986), questioned the necessity of having eight health boards for a population of just over three million. It suggested that health boards should be renamed to take cognisance of their wider brief which encompassed welfare as well as health. While it did not suggest a particular title, it could be inferred that the title of Health and Social Services Boards such as existed in Northern Ireland might be suitable. The strategy document 1994 took a different line in both respects. It maintained, and indeed extended, the pivotal role of health boards, to be renamed health authorities, in the provision of health care, and created three health boards from the Eastern Health Board area with a new element in the structure – that of the Eastern Regional Health Authority (ERHA) having some shared remit for the newly created boards.

However, it was evident that this change to ten health boards did not deal with the structural issues inherent in the health care organisational system as a whole. The fact that the health boards were comprised of mainly locally elected representatives inevitably led to difficulties when rationalisation of services and the development of centres of excellence (involving the upgrading of facilities in some hospitals at the perceived expense of others) were under consideration. Moreover, the fact that no one organisation had responsibility for managing the health service as a whole was an impediment to the development of the health service overall.

The second strategy document published in 2001, *Quality and Fairness: A Health System for You* (Department of Health and Children, 2001c), put forward a vision of health care using the terms 'supportive', 'empowering', 'fair', 'trustworthy' and 'responsive to service users'. Its goals for health services were: (1) improving the health status of the population; (2) ensuring fair access with eligibility broadened and clearly defined; (3) providing responsive and appropriate care and (4) ensuring that the services were of a uniformly high standard by means of quality control and strategic planning. The need for organisational reforms to help achieve these goals was acknowledged in this document.

Organisational change to create a seamless system of health care provision was addressed in the Prospectus Report (2003) and in the Brennan Report (Commission on Financial Management and Control Systems in the Health Service, 2003). Both identified as a core problem the fact that no one organisation had responsibility for managing the health service. Following these reports, the Health Services Reform Programme (Department of Health and Children, 2003b) set out the new structures for health care in Ireland. Henceforth, the Department of Health and Children will play no role in direct service provision. Responsibility for all health services is now vested in the newly created Health Services Executive. The health board structure will be reformed into four Regional Health Authorities which will be directly accountable to the Health Services Executive for both hospital and community based health care.

A further development recommended in the Prospectus Report was the amalgamation of the roles and functions of a large number of health agencies that had been created over time in different aspects of health care. Out of a total of 43 such agencies, the Report (Prospectus Report, 2003: 122) identified 27 whose functions could be subsumed into the newly created Health Services Executive or into the restructured Department of Health and Children. A further five agencies were recommended to be merged while 11 agencies would continue to exist as separate entities within the system. The latter included the Irish Medicines Board, the Institute for Public Health, the Food Safety Authority and the recently established Mental Health Commission.

A further report which has implications for the provision of hospital based care and has got much public attention is the Hanly Report (National Task Force on Medical Staffing, 2003). This report addressed the implications of the European Working Time Directive and its implications for medical practice in the hospital sector. The Directive required that by 1 August 2004, non-consultant hospital doctors were to work for no more than an average of 58 hours per week, and for no more than 13 hours in any one day with required rest intervals within that time. By August 2007, the average hours per week must be reduced to a maximum of 56 hours reducing further to the target maximum of 48 hours per week by 2009. This clearly presents challenges for the provision of hospital-based medical care in Ireland given that, currently, non-consultant hospital doctors in this country work on average 75 hours per week, often for continuous periods of more than 30 hours (National Task Force on Medical Staffing, 2003: 13).

The present system whereby individual doctors work such long hours is clearly undesirable from their viewpoint and, even more importantly, from the viewpoint of quality patient care. However, the Report also points out that there are incentives to continue current practice. At Registrar level, for example, the monetary rewards from high levels of overtime can be substantial. The Report draws out the differences between a consultant-led service (which is what exists at present) and a consultant-provided service which it regards as the way forward. Essentially, the difference between these two is that the former entails the consultant taking overall responsibility for the work of his/her (most commonly the former) medical team but the bulk of the patient contact being undertaken by the other team members. In a consultant-provided service, much more of the direct patient contact is undertaken by the consultant themselves. The implications of recommending the way forward as a switch from the consultant-led service to a consultant-provided service led to the recommendation of substantial increases in consultant posts (2003: 87). It is how such posts would be distributed and the implications for smaller hospitals of this distribution along with the requirement of a consultant-provided service that have led to controversy about perceived winners and losers in the different hospital locations throughout the country. Hospital action groups have been formed in a number of areas in reaction to this issue which is likely to be an ongoing one.

Meeting the health care needs of specific groups

In recent years there has been growing recognition of the health care needs of specific sections of the population. In the mid-1990s, for example, the particular health care needs of women were first addressed. Prior to this, women's health care was subsumed within the general health care system. The discussion document, *Developing a Policy for Women's Health* (Department of Health, 1995b) was designed to redress this imbalance by creating a consultative process for the development of a women-friendly service. The document covered a range of areas relating to women's health including childbirth, menstruation, gynaecological services, breast and cancer screening and family planning. It also addressed the question of women's participation in the formulation and management of health services as well as identifying women who were particularly disadvantaged in terms of health needs and/or access to an appropriate range of health services. The document saw the objectives of a women's health policy to be the identification, planning and promotion of a health policy which ensured that the services provided were appropriate and accessible based on consultation and participation. This approach very much reflected the Department of Health's (1994) health strategy which placed emphasis on greater consumer participation in the planning and delivery of health services generally.

Taking Irish women's health in the EU context, the statistics reported showed that, while there has been much improvement since the middle of the twentieth century, women in Ireland have a lower life expectancy and a higher premature mortality rate than average. Of particular concern was the early mortality of Traveller women. This discussion document ((Department of Health,

1995b) acknowledged the context in which some specific aspects of women's ill health arose. Examples of the importance of context were the health implications of domestic violence and the socioeconomic factors underlying their mental health profile, particularly in relation to gender differences between men and women in the incidence of depression (see Quin, 1995; Cleary, 1997 for further discussion of this). Following the publication of the document, there was consultation with women throughout the country to incorporate their views. This process did at least represent an institutionalised attempt to garner the views of consumers. The resulting policy document *A Plan for Women's Health* (Department of Health, 1997a) aimed to incorporate these views. Included in its plans was a mechanism to institutionalise the process of consultation on an ongoing basis in the creation of a permanent Women's Health Council, as well as the establishment of advisory committees in each health authority area. Considering that it was based on consultation, the new document did not differ greatly in approach from its original. Two important inclusions were a focus on the need for services which were experienced as more accessible and user friendly and the desirability of including alternative treatments and approaches, including the availability of counselling in non-medical settings. The importance of greater accessibility and targeting those at greatest risk/need was amply demonstrated in Wiley and Merriman's (1996) study of women's needs in relation to the reproductive sphere. Two particularly interesting findings were indications that Irish women across geographical and socio-economic boundaries 'may be less traditional than is assumed' and, less surprisingly, that the extent of knowledge about health enhancing practices was less than desirable, most particularly amongst those with low levels of educational attainment. This latter finding indicated the need for health promotion strategies which take account of socioeconomic differentials within Irish society.

It is not just in relation to gender that the particular health care issues and needs arise. It has long been recognised that the morbidity and mortality statistics of members of the Travelling community were unacceptably high in relation to the population as a whole. These issues were addressed in the Traveller Health National Strategy 2002–2005 (Department of Health and Children, 2002a). Other examples of policy documents in relation to specific categories of need include the Report of the Task Force on Suicide (Department of Health, 1998), Report of the National Advisory Committee on Palliative Care (Department of Health and Children, 2001d) and *An Evaluation of Cancer Services in Ireland: A National Strategy 1996* (Department of Health and Children, 2003a).

The relatively recent and significant change in the racial and ethnic profile of the population has posed, and will continue to pose, new and different challenges for Irish health services. This is acknowledged in the health strategy (Department of Health and Children, 2001c: 54) which states that 'Ireland is now moving towards a more multiethnic/multicultural society. In health, as in other areas of public policy, this brings a need to plan for diversity with a wide range of needs to be addressed – affecting both the health workforce and the patient/client group'. For the latter, this relates to both the technical care of patients when the health system is faced with hitherto relatively unfamiliar conditions arising from different genetic and health risks and also ensuring that health care is provided with cultural and ethnic knowledge and sensitivity. The resource implications of ethnically sensitive best practice are important, for example the availability of translation facilities to ensure that patients can be understood and understand is a vital (and costly) element of patient care (Murphy-Lawless and Kennedy, 2002). Understanding of cultural differences in relation to illness, disability, dying and death are core prerequisites of good health care practice (Quin, 2003).

Socioeconomic inequalities in health care

There is evidence of strong links between health status and socioeconomic differentials. As living standards improved during the latter half of the twentieth century, and with them increased access to health services for all, it was assumed that health differentials arising from differences in socioeconomic status would disappear. However, the publication of the Black Report in Britain (Working Group on Inequalities in Health, 1980) indicated that this was not so. This report found that, in spite of overall improvements in health status in the population, health differentials between the higher and lower socioeconomic strata had, in fact, increased during the period 1930 to 1970. The Report cited the multi-causal nature of health inequalities of which material conditions were the main factors. A subsequent report by Whitehead (1992) confirmed these findings and demonstrated that, in the following decade from 1970 to 1980, little had changed in this respect. Research that has been carried out in Ireland on this subject indicates that there is no room for complacency (see Nolan, 1989; Cook, 1990; Nolan, 1992; Wiley and Merriman, 1996; Collins and Shelly, 1997; Balanda, 2001; Barry et al., 2001; European Commission, 2003). Commenting on their study of mortality statistics in Ireland as a whole, Balanda (2001: 11) states that the findings establish 'the pervasiveness and mag-nitude of occupational class inequalities on the island. In both Northern Ireland and the Republic of Ireland the all causes mortality rate in the lowest occupational class was 100–200 per cent higher than the rate in the highest occupational class. This was evident for nearly all the main causes of death.'

The findings that poorer people, on average, live shorter lives and are subject to more ill health at an earlier age than their richer counterparts leads to what Nolan (1989: 2) describes as 'a double injustice – life is short where quality is poor'. The trans-generational nature of the inequalities is reflected in the lower birth weight, smaller stature and poorer nutritional status on average of those who are poor. As Blaxter (1989: 219) points out, 'variation in health is part of the human condition, and the degree or nature of variation which is unacceptable has political and historical dimensions'. The definition of health inequality is ultimately an ideological one concerning qualitative judgements about what is acceptable, preventable and just. It also requires a broad perspective on the concept of health that encompasses inequalities in life chances and in service provision both within and outside the health sphere into, for example, education, housing and income maintenance. Burke et al. (2004: 55) argue that 'while health services alone cannot tackle health inequalities, they have the responsibility to provide leadership in this area and proactively contribute to a reduction in current levels of inequalities'.

Challenges for the future

There is no indication that health care will be perceived as any less important in the future. The potential for new demands on health services is great and Tormey's (1992: 381) prediction over a decade ago that 'demands on health services will continue to outstrip supply' has proven to be correct. There is certainly no sign of reduced spending and it is likely that the coming decades will be characterised by an ongoing preoccupation with ever rising costs and demands. Evans (1996) argues that demands on health services inevitably increase more rapidly than resources are allocated. Further, he argues that from a resource perspective some developments in treatments will result in increased demand in the future. He cites the example of the treatment of renal failure with dialysis and its impact on the demand for health care. A few decades ago, a person with renal failure would make but brief demands on the acute sector as terminal care would be the only requirement. Advances in treatment have extended this condition to a chronic one needing continuing intervention. This example can be applied to other conditions which have become chronic such as AIDS. Indeed, he suggests the very success of health services in contributing to the overall health status of the population has resulted in increased numbers living longer and thereby utilising more health care services.

Caplan (1995: 110) argues that recent medical advances are of the order to challenge 'thinking on living, dying and being human'. These include hitherto uncharted areas such as therapy in the womb, genetic manipulation, construction of artificial organs and innovative techniques for improving or restoring organ functioning. Such developments present formidable challenges for health care in the coming decades of the twenty-first century. The capacity to genetically map predisposition to health risks offers scope for preventative measures which could change the relative position of preventative vis à vis curative practice. The repercussions of genetic adaptation have the potential to change the health profile and status of future generations.

Optimists would suggest that the development in treatments such as genetic manipulation and treatment in the womb might lessen the costs of health care for future generations. Certainly it would be a great deal more economic to correct a genetic disorder such as spina bifida *in vitro* than to provide health care services for the same individual during the course of their lifetime. However, such potential savings are in the future. Pessimists would counter with the point that the alleviation of one set of health problems is likely to be replaced by others, especially related to advanced ageing, the survival of very premature babies with increased risk of severe physical/intellectual disabilities, and continuing 'affluent' disease patterns.

Tormey (2003: 1) comments that 'the most overwhelming feature of medicine in the twenty-first century is the phenomenal pace of change'. In the foreseeable future, therefore, concern with spending on health services is likely to continue. Regardless of the economic conditions which prevail, the debate about fair allocation of resources to different sectors and needs will, if anything, intensify. As discussed earlier, one reason is the projected increase of older people within the population in the coming decades, especially, those over 85 years. However, Fahey (1995) cautions against making the assumption that increased numbers of those over 65 in future decades will automatically create increased demand in the same ratio as at present. He argues that, in the future, there may be a need to redefine 'old age' to take account of improved health status. It may be that, by the year 2020, old age may be defined in terms of 75 or 80, rather than 65 as at present. However, it is still likely that the older person will make disproportionate demands on health care. How society will respond to this will depend upon many factors, not least, the values and ideology pertaining to ageing (see chapter 10).

An issue which has provoked considerable attention in recent times has been concern about individual control over the nature and timing of death and, in particular, questions about the validity or otherwise of voluntary euthanasia. Concern about the process of dying is likely to increase rather than diminish. Avoidance of the prospect of one's own death in Western society, it can be argued, has been facilitated by the removal and sanitisation of death in a hospital setting. Advanced directives, also called living wills, are becoming increasingly utilised to ensure that, should a person be incapacitated to the extent that they are not able to express preferences regarding the giving or withholding of treatment, their wishes in this respect are recorded. As Cusack (1997: 161) points out, the legal standing of an advanced directive is not clear in Ireland although 'the right of a patient to refuse treatment itself is beyond doubt'. An advanced directive can only record a person's wishes regarding the provision or non-provision of what is termed medical interventions; it cannot require that the medical personnel take any steps to hasten death by active or passive means. What constitutes treatment in this context has been the subject of medical and legal debate, particularly in relation to patients who are in what is termed a persistent vegetative state and thus unable to either continue living unaided or be able to express any wish regarding their care. In the case of Anthony Bland, a soccer fan injured beyond recovery when crushed, the British House of Lords in 1993 held that artificial feeding could be stopped as it constituted treatment (Walton, 1995). A similar case in Ireland in 1995 of a woman who had been living for 23 years in a near persistent vegetative state resulted in a judgement by the High Court, upheld by the Supreme Court, that artificial feeding could be lawfully discontinued. This judgement was made without precedent and there is an absence of guidelines in this area in Ireland (Cusack, 1997).

McDonnell (1997) argues that the reluctance of the state to become involved in the debate surrounding the repercussions of contentious issues such as the right to die and the anomalies relating to the practice of new reproductive technology has left a vacuum in which the implied responsibility and power of decision is often left to individual medical practitioners acting within the self-regulatory sphere of medicine. Writing about the United States, Markson (1997: 86) quotes unofficial estimates that between one and 15 per cent of deaths per year are physician-aided ones which are 'typically recorded officially as cardiac arrest'.

The public/private mix of health care has been enshrined in health policy documents as a desirable and permanent feature of our health care system. Inequality of access is thus inbuilt within Irish health services so that those with resources have choice and speed of access to a wider range of health care than others. Private health care has been traditionally endorsed by the Catholic Church in Ireland, both in its support for the principle of subsidiarity and by its provision of actual facilities such as the private hospitals run by religious orders. It has been strongly supported by the medical profession with GPs acting as private entrepreneurs, while many hospital consultants apparently have no difficulty reconciling the fact that they are among the highest paid public employees and, at the same time, can and do reap the considerable benefits of private practice in the same field. It is not simply the issue of 'double-jobbing' which is in question. Consultants interviewed in the study by Brown and Chadwick (1997: 203) claimed that most consultants worked more than the requisite hours in their public capacity. The more important issue is that, by engaging in extensive private practice, they are witnessing and contributing to an unequal system endorsed by the state which condones preferential treatment to those who can afford it. Good health and fast access to high quality care when needed are commodities which are equally precious to all. However, in a variety of respects, they are not equally distributed across the population and the existence of a private health care sector, supported by tax relief on premia, serves to institutionalise and perpetuate socioeconomic inequalities. Together and separately the Catholic Church and the medical profession have acted as a conservative force in Irish health care long after the controversies surrounding the proposals for a comprehensive health care scheme for mothers and children (Whyte, 1980). The profit motive which governs, at least in part, all private provision is hard to reconcile with best possible standard of care and the existence of a two-tier system is surely irreconcilable with the stated desire to provide the highest possible standard of care for all. In view of the advancing knowledge in the area of genetics discussed above, there is real danger that, in future, particularly given the private availability of health care, there will be differences in genetic endowment created which could result in health inequalities unprecedented in the history of health care.

Table 3.1 **Policy developments**

1838	Poor Law (Ireland) Act – first provision of state health services; infirmaries provided in association with workhouses
1851	Unions divided into dispensary districts; physicians attached to each district to provide free service to the poor
1872	Poor Law Commissioners abolished, replaced by Irish Local Government Board
1924	Department of Local Government and Health established
1947	Department of Health established when functions of above were divided into Health, Social Welfare and Local Government
1953	Health Act extended entitlement for health care. Maternity and Infant Care Scheme established
1957	Voluntary Health Insurance Act
1960	Local Authorities responsible for the provision of services reduced to 27
1966	White Paper on the future of the health services
1970	Health Act established eight regional health boards
1986	Publication of Health – The Wider Dimensions
1989	Report of the Commission on Health Funding
1990	Dublin Hospital Initiative Group, proposed organisational structures for the Dublin area
1991	Entitlement to free public hospital care extended to all under the Health (Amendment) Act
1994	Department of Health First Strategy Document
	Health Insurance Act ended monopoly position of VHI
1995	Health Promotion Strategy, 1995–2000
1997	Publication of Plan for Women's Health
1998	Department of Health renamed the Department of Health and Children
1999	White Paper on Private Health Insurance
2000	Health Promotion Strategy 2000–2005
2001	Department of Health and Children Second Strategy Document
	Primary Care: A New Direction
	Audit of the Irish Health System

2003   Commission on the Financial Management and Control Systems in the Health
            Service (Brennan Report)
        Audit of the Structures and Functions in the Health System (Prospectus Report)
        Report of the National Task Force on Medical Staffing (Hanly Report)
        Health Services Reform Programme
2004   Setting-up of the Health Service Executive and abolition of the Health Boards
        Health Act establishing the Health Service Executive

Recommended reading

Barrington, R. (1987) *Health, Medicine and Politics in Ireland 1900–1970*. Dublin: IPA.
Curry, J. (2003) *Irish Social Services*. Dublin: IPA. Chapter 5.
Leahy, A. L. and Wiley, M. M.(eds) (1998) *The Irish Health System in the 21st Century*.
    Dublin: Oak Tree.
Tormey, B., (2003) *A Cure for the Crisis: Irish Healthcare in Context*. Dublin: Blackwater.
Wren, Maev-Ann. (2003) *Unhealthy State: Anatomy of a Sick Society*. Dublin: New Island.

Chapter 4

Housing policy

David Silke

Introduction

Shelter is considered one of the most basic of human needs. Adequate shelter involves a complex series of issues including access, appropriateness, quality, environment, supply/affordability, choice of tenure and sustainability. It is the central goal of housing policy. As we will see in this chapter, adequate shelter was an important issue in the early years of the Republic, but one which was considered largely under control by the end of the 1980s /early 1990s (see, for example, NESC, 1993a: 449). In the mid-1990s things changed and in social policy terms they changed rapidly. Economic growth, increased employment rates, moderate to low interest rates, inward migration and a maturing young population all contributed to increased demand for accommodation. This demand surge was not forecast and was not planned for. Accommodation could not be supplied quickly enough to meet this demand, consequently house prices and rents in the private sector increased sharply, as did waiting lists for social housing. Affordability and access were issues dominating public debate. This resurgence of interest in housing policy should be of particular interest to social policy students, particularly regarding how issues get identified and defined as social problems and how policy is subsequently designed and implemented.

Before focusing in on housing policy, however, it is important to draw attention to its links with other areas of social policy. Studies have pointed to the connection between poor housing conditions and ill health (O'Shea and Kelleher, 2001: 274). The link between housing and employment can be seen at a very basic level by the practical difficulties of sustaining oneself within the work environment while experiencing homelessness and sustaining accommodation while unemployed. Links have also been drawn between employment and address, or location, which has a strong association with housing tenure

David Silke is a Policy Analyst with the National Economic and Social Forum. The views expressed are those of the author and are not necessarily those of the NESF.

in the Irish situation owing to the high degree of geographical segregation of tenures. Policy reviews have examined the interaction of the social welfare system's support of housing costs and financial incentives to take up work (Expert Working Group on the Integration of Tax and Social Welfare Systems, 1996). As part of a multi-dimensional approach to tackling educational disadvantage and early school leaving, the importance of adequate housing has also been highlighted (NESF, 2002a: 26–7). Links can also be traced between housing and the availability of and access to social services. For older people, for example, unsuitable housing can lead to early or avoidable entry to institutional care if problems are not dealt with expeditiously (Silke, 1994).

It is for these reasons that housing is considered as one of the four principal areas of study in social policy, along with health, education and income maintenance. In this chapter, students are offered an analysis of Irish housing policy. The chapter begins with some contextual information. Current housing policy is then outlined and evaluated. The chapter concludes by highlighting some potential challenges for the future.

Definition and scope of Irish housing policy

Housing policy is of relevance to all residents in the country. Housing policy is 'any deliberate course of action which is designed to affect housing conditions' (Blackwell, 1988: 75). This is a very broad definition and gives some idea of the wide scope of policy actions in this area. It includes, for instance, support for owner-occupation and the private rented sectors through tax relief; direct provision of accommodation by local authorities; support for those who cannot afford their accommodation through the social welfare system; and support of the voluntary housing sector.

Blackwell (1988) outlines various reasons why governments intervene in housing markets. These include: a wish to make housing markets work more efficiently (i.e. to correct poor information or to help people secure mortgages); supporting the building industry and related employment in order to achieve minimum housing standards; promoting either private or social ownership as something desirable in its own right; the wish to achieve a different distribution of income than that which would be the outcome of housing market forces; and in particular to help lower income households with their housing costs.

Government intervention can take a number of different forms. The main ones are: regulation (e.g. ensuring minimum building standards are achieved); direct provision (e.g. through local authorities); the provision of information (to customers and providers); subsidies and tax levies (e.g. tax relief on mortgages, urban renewal, grants to the voluntary sector); transfer payments (e.g.

towards the cost of rented accommodation or grants for home improvement); and the direct provision of loan finance for housing on the part of state agencies (NESC, 1988: 141). It should also be noted, however, that interventions can be expensive and can have unintended consequences – for example, favourable fiscal treatment of home-ownership may encourage over-investment in housing and under investment in other forms of savings. This may lead to increased house prices and dampening of other investment, which in turn raises the cost of borrowing to business (NESC, 1999: 487–8).

Housing policy responsibility

Principal actors involved in policy development in Irish housing policy

As housing issues are of central importance to all residents, a large number of different organisations and bodies are active in this area. The Department of the Environment, Heritage and Local Government takes the lead policy responsibility. Other government departments also play an important role in housing policy – for example the Department of Finance in relation to the tax treatment of housing, the Department of Social and Family Affairs, which funds the Supplementary Welfare Allowance rent and mortgage supplement scheme (administered by the health boards), the Department of Justice, Equality and Law Reform, which monitors the implementation of the Report of the Working Group on the Traveller Community and the Department of Health and Children, which provides grants for some special housing needs.

Local authorities, of which there are currently 88, are responsible for the operation and management of public housing policy at the local level. The housing functions of local authorities include: housing management, rent collection, estate management and services for special needs groups; housing provision, construction and purchasing; enabling housing provision through the voluntary and co-operative bodies, tenant purchase / affordable housing schemes; and local level planning such as need assessment, housing strategic planning committees and homeless fora. Traditionally, the Irish system of government was very centralised, but this is changing. The current reform package, which focuses on enhancing local democracy, improving customer services, developing efficiency and local revenue collection, was initiated in the mid-1900s (Department of the Environment, 1996, see also Devolution Commission, 1996).

The Homeless Agency (formerly Homeless Initiative) was established as part of the government strategy on homelessness and is responsible for the management and co-ordination of services to people who are homeless in Dublin. State-sponsored bodies with an interest in the area of housing policy include: An Bord Pleanála (responsible for dealing with planning appeals), the Housing Finance Agency (lends money to housing authorities and other approved bodies to enable the provision of social housing), the National Building Agency (a consultancy specialising in housing, urban design, conservation, and project management), the Private Residential Tenancies Board Rent Tribunal (maintains a register of all private residential tenancies, offers mediation and conducts research) and the Housing Unit (provides advice and guidance on social housing management, undertakes research and training).

The Construction Industry Federation is the management association for the construction industry, and among other activities represents the industry to government. The Irish Business and Employers Confederation (IBEC) and the Irish Small and Medium Enterprises Association (ISME) represent different aspects of the building industry. Banks and building societies would also be expected to keep an active watching brief on housing policy as it is of central importance to their mortgage and lending business. The Irish Property Owners' Association represents the interests of private landlords.

Key voluntary agencies in this area are Focus Ireland, the Simon Community, Respond!, Threshold, the Irish Council for Social Housing (representing over 180 voluntary housing bodies) and the Society of St Vincent de Paul. Many of these organisations undertake research and policy in the area of housing policy and have library facilities open to the public which can be the source of very useful and otherwise difficult-to-find information. The Institute of Public Administration, the Economic and Social Research Institute and the Combat Poverty Agency are also good sources of information on housing policy.

Current housing system

Tenure types

The number of private dwellings (defined for Census purposes as the room or set of rooms occupied by a private household [i.e. a group of persons living together, jointly occupying the whole or part of a private dwellings house, flat or temporary dwelling and sharing a common budget] in a permanent housing unit) has almost doubled between 1911 (the earliest date for which comprehensive records are available) and 2002 from 641,156 to 1,287,958 units. Indeed, from 1911 to 1946 the number of private households dropped by 20,000, mainly owing to depopulation in rural areas, emigration and demolition. The main expansion in the housing stock has taken place since the early 1970s. Table 4.1 charts this increase. It also shows the trend towards smaller households over the same period.

Between 1996 and 2002 the number of private households increased by 164,700 or by 14.7 per cent, the greater increase being among childless couples

Table 4.1 **Main trends in the number of households 1971– 2002**

	Households (,000)	% change	Persons per household	% change
1971	726.4	—	3.94	—
1981	896.1	23.4	3.68	−6.6
1991	1,019.7	13.8	3.34	−9.2
1996	1,123.2	10.2	3.14	−6.0
2002	1,288.0	14.7	2.94	−6.8

Source: Census of Population, various years

(up 58,900 or 38.7 per cent) and lone parents with children (up 25,800 or 24.5 per cent) (CSO, 2003). Table 4.2 shows the distribution of private dwellings or private households by tenure in Ireland, 1946–2002. It demonstrates the steady decline in social housing since 1961 and the growth of owner-occupation as the dominant tenure. There was a slight drop in the percentage of owner-occupied dwellings between 1991 and 2002; however the absolute number of such dwellings increased by a little over one fifth, from 808,385 to 990,723 (see table 4.3). The share of privately rented dwellings declined until 1991, most markedly during the 1940s and 1950s. But a reversal of this trend is now evident, with the number of privately rented units up from 81,424 to 141,459 (or three percentage points) between 1991 and 2002 (see table 4.3).

Not specifically coved in tables 4.2 and 4.3, but important nonetheless, is the voluntary non-profit housing sector. Mullins et al. (2003: 28) estimate that in December 2001 there were about 330 active non-profit housing associations in the Republic of Ireland, managing about 13,000 dwellings or about 10 per cent of the social housing sector. The sector includes voluntary housing organisations, formed out of existing community organisations to provide

Table 4.2 **Private households/private dwellings by tenure type in Ireland, 1946–2002 (%)**

Tenure	1946 %	1961 %	1971 %	1981 %	1991 %	2002 %
Owner-occupied[1]	52.6	59.8	68.8	74.4	79.3	77.4
Social housing	–	18.4	15.5	12.5	9.7	6.9
Private rented	42.7	17.2	13.3	10.1	8.0	11.1
Rent free/not stated	4.7	4.6	2.4	3	3	4.6

1 Including local authority tenant purchase.
Source: Census of Population, various years.

Table 4.3 **Private households/private dwellings by tenure type in Ireland, 1971–2002**

Tenure	1971	1981	1991	2002
Owner-occupied[1]	499,560	667,005	808,385	990,723
Social housing	112,709	111,739	98,929	88,206
Private rented	96,884	90,315	81,424	141,459
Rent free/not stated	17,210	26,995	30,985	59,229
Total	726,363	896,054	1,019,723	1,279,617

1 Including local authority tenant purchase.
Source: Census of Population, various years.

housing and related services, mainly to older people and those with special care needs and housing co-operatives, which were traditionally self-build group housing schemes. Rental co-operatives have developed more recently.

Fahey and Watson (1995: 20–1) noted that home-ownership has been promoted as the main tenure in Ireland in a number of different ways. First, home ownership is generously subsidised through tax relief for mortgage interest payments, first-time buyers' grants (abolished in 2002, but mortgage tax relief increased for this group), waiving stamp duty on purchases of new homes, the non-taxation of imputed income from owner-occupied housing, and the exemption of homes from capital gains tax. In more recent years, initiatives have been targeted at low-income aspiring homebuyers with the introduction first of the Shared Ownership scheme and later the Affordable Housing scheme. The sale of local authority housing to sitting tenants at discount prices has meant that social housing has been used primarily as a route to home ownership for low income households and only in a secondary way as an alternative to home ownership for that sector. Drudy and Punch (2001: 243) refer to this as the 'commodification' of public housing, whereby social housing has become a commodity which can be used for profit-making as opposed to its primary function of providing shelter. It should be noted that entry to the tenure is reserved for low income groups who are deemed not to be able to afford to provide for their own accommodation needs. Since Independence, local authorities have built over 300,000 dwellings; however less than one third are still under local authority ownership (Fahey and Watson, 1995). Finally, the lack of support until recently of the private rented sector has meant that it has traditionally been unable to compete with private ownership.

In addition to local authority social housing provision, some fiscal supports are available to non-homeowners. For instance, Capital Assistance and Capital Loan and (Rental) Subsidy Schemes are open to approved voluntary organisations to build housing for rent to those in need and on low income

(Department of the Environment and Local Government, 2002a). The Capital Assistance Scheme provides 95 per cent funding (to maximum limits) towards the building costs, generally of one or two bedroom units, for special housing needs, including older people, homeless people and those with a disability and in some cases smaller families. The scheme does not help with the maintenance and repair of property. The Capital Loan and (Rental Subsidy) Scheme is used primarily for housing low-income families who are eligible for social housing. Tax relief has been used to encourage investors to buy properties to rent and relief is available to private tenants at the standard rate. A limitation of the former measure is that, by definition, the scheme only applies to tenants who pay income tax (which, for instance, excludes many students,).

The dominance of one tenure type in the Irish situation may have unintended consequences for those who are not in that tenure. It can lead to segregation and marginalisation of certain sectors of the community, or it can mean that some tenures are seen as 'temporary' or 'transitory' – a means to reach owner-occupation, rather than as a legitimate, long-term tenure choice. This can result in some tenures, such as in the private-rented sector, lacking adequate regulation, management and planning, and others, such as the voluntary, non-profit sector receiving less financial aid than others. The stress on the importance of home-ownership has had the effect of reducing the importance attached to considerations of equity in housing policy (see Fahey and Watson, 1995: 21–3). More recently, concern has been expressed that increased debt burden, as home ownership becomes more expensive, may fuel wage demands and reduced competitiveness (NESC, 1999: 501).

Housing need

Under Section 9 of the Housing Act 1988 each local housing authority is required to carry out periodic assessments (at least every three years) of social housing needs. The assessments cover the need for local authority housing in each local authority area, together with the part that can be played in meeting need by other social housing options, the need for residential caravan parks for Travellers and for the number of homeless persons. Six assessments of housing need have been undertaken since 1988, and the results are presented in table 4.4 below.

Table 4.4 shows in general an upward trend in housing need between 1989 and 2002 as defined by the survey. During this period, the total number of households identified as in need of housing has more than doubled. The most dramatic increase has been in the number of households unable to afford their accommodation, which has increased over seven-fold. In two categories – unfit dwellings and the elderly – the assessments show a reduction in unmet need comparing 1989 with 2002. The 2002 survey counted over 48,000 households as being in need of local authority housing, or almost four per cent of all

Table 4.4 **Assessment of social housing need 1989–2002**

Households	1989	1991	1993	1996	1999	2002	% change 1989– 2002
Unable to afford existing accommodation	2,809	4,075	6,432	7,659	13,328	21,452	663.7
In overcrowded dwellings	4,621	5,896	7,075	5,912	8,328	8,513	84.2
In unfit dwellings	4,324	4,590	5,122	4,799	4,796	4,065	−6.0
Involuntarily sharing accommodation	2,000	2,432	3,345	3,120	4,086	4,421	121.1
Elderly	2,349	2,379	2,191	2,140	2,363	2,006	−14.6
Medical/compas- sionate grounds	1,187	1,331	1,861	1,762	2,347	3,400	186.4
Homeless	987	1,507	1,452	979	2,219[1]	2,468	150.1
Travellers	834	748	884	749	1,406	1,583	89.8
Disabled	108	180	194	241	236	423	291.7
Young persons leaving institutional care	—	104	68	66	67	82	—
In institutional care	156	—	—	—	—	—	
Total	19,376	23,242	28,624	27,427	39,176	48,413	149.9

1 The definition of homeless was broadened in 1999 to include those with no accommodation, those in hostels and in Health Board accommodation.
Source: Housing Statistics Bulletin: Department of the Environment and Local Government, various years.

households (Department of the Environment and Local Government, 2002b: 58–85). The majority of these households could be considered to be low-income households – 85 per cent had annual incomes of less than €15,000. Over half were either single person households (32 per cent) or consisted of one adult and one child (29 per cent). In addition 3,406 households were considered suitable for other social housing measures including shared owner-ship, extensions or sale of site. A further 1,025 were considered suited to rent or mortgage supplementation under the Supplementary Welfare Allowance Scheme. This type of information is very important if social policy analysts are to consider how best 'housing need' should be met. However, planners need to be aware of the limitations of the data collected, especially if not all 'housing needs' are included in the survey (see, for discussion, Fahey and Watson, 1995).

Homelessness

Numbers in relation to the homeless category deserve separate comment. One of the problems here is how to define and measure homelessness. The 1988 Housing Act provides a statutory definition, which includes those with no accommodation and those living in hospitals, county homes, bed and breakfast or shelters as they have nowhere else available to them due to lack of resources. The measurement of homelessness can take two forms. The stock measurement, used in the assessment cited above counts the number homeless at a particular point in time. The alternative measure is to count the flow of those who experience homelessness over a period of time. The stock measure is useful to get a snapshot of the problem while a flow measure is more useful at understanding the duration of homelessness people experience and also the dynamics of the problem (see Fahey and Watson, 1995: 99–121). Additionally, it can be useful to consider homelessness on a continuum from street homeless (e.g. rough sleepers) to vulnerable or at-risk households. The latter may include those involuntarily sharing with family or friends, in insecure accommodation, those leaving prison or other long-stay institution and those living in inadequate or substandard accommodation (Focus Ireland et al., 2002).

The March 2002 assessment of homelessness reported the number of homeless households at 3,773, compared to 3,743 in 1999. The number of homeless persons increased from 5,234 to 5,581 over the same period. When considering these trends it is interesting to note that the Department of the Environment and Local Government spent €43 million on accommodation and related services for homeless persons in 2002, compared to about €12.5 million in 1999. Looking in more detail at the 2002 figures, firstly in relation to homeless households, three quarters were one-person households and two thirds were living in the Dublin area. In relation to homeless individuals, three quarters were adults and one-quarter were children (Department of the Environment and Local Government, 2003a: 68–9). A snapshot survey of one night (from 2 to 4 a.m.) in March 2002 found 140 rough sleepers in the four Dublin local authority areas, the majority of whom were in the Dublin City Council (79) and South Dublin County Council (50) areas. Up to 312 people reported that they had slept rough in the week of the assessment (Williams and Gorby, 2002).

Particular groups may be more prone to homelessness then others. Lennon (1998) identified people with mental health problems, young people under 18 years of age, families, people with substance addictions, young single people and older single men as being particularly at risk. Research carried out by the Gay and Lesbian Equality Network and Nexus (1995: 67) found that almost one third (32 per cent) of lesbians and gay men interviewed said that they had left home at one time or another with no certainty as to where they were going to live next. The proportion almost doubled (to 62 per cent) for those who were considered to be living in poverty. O'Sullivan (1998b) has also drawn attention to the problem of child homelessness in Ireland. Those leaving prison have also been identified as an at-risk group (NESF, 2002b; Focus Ireland and PACE, 2002).

Three government strategies have been produced in response to the growing number of homeless people. The first, *Homelessness: An Integrated Strategy* (Department of the Environment and Local Government, 2000a), focused on the development of a more integrated response to the planning and delivery of services covering accommodation, health, welfare, education and preventative measures. Homeless fora were established at county level (they already existed at city level) and three-year action plans were drawn up involving local authorities, health boards and voluntary agencies. New services were introduced and additional funding approved. Local authorities were given responsibility for the provision of accommodation, including emergency hostel and temporary accommodation for homeless persons, and health boards were given responsibility for the provision of health and in-house care needs. An evaluation of the plans was, however, critical that not all local authorities had completed their plans on time, that completion of the plans lacked a statutory requirement, that many lacked a clear vision or specific targets, that data were inadequate for planning and projections and that there was a lack of linkage to the housing strategies (Focus Ireland et al., 2002). The second strategy, *Youth Homelessness Strategy* (Department of Health and Children, 2001), had twelve objectives covering preventative measures, services responsiveness and planning /administrative supports. The third strategy, *Homeless Preventative Strategy* (Department of the Environment and Local Government, 2002c), focused in particular on measures to prevent homelessness among young and adult offenders, those leaving mental facilities and acute hospitals and young people leaving care. It aimed to ensure that no one was released from any type of state care without the appropriate measures in place to ensure they had a suitable place to live and adequate supports if needed.

Homelessness has also been included in social inclusion strategies. Both the Revised National Anti-Poverty Strategy, *Building an Inclusive Society* (Department of Social, Community and Family Affairs, 2002: 13), and Ireland's submission to the EU equivalent, the *National Action Plan against Poverty and Social Inclusion 2003–2005* (Office for Social Inclusion, 2003: 30), set as a target that, by the end of 2004, sufficient and appropriate emergency accommodation would be available to rough sleepers, in each local authority and health board area in conjunction with appropriate outreach services to enable them to access it. A commitment was also made to review progress, with revised mechanisms to be put in place to achieve the target if required. The issue of homelessness is also included in the most recent partnership agreement, *Sustaining Progress* (Government of Ireland, 2003a: 24).

The collection of adequate and reliable data on the extent of homelessness and the type of services required in response and the co-ordination of services, both between statutory and voluntary service providers and between the homeless sector and other relevant sectors (such as health), remain key issues in relation to tackling homelessness. There is also growing recognition of the need for move-on permanent accommodation to progress people out of homelessness as quickly as possible to more stable accommodation provided by local authorities, the voluntary sector or the private rented sector, as appropriate. The increasing use of bed and breakfast accommodation and its unsuitability as a long-term housing option have also been raised as concerns (Focus Ireland, 2000); and recent research has emphasised the links between homelessness, social exclusion and food poverty (Hickey and Downey, 2004).

Housing completions

Moving on from the concept of housing need, it is also important to examine trends in the number of house completions over time. Table 4.5 illustrates the general slowdown in the number of house completions during the mid-to-late 1980s, with local authority completions slowing down in particular. This general decline in completions was attributed to a downturn in the economy, an increase in emigration, a reduction in local authority waiting lists and a general policy across Europe to reduce expenditure on public housing (NESC, 1993a: 452). During the mid-to-late 1990s, house completions recovered to the levels experienced in the early 1980s, and then continued to increase at a steady pace. Social housing (local authority and voluntary completions) also increased, but not at the same rate. Indeed, comparing 1981 and 2003, we see that the proportion of completions accounted for by social housing reduced from about one in five of all completions to about one in eleven. That said, in absolute terms, it is worth noting the recovery in voluntary housing completions since 2000.

The National Economic and Social Council (NESC, 2003: 82–4) has drawn attention to the fact that the spatial pattern of this housing expansion has been more dispersed than the pattern of employment growth, particularly in the Dublin / Eastern region. This has led to large-scale developments in small villages and one-off housing in rural areas within commuting distance of urban-based employment. While this may make home ownership more affordable for some it also has the down side of often inadequate infrastructure and services and long commuting times. The National Economic and Social Forum (NESF, 2003: 107–12) has highlighted the need to consider the

Table 4.5 **Housing completions 1981–2003**

Year	Private houses	Local authority	Voluntary	Total
1981	23,236	5,681	n/a	28,917
1983	19,948	6,190	n/a	26,138
1985	17,425	6,523	n/a	23,948
1987	15,376	3,074	n/a	18,450
1989	17,300	768	n/a	18,068
1991	18,472	1,180	n/a	19,652
1993	19,301	1,200	890	21,391
1995	26,604	2,960	1,011	30,575
1997	35,454	2,632	756	38,842
1999	43,024	2,909	579	46,512
2000	46,657	2,204	951	49,812
2001	47,727	3,622	1,253	52,602
2002	51,932	4,403	1,360	57,695
2003	62,686	4,516	1,617	68,819

Source: Housing Statistics Bulletin (various years) Department of the Environment, Heritage and Local Government.

possible impact these changes will have for social capital, community engagement, support networks and trust in others. A second point to note about this expansion is that, despite the marked increase in the housing stock noted above, Ireland's housing stock is the lowest in the European Union at 341 housing units per thousand population compared to 417 in the United Kingdom and an EU average of 437 (European Union, 2001).

Quality of accommodation
A central issue in housing policy is the quality of accommodation. This concept is often measured in terms of household facilities such as running water, flush toilet, age of dwelling and overcrowding. Census data show a continuing improvement in the quality of Irish dwellings and it is generally accepted that housing policy has been successful in enabling most Irish people to live in reasonable accommodation (NESC, 1993a: 449). A national survey of the housing stock was undertaken in 2001–2 by the Economic and Social Research Institute (Watson and Williams, 2003). It involved a representative sample of over 40,000 householders and collected information about the characteristics and problems of their homes. This survey differed from earlier ones, most noticeably in that it had a larger sample size, was centrally administered rather than through the local authorities and collected residents' assessments of their housing – in previous years housing quality was assessed

by survey staff (see Finn, 1992). In this latest survey, at least one household in eight (13 per cent) reported a major problem with the condition of its housing – dampness, major heating problems, lack of sanitary or food preparation facilities or proper ventilation. These problems were more likely to be experienced by local authority renters (33 per cent), those in pre-1941 accommodation (25 per cent) and those on low income (25 per cent). Over a quarter of respondents (27 per cent) reported a problem with the condition or some other aspect of their accommodation such as cost, space or problems in the area. Local authority tenants were most likely to report experiencing problems in their areas, such as graffiti, rubbish lying about and vandalism (25 per cent), while those privately renting were most likely to indicate problems regarding affordability (29 per cent). Lone parents with dependent children were most likely to find their housing costs a heavy burden (35 per cent), with one in six (17 per cent) reporting that they spent more than one third of their income on housing costs. Overall, however, the majority of respondents (92 per cent) reported satisfaction with the general condition of their accommodation.

Housing affordability

The issue of house prices came to dominate Irish social and economic discussion in the mid to late 1990s, particularly for first-time buyers. Figure 4.1 charts the increase in house prices from 1993 and shows how prices began to pick up in the mid-1990s.

In order to inform the Government's response to these price rises, Peter Bacon and Associates was commissioned to undertake a review of the situation.

Figure 4.1 **Average price of new and second-hand house prices 1993–2003**

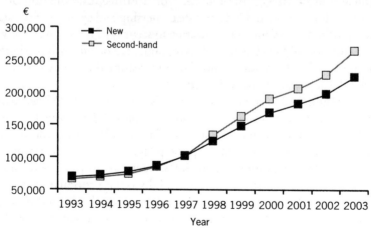

Source: *Housing Statistics Bulletin* (various years) Dublin: Department of the Environment, Heritage and Local Government.

The report, *An Economic Assessment of Recent House Price Developments*, emphasised both supply and demand aspects fuelling house price inflation (Bacon et al., 1998). On the supply side, the shortage of serviced land and inefficiencies in the planning process were identified as constraining new house building. On the demand side, the role of investors in the private housing market was highlighted and it was argued that these investors were contributing to general house inflation and crowding out would-be first time buyers. The Government's response – *Action on House Prices* (Department of the Environment and Local Government, 1998) – was to accept the report's analysis. It doubled funding to the Serviced Land Initiative to open up more land for residential development, allocated extra resources to the planning process and reduced Capital Gains Tax on sales of serviced, zoned residential land for a limited period. Stamp duty payable by owner-occupiers purchasing second hand houses was reduced while at the same time stamp duty was introduced for non owner-occupiers buying new dwellings. In addition, landlords would no longer be able to offset the money borrowed to purchase a dwelling for rent against rental income for tax purposes.

As Figure 4.1 indicates, house prices continued to rise following the publication of the first Bacon report and the Government commissioned a second study. The resulting report – *The Housing Market: An Economic Review and Assessment* – was published in March 1999 (Bacon and MacCabe, 1999). It found that the house price increases had eased following *Action on House Prices* but concluded that further measures were needed to address the supply and demand aspects outlined above. As a result of the second Bacon report, *Action on the Housing Market* (Department of the Environment and Local Government, 1999), further government initiatives were announced, including additional housing sites in the Dublin North Fringe, examination of the potential use for housing of lands in state ownership and agreement to establish a commission to examine issues relating to security of tenure in the private rented sector (see below). The report also commented on affordability in relation to the rental sector and concluded that increasing the supply of housing remained the key factor to be addressed.

The third and final Bacon report was published in June 2000, *The Housing Market in Ireland: An Economic Evaluation of Trends and Prospects*. It found a continuing issue in relation to the supply of affordable private housing and recommended a range of measures, principally: changes to streamline the planning system; the completion of infrastructural projects; revisions to stamp duties to favour first-time buyers and discourage speculative demand and the introduction of an annual tax on dwellings which were not principal primary residences as an anti-speculation tax. The Department's response to this report, *Action on Housing* (Department of the Environment and Local Government, 2000b), again accepted these recommendations on the whole and made provision for the establishment of Strategic Development Zones to fast-track planning and infrastructural provision to develop large-scale residential developments, with a tax levied on sites not developed within specified timeframes. This measure was subsequently given a statutory basis in the Planning and Development Act 2000.

These three reports are interesting from a social policy perspective, both for their content and also for the process involved in their completion. They provide an interesting case study on the potential role of independent consultants in informing and – in this case – leading the development of social and economic policy. It is not possible to expand on this point in greater detail here; however, it is clear that the analysis contained in the Bacon reports was highly influential in the development of housing policy, at a time when the affordability of private ownership was a key political issue.

Private residential rents
As table 4.2 has shown, the relative importance of the private rented residential sector in Ireland declined steadily from the 1940s to the early 1990s. As outlined in table 4.3, results from Census 2002 indicate a reversal of this trend in more recent years, with the sector expanding by about three quarters between 1991 and 2002. Affordability, as rents rose in line with house prices, also became an issue in this sector towards the end of the 1990s (Downey and Devilly, 1999; Bacon and MacCabe, 1999: 54–5), although there was evidence of rent moderation in 2002–3 (Office for Social Inclusion, 2003: 7). Nonetheless, research by Fahey et al. (2004) found that those in the private rented sector spent proportionally more of their available income on housing compared to those in other tenures and that those who privately rented were at greatest risk of experiencing poverty and affordability problems. They found, for example, that in 1999–2000, mortgage payments absorbed on average one tenth of household income while households in the private rented sector used about two fifths (21 per cent) of their income on rent payments. Only one per cent of those with a mortgage experienced financial strain in meeting payments (defined as payment levels over 35 per cent of household expenditure) compared with one in five (20 per cent) of those in the private rented sector (Fahey, et al., 2004: 30–43). Figures released by the Central Statistics Office (CSO, 2004a: table 14) support the view that, on the whole, those prepaying mortgages were not experiencing major affordability problems. Of those recent first-time buyers (who generally bear the highest costs associated with dwelling purchase) who replied to a question regarding perceived affordability of mortgage repayments, the majority (88.4 per cent) considered their repayments either easy (24.2 per cent) or manageable (64.2 per cent); one in ten (10 per cent) said they were difficult and 1.6 per cent said they were very difficult to manage.

In 1999, the then Minister for Housing and Urban Renewal, Mr Robert Molloy, TD, established a Commission on the Private Rented Sector, which published its report the following year. It addressed a number of issues including security of tenure, regulation and enforcement, balancing the rights and responsibilities of tenants and landlords, measures to increase investment in, and supply of, rented accommodation, and the removal of constraints to the development of the sector. The Commission made a number of recommendations, including: the establishment of a Private Residential Tenancies Board to deal with disputes between tenants and landlords; greater security of tenure where the tenancy had lasted more than six continuous months, rent levels to be no greater than the market rate and reviews to be no more frequent than once a year; tax incentives to promote investment and professionalism in the sector and local authorities to give greater priority to the enforcement of statutory regulations. The Government broadly endorsed the package of measures put forward by the Commission and prepared a Residential Tenancies Bill 2003 to implement them. A Private Residential Tenancy Board was established on an *ad hoc* basis in October 2001, and was put on a statutory basis under the Residential Tenancies Act, 2004. The Board will provide a dispute resolution service, have responsibility for tenancy registration, research, the provision of information, policy advice and guidelines in relation to the sector.

Historical origins of Irish housing policy

The 1841 Census was the first to include an assessment of housing quality. Four categories were used. The lowest, category four, comprised houses built of mud or perishable material, having only one room and window; the third category could vary from one to four rooms and windows; category two was the equivalent of a good farm house; and the top category included anything better than the preceding. The results show that in 1841 of a total of 1,328,839 houses: 37 per cent were of category four quality; 40 per cent were category three; 20 per cent in category two and the remaining three per cent were category one. By the turn of the century the total number of houses recorded had been reduced to 858,158. The number of category four houses had been reduced considerably to only 1.5 per cent of the total, category three houses had reduced to 29 per cent, category two houses had increased dramatically to 61 per cent and the top category houses had increased to nine per cent (see, for discussion, Matheson, 1903).

The reduction in the level of poor quality accommodation was related to desolation caused by the Famine, with one million people dying and a similar figure emigrating during this period, many from the poorer housing. The Dwellings for Labouring Classes (Ireland) Acts 1860 enabled landlords to obtain loans for the provision of cottages (see Curry, 1998: 49–50). Government loans were also provided under the Labourers' Housing Act of 1883 and 1885 for the building of labourer cottages. The scheme was not very successful at first, as the initiative for building the cottage rested with the Local Board of Guardians (the predecessors of local authorities), which were heavily representative of the farming community. The farmers were hostile to the scheme because of the possible impact it would have on increasing rates (Daly, 1981: 33). This provides an interesting and early example of the influence of vested interests in the effective (or otherwise) implementation of housing policy. Amendments to the scheme, under the Labourers Act 1906, came about as a reaction to political unrest and led to the introduction of generous loan terms and a dedicated fund of £4.25 million. This did improve matters somewhat, and a surge in the construction of labourer cottages was evident – 23,000 such dwellings were built between 1906 and 1914. Fraser (1996: 43) observes that the success of the scheme 'created a situation in Ireland where there was virtually unanimous support for state-subsidised housing'. This was a substantial break with the laissez-faire tradition, and one which has had a long-term impact.

However, Kaim-Caudle (1967: 79) recounts that 'housing standards in Ireland in the first decade of this [twentieth] century were notoriously poor. The Dublin tenements were among the worst in Europe and many rural dwellings were not much better than hovels'. During the latter half of the nineteenth century, an expanding population living in urban tenement accommodation led to terrible slum conditions. The Census of 1901 provides depressing reading on this topic. It included a special set of questions on tenements of less than five rooms and found that three quarters of families in the country occupied such tenements. Tenements of one room only, numbering 79,149, were identified and of these only 20,994 had one occupant; 41,918 had two to four occupants; 13,351 had five to seven occupants; 2,886 had eight or more. In total, 101,845 people occupied these rooms or 2.3 per cent of the total population of the country (Matheson, 1903: 205–6). Those who are interested in the social history of tenement life may find Kearns (1994) of particular value in his account of tenement life in Dublin during this period.

The Housing Inquiry, established by the Local Government Board for Ireland after the Church Street Tenement disaster in 1913 in which three adults and four children were killed, and in the more general context of industrial upheaval and political unrest of the time, detailed the extent of urban deprivation (McManus, 2002: 24). It estimated that 60,000 people needed to be rehoused in Dublin City, and about 14,000 new dwellings were urgently required. It also exposed the fact that 14 members of Dublin Corporation owned tenements or small cottages, some of which were classified as unfit for human habitation (McManus, 2002: 32–5). The report drew links between poor housing and ill health and recommended the provision of self-contained dwellings of sufficient size to avoid overcrowding and the separation of the sexes (Powell, 1992: 123–7). The Housing (Ireland) Act, 1919 provided substantial subsidies to local authorities for housing, yet progress was slow.

The Free State inherited a poor housing stock and in 1922 set about trying to tackle the problem by introducing the 'Million Pound Scheme'. The scheme empowered local authorities to raise half a million pounds through the rating system and loans matched by £1 million from central government. It enabled 2,000 houses to be built. However, in the early years of Independence the focus was not on slum clearance, but largely on the middle classes, with the state encouraging home ownership. The Housing Act 1924, for instance, focused on the provision of grants for owner-occupiers. In 1929 the Department of Local Government and Public Health carried out a survey which estimated that 43,656 housing units were needed (McManus, 2002: 99).

By the 1930s the housing issue had developed into a housing crisis, particularly slum clearance. Despite increased spending and construction, the scale of the problem was such that a survey in 1938 discovered that 60 per cent of Dublin's tenements and cottages, which provided housing for 65,000 people, were unfit for human habitation. Building was to be dramatically reduced during the Second World War and following the War a White Paper on housing, published in 1948, estimated that a further 61,000 new dwellings were required, 38 per cent (or 23,500) in Dublin, another 35 per cent (21,000) in other urban centres and the remaining 27 per cent (16,500) in the countryside (Curry, 2003: 50). This is, perhaps, a good example of the way in which social policy needs are very difficult to satisfy. It also reflects the way in which need seems to outstrip delivery on an ongoing basis.

Construction of housing picked up again after the War, encouraged by government grant aid to private dwellings and particularly those building dwellings for their own occupation. In the late 1950s a downward trend was again evident, spurred on by an impression that the housing problem had been solved through the successful building programme and increased emigration. Demographic change and economic growth in the 1960s increased the demand for housing, particularly in urban centres. During the 1960s housing completions increased steadily and continued to climb into the early 1970s, reaching a peak of almost 27,000 in 1975. Completion rates remained high for the next ten years and then began to decline in the late 1980s (Curry, 2003: 51). Throughout this period, however, housing policy remained high on the political agenda. In 1977, Fianna Fáil promised to abolish domestic rates and to introduce a £1,000 first-time buyers' grant – both of which were enacted. In 1985, the Fine Gael–Labour government introduced a £5,000 home-improvement grant for houses constructed prior to 1946, which proved very popular.

A £5,000 surrender grant was also introduced in October 1984 to local authority tenants, with at least three years' satisfactory tenancy, who wanted to buy a home of their own. The first corporation sale scheme was introduced in 1968, which facilitated the sale of corporation houses at a discount price (to a maximum of 30 per cent). The surrender grant, however, was different in that it allowed tenants to choose the area in which they wanted to live. While this increased tenant choice, it also had some unintended negative consequences, particularly for those living in disadvantaged areas. Research carried out in Dublin by Threshold (1987) found that the scheme was mainly taken up by people who were in employment and could afford to buy a house. This often meant that they moved from their own area, and those who remained were mainly unemployed. Income levels in these areas then dropped and services deteriorated. Houses that were left behind often remained vacant for some time and were vandalised. These areas then became stigmatised, which provided additional motivation for people to leave and made vacant property hard to let. The impact of the scheme was highly localised with about two thirds of the total applications in the Dublin Corporation area confined to three housing sub-areas – Darndale, Ballymun and Tallaght. This policy is also of interest to social policy students as it offers an opportunity to reflect on the concept of choice, and particularly how extending one person's choice can restrict another's.

This short account of Irish housing policy is interesting in the way in which it shows how it has been seen as natural for the state to intervene in this area, and to encourage and support the development of home ownership as the preferred tenure. It has occurred both through direct subsidies for those entering the market and by selling local authority housing to tenants. It has weakened, until recently, the development of alternative tenures, such as the private rented sector or local authority housing, which have been treated more as temporary staging posts on the way to home ownership rather than as valid tenures in their own right. Readers might find it useful to compare the acceptance of state intervention in the area of housing policy to the opposition to intervention in other areas of social policy, the Mother and Child Scheme in the area of health policy being a good example.

Those interested in a more detailed account of the history of housing policy in Ireland should refer to Meghen (1963), and a good overview of this area is also provided by Curry (2003).

Housing legislation

There is a great deal of legislation of relevance to housing policy. What follows should not be considered as in any way exhaustive, but should be seen as an indication of the level of state intervention in the provision of housing.

The Housing Act 1966 is the principal enabling act covering local authority accommodation and includes sections on: financial provisions; provision and management of dwellings; overcrowding of unfit housing; land acquisition for housing and other uses; local authority housing policy adoption; land/house sales; and assistance to persons wishing to house themselves. Many aspects of the local authority housing services still fall under the remit of this piece of legislation.

The Housing Act 1988 is important in a number of respects, for instance it requires local housing authorities to undertake periodic assessments of housing need (at least every three years) and to draw up a scheme of letting priorities. Section 2 of the Act is also important in that it defines the circumstances in which a local authority may assess a person as homeless. The Act gives additional powers to local authorities to meet the housing needs of homeless persons.

The Housing (Miscellaneous Provisions) Act 1992 requires local authorities to draw up and adopt a written statement of policy on the management of their rented dwellings, allows them to fund social housing providers, carry out improvements to private dwellings in lieu of local authority housing, empowers them to grant shared ownership leases on dwellings, provides safeguards for tenants regarding rent books, standards of accommodation and notice to quit, and also requires landlords to register a house let for rent with the housing authority.

The 1997 Housing (Miscellaneous Provisions) Act introduced special measures to deal with 'antisocial behaviour' on local authority estates. The core aim of the legislation was to enable local authorities to evict tenants and other occupants of local authority dwellings if they were engaged in such behaviour (mainly drug-dealing and intimidation / harassment). The impact of this legislation in the Dublin area was researched by Memery and Kerrins (2000). They found that while the legislation may have provided local authorities with greater powers to tackle anti-social behaviour on estates, it also increased pressures on the homeless services as a result of the exclusion or eviction of anti-social tenants.

The Housing (Traveller Accommodation) Act 1998 requires local authorities to draw up five-year traveller accommodation programmes and obliges them to appoint local consultative communities to advise them on the preparation and implementation of the programme. It empowers authorities to remove temporary dwellings and to provide and operate sites for caravans used by Travellers. The Act also provides for the appointment of a National Traveller Accommodation Consultative Committee by the Minister for the Environment and Local Government to advise on matters relating to the accommodation of Travellers. The Act provides the legislative framework to implement the accommodation aspects of the Report of the Task Force on the Travelling Community (1995). This implementation is subject to regular monitoring by a group under the Department of Justice, Equality and Law Reform (Committee to Monitor and Co-ordinate the Implementation of the Recommendations of the Task Force on the Travelling Community, 2000).

The Planning and Development Act 2000 updates and consolidates the planning laws. It obliges local authorities to produce development plans every six years which set out the planning objectives for their areas, to include a housing strategy which provides for the housing of the existing and future population of the area. Under Part V, it specifies that the strategy should include an assessment of all persons in need of social or affordable housing and empowers local authorities to require that up to twenty per cent of land designated for housing developments is allocated to meet this need. This stipulation was changed in the Planning and Development (Amendment) Act 2002. The amendment allows developers to reserve land or provide houses or sites at another location, make a payment to the local authority to be used for social and affordable housing or a combination of both as alternatives to including social and affordable housing in private estates (see below).

The Equal Status Act 2000 outlaws discrimination in a range of areas including the provision of accommodation on the grounds of age, family status, gender, race, disability, religion, marital status, sexual orientation and membership of the Traveller community. In 2002, the Equality Authority handled 44 such cases (out of a total of 795 cases under the Equal Status Act 2000) relating to the provision of accommodation, up from 26 (out of 675) in 2001 (Equality Authority, 2003: 21)

The Housing (Miscellaneous Provision) Act 2002 enables local authorities to build and sell dwellings at less then their market value under the affordable housing scheme. It provides for the regulation of the re-sale of dwellings purchased under the Shared Ownership Scheme and for grant aid towards the administrative costs of voluntary and co-operative bodies involved in the provision of social housing. It also enables local authorities to serve notices requiring the removal of temporary dwellings in certain circumstances.

The Residential Tenancies Act 2004 sets out minimum obligations that will apply to landlords and tenants, covering issues such as security of tenure, rent review and dispute resolution. The Act also establishes the Private Residential Tenancies Board on a statutory footing, giving it responsibilities in relation to dispute resolution and tenancy registration. The Board will also review the operation of the legislation and will provide policy advice, research and information on the sector.

Current Irish housing policy

As outlined above, the Department of the Environment, Heritage and Local Government takes the lead for policy responsibility in this area. The overall aim of housing policy, as defined by the Department, is 'to enable every household to have available an affordable dwelling of good quality, suited to its needs, in a good environment, and, as far as possible, at the tenure of choice' (Department of the Environment, 1995: 4; Department of the Environment and Local Government 2003b: 36). Statements such as this require some unpacking. What is an affordable dwelling? Who defines and regulates quality? How best might needs be met? What is a good environment? How important is tenure choice?

Current housing policy is underpinned by seven specific objectives:

- to promote home ownership;
- to promote a thriving, more diverse and well-managed rented sector, both public and private;
- to ensure that households, which are not in a position to provide housing from their own resources, have suitable accommodation available to them at an affordable price;
- to promote the conservation and improvement of public and private housing;
- to reduce the extent and effects of social segregation in housing;
- to enable a prompt and adequate response to the accommodation needs of homeless people;
- to enable the provision of suitable housing and halting sites for Travellers.
                                            (Department of the Environment, 1995)

The clear articulation of these policy objectives is commendable. It is less clear, however, how the contradictory nature of these objectives is to be addressed. For example, is the promotion of home ownership consistent with the promotion of the public and private rented sectors? In the context of limited resources, which of the seven objectives should be prioritised? What type of evaluation indicators can be used to measure whether objectives are being met effectively and efficiently?

The Department's strategy statement 2003–2005 explicitly linked addressing housing need with economic and social success. It identified four key housing strategies to achieve housing policy objectives. These are:

- oversee and seek to maintain an efficient housing market.
- facilitate home ownership by those who desire and can afford it
- expand the availability of housing to meet demand

- seek to ensure the existence of appropriate standards in housing provision.
  (Department of the Environment and Local Government, 2003b: 36)

It warned that 'Failure to address the housing needs of a growing population would impose significant costs and constraints on economic growth, competitiveness and social development' (2003b: 37).

Evaluation of current Irish housing policy

Two main measures are traditionally used to assess housing policy: efficiency and equity (see Baker and O'Brien, 1997; Blackwell, 1988). Efficiency refers to the extent to which policy leads to the optimal amount of housing services; equity means the degree to which similar cases are treated in the same way. Efficiency has already been discussed above in the context of the accommodation supply problems experienced from the mid-1990s and the subsequent affordability issues arising from that. Equity can be further subdivided into vertical and horizontal equity. Horizontal equity or equal treatment of equals means the extent to which those in a similar situation (such as a particular income group) are treated in the same way. Vertical equity refers to the way in which people with different incomes are treated. Treatment is considered progressive if those with lowest incomes benefit most, regressive if those with higher incomes benefit most, and proportional if net benefits are the same ratio of income throughout the range of income (Blackwell, 1988: 143).

The Expert Working Group on the Integration of Tax and Social Welfare (1996: 113–22) assessed government housing subsidies. The efficiency of subsidies was questioned on the grounds that subsidisation of housing was likely to lead to increased house prices and some of the benefit would go to existing homeowners and owners of land. The overall system was also criticised in terms of vertical equity as mortgage interest relief was likely to benefit those with higher incomes, who are more likely to be able to take out higher mortgages.

Issues of equity are of particular relevance in examining the treatment of low income groups. Two main sources of assistance with housing costs for those on low income are the differential rent scheme operated by local authorities and the Supplementary Welfare Allowance (SWA) rent and mortgage supplements. Under the differential rent scheme, a tenant's rent is calculated on the basis of housing composition and income. This calculation is not standardised from one local authority to another, so horizontal equity between local authority tenants in different local authority areas cannot be assured. Also rents are capped (that is, there is a cut-off beyond which rents do not continue rising with household income), which raises questions of vertical equity. This is particularly so given the low rents charged by local authorities – in 2001 the average weekly rent was €26.33 per week (Department of the Environment and Local Government, 2002b: 40), but is explained to some degree by the high levels of poverty found among local authority tenants (Nolan and Whelan, 1999; Murray and Norris, 2002).

Those with low incomes in the private rented sector can apply for Supplementary Welfare Allowance rent supplement, operated by the Health Boards for the Department of Social and Family Affairs. The scheme has been the subject of numerous studies and reviews (see, for instance, Guerin, 1999; Inter-Departmental Committee, 1999; McCashin, 2000; Comhairle/ Threshold, 2002), covering issues such as administration, cost and coverage of the scheme. The scheme is considered to have clear positives, such as flexibility and the potential quick response to need. However, negatives are also evident, such as the rising cost of the scheme, its unplanned expansion and lack of integration with other social housing provisions, concern about value for money, the lack of suitable and affordable accommodation, work disincentives and poverty traps which arise because of the way rent supplement is withdrawn as income increases, and variations in practice across health boards.

Finally, equity issues can be raised in comparing the situation of tenants of voluntary housing to those in standard local authority housing on the question of right to buy. Most local authority tenants (excluding flats and special housing schemes) have had the option to buy their property from the local authority, often at a considerably discounted rate. Many have done so and benefited from substantial capital appreciation as house prices increased in the mid-1990s. This option is not open to existing tenants of voluntary housing schemes, so as to build up the voluntary housing stock and because most of these units are for special needs groups such as older people and those with a disability. It does, however, raise questions of equity in principle. Housing co-operatives are distinctive in this regard in that they traditionally provided for ownership under self-build housing schemes. In addition, the Planning and Development Act (Amendment) 2002 permits approved voluntary and co-operative housing bodies to provide new affordable housing for sale.

Challenges for the future

The supply of affordable accommodation remains a key challenge. An increase in the number of social housing completions and alternatives such as shared ownership and affordable housing is evident over recent years. Given the dramatic increase in the numbers identified as in need of social housing because they cannot afford their existing accommodation, the availability of affordable accommodation for low income groups, including those in the private rented sector, is likely to remain a key issue for sometime to come. Despite record private housing completions over the last ten years, demand continues to outstrip supply. In this circumstance, and while interest rates remain low, prices are likely to continue to increase in the near future, albeit at a slower pace. The National Development Plan 2000–2006 estimated that 500,000 additional new dwellings would be required over ten years to meet demand (Government of Ireland, 2000a: 69). Output from recent years is well over 50,000 per annum, indicating that this target should be reached if sufficient zoned and serviced land remains available. A related issue, with long-term implications, is the location of all this new housing and the public service infrastructure required to underpin and support it – road, schools, public transport, health services, leisure facilities. In this regard, the National Spatial Strategy (Department of the Environment and Local Government, 2002d) is important in that it sets out the framework for regional development over the next twenty years and aims to achieve a better balance of social, economic and physical development between regions.

In the event that the housing market does go into reverse, this will bring with it its own set of social policy issues. House price reductions resulting in negative equity (where the current market price is less than the original) can inhibit owner-occupiers' mobility, which in turn can have a negative effect on labour force flexibility as workers are reluctant to take up employment which necessitates moving house. Should this scenario come to pass, however, it is not likely to be severe in the Irish case, given the large amounts of positive equity many owner-occupiers have accumulated over the last decade.

A persistent challenge facing housing policy in Ireland is segregation. Research indicates the highly segregated nature of current provision and the consequent role which housing can play in the social exclusion of low-income households (Nolan et al., 1998; Fahey, 1998a). Part V of the Planning and Development Act 2000 aimed to address the need for social and affordable housing and to do so in a way that would promote social integration by requiring that up to twenty per cent of residential development land be given over to social and affordable housing as a condition of planning permission. The amendments to the Act introduced in 2002 dilute this requirement by allowing local authorities the option of reaching alternative arrangements with developers. Subject to agreement, under the amendment, developers will be able to provide land, houses or sites at alternative locations, exchange land with authorities or make a payment to a local authority fund to provide social and affordable housing. In addition to tenure segregation, particular groups in Irish society, such as members of the Traveller community (Fanning, 2002) and asylum seekers and refugees (Kenna and MacNella, 2004), can experience additional exclusion from mainstream social settlement.

There are also challenges for the voluntary and co-operative housing sector. The National Development Plan set a target that by 2006 voluntary sector output would reach 4,000 accommodation units per year, from 500 in 1998 (Government of Ireland, 2000a: 70). Output declined in the late 1990s but has recovered in more recent years. Traditionally, the sector focused primarily on housing older people and those with care and support needs, mainly in small-scale developments, and many provided additional services to tenants such as day centres or dining and laundry facilities. The sector is changing, however. Through the Capital Loans and Subsidy Scheme, a small number of general needs associations have begun to produce general needs housing (that is housing provided for people who have no particular need other than housing) on a larger scale than before, bigger on average in fact than schemes produced by local authorities. The challenges for the sector include how to: maintain a voluntary ethos in an increasingly professionalised service; maintain independence while drawing heavily on state funding; balance special needs (that is those who have a particular need in addition to a housing need – older, homeless or disabled people, for instance) with general housing provision and balance the needs of small organisations with larger ones (see Brooke, 2001; Mullins et al., 2003).

The lack of hard data for housing policy analysis is another key issue to be addressed. The assessments for housing need, for example, carried out by the local authorities every three years, provide aggregated results with limited ability to disaggregate the data for further analysis. There is a lack of data in relation to the private rented sector: tenant and landlord characteristics, rents and leases, accommodation quality, etc. Difficulties in counting the numbers who are homeless have been highlighted above, but act as a further example here. Evaluation of schemes and initiatives has improved in recent years, but monitoring and evaluation could be integrated more centrally into housing initiatives.

Issues in relation to the current and future housing needs of particular groups are also important. The persistent nature of absolute housing need experienced by, for example, the homeless and members of the Traveller community living on the roadside have been identified and strategic responses designed. The implementation of these responses is ongoing. For people with a disability, accessible and adaptable housing is one key to independent living (Commission on the Status of People with Disabilities (1996: 187–94). Under Part M of the Building Regulations, new houses built after January 2001 should be designed so that the main rooms are accessible for people with a disability. It is important that these basic requirements are implemented and that further consideration be given to building design to address questions of accessibility and adaptability. The suitability of the housing stock profile may also become increasingly an issue as our demographic structure changes.

Smaller family units (see, for instance, Lord Mayor's Commission on Housing, 1993) and the projected increase in the numbers of older people, many of whom will be living alone (Silke, 1994), have implications for the size and type of accommodation required in the future.

The key position of local authorities, as housing planners, direct providers and managers, has also received attention in recent times. They have come under the spotlight because of unprecedented housing demand but also more generally in the context of local authority reform and modernisation. Streamlining the planning process, spatial planning and sustainability, unmet housing need, a shortage in local authority building land, urban renewal and once-off housing in rural areas are examples of the types of issues facing local authorities at the moment. One issue worthy of special mention here is the delivery of housing as a public service. Efforts to introduce more devolved management of social housing, for instance through estate management and tenant participation initiatives, have begun in Ireland, but could be further enhanced (NESF, 2000; Housing Unit, 2001, Norris and O'Connell, 2003). A related issue here is the development of strategies to reduce and deal with anti-social behaviour on some local authority estates (Housing Unit, 2003). At a departmental level, it is clear that housing policy has had to react to rapid change since the mid-1990s and a priority now should be to take stock of achievements and future challenges. A departmental appraisal of the housing system as a whole is required. In this regard, housing policy needs to be considered as a more integral element of social policy, with links to education, health, environmental and employment polices.

Table 4.6 **Irish housing policy: recent important dates**

1966 Housing Act 1966 introduced – this is the main enabling act regarding local
        authority housing
1984 £5,000 Surrender Grant introduced (ended in 1987)
        Capital Assistance Scheme introduced for non-profit and voluntary housing
1988 Housing Act 1988 introduced, which includes a requirement that local authorities
        carry out periodic assessments of housing need.
1989 First assessment of housing need carried out.
        Local authority completions reach an all-time low of 768
1991 *A Plan for Social Housing* published by the Department of the Environment
        Shared Ownership Scheme introduced
        Second assessment of housing need carried out
1995 *Social Housing: The Way Ahead* published by the Department of the Environment
1996 Homeless Initiative established in Dublin
        Publication of the Report of the Expert Working Group on the Integration of Tax and
        Social Welfare Systems.

1997	Measures to deal with anti-social behaviour introduced under the Housing (Miscellaneous Provisions) Act, 1997
1998	The Housing (Traveller Accommodation) Act, 1998 introduced
1998–2000	Publication of three Bacon Reports on house prices and Department of Environment and Local Government responses
2000	National Development Plan 2000–2006 published Planning and Development Act 2000 (amended in 2002)
2002	National Spatial Strategy published.
2003	New social partnership agreement *Sustaining Progress* includes housing and accommodation as one of ten special initiatives. It includes an initiative to provide 10,000 affordable houses for sale by 2005.
2004	Residential Tenancies Act enacted.

Recommended reading

Those who are new to the study of housing policy will find the housing chapter in Curry (2003) and also Meghen (1963) very useful. The Report of the Housing Commission (Drudy, 1999) is another useful analysis of housing policy issues. Those interested in government statements of housing policy should read *Social Housing: The Way Ahead* (1995) and *A Plan for Social Housing* (1991a), both by the Department of the Environment. The Department also publish a *Housing Statistics Bulletin* on a quarterly and annual basis and a *Statement of Strategy* every three years. Volume 13 of the 2002 Census (CSO, 2004b) provides detailed information on housing characteristics. Those particularly interested in housing for low-income groups are referred to work by Tony Fahey. Works by Anne Power *Estates on the Edge* (1997) and *Hovels to High Rise* (1993) provide useful international comparisons of local authority housing policy and practice. The Housing Unit is a useful source on issues relating to local authority housing management. Those interested in reading more about owner-occupation should consult the Bacon reports (1998, 1999, 2000), while Mullins et al. (2003) provide a detailed study of non-profit housing in Ireland. The Homeless Agency commissions and publishes research in relation to homelessness in Ireland. Voluntary bodies such as the Simon Communities, Focus Ireland, the Society of St Vincent de Paul and Threshold are also useful sources in this regard. The Report of the Task Force on the Travelling Community (1995) is a good starting point for those interested in accommodation policy for this group. Two reports were under way as this chapter was being prepared, which students may find useful once available. The first, a review of housing policy since 1990, was commissioned by the Department of the Environment, Heritage and Local Government and undertaken by Michelle Norris and Nessa Winston. The second is a review of housing policy by the National Economic and Social Council (2004).

Many of these organisations now have useful websites. The Department of the Environment, Heritage and Local Government's site can be found at www.environ.ie and includes a section on Irish housing policy, access to recent departmental publications and links to local authorities and other relevant sites. Other useful sites are:

Dublin Simon Community – www.dublinsimon.ie

FEANTSA (European Federation of National Organisations Working with the Homeless) www.feantsa.org

Focus Ireland – www.focusireland.ie

The Housing Unit – www.housingunit.ie

Irish Council for Social Housing – www.icsh.ie

Irish Traveller Movement – www.itmtrav.com

Northern Ireland Housing Executive – www.nihe.gov.uk

Pavee Point Travellers Centre – www.paveepoint.ie

Finally, one of the advantages of studying housing policy is that its outputs are all around you! Students are strongly encouraged to visit as wide a range of housing initiatives as possible and to consider their potential impact from a social policy perspective. Keep abreast of renewal schemes of note, such as the regeneration of Ballymun in Dublin see www.brl.ie.

Chapter 5

Education policy

Patrick Clancy

Introduction

The 1990s initiated a period of intense debate, analysis and policy development in Irish education. While it is somewhat arbitrary to identify a starting
point for the recent flurry of activity in policy analysis and development, the
1991 OECD, *Review of National Policies for Education: Ireland,* report appears to
have served as somewhat of a catalyst. Although the explicit remit of this report
was to deal with teacher supply and training, it was the comments on the
organisation of education and the perception of the weak administrative and
policy-making capacity of the system which attracted most attention. These
issues were to figure prominently in the 1992 Green Paper, *Education for a
Changing World* (Government of Ireland, 1992), the publication of which
initiated an unprecedented consultation process. About 1,000 written submissions were made in response to the Green Paper and the national debate on education culminated in a high profile National Education Convention where 42
interest groups and organisations were involved in public discussion on key
issues of educational policy in Ireland. The Report by the Convention Secretariat (National Education Convention, 1994) formed a major input to the 1995
White Paper, *Charting our Education Future* (Government of Ireland, 1995b).

The overall analysis of the educational system was complemented by more
focused analysis of separate elements of the system. By the end of the decade
a White Paper on Early Childhood Education (Government of Ireland, 1999d)
and a White Paper on Adult Education (Government of Ireland, 2000b) were
published. The higher education system was also the focus of several separate
analyses, amongst which were a Report of the Steering Committee on the
Future Development of Higher Education (Standing Committee, 1995), a
report from the Commission on the Points System (1999), a Report of the
Action Group on Access (2001) and the Skilbeck (2001) report. Special
Education was also the subject of several reports, including the Report of the
Special Education Review Committee (1993) and the Report of the Taskforce
on Autism (2001).

This intense debate has paralleled continuing rapid increases in enrolment in post-compulsory education. The centrality of education in Irish public policy reflects a continuing belief in the relevance of education for economic development and societal transformation. This policy orientation has had continuing public support since the 1960s when the state-led project of modernisation first signalled a commitment to a restructured, diversified and greatly expanded educational system. This continuing affirmation contrasts with considerable oscillation in support in many other countries, ranging from periods of unbridled confidence (OECD, 1965) to profound pessimism (Murphy, 1993) about the potential of education to contribute to economic and social development.

The massive expansion in enrolments provides an indicator of the importance of education in Irish life. In 2000–1 a total of 920,356 students (24 per cent of the total population) were receiving full-time education. The distribution of these students, by sector, is shown in table 5.1, which also demonstrates the pattern of growth since 1965–6. The most spectacular growth has occurred in the third-level sector with a six-fold increase over the 35- year period. Second level enrolments have also grown dramatically, by a factor of about 2.4. Currently about 82 per cent of the age cohort complete second-level education and about 50 per cent of the age cohort go on to full-time higher education. The growth in enrolment is matched by a corresponding increase in the financial contribution made by the state to education. Government expenditure on education has grown from 3.7 per cent of GNP in 1966, to 4.9 per cent in 2001. Over this 35-year period expenditure per student (in constant 2001 prices) had grown by 361 per cent at first level, 234 per cent at second level and 70 per cent at third level to reach €3,018, €4,310 and €6,287, respectively, in 2001.

Table 5.1 **Enrolment in full-time education by sector, 1965–6 and 2000–1**

Level	1965–6	2000–1
Primary	504,865	444,782
Second Level	142,983	349,274
Third Level	20,698	126,300
Total	668,546	920,356

In prioritising public expenditure on education in the late 1990s Irish policy is supported by the current consensus in most Western countries. This is especially evident in OECD publications, but also finds expression in the EU *White Paper on Education and Training* (1996). Two principal substantive concerns underpin this consensus. The first and dominant concern is the relationship between education and the labour market and focuses on education's contribution to economic growth and competitiveness. A second concern centres on considerations for equity, social justice and the needs of the disadvantaged. The pursuit of these twin economic and social objectives has legitimated the expansion of educational provision. These are not, of course, the only objectives of educational policy. The 1995 White Paper (Government of Ireland, 1995b: 10) sets out the principles which should underpin the formulation and evaluation of educational policy and practice – principally, the promotion of quality, equality, pluralism, partnership and accountability. More specifically, it sets out the following statement of educational aims:

- to foster an understanding and critical appreciation of the values – moral, spiritual, religious, social and cultural – which have been distinctive in shaping Irish society and which have been traditionally accorded respect in society
- to nurture a sense of personal identity, self-esteem and awareness of one's particular abilities, aptitudes and limitations, combined with a respect for the rights and beliefs of others
- to promote quality and equality for all, including those who are disadvantaged, through economic, social, physical and mental factors, in the development of their full educational potential
- to develop intellectual skills combined with a spirit of inquiry and the capacity to analyse issues critically and constructively
- to develop expressive, creative and artistic abilities to the individual's full capacity
- to foster a spirit of self-reliance, innovation, initiative and imagination
- to promote physical and emotional health and well-being
- to provide students with the necessary education and training to support the country's economic development and to enable them to make their particular contribution to society in an effective way
- to create tolerant, caring and politically aware members of society
- to ensure that Ireland's young people acquire a keen awareness of their national and European heritage and identity, coupled with a global awareness and a respect and care for the environment.

This statement of educational aims, which gives recognition to personal development and cultural objectives, seeks to go beyond the narrow concern with economic and social objectives which are frequently and sometimes exclusively invoked in educational debate. Many commentators have identified the marginalisation of personal development and cultural objectives as a major weakness of contemporary educational policy in western countries (Bailey, 1984). In the Irish context, O'Sullivan (1992) has examined how the

OECD report, *Investment in Education* (1965), may have been a modernising force in changing the paradigm governing Irish education policy, in particular replacing the personal development with the human capital paradigm as the institutional rationale for education.

Following a prolonged period of consultation, the 1995 White Paper set out the future direction of educational policy. The most recent period could be characterised as the 'implementation phase'. An important feature of this phase is the enactment of legislation, until recently a very scarce phenomenon in Irish education. This legislation is designed to underpin significant structural transformations in the educational system. The Universities Act was passed in 1997 and an Education Bill was introduced by the outgoing Rainbow Coalition government. This Bill was not enacted prior to the change in government and a new Bill, Education (No. 2) Bill 1997, was introduced by the new government. The important Education Act 1988 was followed by a range of further legislation including the Qualifications (Education and Training) Act 1999, and the Education for Persons with Disabilities Act 2002.

Initially the main focus of educational policy and debate was on the formal system at first, second and third level. By comparison, pre-school education and adult and continuing education received little attention. This imbalance has been rectified with the publication of a White Paper on Early Childhood Education (1999) and a White Paper on Adult Education (2000). Because of the limitations of a single paper, the latter areas will not be examined in any detail here. The scope of the paper is further delimited. For example, our consideration of disadvantage is limited to socio-economic disadvantage – gender issues, children with special needs and children of the Travelling community are not considered. Other important topics not examined include: in-school management, curriculum reform at first and junior cycle level, assessment, the inspectorate and the school psychological service.

Following this introductory section the rest of the paper is divided into four sections. The next section reviews the historical origins of policy. This is followed by an analysis of the role of the partners in education. Current policy concerns are addressed in the next section while the final section looks to challenges for the future.

Historical origins of policy

Before examining current policy developments, it is appropriate to look at the historical evolution of educational policy. This brief venture into history is necessary since the nature of some of the key issues in contemporary policy is a direct legacy of historical experience.

The Irish educational tradition is a long one which dates back to the pre-Christian Bardic schools. After the introduction of Christianity, a thriving system of monastic schools was developed which, during Christianity's darkest days on the continent of Europe, led to the designation of Ireland as 'the island of saints and scholars'. From the time of Henry VIII there followed a long darker period during which the monastic schools were suppressed and 'thus began a definite English state policy in Irish education, namely, the Anglicisation of the Irish people and the suppression of Catholic ideals in education' (Council of Education, 1954: 12). During the Penal Laws, which forbade any Catholic from acting as a schoolteacher, recourse was made to the 'Hedge Schools' which were so named because they were often conducted in the open air under the protective cover of hedges. These schools were funded by students' contributions. This independent tradition persisted, even after the Penal Laws were ended, with Irish Catholics being distrustful of the educational initiatives of the state and the various charitable trusts and foundations and proselytising agencies. In the early 1890s a number of religious orders, devoted specially to education, were founded. These included the Presentation Sisters in 1800, the Christian Brothers in 1802 and the Sisters of Mercy in 1828.

The system of National Schools, which in essence has survived to date, had its origin in the letter of the Chief Secretary, Lord Stanley, in 1831. Stanley made it clear that the state's role was that of assisting local initiatives on the basis of local schools adhering to the rules and regulations of the newly appointed Commissioners of National Education. While the national school system was intended to be non-denominational, this was resisted by the churches, especially the Presbyterians and Catholics. This opposition was ultimately successful and by 1870 the Powis Commission accepted that the attempt to establish a non-denominational system had failed and declared the system to be *de facto* a denominational one. It is of interest to note that the establishment of a national system of education in Ireland predated its establishment in England and Scotland. While there are several possible reasons for this, including the fact that, as a crown colony, Ireland was well used to state intervention and that 'the Irish peasantry showed a striking desire for their children to be schooled' (Akenson, 1970: 17), it is likely that the main motivating factor was the government expectation that the schools could serve politicising goals, cultivating attitudes of political loyalty and cultural assimilation (Coolahan, 1981: 4).

The centrepiece of the national school system was the managerial system through which state aid was disbursed by the Board of National Education to schools established and managed locally. The system was an aided one. State aid was contingent on a local contribution towards the cost of building and maintenance. In addition a site, approved by the commissioners, was to be provided and the school was to be vested in trustees approved by the Board.

The system evolved into one of denominational management under parish priests or Protestant clergymen. State control was exercised via control of curriculum and textbooks and via an examination system whereby, for a long time, teachers' salaries were in part determined by pupils' results on examinations conducted by the Board's inspectors. After some time it was determined that schools operated by Catholic religious orders would be eligible for state aid, just as any other school, as long as the rules set down by the Board were complied with. However, the Irish Christian Brothers, after initially attaching some schools to the Board, withdrew them and operated their schools independently of the Board until 1925, after political independence.

The evolution of state aid to secondary education follows broadly the pattern established by the national school system. The Intermediate Education Act of 1878 established an Intermediate Education Board to distribute state funds on the basis of written examinations. However, in this case the level of funding was small and the operation of these schools required students to pay fees and/or personal sacrifices were made by members of religious orders. During the nineteenth century, secondary education was primarily a middle-class aspiration. An 1871 census listed a total of 186 schools which catered for about 21,000 students.

While the present system of vocational education dates from 1930, its antecedents go back to 1898 when the Local Government (Ireland) Act empowered local authorities to levy rates for the purpose of technical education. In the following year the Department of Agriculture and Technical Instruction for Ireland was established. The result was a system in which local committees, under the local rating authorities, planned and built schools called Technical Schools. At the time of transition to the Irish Free State some 65 schools existed. About two thirds of the costs of these schools were borne by the state, with some 27 per cent coming from local rates and about six per cent from student fees.

Ireland's oldest university, the University of Dublin (Trinity College), received its royal charter in 1592. While some Catholic students were admitted to Trinity in the early years, the operation of religious tests in the seventeenth and eighteenth centuries meant that only members of the Established Church could avail themselves of university education in Ireland. The first concession to allow higher education for Catholics was the granting of direct funding for the establishment in 1795 of a Catholic college at Maynooth. This college was founded to educate Catholic priests, the view being that it was preferable to provide this education at home rather than risk Irish students being 'exposed' to revolutionary thought and fervour which was sweeping Continental Europe in the wake of the French revolution. The problem still remained of providing university education for lay Catholics, as the atmosphere and control of Trinity College remained essentially Protestant. During the course of the nineteenth century several attempts were made to provide a form of university education which would be acceptable to Catholics. Three Queen's colleges at Belfast, Cork and Galway were opened in 1849, with the Queen's University established as the examining and degree-awarding body for the colleges. The Queen's University was replaced by the Royal University of Ireland in 1879. This was purely an examining body and students attending the Queen's colleges as well as other students could enter for its degrees. The Catholic University was established in 1854, with John Henry Newman as its first rector. While Newman's stewardship was short-lived, the Catholic University, as well as a number of other institutions, evolved to become University College Dublin. Finally, the university question was resolved in 1908 with the passing of the Irish Universities Act. A federal university, the National University of Ireland, was formed, with three constituent colleges: the former Queen's colleges at Cork and Galway, and University College Dublin. The other Queen's College, Belfast, became Queen's University of Belfast and the University of Dublin continued its existence unaffected. Until recent decades higher education in Ireland was almost synonymous with university education. The only other significant elements were the Training Colleges (now called Colleges of Education) and a small technological sector, mainly composed of the Colleges of Technology under the control of the City of Dublin Vocational Education Committee.

Partners in education

The education system is constituted from a large number of interest groups, referred to collectively as partners in education. The White Paper (Government of Ireland, 1995b: 213) differentiates between those involved in the policy-formulation process and the delivery and practice of education in a direct and continuous way, and those with a more broadly based interest and involvement arising from their participation in the social, economic and political fabric of our society. In their 1996 strategy document, the Department of Education (1996a) gave a figure of 120 groups whom it had identified as having an active interest in the educational service, while a total of 42 groups were given invitations to participate in the National Education Convention. In practice, of course, a much smaller number of groups can be identified as key players in the policy process.

Churches and the state
Perhaps the most distinctive feature of the Irish education system is the level of church involvement and control. Church control of education is rooted in the ownership and management of schools. After independence in 1922, the

new state institutionalised the denominational school system which it inherited. Successive ministers of education adopted the view that the role of the state in education was a subsidiary one of aiding agencies such as the churches in the provision of educational facilities. The classic expression of this position is outlined in Minister for Education, Richard Mulcahy's speech to Dáil Éireann in 1956:

> Deputy Moylan has asked me to philosophise, to give my views on educational technique or educational practice. I do not regard that as my function in the Department of Education in the circumstances of the educational set-up in this country. You have your teachers, your managers and your Churches and I regard the position as Minister in the Department of Education as a kind of dungaree man, the plumber who will make the satisfactory communications and streamline the forces and potentialities of educational workers and educational management in this country. He will take the knock out of the pipes and will link up everything. (Dáil Debates, 159: 1494)

Currently about 98 per cent of children of primary-school going age (4–12) attend state-supported national schools, although the term 'national' is somewhat misleading since the schools are not owned by the state. Almost all of these schools are denominational, with 93 per cent under the patronage of the Catholic Church. At second level, about 57 per cent of students attend secondary schools, the vast majority of which are owned and controlled by Catholic religious communities; the remainder are divided between those which belong to other religious denominations, and those which are either privately or corporately owned by lay Catholics. The churches are also involved, in partnership with vocational education committees, in the management and control of Comprehensive and Community Schools which educate about 15 per cent of students in this sector. While the churches have no formal involvement in the control of vocational schools, which are publicly owned, it is of interest that in some of the newly established vocational schools, called Community Colleges, the VECs have been prepared to enter into agreements with religious authorities in relation to agreed places on boards of management. Thus, the primary sector and the major part of the second-level sector consist of privately owned state-aided schools, with the state now paying over 80 per cent of capital costs of buildings and facilities and over 90 per cent of current expenditure.

The issue of governance came to occupy centre-stage in the policy debates during the 1990s. Part of this concern arose from demands for more democratic participation by parents and teachers in the management of schools. The debate also reflected an attempt to redefine the appropriate role of the state and of denominational authorities in the control of education. The demands for greater democratisation represented a challenge to the traditional managerial system. Traditionally the patron (usually the bishop of the diocese) appointed the manager who administered the school in accordance with the regulations laid down by the Department of Education. Typically the manager was the parish priest or, in the case of the schools operated by religious congregations, the superior of the religious community. More recently (from 1975 in the case of primary schools and 1985 in the case of secondary schools) the single manager has been replaced by a board of management. This change did not significantly alter the power structure, since the patron's nominees constituted a majority of the board. The other members were elected parents and teacher representatives.

In responding to these demands for greater democratisation and to the continuing insistence by the patrons and trustees on their need to appoint majorities on the boards so as to safeguard the ethos of their schools, the Secretariat of the National Education Convention suggested that both concerns might be accommodated by a clearer specification of the functions of patronage and management. It was suggested that the interests of patrons and trustees could be safeguarded by the drawing-up of agreed Deeds of Trust and Articles of Management, within the ambit of which a board of management could operate and departures from which could lead to its being called to account. In this context it was suggested that boards could be equally representative of patrons, teachers and parents (National Education Convention, 1994: 29). Agreement was finally reached on the composition of boards of management for National Schools in 1997, after several years of negotiations. The boards would in future be made up of two direct nominees of the patron; two parents of children enrolled in the school elected by the general body of parents; two teachers, one the principal and one elected by the teaching staff; and two extra members proposed by these nominees. The patron would then appoint one of the members so appointed as Chairperson of the Board of Management. The final element of the agreement included a model deed of trust, which provides a legal basis for guaranteeing the specific ethos of each school. No universal agreement has yet been reached on the composition of boards of management for second-level schools.

The controversy surrounding the constitution and rules of procedure of boards of management brings into sharp relief the respective role of the partners in education. Some of the legal and constitutional issues which arise are discussed in an incisive final chapter of the White Paper (Government of Ireland, 1995b: 214) which sought to prepare the ground for the drafting of the Education Bill. Here it is argued that:

> legislation must have regard to the constitutional rights and duties of parents and of the state; property rights and the rights of religious denominations to manage

their own affairs; the legal principles of estoppel,[1] legitimate expectation and proportionality as well as equality principles and the interests of the common good. Any provisions must reflect a careful balancing of the many legitimate rights and interests in education – rights and interests which at times may be in conflict with one another – so that the exercise of rights by one of the partners in education does not unreasonably delimit the exercise of their rights by any other.

The difficulty in reaching a 'harmonious interpretation' in respect of conflicting rights is illustrated by the different positions that were taken, in respect of boards of management, by Minister Bhreathnach and Minister Martin in the preparation of their respective Education Bills. Education Bill 1997, presented by Niamh Bhreathnach, upheld the right of the Minister for Education to require all recognised schools to establish boards of management appointed by the patron and composed as determined by ministerial order. However, it acknowledged that before making an order the minister had to seek agreement with the patron, national association of parents, and unions and associations representing teachers. The Bill provided for the fact that if agreement could not be reached then the Minister could make an order which would be subject to ratification by the Houses of the Oireachtas. Notwithstanding this provision, the proposed sanction in respect of a failure to establish a board was limited. The Bill specified that where a school did not have, or ceased to have, a board of management constituted in accordance with the Act, public funding to the school and the number of teachers paid from public funds would be fixed at the level obtaining at the time of the passing of the Act or the date on which the school ceased to have a board of management.

In the debate on the Education Bill, prior to the 1997 General Election, spokespersons for both Fianna Fáil and the Progressive Democrats argued that the Education Bill, as tabled, was unconstitutional in view of the excessive powers appropriated by the Minister for Education. Thus, it was no surprise that when Micheál Martin introduced his new bill, Education (No. 2) Bill 1997, these provisions were changed. The new Bill proposed that 'it shall be the duty of a patron . . . to appoint where practicable a board of management the composition of which is agreed '. There is no provision for sanctions where a board is not established. It is clear that in this Bill the state has settled for a less-controlling position vis-à-vis the churches.

The successful reassertion by the churches of their rights in education does not, of course, represent an overwhelming constraint on the powers of the state to act by virtue of its role as promoter and guardian of the common

1 Estoppel arises when a person makes a promise or a representation as to intention to another, on which that other person acts. The representor is bound by that representation or promise.

good. It is also clear that the scale of state intervention has increased dramatically since the 1960s, making redundant the image of the dungaree man. The
OECD examiners (1991: 37–8), while being intrigued by the degree of private
(church) control, recognised that there was not a private monopoly and that
the state exercised a much tighter control than appeared at first sight. The
state's prerogative gains particular legitimacy in view of the fact that it provides
most of the funding for education. It pays teachers' salaries, determines teacher
qualifications and pupil/teacher ratios; it controls curriculum and employs
inspectors to monitor standards; it has *de facto* control of building policy and
establishes rules for the management and maintenance of schools (p. 37).

While most of the state's power is exercised directly by the Department of
Education and Science (formerly Department of Education), representing a
high level of administrative centralisation, a number of its functions have
been allocated to specialist agencies which operate under its aegis. These
include the National Council for Curriculum and Assessment (NCCA), the
National Educational Psychological Service, the Further Education and
Training Awards Council (FETAC) and the Higher Education and Training
Awards Council (HETAC) which operate in association with the National
Qualifications Authority, and the Higher Education Authority (HEA).

Apart from the Department of Education and Science and its associated
national agencies, public control of education is also reflected in the operation
of the Vocational Education Committees. The VECs are largely controlled by
members of the local authorities – at least five and not more than eight of
their 14-member committee must be members of the local rating authority.
The remaining members are selected from employers, trade unions or individuals with a special interest or expertise in education. The VECs represent a
unique element in the Irish educational structure, being non-denominational,
regionally based and publicly controlled. Currently vocational schools cater
for some 28 per cent of second-level students and also provide continuing
technical and vocational education, as well as a range of adult and community
education and out-of-school services. At the time of their establishment, vocational schools were not intended to compete with existing denominational
schools in the provision of 'general education'. Since the 1960s successive
attempts have been made to end the essentially binary system which differentiated between Secondary/academic and Vocational/technical schools. The
system remains, however, highly differentiated in terms of social selectivity,
prestige and academic emphasis (Clancy, 1995a: 490). Vocational schools still
cater disproportionately for students from working-class backgrounds and
appear to have a higher incidence of social problems among pupils (Hannan
et al., 1996: 82–3).

This commitment to meeting the needs of the disadvantaged has been
identified as one of the perceived strengths of the VECs, in a study by two

Scottish researchers (Brown and Fairley, 1993). Other perceived strengths include the contribution to providing vocational education, being innovative and flexible in their response to change, providing a co-ordinating and supportive function for local schools in their area, and facilitating links between local schools and the local labour market and economy. A principal criticism identified was the so-called 'politicisation' of the VECs, especially in relation to the appointment of teachers and principals. While the VECs represent an extension of public control in education, their concern for survival, as a distinctive entity in a system which is predominantly privately owned, means that their interests are not synonymous with that of central government. In commenting on the mediating powers of the VECs, Lynch (1989) suggests that while their democratic representativeness serves to legitimate the functioning of the educational system it is the case that, like all local authorities, the VECs are dominated by middle-class personnel who are unlikely to seek to seriously challenge the status quo.

Teachers

While the churches and the state appear to have dominated some aspects of policy making, it is also necessary to bear in mind the powerful role of teachers as an interest group. The power of the teacher unions was identified by the OECD examiners, who noted 'the very active and well-organised professional teacher associations with their formidable negotiating skills' (OECD, 1991). Four unions representing the different sectors represent teachers. The Irish National Teachers Organisation (INTO) represents teachers in national schools; the Association of Secondary Teachers of Ireland (ASTI) represents teachers in secondary schools, while the Teachers Union of Ireland (TUI) represents teachers in vocational schools and lecturers in the third-level technological sector. Teachers in comprehensive and community schools are represented by either the ASTI or the TUI, the choice being largely determined by the former sector to which they belonged prior to school amalgamation. The fourth, and very much the smallest, union is the Irish Federation of University Teachers (IFUT) which represents university staff.[2]

Burke (1992) has pointed to the dilemma which confronts professionals in bureaucratic organisations who are torn between maintaining their professionalism and at the same time striving for working conditions which befit their status and responsibility. The latter orientation forces them into a trade union model of organisation which has been especially significant in Ireland. The main teacher unions are among the most powerful white-collar unions in

2   A minority of university staff are represented by SIPTU (Services Industrial Professional Technical Union), while the Teachers Union of Ireland represents teaching staff in the RTC/DIT sector.

the country. Their influence is reflected in their establishment of direct negotiation rights with government (Lynch, 1989) and in their representation on statutory and investigative bodies on various aspect of Irish education. Barry (1989) has detailed this growing influence in respect of one union (the ASTI), while Burke (1992) has described the overall trend as involving a change from a position of inadequate representation on bodies such as the Council of Education in the 1950s to the current situation, in which teacher unions (and other special interest groups such as managerial bodies) enjoy a virtual veto on the formulation of educational policy. One of the implications of involvement in statutory bodies such as the NCCA and investigative bodies such as the Primary Education Review Body is that it serves to prevent certain issues getting on the policy agenda and circumscribes the range of solutions which are considered.

A further increment in the power of the main teacher unions is their growing influence within the Irish Congress of Trade Unions (ICTU) in helping to set the agenda of the various national understandings negotiated since the late 1980s. This influence reflects a dual agenda. At one level it supports a number of initiatives designed to tackle the problem of disadvantage in Irish education. At another level many of the initiatives which have been negotiated, such as improved staffing levels, are also designed to improve the working conditions of teachers. While on occasions there may be a happy coincidence between both objectives, sometimes the latter consideration may dictate the choice of measure adopted. For example, an increase in staffing levels can be used to achieve an across-the-board reduction in pupil-teacher ratios or the extra personnel can be exclusively targeted to schools in disadvantaged areas. The options represent a choice between the pursuit of trade union interests versus the pursuit of an equality agenda.

Recently the ASTI broke ranks with the other teacher unions in pursuit of a 30 per cent increase in salary. It boycotted the benchmarking process, resigned from ICTU and pursued a protracted independent struggle to achieve its objectives. This campaign, which was ultimately unsuccessful, resulted in a bitter internal dispute between its General Secretary and the elected officers.

A highly significant development for teachers, which offers the potential to enhance their professional status, is represented by the decision to establish a Teaching Council which will act as a professional regulatory body. Following the report of a technical working group in 1998, the Teaching Council Act 2001 was enacted by the Oireachtas although at the time of writing the Council has not yet been established. The establishment of a Teaching Council will entitle teachers to appropriate regulation of their own affairs. It is envisaged that the Teaching Council will take over a range of functions previously performed by the Department of Education and Science, including the registration of teachers. It will advise the government on the induction of newly qualified teachers and devise a framework for in-service training. It will draw up codes of professional practice and conduct and will have powers to investigate and adjudicate on complaints that teachers have failed to meet professional standards and to take disciplinary action in cases of serious misconduct. The establishment of a Teaching Council has been a long-standing demand of the INTO and the ASTI for many years, although the TUI has always had reservations about the idea.

Parents

While students are the principal clients of the education system, with the exception of third-level students who have their own representative organi-sation (the Union of Students in Ireland), they have not been seen as an organised interest group. However, the Education Act 1998 (Section 27) does give students some consultative rights in schools. Boards of management are required to facilitate the involvement of students in the operation of the school 'having regard to the age and experience of the students' and, in the case of post-primary schools, they are obliged to encourage the establishment by students of a student council. In addition, in the case of a student who has reached the age of 18, a right of appeal to the board of management is given in respect of a decision of a teacher or other member of staff of a school. In practice, parents who are secondary clients of the educational system are expected to act in respect of the interests of their school-going children. However, as an interest group, parents as a collectivity have only recently become accepted as a part of the policy community in education.

The limited level and recency of involvement of parents in education policy making and administration represent something of an anomaly given the fact that the Constitution acknowledges that the primary and natural educator of the child is the family, and that Article 42.1 states that it is the inalienable right and duty of parents to provide, in accordance with their means, for the religious and moral, intellectual, physical and social education of their children. For a long time the representatives of the churches, acting as patrons and managers, saw themselves as representing the interests of parents. More recently, with more educated parents desiring a more active involvement in their children's education, the older model of patron 'acting on behalf of such people is coming under challenge' (National Education Convention, 1994: 25). A difficulty remaining arises from the heterogeneous nature of the parent body and the problem of securing spokespersons who are truly repre-sentative. It has long being established that middle-class parents take a more active interest in their children's education and, while we lack research evidence on the characteristics of those involved on parents' councils, it would appear that the great majority of activists are from middle-class backgrounds. Parent input into decision-making at national level is via the National Parents

Council (NPC) which has separate primary and post-primary tiers. The NPC-Primary has a branch in every county and currently has over 900 parents associations affiliated while the NPC Post-Primary is composed of delegates elected from the six national bodies representing second-level parents' associations. The Education Act 1998 marks an important milestone for the NPC in that it formalises its inclusion within the policy community. The Bill stipulates that the exercise of discretion by the Minister in a whole range of areas requires prior consultation with national associations of parents, as well as with the other partners.

Current policy concerns

Creation of new legislative and administrative framework
A central objective of the recent intense activity in education policy has been to establish an appropriate legislative and administrative framework for the educational system. The absence of a proper legislative framework for primary and most of second-level education and the unease of relying on administrative circular as the main regulatory and administrative instrument have been the subject of frequent comment, most notably by the influential Report of the Constitution Review Group (1996). A key objective of the Education Act (1998) was to provide, on a legislative basis, for the respective roles and functions of all of the partners in the educational system. In introducing the Bill in the Dáil, Minister Martin stressed that it sought to promote and give statutory recognition to the principle of partnership as a principle which underpins the operation of the system. The role of the respective partners has been described in the previous section of the chapter; this section will thus confine itself to describing some of the debate surrounding the reform of the administrative system. However, before doing so it is appropriate to set out some of the main parameters of the Education Act. The main provisions of the Act provide for: the recognition of schools for the purpose of funding by public funds; the establishment of the inspectorate on a statutory basis; the establishment of boards of management of schools; the establishment and role of parents associations; the functions of principals and teachers; appeals by students and their parents; the making of regulations by the minister; the establishment of the National Council for Curriculum and Assessment; and regulation of the state examination system.

The publication of the OECD (1991) report, which was highly critical of the weakness of the policy, decision-making and planning system in Irish education, initiated a major debate on the administrative system. The report noted that the Department of Education functioned like a classic, highly centralised bureaucracy and suggested that if it was to concentrate on the strategic policy-making role it would be necessary to shed much of the routine administrative responsibility. Such a change, the report argued, would require an administrative layer interposed between it and individual schools. While the then Minister for Education, Mary O'Rourke, did not accept the need for a local or regional administrative system, much of the discussion following the publication of the Green Paper seemed to reflect a growing consensus that it was appropriate to transfer substantial co-ordination and support service functions to regional boards. This rationale was outlined in the White Paper, and the establishment of ten Education Boards was a central feature of the Education Bill 1997 introduced by Minister Niamh Bhreathnach, which, as we have already noted, was not enacted prior to the General Election. The rationale for the establishment of the Education Boards as set out in the White Paper (Government of Ireland, 1995b: 165) includes:

- a need for greater awareness of and sensitivity to the needs of local and regional communities in order to improve the quality, equality, efficiency, relevance and flexibility of delivery of all educational services
- the value of further involvement and empowerment of local and regional communities, in addition to their current and continuing involvement at school level
- the desirability of releasing the Department of Education from much of its current involvement in the detailed delivery of services to schools, in order to allow it to concentrate on the development and monitoring of the education system at national level
- a realisation that the demands of educational provision cannot, in many instances, be met at the level of the individual school

The proposal to establish a regional structure of administration was opposed by Fianna Fáil and the Progressive Democrats while in opposition, thus it came as no surprise that it did not feature in the new Education (No. 2) Bill 1997. In introducing his Education Bill, Minister Martin rejected the many 'inflated claims' which had been made in respect of the potential of regional education boards, arguing that their establishment 'would have involved a massive extension of state control and would have increased greatly the level of bureaucracy'. In addition, he argued that it had been estimated in 1995 that they would have cost about £40 million annually and that this cost would not have been justified, his preference being to use scarce resources where they were most needed, in the classroom (Dáil Debates, 5 Feb. 1998: 1287–8).

Part of the difficulty with the proposal for the establishment of regional education councils made by the Rainbow Coalition government, and which was mediated via a special roundtable discussion on a position paper issued by the Minister (Coolahan and McGuinness, 1994), was the problem of integrating within a single council a system of primary and post-primary privately owned schools with the VEC structure which was already regionalised and in public control. A decision to subsume the VECs within the regional councils in the interests of avoiding duplication of regional structures seemed to be unacceptable both to the VECs and to the patrons and managers of private schools. The latter feared that a regional council which owned some of the schools within its jurisdiction might not be impartial or be seen to be impartial in its allocation of resources and services, while the former had a vested interest in their own survival. The final proposals did not envisage the abolition of the VECs or their incorporation within the regional councils, although a limited rationalisation was effected by the decision to amalgamate five town VECs – Bray, Drogheda, Sligo, Tralee and Wexford – with their respective county VECs.

The decision to abandon the attempts to establish regional education boards makes it difficult for the Department of Education and Science to achieve the kind of administrative devolution which it seemed to endorse, to enable it to concentrate on its more strategic planning and policy-formation role. This difficulty was discussed more recently in the Cromien Report (2000) which reviewed the operations, systems and staffing needs of the Department of Education and Science. This report highlighted the extent to which the Department was overwhelmed with detailed day-to-day work which had to be given priority over long-term strategic thinking (p. 2). In recommending the devolving of work outside the Department the Report endorsed a more extensive use of a process which had already commenced, namely the setting up of specialist agencies to carry out certain functions. An early example is the Commission on School Accommodation which was set up to plan, in an ordered way, for future school provision. It consists of a steering group representative of the partners in education and technical working groups which report to the steering group. More recent examples of significant specialist agencies include the National Educational Psychologist Service, the State Examinations Commission and the National Council for Special Education. While the Report did not revisit the controversy surrounding the establishment of Regional Education Boards it did endorse the establishment of a Local Office Network of 'one-stop-shops' of educational services including psychologists from the National Education Services, special needs organisers and representatives from other educational services to provide an integrated access to services for those in a particular area.

Increasing participation and programme diversification
Turning to substantive policy developments, the most emphatic trend, as suggested in the introduction, has been the increase in participation rates in the post-compulsory years. This trend is driven both by labour market and

equality considerations and is also associated with curriculum reform and programme diversification, especially at senior cycle level, and by attempts to develop a co-ordinated certification framework. Much of the impetus behind the increasing participation rates arises from repeated research findings on the relationship between level of education and employment levels. High levels of unemployment are disproportionately concentrated among those who leave school with no qualifications. The recent and unprecedented upsurge in job creation (Sweeney, 1998) is associated with a demand for highly skilled workers; those with minimal qualifications are not in demand. In this context the number-one policy priority is to eliminate the problem of early school-leaving and to increase the numbers staying on to take the Leaving Certificate. However, the success of the policy of increased participation rates has greatly increased the diversity, ability and aspirations of students in secondary education posing an ever-increasing challenge to provide an appropriate and beneficial education for all. A feature of second-level education has been the dominance of the traditional academic curriculum. The NESC (1993c) study pointed to the low percentage of students enrolled on vocational programmes by comparison with other European countries, while the influential *Report of the Industrial Policy Review Group* (Culliton, 1992) argued that the inadequate provision for vocational education at second level demonstrated that the educational system was not attuned to the economic needs of society. It called for the development of a separate vocational stream at second level to rival the existing dominant academic stream. Also relevant are the findings of an ESRI study of school leavers' levels of satisfaction with their education, which reveal low levels of satisfaction among those whose experience was confined to the ordinary (lower) level academic Leaving Certificate programme (Hannan and Shortall, 1991).

A major restructuring of the senior cycle involving four main elements has been effected. This involves the availability of the transition year programme for all second-level schools; the revision of syllabuses for the established Leaving Certificate programme; the development of the Leaving Certificate Vocational programme; and the introduction of a new Leaving Certificate Applied programme.

The transition year, which is an optional year between the Junior Certificate and senior cycle, was first introduced in the mid-1970s, but was available only in a limited number of second-level schools. While it remains an optional programme, since 1994 all schools have been free to offer the programme and by 2000–1, about forty per cent of the appropriate second-level cohort were taking the programme. The transition year programme is interdisciplinary and student-centred, emphasising interpersonal and experiential learning and practical skills which are difficult to accommodate in the pressurised Leaving Certificate cycle.

The introduction of the Leaving Certificate Applied (LCA) represents the most radical restructuring at senior-cycle level. This programme, which was first introduced in 57 schools in 1995, differs fundamentally from the conventional Leaving Certificate and replaces the experimental Senior Certificate and the Vocational Preparation and Training (VPT 1) programmes. The new LCA programme is built around three main strands: vocational preparation, which includes work experience, enterprise education, and oral and written communication skills; vocational education which is concerned with the acquisition of knowledge and skills in vocational specialisms such as horticulture and tourism; and general education which involves arts, civic, social and economic education and languages. It is envisaged that students on the LCA will spend a minimum of 55 per cent of their time on vocational preparation and vocational education, compared to a minimum of 30 per cent on general education. The LCA is designed as a separate and distinct form of Leaving Certificate, a vocationally oriented stream which will provide for the needs of those students for whom the traditional Leaving Certificate was deemed inappropriate. Notwithstanding the reservations of many educationalists, whose concerns were reflected in the Green Paper (Government of Ireland, 1992) proposals which sought to avoid completely separate tracking, the introduction of the LCA has reinstated the dual system in second-level education (albeit now at senior cycle in contrast to the junior cycle differentiation which prevailed from the 1930s to the late 1960s). While students who complete this programme will not gain direct entry to third level, they will be able to proceed to Post Leaving Certificate programmes.

A second and less radical alternative to the traditional Leaving Certificate, the Leaving Certificate Vocational programme, has been available in schools since 1989. It was originally devised as a subset of the Leaving Certificate course with an emphasis on a limited number of technical subjects. It has now been developed and restructured and, following piloting in September 1994, was made available nationwide in 1996. In its restructured form it involves five subjects from the existing Leaving Certificate programme, including two subjects chosen from a set of vocational subjects, a recognised course in a modern European language and three mandatory link modules (enterprise education, preparation for work, and work experience). In 2000–1 of the total 54,506 students in the final year of the senior cycle about five per cent were taking the Leaving Certificate Applied while a further 26 per cent were taking the Leaving Certificate Vocational Programme.

Tackling disadvantage

The drive to eliminate the problem of early school-leaving and to greatly increase overall qualification and skill levels of school-leavers is an intrinsic part of the strategy of tackling the problem of disadvantage. In spite of considerable progress in recent years, the best estimates for 1999 suggest that more than 3,000 students each year leave school without any qualification and that a further 10,600 leave before taking the Leaving Certificate. These differential qualifications of school-leavers are directly related to parents' social backgrounds. In an analysis of three cohorts of school-leavers over the period 1996–8 it was revealed that while almost four per cent of school-leavers had left without any education qualifications, this was the case with nine per cent of the children of unskilled manual backgrounds compared with less than a third of one per cent of those with parents from higher professional backgrounds. Furthermore, for those who did persevere to Leaving Certificate, the levels of attainment were strongly related to social background, with significantly higher levels of attainment for those from higher socio-economic groups. Finally, for those school-leavers who attained a Leaving Certificate, the percentage going on to third-level education varied by socio-economic group and level of attainment in the Leaving Certificate. The socio-economic group disparities in percentages making this latter transition was especially marked for those with low levels of attainment. In contrast, the class differentials in making this transition were very modest for those with a high level of attainment in the Leaving Certificate (Clancy, 2001).

Policies to counter disadvantage in education have evolved over time. Initial efforts were concerned to eliminate barriers to access. Thus, there was a concern with increasing the provision of places, and initiatives such as 'free' post-primary education and a school transport system were introduced. However, as in other countries, research demonstrated that equality of access does not guarantee equality of participation, much less equality of performance. More recently, many policy initiatives have been characterised by the acceptance of the need to provide additional resources to students who experience difficulty in adapting to and who make poor progress at school. The Department of Education and Science (2003a) lists a total of more than 60 initiatives which it funds. While the plethora of schemes suggests that this is a matter of some priority in public policy, it may also point to some overlap and lack of systematic focus, a matter that was raised by the Education Disadvantage Committee (2003) in its report on the inaugural meeting of the Educational Disadvantage Forum.

Most policy analysts have come to accept that the earlier one intervenes in tackling disadvantage the better the results. Following this logic and following the example of the innovative Rutland Street project which, since 1969, has served a severely disadvantaged area in Dublin's north inner city, the government in 1994 introduced its pilot pre-school intervention programme, Early Start, in designated disadvantaged areas. The curriculum in the pre-school makes language and literacy a priority and parental involvement is a key objective, thus striving to create a shared exchange of expertise between staff and parents. By 1996, Early Start operated in 40 locations. At primary level a range of initiatives are in place. These include the provision of remedial teachers, the designation of disadvantaged areas which qualify schools for additional capitation grants and some concessionary teaching posts, the home–school–community liaison programme and, in 2001, the Giving Children an Even Break programme which represents an extension to 569 schools of the initiatives piloted under the Breaking the Cycle scheme. Under this latter scheme, which represents the most extensive form of affirmative action, a number of selected primary schools in urban and rural areas have been targeted for an intensive package of additional supports including additional staffing and reduced class sizes in large urban schools, special additional funding for materials and equipment and a special programme of in-career development. The urban dimension of this programme involves 33 large schools from Dublin, Cork and Limerick, while the rural dimension involves 118 small schools grouped into 25 rural clusters. As an example of the special targeting, in the urban schools chosen, all infants, first and second classes will have a maximum of 15 pupils.

An important dimension of the intervention in schools in disadvantaged areas is the involvement of parents. This policy is reflected in the development of the home–school–community liaison (HSCL) scheme which was initiated in 55 primary schools in 1990 (Conaty, 2002). The scheme allows schools to appoint a teacher as co-ordinator with the full-time task of developing relationships between schools, homes and communities and represents an acknowledgement of the role of the family and community as agents of learning and development. By 1999 a total of 277 primary schools were parti-cipating in the HSCL scheme which had a national co-ordinator and two assistant co-ordinators to work with teachers seconded to the programme.

Traveller children represent a disproportionate number of those who are educationally disadvantaged in Ireland. It is estimated that about 5,000 Traveller children attend primary schools while only 1,178 attend second-level schools (Department of Education and Science, 2003a). This ratio of 4.2:1 is very different from the overall national ratio (1.3:1) of first level as to second level enrolments, as calculated from table 5.1 (p. xx above), and reveals the very low participation rate of Traveller children at second level. With the exception of four special schools dedicated to Traveller children almost all attend ordinary national schools reflecting the official policy of integration. An additional 465 resource teachers are deployed in these schools to cater for the special educational needs of Traveller children.

Many of the interventions at post-primary level parallel those found at primary level. Thus, there is provision for remedial teachers and HSCL teach-ers. A Scheme of Assistance to Schools in Designated Areas of Disadvantage has operated since 1990–1. By 1999 some 211 post-primary schools, catering for 28 per cent of the post-primary population, were in the scheme. Many of the curriculum initiatives at second level are at least partially designed to assist the disadvantaged. As discussed above, most of the recent activity has taken place at senior cycle level, although the revamped junior cycle was introduced in 1989. A recent initiative was the introduction of the Junior Certificate School Programme, offering a more flexible approach to curriculum and its assessment which is particularly targeted at students who are at risk of leaving school early. Students following this programme take at least two subjects in the Junior Certificate Examination and may take other subjects as appropriate. A student profile is kept as a positive record of school achievement. On completion of the programme students receive both state certification for subjects taken in the Junior Certificate examination and a school-assessed student profile.

A more system-wide initiative, which also focuses on young people who are at risk of leaving school early, is the new School Completion Programme. This programme aimed at those between the ages of four and 18 spans first and second level and incorporates elements of best practice established in two earlier programmes: the 8–15 year old Early School Leaver Initiative (ESLI) and the Stay in School Retention Initiative at Second Level (SSRI). A Local Management Group is established to manage each of the 82 projects. Each group will be required to assess the needs of marginalised educationally disadvantaged young people at local level and to devise an integrated, costed and focused targeted Retention Plan that will support these people in their school, home and community life. In all a total of 288 primary and 112 post primary schools are participating in this scheme.

The concern for early school leaving and absenteeism finds legislative expression in the Education (Welfare) Act 2000 and the setting up of the National Education Welfare Board. The Board is charged with responsibility to ensure that every child either attends school regularly or otherwise receives an education. The Board also has responsibility for children who are educated outside recognised schools and for the continued education and training of young people who leave school early. By the end of 2003, 58 Education Welfare staff had been appointed, including 31 former school attendance officers, and it is planned to bring the total number of staff in the Board to 84.

While the emphasis in present policy is to reduce the incidence of early school leaving, the level of earlier failure has left a large minority of older age groups who are poorly equipped to take advantage of the new employment opportunities in the economy. A number of post-school programmes are in operation. Youthreach, a programme for unemployed early school leavers aged 15–18 with no formal educational qualifications, was first introduced in 1989. In recent years this target group has been seen as a policy priority and the programme has been extended. In 2002 about 3,000 were on the

Youthreach programme with a further 4,162 on two parallel schemes, FÁS-funded Community Training Workshops and the Senior Traveller Training Centres. A second scheme, the Vocational Training Opportunities Scheme (VTOS) catering for adults over the age of 21 and who were unemployed for at least six months (12 months in the original scheme), was also introduced in 1989. In 2002 some 5,700 VTOS places were provided. The scheme provides an opportunity for participants to update their general education while retaining their Social Welfare entitlements. The most extensive provision for second-chance education is through the Adult Literacy scheme. This scheme was given a fresh impetus following the publication of OECD Adult Literacy Survey which showed that 25 per cent of the Irish adult population were operating at the minimum level of literacy and that, with the exception of Poland, the Irish sample was significantly less literate than that from eight other comparator countries (Morgan et al., 1997). Participation in the adult literacy programme increased from about 5,000 in 1997 to 22,733 by the end of 2001.

Inequalities in participation in higher education, which were first examined in *Investment in Education* (Department of Education, 1965), have been well documented by the present author in a series of studies (Clancy, 1982; 1988; 1995c; 2001). While it is widely accepted that these inequalities represent merely the end of a cumulative process which first manifests itself early in the educational career, and that early intervention represents the best policy option, it has also been accepted that third-level institutions have some responsibility for helping to redress the inequalities. Two pioneering schemes, which have been in operation since 1990, have attracted a good deal of attention. The Ballymun Initiative for Third Level Education (BITE) and the Limerick Community-Based Educational Initiative (LCBEI) focus on post-primary schools in disadvantaged areas close to Dublin City University and the University of Limerick. These interventions, which are designed to counter early drop-out from post-primary school, include supervised evening study facilities, supplementary tuition by university students, summer schools to familiarise second-level students with third-level courses, briefing sessions for parents, and financial assistance for some students from the age of 15. More recently, almost all third-level colleges have introduced their own access programmes and the success of these schemes in the university sector have been reviewed by Osborne and Leith (2000). This policy development followed the admonition in the White Paper that all third-level colleges would be encouraged to develop links with second-level schools building upon existing good practice and the passing of the Universities Act 1997 which places an obligation on all colleges to put in place arrangements which facilitate an increase in participation of students from disadvantaged backgrounds.

The strongest form of affirmative action recommended to date is that of the Steering Committee on the Future Development of Higher Education

(1995) which suggests a pool of reserved places for students from disadvantaged backgrounds for which there would be alternative entry requirements with, where appropriate, success in a special access programme a prerequisite for a place. This pool of reserved places would represent about two per cent of total entrants in each institution. This policy is being implemented in most colleges which operate a direct entry scheme for certain under-represented targeted groups where the CAO points requirement is not strictly adhered to. These targeted groups extend beyond that of social disadvantage to include those with disabilities and mature students. Current policy in this area follows from the advice of the Action Group on Access (2001). Their report endorsed the value of existing 'targeted initiatives' taken by third-level colleges working with selected designated disadvantaged schools to stimulate college-going aspirations among young students and facilitating access, frequently via nonstandard entry procedures. It also endorsed the community-led initiatives involving partnership companies and community groups which have developed support schemes for students, additionally to those available nationally. Perhaps the most important recommendation of the Action Group, which has recently been implemented, is the establishment within the HEA of a National Access Office. The remit of this office will be to put in place and oversee an integrated national programme to bring about significant improvement in equity in access to higher education among the target groups.

Further education sector

Efforts to strengthen the vocational element of the senior cycle curriculum have been complemented by developments in certification and the evolution of a further education sector. The latter development stems largely from the provision of Post Leaving Certificate (PLC) courses. These courses seek to provide vocational training to enhance students' employment prospects. The emphasis in these programmes is on technical knowledge – the development of vocational skills needed for a particular discipline; work experience – including on-the-job training, where feasible; and personal development – fostering interpersonal skills, computer familiarisation, adaptability and initiative etc. The number of students on PLC courses increased very rapidly to 25,410 in 2000–1.

A feature of the evolution of PLC programmes was the ad hoc and relatively unstructured nature of the development. This was most evident in respect of certification arrangements. While all students received a certificate of participation from the Department of Education, a range of other external bodies were sometimes involved in certification. These included the Business and Technology Education Council (BTEC), City and Guilds of London, Royal Society of Arts and the Marketing Institute of Ireland. In 1991 a National Council for Vocational Awards (NCVA) was established for the certification and assessment of vocational and training programmes provided outside the second level system. In addition to the PLC courses, programmes within the remit of the NCVA included the Youthreach Foundation Year, the Vocational Training Opportunity Scheme (VTOS), and Programmes in Travellers' Training Workshops. All of the programmes validated by the NCVA came to consititute the main elements of what is now formally designated as the Further Education sector. This sector also includes Apprenticeships and the greatly expanded Adult Education sector. The latter sector, long the Cinderella section of Irish education has become the focus of significant policy development following the publication of the White Paper on Adult Education (Government of Ireland, 2000b). The National Education Learning Council, an executive agency of the Department of Education and Science, was established in 2002 to co-ordinate strategy in this sector.

A major development in 2001 was the establishment of the National Qualifications Authority of Ireland (NQAI) with the remit to establish and maintain a national framework of qualifications and to promote and facilitate access, transfer and progression. The framework developed incorporates ten levels designed to accommodate 'awards gained in schools, the workplace, the community, training centres, colleges and universities, from the most basic to the most advanced levels of learning' (NQAI, 2003). Two new awards councils have been established, the Further Education and Training Awards Council (FETAC) and the Higher Education and Training Awards Council (HETAC). The framework also incorporates the awards made by the State Examination's Commission (the Junior and Leaving Certificate Examinations), the universities and the Dublin Institute of Technology. FETAC has assumed the awarding power of the former NCVA and also incorporates the awards previously given by FÁS, Teagasc, CERT and BIM. Level 1 and 2 awards cater for those without any formal educational qualifications and offer a progression option for those who wish to gain higher awards while levels 3, 4 and 5, correspond to those awarded the Junior and Leaving Certificates. HETAC is the qualification and awarding body for third-level and training institutions outside the university sector and incorporates the functions previously performed by the National Council for Educational Awards (NCEA). It offers awards from Level 6 (Higher Certificate) through to Doctoral Degree (Level 10) while the universities' awards range from Level 7 (Ordinary Bachelor's Degree) through to Doctoral Degree (Level 10).

Higher education
As was indicated in the introduction, the rising participation rates have had their most dramatic impact on the higher education sector. Thus it is not surprising that higher education issues have been the focus of policy analysis, not just in the 1995 White Paper, but have also been the subject of specialist analysis in several reports. Over the past decade the report of the Steering

Committee on the Future Development of Higher Education (1995) and the report of its Technical Working Group (1995) were especially significant. More recently the Skilbeck Report (2001), jointly sponsored by the HEA and the Conference of Heads of Irish Universities, has stimulated considerable debate (Skilbeck, 2001). This report presents an overview of trends and issues arising in the international domain of university education with a view to focusing on possibilities for action in the Irish university system. In 2003, at the request of the Minister for Education and Science, an OECD survey team was appointed to carry out a review of higher education in Ireland. This report is expected in 2004 and is likely to impact significantly on policy development in the future. The context of the review, as set out in the terms of reference, is provided by 'Ireland's strategic objective of placing its higher education system in the top rank of the OECD in terms of both quality and levels of participation and by the priority to create a world class research, development and innovation capacity and infrastructure in Ireland as part of the wider EU objective for becoming the world's most competitive and dynamic knowledge-based economy and society.'

The continuing growth in higher education enrolments even in the face of the significant decline in the size of the school leaving age cohort, which commenced in 1999, has surprised some analysts. The size of the 15–19 age group recorded in the 2002 Census was eight per cent less than that recorded in the 1996 Census and, discounting possible migration, is likely to decline by a further 16 per cent over the next decade. An important basis for continued expansion, in the considerations of the Steering Committee, was the need to provide enhanced opportunities for mature students who have been very poorly represented. Its projections provide for an increase in the percentage of mature students among full-time entrants, to rise from less than four per cent in 1994 to about 15 per cent in 2010 (Steering Committee, 1995).

Growth in higher education has been accompanied by diversification, evolving into an essentially binary system, following the establishment of the Regional Technical Colleges in the early 1970s (Clancy, 1993). While there is some evidence internationally for binary systems to evolve into more unified systems (Scott, 1995), both the White Paper and the Steering Committee Report strongly endorse the binary system. The White Paper argues that because of the multiple purposes of higher education there was a need for diversity of institutions, with distinctive aims and objectives. It specifically affirmed the remit of the RTCs with their primary focus on sub-degree programmes and only a limited level of degree provision. The Steering Committee targeted the RTC/DIT sector for two thirds of the recommended increase in admissions. By 2000, however, while the RTC/DIT sector intake was broadly in line with projections, entrants into the HEA sector were some 2,400 ahead of projections. The Steering Committee recommended that the proportion of students graduating from the RTCs with degrees should rise to 20 per cent, from the mid-1990s level of 16 per cent. The process of 'academic drift' has been observed in many countries and is also evident in Ireland. The former National Institutes of Higher Education (NIHEs) have become universities (University of Limerick and Dublin City University), the former Colleges of Education have all become affiliated with universities, and the Dublin Institute of Technology has been given degree-granting power and aspires to designation as a university.

The future status of the RTCs has become a matter of great controversy since the initial decision to 'upgrade' Waterford RTC to Institute of Technology status. This decision, which followed from a recommendation of the Steering Committee, was made to legitimate the provision of a greater concentration on degree level courses there to cater for the under-provision in the south-east region. The decision evoked a storm of protests from staff and local communities in the other RTCs, who interpreted the 'sponsorship' of one college as an effective downgrading of status for all of the others. All former RTCs have now been given a change of title, to Institute of Technology (IOT). The qualifications awarded by the IOTs have been validated by HETAC, which also has the power to delegate authority to make awards to individual institutes, subject to periodic review by the council.

A further development, which may ultimately have implications for the future of the binary system, is the decision by government to extend gradually the remit of the Higher Education Authority until it has executive responsibility for the entire higher education sector. To date, the executive responsibility of the HEA has been mainly confined to the university sector, leaving the majority of higher education institutions, which cater for almost half of total enrolments, under the direct control of the Department of Education and Science. Most of the Colleges of Education have now been brought within the scope of the HEA and it is envisaged that the DIT and then the other IOTs will follow, to create a unified administrative structure. The incorporation of all of these colleges within the scope of the HEA may be viewed as a growth in autonomy for this sector and as such might be interpreted as a counter-trend to the apparent contraction in the autonomy of the universities. One interpretation of the partial trend towards 'self-regulation' is that when government is satisfied that it has achieved satisfactory *product control* (as in the case of the more vocationally oriented IOT sector), it may be willing to grant greater *process control* to these colleges (Clancy, 1991).

An important development for the universities was the passing of the Universities Act 1997. This Act sought to restructure the National University of Ireland, introduce new governing structures at college level and set out a revised statutory framework governing the interaction between the colleges and government, providing for autonomy and accountability. It was in respect of the latter element that the Universities Bill, in its original version, faced concerted opposition, especially from spokespersons from the universities, who argued that it represented an unwarranted intrusion by the state on university autonomy. In the course of its passage through the Oireachtas, the Bill was amended very substantially largely to the satisfaction of the academic community (*IFUT News*, 1997).

The form of financial support available to support students in higher education has been a matter of recurring controversy and has been an area of policy development in recent years. Until the mid-1990s financial support for students in higher education came via three separate schemes. Both the Higher Education Grant Scheme and the Vocational Education Scholarship Scheme were means-tested and were targeted mainly at students in the university and technological sectors, respectively. With the support of the European Social Fund a third scheme evolved and came to be the main source of financial support for certificate and diploma students in the IOT sector. Initially neither the tuition nor maintenance element of this scheme was means-tested, but in 1992 the maintenance element of the ESF grant was means-tested. The assessment of eligibility for all means-tested third-level student support has long been a matter of controversy, arising from a widespread perception that the system discriminated against the PAYE sector. This was the subject of a report by the Advisory Committee on Third Level Student Support which reported in 1993 (the report was published in 1995). The main recommendation of this committee was for the introduction of a capital test as well as an income test to determine eligibility for all means-tested student support. The committee also recommended that the grant in respect of the tuition element for ESF-funded courses be means-tested, subject to a review of the effect of means-testing the maintenance element.

These recommendations have not been accepted. Instead, in 1995 the Government announced its intention to abolish all undergraduate fees from 1996–7 (these fees were halved in 1995–6). This decision was taken in tandem with a decision to abolish tax relief on covenants which had been increasingly used by high and medium-income families as a way of subsidising third-level education. An important rationale for the abolition of tuition fees was that it would 'remove important financial and psychological barriers to participation at third level' (Government of Ireland, 1995b: 101). The decision to abolish tuition fees applies only to full-time undergraduate courses in colleges deemed eligible for state support. However, subsequent decisions taken include the granting of tax relief on tuition fees paid by part-time students and for NCEA-validated courses taken in private colleges. In addition, the government decided that students attending full-time higher education courses in overseas colleges would, from 1996, be eligible for a maintenance grant, subject to the normal means-test requirement.

While the populist decision to abolish undergraduate fees neutralised the controversy surrounding the equity of the means test, it attracted a good deal of criticism. Many questioned the wisdom of substituting public expenditure on higher education for existing private expenditure by families who are well positioned to meet current fee levels (Clancy, 1995c: 166). Furthermore, while it was widely accepted that the existing means test excluded some families who required support, this could have been rectified by an increase in the income threshold governing eligibility. Perhaps the strongest claim for additional state support for higher education was that made for an increase in the level of the maintenance grant for students from disadvantaged backgrounds. The report of the Technical Working Group (1995: 127) identified this as the number-one priority in any revamping of the student support system.

Because of differential participation rates by social class, one effect of the decision to abolish undergraduate fees is that it will further increase the already disproportionate (Callan, 1992) amount of state support going to middle-class families. Furthermore, because of the very substantial private rates of return to expenditure on higher education (Callan and Harmon, 1997), it seems reasonable that those who stand to benefit, and who can afford it, should pay some contribution to the cost of their higher education. One of the 'unintended consequences' of the abolition of undergraduate university fees is that it has altered the 'pricing structure' of different forms of higher education. Previously all certificate and diploma courses in the IOT sector were exempt from tuition fees for all students irrespective of means and this may have stimulated demand for these courses, especially from those who would not meet the means-test requirement. The effect of the elimination of university fees is to make university courses relatively more attractive since they are no longer less favourably priced. Thus it is no surprise that client demand has been influenced – the points requirement for very many degree courses increased in 1997, while an increasing number of certificate-level courses were admitting all qualified candidates, in spite of the apparent skills shortage at technician level.

In 2003 the issue of student support was again a matter of major controversy. The Minister for Education, Noel Dempsey, indicated his wish to reintroduce fees for high-income families and to redistribute the money saved to students from disadvantaged backgrounds. Notwithstanding the preparation of a report, which was meant to legitimate this decision (Department of Education and Science, 2003b), the proposal had to be abandoned because of insufficient support from his cabinet colleagues. The abandonment of the proposal was accompanied with an announcement of a special package for disadvantaged students. The grant levels were increased by 15 per cent; the income thresholds were extended and the gradations for varying levels of support increased; the top-up grant for students from very low-income families was increased to the maximum personal rate of Unemployment Assistance; and the exemption threshold for paying the student service charge was raised. The controversy relating to the funding of higher education has not dissipated. At the time of writing the universities have been notified that the level of state grant for 2004 has been frozen at 2003 levels, representing a cut in real terms of about nine per cent. It is being argued that if the state is unwilling or unable to meet the full cost of higher education it is inevitable that those who benefit will have to pay a significant payment. It is likely that this matter will be high on the agenda of the OECD survey team.

The instability in respect of current funding for third-level colleges has been countered by recent positive achievements in respect of research funding. This represents a significant change from that which prevailed until the mid-1990s as revealed by a CIRCA (1996) report, which, in a comparative assessment of Irish research, noted that the public funding of higher education research in Ireland was among the worst in the OECD. The problem was also addressed in the report of the STIAC Advisory Council (1995) and in the White Paper on Science, Technology and Innovation (Government of Ireland, 1996f). Currently there are four strands of support for research: the long established unified budget for teaching and research allocated to universities by the Higher Education Authority; the funding of individual research projects following a competitive application and peer review assessments; the funding of institutional research strategies on the basis of competitive peer-review evaluation; and 'mission oriented' research, where institutions and researcher respond to invitations for research proposals in priority areas identified by government. While both of the latter categories have attracted substantial funds, predictably it is the 'mission oriented' research which has been most privileged through the establishment of Science Foundation Ireland. This is a new initiative by the Irish government to establish Ireland as a centre of research excellence in strategic areas relevant to economic development particularly biotechnology and information and communication technologies (ICT). The government has allocated a budget of €635 million to the Technology Foresight Fund to be disbursed by SFI. The second major source of dedicated research funding is that funded through the Programme for Research in Third Level Institutions (PRTLI). A third major research initiative is the setting up of two research councils, the Council for the Humanities and Social Sciences (IRCHSS) and the Irish Research Council for Science, Engineering and Technology (IRCSET) which offer funding for research projects, postgraduate students and fellowships.

Facing the future

The substantial achievements in educational policy over recent decades are matched by the myriad challenges for the future. Many of these challenges facing educational systems in the future are outlined in a report by an EU Study Group on Education and Training (1997) which identified three major imperatives that Europe's education and training systems must take into account: (1) the need to strengthen European competitiveness in economic, technological, innovatory scientific and organisational terms, (2) the need to appreciate the difficulties of the current situation, and (3) the need to respect the basic principles of education, whose aims go far beyond a purely utilitarian perspective. While this report gives consideration to the problems of developing personal autonomy, citizenship and social cohesion, inevitably much of the focus is on the problem of reinforcing European competitiveness within the world system. This will remain a central concern of Irish national policy where much of the success of the Irish economy in the last decade has been attributed to the quality of the educated workforce. The IDA has identified this as one of the key factors which is influencing multi-national investment in Ireland (Sweeney, 1998). The recent success gives no grounds for complacency since with the weakened power of the nation state vis-à-vis economic policy, more and more countries have come to realise that the development of human capital is the main weapon available to individuals and governments in the fight for economic prosperity (Brown and Lauder, 1996). Since increasingly the competitive advantage of nations is being redefined in terms of the quality of national education and training systems, the struggle to enhance the operation of educational systems will be an ongoing battle.

Public policy will have to focus on eliminating existing system weaknesses. Firstly, the concern with the problem of unqualified school leavers will call for even more targeted attention. And even if this problem can be eliminated in relation to the present school-going cohort, there remains a large deficit with older cohorts, many of whom have experienced long-term unemployment because their low level of education and skills leaves them ill-equipped to compete for jobs in the present economic environment. The educational needs of adults, whether this is for basic literacy or numeracy skills or for professional recurrent education, are poorly catered for. Future policy will have to see a shift in the balance of attention, investment and organisation between initial and continuing education, with an increased importance being attached to the latter. A particular difficulty which faces many types of adult and continuing education, including part-time higher education, arises from inadequate funding. In many cases part-time courses will only be provided where they are self-financing and consequently tend to command relatively high fees for which the student grant system does not apply. The failure to apply the free-fees initiative to part-time courses seems shortsighted because of their potential to provide second-chance education for mature students, for whom the part-time route is frequently the only viable option.

While most of the challenges for the future will call for additional resources, the demographic decline offers some scope for curtailing spending. Over the past decade primary school enrolments have declined 17 per cent and although this decline will soon be arrested the consequences of the decline in the birth rate through the 1980s and early 1990s will carry through into declining second level enrolments for about a decade. And while third-level enrolments are projected to continue growing through this decade the rate of increase is likely to be much slower than that experienced in the 1990s and there is unlikely to be any further growth in the following decade. There has been much talk about how best to utilise the 'demographic dividend'. A principal target must be the continued improvement in the relative level of funding for primary education (see p. 100 above). Comparative OECD data reveal that while, in 2000, public expenditure on third-level education in Ireland, as a percentage of GDP, was 20 per cent above the average for OECD countries, public expenditure on primary and secondary education as a percentage of GDP was 15 per cent below the country average (OECD, 2003a). However, to reallocate existing levels of expenditure in order to improve provision for the smaller cohort of students is not a straightforward process. It will involve school closures and amalgamations to achieve the optimum use of resources. An additional difficulty arises because of a growing demand for a wider choice of schools. Thus, while the national need is for fewer schools there is an increasing demand for gaelscoileanna and multidenominational schools. The Commission of School Accommodation Needs is currently addressing these difficult issues.

In looking to the future, a further important consideration arises in respect of the implications of the sharp decline in religious vocations. Some of these implications were explored in a reflection paper published by CORI (1997b). It pointed out that current levels of involvement cannot be maintained, taking account of the decline in personnel. For example, by 1995–6, less than six per cent of teachers (753) in voluntary secondary schools were members of religious orders, compared with one third (2,300) in 1969–70. In addition, of the religious working in secondary schools, about 40 per cent were within ten years of compulsory retirement, whereas fewer than five per cent were aged under 35. The challenge extends beyond the issue of the religious congregations providing teachers, as the report argued that religious congregations will find it increasingly difficult to find the personnel and resources necessary to discharge their responsibilities as trustees of schools. Some congregations have already responded to these changed circumstances by putting in place lay Boards of Trustees to take over the functions previously fulfilled by religious personnel.

In the final analysis, perhaps the most generic challenge facing the educational system concerns the system's administrative capacity to provide for both strategic planning and policy implementation in a constantly changing environment. In this context the problems posed for the Irish system are in some ways the opposite to those posed in many other countries where, over the past decade or more, the ideological climate has questioned the efficiency of democratically elected and publicly controlled education systems and championed the virtues of privately owned market-led providers (Chubb and Moe, 1988). In contrast, invoking the distinction made by Evans et al. (1985) between state autonomy and state capacity, one of the critiques of Irish public policy (including education policy) is that notwithstanding the more active role of the state in establishing policies and providing resources for social change, it did not establish effective control over the institutions that would use the resources and implement the policies (Breen et al., 1990). More recently, Lynch (1998) has provided an example of one aspect of this dilemma when she points to the difficulty of dealing with the problems of inequality in a system which is privately owned. She argues that one of the indirect effects of the principle of subsidiarity in education, and the voluntarism flowing from it, is the development of significant differences in the quality and range of resources and facilities across schools (Lynch, 1998: 335). The challenge of achieving a correct balance between maximising individual freedom and institutional autonomy, on the one hand, and simultaneously catering for the common good, will remain a touchstone by which the educational system will be evaluated as we face the future.

Table 5.2 **Chronology of developments in Irish educational policy**

1591	University of Dublin (Trinity College) founded
1795	Foundation of Maynooth College
1831	Establishment of National School system
1850	Queen's University established
1854	The Catholic University formally opened
1899	Agricultural and Technical Instruction Act
1879	The Royal University set up
1908	The Irish Universities Act
1924	Department of Education set up
1930	Vocational Education Act
1954	Report of Council of Education on Function and Curriculum of the Primary School
1962	Report of Council of Education on Curriculum of Secondary Schools
1965	Investment in Education Report

1967 Introduction of 'Free Education' Scheme and School Transport Scheme
Report of Commission on Higher Education
Report on Regional Technical Colleges
1968 Higher Education Authority set up on ad hoc basis (statutorily in 1971)
1970 National Institute of Higher Education, Limerick receives first students
Establishment of first Regional Technical Colleges
1971 New Curriculum for National Schools
1972 National Council for Educational Awards established on ad hoc basis
(statutorily in 1979)
1976 Establishment of Central Applications' Office
1980 White Paper on Educational Development
1987 Establishment of National Council for Curriculum and Assessment
(statutorily in 1999)
1989 Introduction of new Junior Certificate Programme
Introduction of Youthreach
Introduction of Vocational Training Opportunities Scheme
1990 Introduction of Home School Community Liaison Scheme
1991 Establishment of National Council for Vocational Awards
1992 Report of the Industrial Policy Review Group (Culliton Report)
1992 Green Paper: Education for a Changing World
1993 Report of the Special Education Review Committee
1993 National Education Convention
1994 Introduction of Early Start Programme
1995 Introduction of Leaving Certificate Applied Programme
Report of the Steering Committee on the Future Development of Higher Education
White Paper on Education: Charting our Education Future
Establishment of TEASTAS, as interim authority
1997 Universities Act
1998 Education Act
1999 Qualifications (Education and Training) Act
White Paper on Early Childhood Education: Ready to Learn
2000 Education (Welfare) Act
White Paper on Adult Education: Learning for Life
2001 Teaching Council Act
Establishment of National Qualifications Authority of Ireland
2002 Establishment of National Education Welfare Board
Establishment of National Adult Learning Council
Establishment of State Examinations Commission
Establishment of Educational Disadvantage Committee

Recommended reading

Coolahan, J. (1981) *Irish Education: Its History and Structure.* Dublin: IPA.

Drudy, S. and K. Lynch (1993) *Schools and Society in Ireland.* Dublin: Gill & Macmillan.

Government of Ireland (1995) *Charting our Education Future: White Paper on Education.* Dublin: Stationery Office.

Mulcahy, D. G. and D. O'Sullivan (1989) *Irish Educational Policy: Process and Substance.* Dublin: IPA.

O'Buachalla, S. (1988) *Education Policy in Twentieth Century Ireland.* Dublin: Wolfhound.

National Educational Convention (1994) *Report.* Dublin: Convention Secretariat.

Steering Committee on the Future Development of Higher Education (1995) *Report.* Dublin: HEA.

Chapter 6

Employment policy

Eithne Fitzgerald

Introduction

Unemployment and emigration were dominant issues in Irish economic and social policy from Famine times until the late 1990s. Emigration was for many years the safety valve which kept unemployment rates relatively low in an economy which had never succeeded in offering all who wanted it work. During the 1980s, with worsening economic conditions at home and abroad, domestic unemployment rose sharply and long-term unemployment became entrenched. Policy began to focus on the wider context of disadvantage associated with persistent unemployment, and on tackling social as well as economic factors. Examples of this policy shift were the setting up of Area-Based Partnerships (1991) and the National Economic and Social Forum's (NESF) seminal 1994 report *Ending Long-Term Unemployment*.

Unemployment represents a waste of the talent and potential of individuals. It imposes severe costs on society. Direct financial costs include social welfare provision (over €900,000 in 2002), the loss of potential output, income and tax revenue. There are social costs of neighbourhood blight, vandalism, crime, and drug abuse whose roots lie in social alienation and high unemployment. Although as unemployment has fallen, unemployed people account for a diminishing share of the poor, the risk of poverty for unemployed households is over three times the average. In 2001, 18 per cent of those in households headed by an unemployed person were in consistent poverty compared with five per cent for households generally (Office for Social Inclusion 2003, tables 1.5, 1.7).

Prolonged unemployment is corrosive of individual self-esteem, and unemployed people are five times more likely to reach clinical levels of psychological distress than those in employment (Whelan et al., 1991). People who have had years of job refusals may withdraw from the labour force altogether and say they no longer want work. There is a clear continuum from long-term unemployment to withdrawal from the labour force.

When Ireland's economic boom began in the early 1990s there were initial fears about jobless growth, as economic recovery was initially slow bringing about any reductions in unemployment. From the middle of the 1990s, the economic success of Ireland's Celtic Tiger period began to translate into a major growth in jobs, achieving virtually full employment by the turn of the millennium. Long-term unemployment fell in tandem with overall unemployment. With economic causes of unemployment successfully addressed, attention has switched to the contribution which social policies can make towards preventing its re-emergence among the most vulnerable, and towards tackling the residual and hidden unemployment which has persisted during a jobs boom.

Economic explanations of unemployment

Unemployment arises from a mismatch between the supply of labour and the demand for labour. There are different economic theories and explanations for why such a mismatch persists, each with different economic prescriptions for reducing unemployment. The demand for labour depends on the level of economic activity in the economy, the skill levels of the workforce, and the cost of employing workers. It is a derived demand – employers employ workers for what they can produce. If wage costs rise or the price of equipment falls, employers may switch to more capital-intensive production, substituting machines for labour, and employing fewer workers for any given level of output. An economy which taxes labour and subsidises capital investment encourages firms to switch from more labour-intensive production.

Employers are interested in the gross cost of hiring workers, including wages, pension contributions, and employer's PRSI. Workers are interested in the net take home pay from the job. The gap between what it costs to hire a worker, and what the worker receives is called the 'tax wedge'. Growth in the tax wedge usually leads to higher unemployment.

It pays an employer to take on workers up to the point where the marginal revenue product of labour – the value of the output of the last worker taken on – exactly equals the wage rate. If an additional worker's contribution to output is higher than the wages paid, it pays to expand the workforce. If the worker's addition to output is worth less than the pay rate, the worker is likely to be laid off, and employment will fall. Thus, if a minimum wage is set which is above the value to the employer of having the worker on the payroll, the result may be that low-productivity workers are laid off or more skilled workers hired in their place.

Labour supply
Economic theory suggests that labour supply is primarily determined by real wage levels. At higher wages, more people are attracted into the job market. Higher wages may encourage the existing workforce to work longer hours,

but may also allow workers to trade off extra income for more time off once they have reached a target income level. A long-term social trend has been increased participation by women in employment but a tighter job market with resulting higher wages accelerates the rate of participation, and conversely a slowdown leads to reduced participation rates from year to year.

Frictional unemployment

The job market is not static – there are new job openings and redundancies occurring all the time as some products, service or firms prosper and others go into decline. Even in a well-functioning job market there will always be some unemployment – frictional unemployment – with people between jobs. The level of frictional unemployment reflects the time it takes for employers to match workers to vacancies, and for workers to find a vacancy that suits them. An economy with no frictional unemployment would probably mean a lot of square pegs in round holes, and significant numbers of people working in jobs which do not make best use of their talents.

Classic economic theory

In normal markets for goods and services, the price is set by the interaction of demand and supply and the market tends towards an equilibrium price which balances supply and demand. In the labour market, the price of labour is the wage rate. Classical economic theory suggests that in the long run wage rates will fall to equate the supply and demand for jobs, and virtually eliminate unemployment.

This theory holds that unemployment is primarily due to an imbalance between the supply of labour at the going wage, and the demand for labour at that wage. If unemployed people were willing to work for less than the going wage rate, that would put a downward pressure on wage rates and that in turn would increase the demand for labour and help clear the jobs market.

Flexible wage rates, the theory goes, should prevent the emergence of mass unemployment by allowing wages to fall to market-clearing levels. The demand from unemployed people for work creates this downward pressure on wages. Minimum wage laws, trade union power, or the existence of a social welfare safety net may prevent wages from falling to market clearing levels, and give rise to unemployment. Classical economists argue there would be no involuntary unemployment if wages were allowed to find the proper levels.

Keynesian theory – unemployment and slumps

The emergence of mass unemployment during the Great Depression after the 1929 crash led to a questioning of classic economic theory and its prescription of further wage cuts during a slump. Keynes, in his 1936 book *The General Theory of Employment, Interest and Money*, argued that in the short run, wages and the price level are not flexible, and that automatic mechanisms to clear the job market may take a very long time to take effect. In the meantime a shortfall in spending power in the economy can lead to mass unemployment. Keynes argued that, in the short run, the level of output and employment in the economy depends on the level of spending, or aggregate demand. He saw the main cause of unemployment in the short run as being in the goods market, not the labour market. Cutting wages in a depression would lead to a fall in consumer spending and exacerbate the slump.

In a closed economy running below full capacity, injecting extra spending power into the economy would have a multiplier effect in increasing demand for goods and services and getting people back to work. Overall spending in the economy could be raised by directly raising government spending, or by raising consumer or investment spending through expanded credit or lower interest rates. If the economy is already running at capacity, an extra spending injection would simply raise inflation. Social welfare systems act as automatic stabilisers adding extra government spending in a downturn, and leading to falling government spending in an upturn.

In a very open economy like the Irish one, however, a spending injection leads to a significant increase in imports, and has little or no multiplier effect in the domestic economy. Attempts in the late 1970s to inflate the Irish economy through expanded public spending brought no lasting increase in employment; in fact the resulting problems created for the public finances, and the corrective measures on the tax side to bring the finances under control, contributed to the steady growth in unemployment during the 1980s.

The postwar Western world was characterised by steady growth and low unemployment, and a belief that unemployment could be minimised through appropriate Keynesian demand management policies. The oil price shocks of 1973–4 and 1979 led to the emergence of simultaneous high unemployment and inflation, which has left a legacy in Europe of high unemployment. The popularity of Keynesian policies waned, and a new emphasis on tackling underlying structural causes of unemployment has characterised reports like the OECD *Jobs Study* (1994).

Structural or 'natural' unemployment
Modern macroeconomics does not assume that the labour market clears automatically although it may over the long run. Structural features of the economy such as the degree of monopoly and excess mark-up, the tax wedge (the gap between an employer's labour costs and what a worker takes home), the efficiency of the process of matching unemployed workers to vacancies, and the extent to which the level of unemployment in fact exerts any influence on wage levels set an underlying structural or 'natural' rate of unemployment. If unemployment is above its underlying structural rate, active demand management policies, or monetary policies which lower interest rates or

increase credit, can be effective in raising output and jobs and in recovering from a cyclical downturn or short-term fluctuation. If unemployment is already at its underlying structural rate, then any attempts to lower unemployment through expanding spending or monetary policy simply lead to extra inflation, and the economy reverts to its underlying unemployment rate, but with higher inflation. This is why the 'natural' rate of unemployment is also called the non-accelerating inflation rate of unemployment or NAIRU. The evidence suggests that following the oil price shocks, Europe's underlying structural unemployment rate or NAIRU has risen (OECD, 1994). Reducing structural unemployment involves addressing underlying structural issues.

One explanation for increasing levels of structural unemployment is *hysteresis* or the theory that today's unemployment rate depends not only on other economic factors, but on last year's unemployment rate – that economies do not respond symmetrically to economic shocks, but that jobs lost in an economic downturn are not all regained in an economic upturn. The adjustment mechanisms in the economy become more sluggish, and wage rates become less likely to adjust downwards in response to growing unemployment. This may be due to *efficiency wages* – it is worth an employer's while to pay more to hold the loyalty, commitment and skills of the existing workforce than the wage for which those outside the factory gate are prepared to work.

High unemployment means many people living on low welfare payments for prolonged periods. This increases the pressure to raise welfare rates relative to other incomes, in turn making low-paid jobs less attractive to unemployed workers. As unemployment remains high for a period, some workers lose heart and drift out of the active workforce, and employers use age or length of unemployment as a proxy for regarding someone as unemployable. Long-term unemployment becomes a condition from which it is harder and harder to escape. And the rising burden of paying for unemployment and the lower tax revenues puts pressure on tax rates and the tax wedge, making it less attractive for employers to take on workers.

Labour supply and incomes
The number of people in the active job market is affected by net income from work, which in turn reflects both prevailing wage rates and the level of taxation on income. At higher take-home pay rates, more people come into the active job market. For low-paid jobs in particular, the supply of labour is affected when people see themselves as little better off than on welfare.

The *reservation wage* is a term for the minimum wage below which someone will not take a job. Classical economic theory argues that unemployment payments keep wages too high to allow the labour market to clear, because workers will not work unless they get a reasonable margin over what they would have earned on the dole.

The welfare system and replacement rates

The replacement rate is defined as the ratio between what someone receives on the dole and what they would earn if in a job. Since the unemployed are disproportionately drawn from those with poor education or skills, the income they are likely to command in the open market will be lower than average industrial earnings. Callan et al. (1996b) found unemployed people on average could expect to earn two thirds of average earnings if in work. This study also found that about 30 per cent of the unemployed (and 16 per cent of current employees) had a replacement rate above 70 per cent. High replacement rates and the potential loss of secondary benefits can form a barrier in moving from welfare back to work. A number of separate schemes are designed to help this transition or lower replacement rates – Back to Work Allowance and Revenue Job Assist for those taking up a job following long-term unemployment, and Family Income Supplement which raises the take home pay of low-paid workers with children.

Developing a strategy on long-term unemployment

Since the early 1990s, national policy has begun to see long-term unemployment as requiring a different response compared to short-term unemployment. Whereas previously unemployment policy had concentrated on getting the economy right and creating enough jobs, greater attention began to be focused on social policies, and on what was different about long-term unemployment. Area-based Partnerships in unemployment blackspots were a product of social partnership, set up under the Programme for Economic and Social Progress (PESP) in 1991.

The first major strategic policy on long-term unemployment was enunciated by the NESF (1994) and further developed by the Task Force on Long-Term Unemployment (Office of the Tánaiste, 1995a). This strategy had four main pillars:

- sound macroeconomic policies for sustainable jobs growth
- early intervention in education to minimise the numbers leaving school without qualifications
- targeted measures to bring the long-term unemployed into jobs
- preventing the drift from short-term into long-term unemployment

These reports also led to specific policy changes such as the setting-up of the Local Employment Service, the recasting of Community Employment and the Whole-time Jobs Initiative; they also fundamentally changed official thinking on the need to address long-term unemployment as a specific policy issue.

However, as national policies began to gear up to the challenge of long-term unemployment, different government departments proposed different measures to address the problem, with little co-ordination between them, or little understanding of how this patchwork of policies might come together on the ground. Today, separate measures designed by Foras Áiseanna Saothar (FÁS), by the Department of Education and Science, by the Department of Social and Family Affairs, by the Department of Enterprise, Trade and Employment, by the Department of the Taoiseach and by the Revenue Commissioners form a complex web of measures in which it is all too easy to get lost. Although there is an interdepartmental Strategy Group on Employment and Unemployment, little has been done to weld the different initiatives into a single coherent policy, to rationalise overlapping programmes, to prioritise the most effective programmes and to make them coherent from the point of view of those out of work.

Unemployed organisations and social partnership

The Irish National Organisation of the Unemployed (INOU) has become an increasingly influential voice in articulating policy on unemployment and focusing attention on long-term unemployment, together with the Irish Congress of Trade Unions (ICTU), which has a network of unemployed centres and has built on their experience in lobbying for change. The involvement of unemployed representatives from both the INOU and the ICTU centres for the unemployed in the National Economic and Social Forum (NESF) was a key influence in shaping the analysis of long-term unemployment which now underpins public policy. Involvement in the NESF has also been a stepping-stone for unemployed organisations into a wider consultative role and into fuller social partnership, and since 1996 unemployed organisations have been involved as social partners in negotiations on successive national agreements. Social partnership has also been a vehicle for involvement of unemployed representatives in making an input into detailed policy through membership of various partnership working groups, dealing with issues as varied as childcare and the benchmarking of social welfare payments to a proportion of average wages.

Historically low levels of unemployment reached

Following the peak in unemployment reached in 1993, Ireland's economy began a remarkable growth performance. On the jobs market, it showed first with a dramatic rise in the numbers at work, and later on there began a steady fall in the numbers of unemployed. By 2000, both unemployment and long-term unemployment as measured by the International Labour Office definition (which counts those actively looking for work) had fallen to levels close to full employment. As the Irish economy moved from a position of job scarcity to one of labour shortage, addressing unemployment became no longer an issue primarily of job creation, but of dismantling the barriers which prevent those without work from accessing job opportunities.

Figure 6.1 **Unemployment and long-term unemployment, 1983–2003**

'000s

Sources: Labour Force Survey; Quarterly National Household Survey

Frictional unemployment, where people in a dynamic economy are between jobs, explains some of the unemployment still being experienced at the turn of the millennium while simultaneously there was a labour shortage in other areas of the economy. Some of those left behind by the jobs boom would have experienced multiple disadvantages in accessing a job – poor education, low self-esteem, literacy problems, substance abuse, crime history or family problems. However, measuring those who are actively looking for work does not tell the whole story about unemployment.

Crucially, some people who regard themselves as out of work are not counted among the unemployed when the criterion used is active job search. Unemployment shades into economic inactivity. The EU Employment Guidelines were amended in 2001[1] to make it explicit that policy should reach out to the economically inactive as well as to the unemployed. In a study in the mid-1990s of economically inactive unemployed, Murphy and Walsh (1997) concluded they had characteristics similar to the long-term unemployed, but somewhat more disadvantaged – they were predominantly men, generally either single or with a large family, had poor levels of education, were long-term out of work, and were more likely to live in local authority housing and in jobless households.

Others among the hidden unemployed are people who are not actively seeking work because they believe work which meets their circumstances is

1   Guideline 5; see Proposal for Guidelines for Member States Employment Policies 2000, p. 3

not available – people with a disability, women with no access to childcare, and people who consider they stand to lose financially by taking a job (Fitzgerald, Ingoldsby and Daly, 2000).

Asylum seekers would see themselves as unemployed, although the majority of them are forbidden to work. Ironically while there has been a determined effort under the Employment Action Plan to systematically refer the registered unemployed to FÁS placement service in order to encourage them into employment, in contrast, there are tens of thousands of asylum seekers who are forbidden from taking up a job.

Measuring unemployment

There is no single agreed measure of unemployment. Three main measures of unemployment are in common use

- International Labour Office (ILO) measure – recent active job search.
- Principal Economic Status (PES) – self-described status
- Live Register (LR) – those signing on for unemployment payments or social welfare credits

Alternative ways of measuring unemployment are discussed in detail in NESF (1997b). Economic definitions of unemployment concentrate on those who are actively seeking work. However, the social and financial problems of unemployment apply equally to the economically inactive as to those out of work who are in the active job market.

In the 2002 Census, a total of 159,000 described themselves as unemployed (including 21,000 first-time job seekers) while official unemployment (ILO measure) from the Quarterly National Household Surveys (QNHS) taken at the same time was only 77,000.

Discrepancies between the different sets of figures may be for a number of reasons:

- The ILO measure counts only those taking active steps to get a job. This excludes people who describe themselves as unemployed but who have withdrawn from job search or are not currently looking for work.
- The Live Register includes people who work part-time and are entitled to sign on and claim for part of the week. Some of those who sign for credits may primarily see themselves as retired or on home duties rather than as unemployed, and may not be interested in getting work. People signing on and working in the black economy may also account for a proportion of the divergence between this and other measures of unemployment.

While unemployment under all three measures has fallen dramatically since the peak of 1993, each measure has fallen at a different pace. There has emerged a significant divergence between the number of people who describe themselves as unemployed and those officially counted as unemployed using the job search criterion.

Table 6.1 **Unemployment, Ireland 1993 and 2003**

	ILO basis	PES	LR
1993	220,000	230,000	295,000
2003	81,000	113,000	171,000

Sources: Labour Force Survey; Quarterly National Household Survey, Live Register
Figures are for April or the March–May quarter

The divergence between self-described unemployment and ILO unemployment is more marked when the two measures are cross-tabulated, as shown in table 6.2, which shows this 'hidden' unemployment is now at two thirds the level of official unemployment. When a substantial share of those who see themselves as unemployed are not actively looking for work, clearly it takes more than a buoyant economy to overcome the barriers to their participation in the job market.

Table 6.2 **People giving 'unemployed' as their Principal Economic Status (PES), Spring 2003**

	ILO unemployed	Others	Total
Male	46,700	33,100	79,800
Female	18,500	14,400	32,900
Total	65,200	47,500	112,700

Source: Quarterly National Household Survey

Social factors and unemployment

As in other countries, Ireland's unemployed are disproportionately drawn from those with poor education or skills levels. There is also a significant degree of geographical clustering. Census 2002 has identified 88 unemployment blackspots, census districts where unemployment exceeds 20 per cent of the workforce. Dublin, Cork and Limerick cities and County Donegal together account for two thirds of these, with significant clustering of unemployment in particular neighbourhoods characterised by multiple deprivation and lack of amenities. Local authority estates account for many of these clusters. Only one in five adults in households renting from a local authority has a job (1999–2000 *Household Budget Survey*). While clustered urban unemployment is important, some of the highest individual rates of unemployment are in isolated rural areas, with rates of 37 per cent and 40 per cent scored in areas near Belmullet, County Mayo.

Among the policies being developed to respond to the geographical concentration of unemployment and disadvantage are the funding of community development projects in disadvantaged areas, moves to delegate power and responsibility to tenants through estate-based tenant management, the targeting of funds to tackle educational disadvantage to such neighbourhoods, and the development of Area-based Partnerships in unemployment blackspots.

Area Partnerships

Twelve Area Based Partnerships set up under the Programme for Economic and Social Progress (PESP, 1991) were given the remit to develop area-based responses to long-term unemployment, and were given substantial freedom to innovate. In 1994, Area Partnerships were extended to a total of 38 unemployment blackspots. Apart from the model of bringing local actors from the community and statutory sectors together with local social partner representation, there is no single 'model' of what a partnership should do. Some partnerships see their role as a catalyst, to get the statutory sector to move on ideas they have piloted. Others put more emphasis on service delivery rather than innovation. Some partnerships have a greater enterprise focus, others put a lot of emphasis on community development and capacity building. The Contactpoint service developed in Coolock by the Northside Partnership became the model for the Local Employment Service, matching local unemployed to the job needs of local employers, and offering long-term unemployed people a personalised assessment, development and job placement service. As the profile of poverty and disadvantage has changed, partnerships have piloted childcare facilities, school meals programmes and after schools activities. While many interesting interventions have been piloted by partnerships, their impact on the causes of disadvantage and unemployment will remain small-scale unless successful innovations are taken on board by mainstream statutory service providers.

Education and unemployment

Rising average education levels have been an important engine driving Ireland's economic growth. However, unemployed people and in particular the long-term unemployed come disproportionately from those who left school early with no or minimal qualifications. There is a direct relationship between the standard of education achieved, and the probability of unemployment. Poor education levels or limited skills lower earnings potential. People whose earning prospects are poor may perceive they will be little better off if they take up a job, particularly once any transitional back to work supports have been withdrawn.

The lifetime cost to the Exchequer of the higher unemployment associated with early school leaving means that investment in effective measures to prevent early school leaving offers a high economic return. The Economic and Social Research Institute (ESRI, 1993) estimated the cost of the excess lifetime unemployment experienced by those who leave school without qualifications compared to getting a Junior Certificate would be €36m (1988 prices), or €56m in 2003 terms, for a given year's cohort of early leavers.

Figure 6.2 **Unemployment rate by highest education received, 1998–2002**

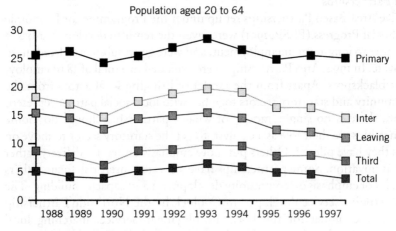

Population aged 20 to 64

Sources: Labour Force Survey micro data; Census 2002

Almost 40 per cent of the generation born in 1945 and a third of those born in 1950 did not go to second-level school. The poor literacy scores recorded for Irish adults in the OECD's International Adult Literacy Survey (1997) where one in four scored at the lowest level of functional literacy (Level 1) is closely linked to the level of education received. Poor literacy in turn is a significant barrier to employment, particularly as service jobs replace the unskilled manufacturing jobs done by a previous generation.

Lack of skills and education give rise to a number of linked barriers to getting work

- loss of self confidence, particularly where literacy is a problem. That makes people more reluctant to take up training offers, and more reluctant to look for work
- it is harder to get and keep work
- unskilled work is not well paid. Given a lack of skills, in general unemployed people can expect to earn about 70 per cent of average earnings, according to ESRI research

- poor education is a barrier to training. Those who are least qualified face difficulties in accessing mainstream training and many will not last the course without participation on a pre-training programme

Active labour market programmes
Active labour market programmes, to provide education, training or work experience for unemployed people began to develop in Ireland in the 1970s and the scale of provision and the variety of schemes have particularly accelerated in the 1980s and 1990s as unemployment lifted off. Such policies have long been a feature of Scandinavian approaches to unemployment which emphasise the importance of active measures to assist unemployed people to get work rather than passive income support. A switch from passive to active measures forms a common theme of the Delors White Paper on *Growth Competitiveness and Employment* (EU Commission, 1993), the OECD Jobs Study (1994), and the EU's five-point programme on unemployment adopted at the 1994 Essen summit. By 1994, about 90,000 people a year in Ireland participated in some kind of active programme, accounting for 6.5 per cent of the workforce (O'Connell and McGinnity, 1997). The variety of such schemes in Ireland stems partly from a wish to try out different approaches, and partly because different agencies (FÁS, and several separate government departments) each developed their own proposals on unemployment independently of each other. These programmes are in a number of categories:

- job placement strategies
- training programmes, in general or specific skills
- work experience and direct employment schemes
- wage subsidies to employers
- wage subsidies for employees or self-employment

Job placement strategies
In the late 1960s, responsibility for filling job vacancies moved from the Labour Exchanges, now Social Welfare offices, to a new National Manpower Service, which is now part of FÁS, the national employment and training authority. FÁS placement services range from walk-in job noticeboards to personal interviews, but for a majority it remains a low-intensity process.

Following recommendations from the National Economic and Social Forum (1994) and the Task Force on Long-term Unemployment (1995), the Local Employment Service was set up in 1996 in a number of Partnership areas, modelled on successful initiatives by Partnerships like Northside's Contactpoint and Ballymun's Jobcentre. A central feature was to be personalised guidance, training and support where the individual's needs rather than the training provider was to be at the centre of the service. It was envisaged that individuals would follow a personalised pathway through appropriately tailored supports towards the job market. Engaging with local employers to employ people coming through the local employment service process was also to be a central feature.

The in-depth engagement with very deprived clients has been a strength of the service. However, the degree of involvement with local employers has been mixed. Relying on drop-in service and word of mouth referrals has not been the most effective way to reach the target client group, and there has been no systematic branding of the service. Set up as an alternative to the FÁS approach, the Local Employment Service has now been placed under the FÁS umbrella. The Local Employment Service process in principle involves a more in-depth engagement over time with unemployed clients who are further from the labour market than the FÁS manpower service. Following a review by Fitzpatricks' Consultants which highlighted the difference in costs between the two services, a withdrawal towards the FÁS model of engagement and a scaling back of LES is under way from 2003.

Employment Action Plan

The European Employment Strategy adopted in 1988 called for a refocusing of unemployment policy towards preventing the drift into long-term unemployment. Ireland's Employment Action Plan to give effect to this policy provides for referral of people receiving social welfare payments for unemployment to FÁS once they have reached a particular unemployment threshold. FÁS provides career advice and referral to jobs, work experience or training. This process has been in place for under 25s since 1998 once they reach six months out of work. Since July 2000, those aged over 25 are referred to FÁS once they have been nine months out of work, and the threshold was reduced to six months in March 2003.

A FÁS analysis (Corcoran 2002) of the Employment Action Programme for those registered with FÁS in 1999/2000 showed that, overall, 64 per cent of those referred left unemployment within three months, and 93 per cent did so within 12 months. These proportions vary relatively little by age or by gender. A large majority of those leaving unemployment – 85 per cent overall – were still off the Live Register twelve months after their original referral to FÁS. This includes those who moved to training, education or a FÁS employment scheme as well as those who got open market employment. These figures were achieved at the peak of the employment boom, and the success may be due to economic conditions rather than FÁS intervention.

Training the unemployed
- FÁS has been the main training provider for the unemployed, with a range of programmes offering general training, and more market-driven specific skills training.

- FÁS training for the unemployed has had little success in reaching the most disadvantaged of the unemployed. Trainees are predominantly under 25, with better education than the average unemployed. In 1996, only 15 per cent of long-term unemployed got specific skills training. McCann and Ronayne (1992), however, reported a clear preference among older unemployed for work rather than training
- the system is provider-centred not client-centred
- FÁS training centres open at 8.30 in the morning to facilitate a four and a half day week for staff, making it very difficult for women who have to get children to school to access training.
- O'Connell and McGinnity (1997) conclude that general training programmes have had little or no impact on future employment chances, but that specific skill training programmes are worthwhile
- severely disadvantaged people may need personal development, confidence building, and basic skills before they can benefit from specific skills training. Such general programmes and specific skills training are poorly linked

Research points to the reluctance of older workers to go on training courses. Over the years, many older unemployed have participated in courses that led nowhere, particularly in the days when there were few job openings (Census, 1997). This makes them reluctant to engage in open-ended training with no guarantee of work at the other end. In contrast to the supplier-centred approach, Ballymun Job Centre (Davitt, 1998) developed an employer-led approach to training where long-term unemployed people were trained to meet specific identified job opportunities, for example forklift training. Long-term unemployed people have had more confidence in participating in training with definite jobs at the other end rather than in open-ended training.

Work experience programmes
The largest single labour market programme has been Community Employment (CE), which began in 1984 as the Social Employment Scheme, offering half-time work experience in community projects to people who have been out of work for at least a year. The Whole Time Job Initiative introduced in 1996 was a full-time variant of CE, aimed at older unemployed out of work for at least five years.

These schemes have been remarkably successful at recruiting highly disadvantaged workers back into the dignity of paid employment. These programmes form the backbone of thousands of voluntary organisations and community groups right around the country. They have, however, been less successful at bringing participants along the next step into the open job market.

Community Employment

The Community Employment (CE) Programme expanded up to 40,000 places in the mid-1990s, but from 2000 onwards the number of participants has been halved.

In its original design as the Social Employment Scheme in 1984, it was set up as a half-time work experience programme, paying half the then average industrial wage. The intention was to kill two birds with the one stone – to provide and share out job openings where there was a chronic shortage of jobs, and to get work of value to the community done. The scheme was reshaped and renamed Community Employment (CE) in 1994 and the numbers on the programme were virtually doubled. The programme was again restructured in 1996, on the advice of the Task Force on Long-Term Unemployment to refocus on the long-term unemployed and it was given the explicit goal of achieving progression into the open job market. Lone parents and people with disabilities as well as registered unemployed were eligible to participate. The scheme has been particularly popular with lone parents as it offers flexible local part-time work which fits in with family commitments while similar openings are less easy to find on the open job market.

Direct employment schemes and progression

Successive research by the ESRI (O'Connell and McGinnity, 1997; O'Connell, 1999) has evaluated how successful different labour market programmes are, having standardised for the different composition of participants on the different programmes according to age, education and so on.

The research examined the success of the different programmes in terms of placing people into work or further training. They found that work experience made a negligible difference to future job chances, once the different composition of participants on the different programmes was taken into account. They argued that the current mix of active labour market programmes is overwhelmingly weighted in favour of those programmes which are least effective in terms of subsequent job placements.

> the category of labour market programmes which has expanded most in recent years – direct employment schemes — is the programme type we have found least effective in improving the employment prospects of their participants . . . Accordingly we believe that the recent expansion of direct employment schemes is a policy choice which favours high volume programmes at the expense of quality and effectiveness . . . While many of those most marginalised in the labour market may need work experience programmes (or, indeed, basic training), our analysis shows that unless participation in such a programme facilitates subsequent progression to programmes with strong market linkages in an individually tailored reintegration path, they are unlikely to convey durable benefits on their participants (O'Connell and McGinnity, 1997: 142).

In a programme covering so many different sponsors and individual job titles, there can be substantial variation in the quality of worker development and work experience from one sponsor to another. Work experience as a secretary or accounts assistant is likely to transfer more easily to the open job market than work experience as a community worker. A sponsor who puts a lot of emphasis on career development, on goal setting, and on progression is likely to have a higher success rate into open jobs than one who takes a hands off approach to staff development and supervision.

The ethos of the community sector is a major strength in attracting people who had been detached from the job market back into the world of work. Participants see the sector as offering a supportive environment and job satisfaction. That very ethos, however, often makes for poor experience of and poor links into the world of mainstream employment.

Another structural issue is the half-time nature of the work. This is clearly a very attractive feature for lone parents and others with family responsibilities. Many lone parents find it difficult to access equally convenient work in terms of location and hours when their period on CE is over. For those whose goal is full-time employment, however, CE offers a less than ideal preparation. The key attributes employers are looking for, irrespective of the job, are reliability, punctuality and consistency in putting in the time and effort required; part-time work offers only a limited introduction to this basic work discipline in respect of full hours. The short hours worked also limit the potential to deliver training within the prescribed hours.

The design of work experience programmes should build in clear progression paths through progressively more challenging work with a focus on progression into open employment.

As labour shortages began to emerge in the tighter labour market of the late 1990s, the current scale of the CE programme was queried by Deloitte and Touche (1998), who recommended a significant scaling-down. That reflects concern that programmes like CE compete with employers for low-skilled labour, by offering a more attractive financial package, particularly to lone parents. Restrictions on eligibility and duration on CE were put in place after this review, and the halving of the number of participants began.

For people with poor experience of the education system, work experience programmes can give the confidence to go on to further training. However, while Community Employment has been markedly more successful than FÁS training or other labour market programmes in reaching long-term employed people with poor educational qualifications, its training content has been very limited, and links into mainstream training have been very poor (EU Social Fund Evaluation Unit, 1998).

Whole Time Job Initiative

The Whole Time Job Initiative, a full-time work experience programme for the older very long-term unemployed, began in late 1996 on the recommendation of the Task Force on Long-term Unemployment. This programme offers temporary (three-year) full-time work on community projects for the very long-term unemployed in the older age groups – those aged 35 or over, and over five years out of work. Job Initiative effectively operates like a full-time version of CE in terms of the kinds of work done, but participants are paid the rate for the job

The Whole Time Job Initiative caters for a very disadvantaged group in labour market terms, yet in terms of sponsor support, fewer resources are available than for the half-time CE. Like CE, the quality of work experience is critically dependent on the ability of the sponsor to successfully manage a highly disadvantaged workforce (Fitzgerald and Ingoldsby, 1999)

Need for a supported work option

A proportion of those who remain out of work will be people who experience major difficulties in accessing or retaining open market jobs. Those difficulties can arise for such reasons as age, illiteracy, physical or mental illness, inability to deal with stress, or alcohol or drug abuse. Experience with the Job Initiative programme which has recruited from a very disadvantaged group has shown there are people who in spite of difficulties in their lives want to work and can make a contribution. It is important not to write anyone with difficulties off as 'unemployable' but to see under what circumstances can people be encouraged and supported and offered the chance to participate.

While, for some, supported employment may be a transitional stage on the road from unemployment into an open market job, there are others who will never make that transition. Supported and sheltered employment has been an accepted part of the employment landscape for people with physical and intellectual disabilities, but there is only limited recognition of the need to offer long-term semi-sheltered work for those whose barriers to open employment are more social than physical or medical.

In a limited move towards longer-term high support employment, people over 50 who, having spent three years on the Community Employment continue to experience difficulties in getting employment, may have their participation in the scheme extended at the discretion of FÁS subject to continued annual review. There is a ceiling of 20 per cent of participants who may be offered such an extension.

Wage subsidies

Generalised wage subsidies have a high risk of *displacement* – where A's subsidised job undercuts B, and puts B out of work, and *deadweight* – where the jobs attributed to the subsidy would have been created in any case. Breen's (1991) study of the Employment Incentive Scheme found that 90 per cent of expenditure was accounted for by displacement or deadweight, and the scheme was abolished.

Targeted wage subsidies for long-term unemployed have been introduced with the aim not of increasing overall employment but of increasing the share of long-term unemployed taking up job vacancies. (Department of Enterprise and Employment, 1997). The Jobstart subsidy to employers had limited success, with about 1,100 employed in April 1998, 18 months after its introduction. For employees, it is far less attractive than the Back to Work Allowance discussed below. Another subsidy scheme, Revenue Job Assist, introduced from April 1998, offers increased tax allowances to employees as well as new incentives to employers. Burtless (1985) reports on a randomised experiment in Dayton, Ohio which showed that subsidy vouchers actually had a detrimental effect on the employment probability of recipients. One possible explanation is that rather than countering employer prejudice, the subsidy might be taken by employers to signal a potentially difficult or unproductive worker.

Back to Work allowance

The Back to Work allowance, introduced in 1994, allowed long-term unemployed returning to work to keep a proportion of their dole over a three-year period. This was subsequently merged with the Area Based Allowance operated as an enterprise support in the partnership areas, to form a single national scheme of income support to unemployed people setting up in business for themselves. Participants retain their unemployment payment on a sliding scale (100 per cent, 75 per cent, 50 per cent, 25 per cent) while starting a business or taking up a job (75 per cent, 50 per cent, 25 per cent). The scheme proved popular and expanded to reach a total of 39,000 participants by 1999 falling back to 30,000 by 2002, and evenly divided between the self-employed and employee strands. A particularly popular feature has been the retention of secondary benefits for the duration of the scheme. There has been a high dropout rate from the scheme – a third in year one, a further 21 per cent in year two, and eight per cent in year three, with redundancy the major reason for drop-out. A majority of those who dropped out returned to unemployment or transferred to another welfare payment (Indecon, 2000). From the start of 2003, the scheme is confined to long-term unemployed over five years on the Live Register with other categories of welfare recipients generally eligible after 15 months on a payment (three years in the case of Disability Benefit). Transitional schemes like this have a useful role to play in encouraging people to take a step from the certain income from social welfare to the uncertainties of employment or self-employment; however, for low skilled workers as benefits are withdrawn they are unlikely to be compensated by corresponding improvements in earnings.

Perceived poverty traps

In a very complex welfare system, fear of less security and a lower standard of living is a powerful obstacle. People fear the loss of existing benefits, including secondary benefits like the medical card and rent allowance, and can see taking up a job as trading the security of the welfare system for the uncertainties of the job market.

There are several schemes to cushion the transition from welfare to work – Back to Work Allowance, Family Income Supplement and Revenue Job Assist. In general, people are financially better off from taking up a job – provided they are getting all they are entitled to. Knowledge of and take-up of Family Income Supplement and Revenue Job Assist is very poor. ESRI research suggests that only half of potential FIS claimants actually receive it (and administrative records suggest that half those in turn are public servants). In 1999, only 1,066 people were receiving Revenue Job Assist in the whole country.

The reality on the ground is often a poor level of accurate knowledge by unemployed people of the various welfare to work incentives (Fitzgerald et al., 2000) It is hardly surprising then that many unemployed people concentrate on the gross wage to calculate the net financial value of taking a job. The jobs on offer to them are usually on the face of them unattractive when compared with a welfare income, unless the net effect of the package, after all benefits, can be spelled out. One effective innovation was the employment for 1999 by Blanchardstown Local Employment Service of a welfare rights worker on secondment from the Department of Social, Community and Family Affairs, who could work out authoritatively what people would receive if they moved to a job or on to a FÁS programme.

Likewise, few employers are familiar with the complexities of the social welfare code and its secondary benefits, or appreciate how central are worries about loss of benefits to those they seek to recruit. In response to this need, Northside Partnership prepared an employers' guide to employment incentives and supports.

Table 6.3 **Barriers to taking up work or training**

Individual	Employer/Trainer	External
Lack of basic skills, including literacy and other core skills	Job specifications based on tradition rather than needs.	Financial costs/ benefits
Lack of specific skills required for job	Expect people to be available with required skills on demand	Lack of information on options
Low expectations of own prospects	Unsuitable hours/timing	Childcare availability, cost and tax treatment
Early school leaving	Unaware of skills/work habits gained via CE/JI	Location/transport issues
Drug/alcohol/prison background	Unaware of financial incentives – FIS, RJA, BTWA – which form part of their job offer	
Poor time management due to absence from workforce	Unaware of existence of LES or Job Clubs as source of motivated people	
Expectations of CE	Training courses: waiting lists, unavailable (forklift, construction) or entry requirements too high Reluctance of employers to take certain types of person – people with disabilities, Travellers, people with history of crime or substance abuse, older people.	

Conclusion

Social as well as economic policies have an important role to play in over-coming unemployment and, in particular, in addressing the multi-faceted problem of long-term unemployment and the multiple barriers to employment faced by many of the hidden unemployed.

In a full-employment society, tackling residual and hidden unemployment means dismantling the barrier that prevents people taking up the work that is available. In a society with less than full employment, those with least skills, both formal and personal, are likely to stay at the back of the jobs queue unless active steps are taken to enhance their chances of gaining sustainable employment.

Table 6.4 **Chronology**

1933   Unemployment Assistance
1953   Social Insurance
1968   National Manpower Agency set up, taking job placement out of Labour Exchanges
        AnCo set up (both later subsumed into FÁS)
1973–4 Oil price crisis
1979   Oil price crisis
1975   Live Register goes over 100,000
1983   Social Employment Scheme
1984   Live Register goes over 200,000
        Youth Employment Agency set up (later subsumed into FÁS)
1986   Report of Commission on Social Welfare published
        Equal Treatment Directive adopted giving equal rights to women in the social
            welfare code
1991   Area-based Partnerships set up in 12 pilot areas under Programme for Economic
            and Social Progress
1993   National Economic and Social Forum set up with Oireachtas, social partner, and
            unemployed representatives, and a mandate to address long-term unemployment
        National Development Plan contains Operational Programme for local urban and rural
            development, extending the Area Partnerships to 38 unemployment blackspots
        Back to Work Allowance introduced
1994   NESF Report no. 4 'Ending Long-term Unemployment published'.
        Task Force on Long-term Unemployment set up to address its detailed
            recommendations
        Replacement of Social Employment Scheme by Community Employment.
            Expansion from 17,000 to 34,000 places.
1995   Part-time Job Initiative set up with 1,000 places, on model recommended by
            Conference of Religious of Ireland
        Interim Report of Task Force published.
        Final report of Task Force published.
1996   Local Employment Service set up on pilot basis in 14 areas
        Recasting of Community Employment on lines recommended by Task Force.
        1,000 places on Full-time Job Initiative for very long-term unemployed
        Youth Progression programme introduced for 18–19 year olds out of work
1997   Luxembourg Summit on unemployment sets targets for EU states on reducing
            inflow into long-term unemployment
        Unemployed representatives involved in negotiating Partnership 2000
1998   Employment Action Plan, giving effect to EU guidelines on referring unemployed for
            guidance before reaching long-term unemployed threshold
        Amsterdam Treaty ratified, with chapter on EU unemployment policy
2000   Unemployment bottoms out at 3.9 per cent. Reduction in Community Employment
            begins

Recommended reading

1 Unemployment in Ireland: economic perspectives

Leddin, A. and B. M. Walsh (1998) *The Macroeconomy of Ireland*, 4tth edn. Dublin: Gill & Macmillan. Ch. 14.

O'Hagan, J. (1995) *The Economy of Ireland: Policy and Performance of a Small European Economy*, 8th edn. Dublin: Gill & Macmillan. Ch. 8.

Tansey, P. (1998) *Ireland at Work: Economic Growth and the Labour Market 1987–97*. Dublin: Oak Tree. Ch. 3.

2 Unemployment in Ireland: development of social policies

Allen, M. (1998) *The Bitter Word*. Dublin: Poolbeg.

National Economic and Social Forum (NESF)

(1994) *Ending Long-term Unemployment*. Dublin: NESF Report no. 4.

(1996b) *Long-term Unemployment Initiatives*. Dublin: NESF Opinion no. 3.

(1997) *Early School Leavers and Long-term Unemployment*. Dublin: NESF Report 11.

Office of the Tánaiste (1995a) *Interim Report of the Task Force on Long-Term Unemployment*. Dublin: Stationery Office.

Office of the Tánaiste (1995b) *Report of the Task Force on Long-term Unemployment*. Dublin: Stationery Office.

Department of the Taoiseach (1998) *Report of Partnership 2000 Social Economy Working Group* (1998). Dublin: Stationery Office.

3 Replacement rates

Callan, T., B. Nolan and C.T. Whelan (1996b) *A Review of the Commission on Social Welfare's Minimum Adequate Income*. Dublin: ESRI, Policy Research Series Paper 29, ch. 7: 106–203.

Government of Ireland (1996c) *Integrating Tax and Social Welfare: Expert Working Group Report* Appendix 5.

4 Active labour market policies

Deloitte and Touche (1998) *Review of Community Employment Programme*. Dublin: Stationery Office.

EU Social Fund Evaluation Unit (1998) *ESF and the Long-term Unemployed*. Dublin: Department of Enterprise Trade and Employment.

O'Connell, P. and F. McGinnity (1997) *Working Schemes? Active Labour Market Policy in the Republic of Ireland*. Ch 3; Ch.8. Aldershot: Aldgate.

O'Connell, P (1999) *Are they working?* Dublin: ESRI Working Paper 102.

Chapter 7

Disability and social policy

Suzanne Quin
Bairbre Redmond

Introduction

Within the past ten years there have been significant attempts to design and implement policies in the area of disability which have been influenced by the concepts of rights, partnership and integration. This chapter covers some of the major issues relating to disability in present day Irish society. It challenges some of the traditional thinking about the nature of disability, particularly in relation to service provision. The key principles of full participation and consultation are identified as central to the policy-making process for those with disabilities. We will examine the impact of the most recent Irish policy developments that have importance for those with disabilities, namely the Employment Equality Act 1998, Education Act 1998, Equal Status Act 2000, Education for Persons with Disabilities Bill 2003 and the Disability Bill 2001.

Defining disability

This chapter deals with policies that relate to individuals who have lifelong disabilities, either intellectual or physical. The terms 'intellectual disability', 'learning disability', 'physical disability' or 'physical impairment' are used to describe a range of people who may have very different needs. On the one hand are those with disabilities so severe that they need considerable help in activities of basic living throughout their lives. At the other extreme are individuals who appear no different from any other citizen and who are able to live and work either independently or with some support. Disability is not an illness: it is a lifelong condition which usually cannot be treated or cured and it can be caused in a number of ways. Some people with disability have genetic disorders, some of the most commonly known are Down's Syndrome and Cystic Fibrosis. Other types of disabilities are caused by damage during pregnancy or at birth such as Cerebral Palsy, as well as from biological metabolic disease such as severe meningitis or encephalitis or from head injury. In many cases, the specific cause of a disability is unknown. Others may develop during childhood (such as Muscular Dystrophy) or adulthood (for example, Multiple Sclerosis or Motor Neurone Disease).

An individual with an intellectual disability (previously known as mental handicap) has a greater than average difficulty in learning and has a below average intelligence. This results in a delayed or incomplete development of a person's mind and presents difficulties for the individual in acquiring adequate social competencies and self-help skills. Intellectual disability is sometimes incorrectly confused with mental illness. Mental illness is characterised by inappropriate emotional reactions and emotional disturbance, whereas intellectual disability is marked by lack of understanding and communication.

The term 'physical disability' incorporates a wide range of diagnostic conditions which impact to a greater or lesser degree on a person's physical capacity to engage in social, economic and cultural life (Review Group on Health and Personal Social Services for People with Physical and Sensory Disabilities, 1996). A condition may be static, variable or progressive in its effects. Some conditions may impact on the person's intellectual as well as physical capabilities. Examples of this are children with severe congenital conditions which may result in profound physical and learning disabilities, or adults with a progressive degenerative condition such as multiple sclerosis which at the later stages of the disease can result in considerable physical and mental impairment.

The words that a society uses to describe those with disability can often reveal the attitudes of the society towards that individual. Despite changes in the actual words used, the terminology used to describe disability has continued to label those with a disability as being different from and considerably less able than the rest of society. Words such as 'moron', 'idiot', 'imbecile', 'spastic' or 'retard', which were once simply clinical terms denoting categories of disability, now exist in the language as expressions of derision. The Review Group on Mental Handicap (1991) warned that any new term can be debased over time and a simple change of label in itself will not have a long-lasting positive effect unless a concurrent attempt is made to change professional and public attitudes (1991: 14). Likewise, the Commission on the Status of People with Disabilities (1996) recommended that in defining disability care should be taken to use language that reflects the right of people with disabilities to be treated as full citizens and to be included in all aspects of society. The Commission Report went on to recommend that all definitions of disability should be reviewed and inappropriate or offensive language replaced (1996: 75)

Irish disability policy and legislation
The period from 1998 onwards has seen an unprecedented increase in policy legislation relating to people with disability. The impact of the Employment Equality Act 1998 and the Education Act 1998 will be discussed later in this

chapter. Perhaps the most significant piece of disability legislation has been the Disability Bill (2001) which was subsequently withdrawn. This Bill was published on Friday 20 December 2001 and was met with a storm of protest over the government's perceived failure to underpin the rights-based approach in the Bill which had been advocated by the Commission on the Status of People with Disabilities (1996). Particular criticism was levelled at section 47 of the Bill that purported to deny people with disabilities the right of appeal through the courts to seek improved services or judicial redress. A number of advocacy groups,[1] under the banner of 'Get Your Act Together', organised a high-level publicity information campaign. This campaign, along with a growing sense of unease about the Bill from the public in general, put pressure on the government to withdraw the Bill on the evening of a mass meeting in Dublin in February 2002. An extensive consultation process was then initiated.

Prevalence of disability in Ireland

In 1997 Colgan remarked that 'every report on disability and policy that has been produced in the past twenty years in Ireland has expressed concern about the lack of data on disability, for the purpose of planning services' (1997: 121). Since the late 1990s the measurement of the numbers of people with intellectual disability and those with physical and sensory disability in Ireland has been undertaken by the Health Research Board (HRB). The HRB also researches current and future service needs of the disabled community. In 1995 the HRB began compiling a National Database of individuals with intellectual disability in the country, and the Board has produced three reports on their findings (National Intellectual Disability Database Committee, 1997; Mulvany, 2000; Mulvany, 2001). The most recent report (Mulvany 2001) shows that there were 26,668 people registered on the National Intellectual Disability Database in 2001, representing a prevalence rate of 7.35 per 1,000 of the population. The report noted that the total numbers with more severe levels of intellectual disability had grown by 31 per cent from 1974 when the first census of this population was conducted. This increase is attributed to the general population increase over the period, improved standards of care and an increase in the lifespan of people with intellectual disability.

The report also shows an increase in longevity in those with intellectual disability with those aged 55 years and over now representing 11.3 per cent of all those with intellectual disability in Ireland. However, a most significant change is the large increase in those with disability currently in the 34–54 year group. This cohort has grown from 19 per cent of the overall population of those with intellectual disability in 1974 (Mulcahy, 1976) to 32 per cent of

1   'Get your act together' comprised the Forum of People with Disabilities, Disability Federation of Ireland, NAMHI and People with Disabilities Ireland with support from the NDA and Comhairle.

the overall population in 2000. The impact of this ageing population of people with intellectual disability has major implications for service planning and provision. For a more detailed discussion on the topic of ageing and disability in contemporary Ireland, the reader is directed to 'Ageing and Disability' (Redmond and D'Arcy, 2003: 113–28). As a companion resource to the Intellectual Disability Database the HRB is also compiling the Physical and Sensory Disability Database (Gallagher, 2001, 2002). Launched in 2002, the Database comprises information on the specialist services currently being used or needed within the next five years by people with a disabling conditions. This database will be used for planning developments, prioritising service needs and assisting in resource allocation decisions at national, regional and local level. By mid-2003, just under 16,000 individuals had been registered on the database, with an expectation that over 40,000 will eventually be registered (Comhairle 2003: 8).

How Irish society will deal with such demands will be dependent on a number of issues: the policy commitment to provide and design the most appropriate services; the level of funding made available for such service provision; and, most importantly, the attitude of society in general towards those who have an intellectual disability. Such attitudes have changed considerably over the past two hundred years, not always for the better, and any examination of major issues surrounding intellectual disability will be illuminated by a brief historical overview of the development of such attitudes.

Historical overview

For as long as the human race has existed, some of its members have had disabilities, but the notion of seeing disabled people as a separate group needing special treatment is a relatively new phenomenon. In both European and American cultures prior to the mid-nineteenth century, local 'idiots' existed in most small communities, many of them usefully incorporated into the largely manual labour of rural society. Some became the butt of ridicule, while others were prized for their perpetual innocence (Trent, 1994: 9). The old Irish term for those with intellectual disability, *Duine le Dia* [person of God], suggests an innocence which transcends the mortal.

The Industrial Revolution of the mid-nineteenth century saw many societies becoming more technical with an increased value being placed on the abilities to read, write and complete more complex physical and technical tasks. These changes made the assimilation of those with a physical or intellectual disability more problematic. By the mid-nineteenth century, societies in both Europe and the United States responded with the establishment of institutions where those with a disability could be cared for and trained in simple tasks (Malin et al., 1980: 39). This was in contrast to the Irish situation where, from the early nineteenth century, most people with a disability who were not living at home were cared for under the Poor Law, primarily in the workhouse or the insane asylum. It was not until the early twentieth century that any type of special provision for those with a disability in Ireland was made available. Despite this, there were still 3,165 people categorised 'mentally handicapped or insane' in Irish workhouses in 1905 (Robins, 1992: 29). By the end of the nineteenth century there was strong support for eugenic ideals which sought to protect society from those with physical or intellectual 'defects'. Large custodial institutions were established which were less concerned with the care and education of those with disability than with wider society's need not to be corrupted by their inmates. Eugenic ideals such as these continued to inform attitudes to those with disability well into the late 1940s, especially in academic and medical circles. They found their last and most horrific outlet in the policies of euthanasia for the 'unfit' in Nazi Germany where hundreds of thousands of people with physical and intellectual disability were exterminated to protect the purity of the Aryan race (Ryan and Thomas, 1980: 109; Race, 1995: 51).

By the 1950s writers on both sides of the Atlantic were beginning to comment on the major problems created by custodial institutional care for those with disability. Erving Goffman's seminal work, *Asylums* (Goffman, 1961) argued that the institution robbed patients of their individuality and, in the United Kingdom, writers such as Jack Tizard (1960, 1964) were studying the detrimental effects of institutionalisation on children with intellectual disability. The conditions of many institutions caring for those with disability had begun to come under public scrutiny in the 1970s. In Scandinavia Kugel was comparing the conditions in institutions for those with intellectual disability to those of animals in the zoo (Kugel and Wolfensberger, 1969). In the United States, in 1972, Geraldo Rivera, now better known as a chat-show host, made a TV programme which exposed the appalling conditions of those with intellectual disability in two large institutions in New York State. Mansell and Ericsson (1996: 7) considered Rivera's TV exposé, which attracted over two and a half million viewers, as the single most important event to give impetus to the development away from institutional services. The reader is directed to the works such as Joanna Ryan and Frank Thomas's *The Politics of Mental Handicap* (1980, 1987), an arresting and often horrific account of the inhumanity and degradation suffered by many of those with intellectual disability being cared for in old-style 'mental handicap hospitals' in the United Kingdom at around the same time. Similarly, Paddy Doyle's *The God Squad* (1988) presents an autobiographical account of the emotional, physical and sexual abuse suffered by a young disabled boy while in residential care in Ireland. Raftery and O'Sullivan's (1999) *Suffer the Little Children* also exposes the systematic abuse of children, some with physical and intellectual disability, incarcerated in Ireland's industrial school system from the foundation of the state to the mid-1970s.

Running parallel with the growing public disquiet with conditions of care for those with disability was political pressure to move services – not only for those with disability but also for those with mental health problems – out of institutions and into smaller, community settings. Such moves were not only in response to the demands for better quality care, but they were also related to the escalating costs of running large institutions and the belief that services could be provided at less cost within the community (Mansell and Ericsson, 1996; Walker, 1993). In Ireland the Government White Paper *The Problem of the Mentally Handicapped* (Government of Ireland, 1960) and the *Report of the Commission of Inquiry on Mental Handicap* (Commission of Inquiry, 1965) were tackling growing numbers of those with intellectual disability in need of both better day services and residential care and noting the cost with some alarm. The *Report of the Commission of Enquiry on Mental Handicap* specifically favoured the provision of these services through religious orders and voluntary bodies (Robins, 1992: 55), a policy decision which still has a considerable impact on Irish service provision to the present day. Likewise *Towards a Full Life* (Department of Health, 1984c) supported joint statutory/voluntary involvement in service provision, favouring the enabling rather than mandatory approach to service provision

Throughout the 1970s and 1980s in Europe and the United States, the numbers of people with disability in institutional care dropped sharply, large institutions closed and care in smaller units and houses based in the community was introduced (Emerson and Hatton, 1994). The cost savings of deinstitutionalisation were often being achieved, however, not because care in the community was in itself a cheaper option, but because many of the services needed to support those with intellectual disability adequately in the community were not being fully developed. Doyal (1993) comments that for care in the community to operate effectively it is necessary for individuals in that community to have access to adequate goods and services which allow them to flourish as persons in their own right and participate as full citizens. He adds, however, that none of the aims of community-based care will be achieved unless sufficient capital is made available and 'thus far this [finance] has not been forthcoming and there are good arguments for believing that it will not be forthcoming in the future' (Doyal 1993: 283).

Disability in context

The Commission on the Status of People with Disabilities noted that

> People with disabilities are the neglected citizens of Ireland . . . many of them
> suffer intolerable conditions because of outdated social and economic policies and
> unthinking public attitudes (1996: 5).

The Commission was the first major report on the overall situation and
service provision for people with disabilities in Ireland since the publication
of Department of Health's Green Paper, *Towards a Full Life*, in 1984. The
contrast in the thrust and approach of these two documents to service delivery
is stark and reflects major changes in thinking about the nature of disability
and its consequences that occurred in the intervening decade. One of the
most interesting and critically important features of the Commission Report
(1996) was the composition of the Commission itself, with 60 per cent of its
membership consisting of people with a variety of different disabilities, and
carers. The consumer voice was clearly represented. The fact that the majority
were service users ensured that it was, as Colgan describes, 'in tune with modern
thinking and values concerning participatory democracy, equality and self-
determination for people with disabilities' (1997: 122). The result is a document which highlights the multitude of problems facing those with a disability
in Irish society, and presents a number of policy measures to address them
based on the fundamental concept of rights.

Disability rights movement

The concept of rights has been of central importance in switching the focus
from the individual's 'inability' to perform a range of physical and intellectual
tasks to a society which takes little or no account of such differences, organising
itself in such a way that those who may need to do things differently from the
norm are hampered. The right to participate equally in society and to promote
conditions which would facilitate this process are seen as the issues to be promoted. Key players in advocating these rights have been people with disabilities
and families of those with disability, who have been the recipients of inadequate
and/or inappropriate services. The politicising of disability has been particularly strong in the United States, where a combination of factors such as the
lobbying process, the influence of other rights movements and the number of
young men disabled as a result of the Vietnam War resulted in a groundswell
movement towards the recognition of disability as a rights issue. Oliver (1989)
argues that this is the last major rights movement following on from the civil
rights movement in the 1960s, and the women's and gay rights movements.
He identified the three main features of the disability rights movement as

- offering a critique of existing service provision
- redefining the problem of disability as social rather than med
- encouraging autonomy and the movement away from the d
  professionals as planners and providers of services

Rights and citizenship

T. H. Marshall (1952) identified the three key rights of citizenship as civil, political and social. Oliver (1996) applies Marshall's categorisation to a person with a disability in society. Focusing on civil and political rights, Oliver points out that those with disability appear to enjoy the same rights as others, yet closer inspection indicates that this is not so. People with disability share the common rights of freedom of association, thought, speech and ownership of property. However, in reality their civil rights are curtailed by such factors as being unable to obtain a mortgage on account of unemployment or temporary work contracts, and the difficulty of meeting together because of inadequate transport facilities. With respect to political rights, although in theory they have the right to exercise their political franchise fully, inaccessible polling stations and infrequent attempts by political parties to involve them means that they have to vote earlier and in a different way from the rest of the electorate.

It is in the third area – of social rights – that the situation of people with disabilities is particularly problematic. The concept of social rights encompasses what is required to be able to participate in social living in its broadest sense, including having a standard of living or lifestyle compatible with current social expectations as well as the use of social facilities similar to everyone else. That this is not so for people with disabilities in Irish society is all too evident, and specific aspects of this problem are discussed on pp. 151–5.

Which rights are most important for social life and service provision can be debated at length. Bruce (1991) suggests they are:

- The right of access, which includes, but goes beyond, the physical accessibility of buildings. It covers such areas as access to communication which takes cognisance of differing physical impairments and access to participation in the social and cultural life of the community.
- The right to self-determination which requires the active participation of people with disabilities in determining the type and range of services suited to their needs. Ultimately, it is about the right to decide one's own lifestyle as an adult including the balancing of risks to health vis-à-vis achieving life goals.
- The right to resources to cover the extra costs of having a disability. Studies of poverty consistently demonstrate a clear relationship between having a disability and the likelihood of being poor (Oliver and Barnes, 1993; Irish Wheelchair Association, 1994, Elwan, 1999, Harbison, 2003).

This is related to the high rates of unemployment amongst people with disability. It is also because having a disability is costly in itself owing to the need for extra or different clothing, special dietary requirements, more than average heating and transport costs, and lack of time, energy and access to a range of shopping giving best value for money.

- The right to be recognised as an individual. Social policy is geared to providing for categories of need, not for individuals. However, each person has a unique set of characteristics of which the disability is but one element. Those involved in service provision must therefore ensure that individual differences and preferences are taken into account and that the assessment of what is possible does not rest solely or primarily with the professional service provider. The focus on consumer rights and consumer input into service planning, which was evident in the health policy document *Shaping a Healthier Future* (Department of Health, 1994) and further emphasised in the second Health Strategy *Quality and Fairness: A Health System for You* (Department of Health and Children, 2001c). This new approach to service delivery put the onus on professionals to share decision-making power with service recipients. This will help to ensure that individual preferences will be a central consideration to a much greater degree than in the past.

Before leaving the subject of rights, it is important to consider particularly vulnerable categories of people with disabilities, for example women who have to deal with the double disadvantage of being a woman and having a disability. Morris (1991), already part of the feminist movement when she acquired a disability as a result of an accident, argued that because the disability movement had been dominated by men who had a male perspective on disability issues, the feelings and subjective experiences of the disabled woman have tended to be excluded from consideration. In her view the disability movement should adopt the feminist principle that 'the personal is political and, in giving voice to such subjective experiences, assert the value of our lives' (1991: 68). Kennedy (2002) discusses the particular issues for women with disability in relation to pregnancy and maternity. An recent example of qualitative research tapping the lived experience of disability is offered by Horgan (2004), herself a mother of a child with a disability, who describes the effects of a disabling society on both women with a disability who are mothers and mothers of disabled children.

Another category of potential double disadvantage is that of people from ethnic minorities who have a disability. The marginalisation and poverty experienced by those of racial and ethnic minority is discussed by Moran (see chapter 12) and by Crowley (see chapter 11) in relation to Travellers in Ireland. At present, there is a lack of general data on ethnic populations in Ireland (Fanning, 2002) and very little is known about the incidence of disability among minority ethnic communities in this country. Pierce comments that 'people with disabilities among minority ethnic communities are largely invisible in Irish society' (2003a: 19). Among those who are refugee or asylum seekers will be those with pre-existing disability as well as those whose disability is a direct result of war, conflict or torture (Pierce, 2003b). Whatever its cause, the impact of disability is likely to pose particular difficulties and challenges for them. Pierce's (2003a) study of people with a disability from ethnic minorities found that they had to contend with racism, language barriers, difficulties in accessing information and lack of awareness and cultural sensitivity on the part of service providers and society in general about disability as well as ethnicity.

As already discussed, there is evidence that those with disabilities, living in residential care, may be at significant risk of having their rights infringed (Clements and Read, 2003). Basic, everyday decisions about when and what to eat, when to get up and go to bed, have a bath or shower, deciding where and when to go out may be determined by staff rostering rather than the wishes of adult residents. The Commission in its Report on the Status of People with Disabilities pointed out that even the right to a basic income for those without resources was limited to discretionary pocket money for those in residential care (Commission, 1996). The restrictions created by living in such a controlled environment which take little account of adult rights led to the creation of the Independent Living Movement in the 1970s in the United States. This movement spread to other countries, including Ireland, and now informs thinking about alternative care facilities for adults with disabilities. Its basic premise is that, as adults, people with disabilities have the right to make decisions, major and minor, about their lifestyle. The purpose of caregiving, therefore, is to enable each person to maximise their choices by having available to them help in the activities of daily living. This help may be specially designed living quarters and/or having someone to carry out tasks such as dressing, cooking, feeding and so on at the behest of the person with the disability. The Report of the Review Group on Health and Personal Social Services for Physically Disabled People (Review Group, 1996) regarded the independent living arrangement as offering the disabled person 'the opportunity to live in a domestic dwelling, supported with the necessary health and social services' (1996: 79). The Review Group supported the development of independent living 'because it promotes independence and respects the service user's right to choose the form of care most appropriate to him or her' (1996: 80). In the independent living approach, the relationship between the person with the disability and his or her helper may be that of employer or employee with reciprocal rights and responsibilities. Increasingly the trend is towards giving resources directly to those not in the paid labour market, who are in need of personal assistance to enable them to purchase the required care.

Family care

The closure of many institutions was not accompanied by the provision of well-financed community based supports. Subsequent gaps in services for those with disability in the community had to be filled from some other source and, in most cases, meant that the work of caring for those with a disability has been increasingly performed by unpaid family carers. The ideal of care in community in which those with disability could live a full, inclusive life nurtured by those around them has never been fully achieved. Community care became a synonym for family care, without the promised support and resources necessary for the system to function properly. Looking at the situation in the United Kingdom, Walker notes that 'despite the rhetoric concerning the needs of carers, there are no proposals designed to ensure that their needs are taken into account' (Walker, 1993: 220).

Most families would say that, given enough appropriate services, they would be able to cope well and it is important to remember that many families would prefer their family member with a disability to live at home, particularly up to young adulthood. (McConkey and Conliffe, 1989: 37; Redmond, 1996: 38–50, Horgan, 2004). However, problems occur when the basic services are inadequate and when mothers become exhausted from heavy burdens of physical care (Redmond and Richardson 2003). Providing families with well-designed support services must be done so that they do not experience restricted and diminished lives just because they have chosen to care for their family member with disability. Professionals must also remember that families have to be fully included in decision-making processes – not as subordinates, but as full partners in the process (Dale, 1996: 42–3). Offering adequate support and recognition to families also has an impact on the quality of life of the person being cared for. Families who are not under great pressure and stress would find it easier to help their family members with disabilities to pursue their own interests and develop their maximum potential.

The most recent report of the National Intellectual Disability Database (Mulvany, 2001) notes that 31 per cent of people with intellectual disability aged 35 years and over are still living in the family home and another 1,638 residential places are needed in the period 2002–6. In many of these cases, family carers are continuing to provide care in the absence of the needed service. These figures also highlight an increase in the age of parents, with the attendant difficulties of providing care on a long-term basis. Redmond's study of parents of teenagers with intellectual disability showed that one of their greatest concerns was how their young adult would be cared for after their death (Redmond, 1996: 67). Many parents approached old age without the reassurance of services available when they could no longer take care of their child, resulting in adults with disability remaining in the family home whether or not their parents were able to cope, or, indeed, whether the individuals themselves liked the arrangement. Most young adults begin to leave the family home from their early twenties onwards, yet those with disability rarely have the option to do so. Scarcity of appropriate accommodation has meant that many adults with disability leave home as a result of a crisis, primarily the illness or death of one or both parents. Making available alternative-to-home accommodation at an earlier stage, when families are around to support such a move, would undoubtedly be expensive. It would, however, give the person with disability the chance to establish their own adult home with dignity and support. Family members would then be able to live out the remaining years of their lives without the nagging worry of what would happen when they died.

Problems regarding practical care also arise where a person with a disability lives with relatives, be they parents, siblings, spouses and/or children. The fundamental issue in the case of a person with a physical disability who requires help with activities of daily living is the juxtaposition of adult status with physical dependency. This is where the element of choice is critical for both the cared-for and the carer. Lack of real alternatives and inadequate support services for those with relative carers can put enormous strain on both parties. The National Rehabilitation Board document *Righting the History of Wrongs* (1991) argues that if the right to adequate services for physical care is not provided, then the rights of family carers are also usurped in that they may feel that they have little or no choice in the matter. Indeed, prevailing ideologies about the family may make them feel guilty if they even wish it to be otherwise. Dalley (1988) uses the term 'compulsory altruism' coined by Land and Rose to describe this. While the policy of community care which has now been in existence for almost half a century has many positives, its downside has been its tardiness in having sufficient alternatives to family-based care (i.e. independent living) and its failure to provide adequate support service to families providing care. This is not only in respect of direct service provision in relation to community care. In the matter of housing adaptation grants, for example, a grant may be paid to adapt only one accommodation unit which makes economic sense but may effectively prohibit shared care by adult children of a parent with a disability (Owens, 1987).

Agency provision

Voluntary organisations have played a major role in the development of services for those with disability and their families. The growth of such organisations is often derived from the work of individuals, concerned groups and religious orders trying to address gaps in state service provision. Some of these organisations have grown very large over time and now employ a range of personnel. These include St Michael's House, Brothers of Charity Services, Daughters of Charity Services, Irish Wheelchair Association, COPE, Central Remedial Clinic and Enable Ireland.

One of the major advantages of the voluntary sector is its ability to develop innovative services in response to identified needs, for example the Personal Assistant scheme, independent living initiatives, the original Breakaway scheme and subsequent nationwide home-based respite schemes such as Take-A-Break and Home Choice. The provision of professional community-based services such as social work, physiotherapy, driving instruction for specially adapted cars, and educational and training services have also been provided in the field of disability by voluntary rather than statutory services.

The development of services provided by such voluntary bodies has been limited by unreliable and often inadequate state funding. Seeking sufficient funding can be very time-consuming for many voluntary agencies and considerable energy may be used up in continual fund-raising. Moreover, the need to raise funds can result in the portrayal of people with disabilities as dependent and needy, rather than promoting a positive image of disability, including the basic right to adequate resources. This lack of funding has also made it difficult for agencies to plan services in the medium to long term. It is arguable that the widespread use of voluntary organisations to provide services has also resulted in an unequal, or variable, distribution of services geographically, with some families moving to areas with better services.

A further issue regarding voluntary provision is the extent to which people with disability and their family carers have a voice in policy planning. Critics of traditional charities point to a lack of people with disabilities in positions of power in voluntary agencies (Drake, 1996). They argue that there should be a commitment to enabling and encouraging people with disability and their family carers to become involved in the process of policy making. This does not mean political lobbying alone; it means ensuring that those with disability and their families have adequate representation at the highest level of decision making at region and national levels.

A large number of voluntary bodies are involved in service provision for people with disabilities in Ireland. Most address the specific needs and issues of a single condition such as Cystic Fibrosis, Muscular Dystrophy or Multiple Sclerosis. Fewer, larger organisations encompass a wider range of disabilities in their brief. Examples of the latter would be the Irish Wheelchair Association for adults with a variety of physical conditions which impact on their mobility and Enable Ireland which provides a wide range of services for children whose primary disability is physical.

Traditionally, voluntary organisations have played both a pioneering and a reactionary role in the development of services for people with disabilities in Ireland. They have also played a key role as pressure groups, trying to keep the issues of people with disabilities on the political agenda. In the absence of state provision, they have played a major part in creating and providing a wide range of health and personal social services such as physiotherapy, occupational therapy, speech therapy, social work, family support and respite care. Voluntary organisations rely on a combination of state funding and resources raised from fundraising (Faughnan and Kelleher, 1993). Over time, state funding has become an increasingly significant factor in service provision and the laissez-faire arrangements for such funding has been replaced by contractual agreements between the statutory payers and the voluntary providers in which the respective obligations of accountability and transparency are defined (O'Farrell, 2000).

Experiences of those with disabilities

There is now a growing literature on the subjective experience of physical disability (see Nolan, 1987; Doyle, 1988; Horgan, 2004, for example, in relation to Ireland, and Bauby, 1997; Reeves, 1998, for recent and notable accounts based in other countries). Tubridy (1996) provides a qualitative study of 30 young people with different physical disabilities in the Irish context. What is important about this area of literature is that it offers some insight into the experience of disability and illustrates the way in which individual people, professionals and society as a whole respond to the person. They also illustrate the barriers that can impede participation in social life.

A study of its members by the Irish Wheelchair Association (1994) raised particular concerns regarding participation. It found that one half of respondents identified themselves as not being involved in common or popular activities in Irish social life. Reasons given included: lack of interest (52 per cent); lack of opportunities (40 per cent); inadequate transport (33 per cent); shortage of personal assistance (24 per cent); and absence of encouragement (19 per cent). These findings led the researchers to question whether members 'are so isolated and apathetic that they have just given up or have never had the chance to participate' (Irish Wheelchair Association, 1994: 52). Such lack of participation clearly impedes the opportunity to forge adult relationships. Tubridy (1994), in comparing the lifestyles and views of people who had a disability from birth or early childhood to those who acquire one as an adult, found that only one person in ten of the first group was married. The other nine in this group saw themselves as unlikely to marry because of the social problems associated with the disability. Many in the latter group were married before the onset of the disability which was regarded as posing serious difficulties for the existing relationship. Parker (1993) remarks on the relative dearth of knowledge about marriage and disability generally. She undertook a small, qualitative study of couples where one spouse acquired a disability subsequent to the marriage. Her findings highlight the importance of the pre-existing relationship as well as the effect of the disability on reciprocal roles within marriage.

Physical access

'One of the greatest forms of discrimination which many people with disabilities face is having lack of access to buildings and functions' (Lonsdale, 1990: 148). 'Access to the built and external environment', states the Commission Report, 'is a pre-requisite condition necessary to enable their [people with disabilities] access and participation in any or all of the other aspects of social and civil society' (Commission on the Status of People with Disabilities, 1996: 153). It comments on the 'frustration and anger caused to people with disabilities by the inaccessibility of buildings' as being very evident in the submissions made to it by both individuals and organisations representing people with various disabilities. The Building Regulations (Department of the Environment, 1991b), Part M, require all new buildings for public use to be accessible to people with disabilities. However, as the Commission (1996) points out, the approach to access in the Regulations 'is not aimed at establishing an enabling environment for everyone but of making special provision for special cases' (1996: 153). This, it argues, 'generally results in designers and others interpreting the cited minimum requirements as being optimum or even maximum requirements' (1996: 154). Lack of enforcement of Part M by the local authorities is also cited as a problem. Part M of the building regulations was amended in 2000 to make houses 'visitable' by people with disabilities. It requires that all new building, subject to planning permission, must now comply with Part M. However, the lack of enforcement of the building regulations, coupled with few sanctions for non-compliance, removes much of the power from Part M which is effectively ignored in relation to creating a more accessible built environment for disabled people. As McGettrick notes 'current Irish social policies in relation to access clearly point to deficient and ineffectual statutory controls governing access needs' (2003: 76).

Education

The right to education for young people with disabilities has been one of the most contentious issues in the area of disability policy over the past twenty years. In the 1980s the main educational debate revolved around the value of specialist versus mainstream education for disabled pupils. Since then, the trend has been towards the development of special classes within mainstream schools rather than increased provision of special schooling for children with physical and/or intellectual disabilities (Department of Education and Science, 2001). This was in line with the Special Education Review Committee (Department of Education, 1993: 22), which recommended 'as much integration as is appropriate and . . . as little segregation as is necessary'.

In 1990, two landmark legal challenges were instigated that highlighted a lack of any education for children with severe and profound disability. The first of these, the O'Donoghue case (1994) resulted in many children with severe and profound learning disability being granted the right to a formal education for the first time. In the second, (Sinnott *v* Minister for Education [2000 SC] – July 2001), the Supreme Court held that the state's constitutional obligation to provide for free primary education ceased at the age of 18. Both of these cases attracted much public attention and pressurised the government into reviewing its education provision to disabled pupils. Many of these reviews have been integrated into aspects of the Education for Persons with Disabilities Bill 2003.

The Education Act 1998 requires schools to provide education to students that is appropriate to their abilities and needs. It specifies that a school must use its available resources to ensure that the educational needs of all students, including those with disability or with other special needs, are identified and provided for [section 9]. However, the level of actual provision leaves a gap between aspirations and reality. The particular challenges facing small schools were evident in the Report of the Special Education Review Committee (1993). McDonnell is critical of this Report for the lack of representation of service users i.e. past and present pupils in the composition of its member-ship. He attributes the paternalistic approach to the educational provision for people with disabilities to the dominance of the psycho-medical model. Such expert perspectives, he states, 'exert a profound influence on social and cultural responses to disability and constitute a powerful counter-resistance to a disability rights discourse' (McDonnell, 2003: 41).

Employment

Lack of employment is a major issue for people with physical disability. The Commission on the Status of People with Disabilities (1996) states that surveys of organisations for people with disabilities in Ireland indicated unemployment rates of over 70 per cent. Eurostat figures for people with disability in Europe for 2002 indicate that labour force participation is much lower for disabled people. Seventy-eight per cent of those with severe disability aged 16–64 are outside the labour force, compared to 27 per cent of the able-bodied and only 16 per cent of those who are faced with work restrictions are given any assistance (such as specially adapted computers, special access or personal supports) to help them to enter the labour force (Eurostat, 2001). It has recommended that there should be further initia-tives to create employment for people with disabilities similar to the Pilot Programme on Employment of People with Disabilities. Since 1977, there has been in the public sector a three per cent quota scheme for people with disabilities. Yet the three per cent has not been achieved overall during the past twenty years (Commission, 1996). This quota does not apply to the private sector where efforts to secure jobs for those with disability have concentrated on facilitating and encouraging employers to take them on voluntarily. The Commission's view was that the quota requirement should not be extended immediately to the private sector, but that it should be reviewed after a three-year period. Quota schemes have their advantages and disadvantages as means of creating employment opportunities for a disadvantaged group such as people with disabilities. On the one hand, they force employers to take on such workers who might otherwise never do so, and a positive experience might encourage the reluctant employer to reach or exceed the required numbers. On the other hand, the employers and fellow employees of workers taken on, on this basis, may view them as less than equal/competent for the task or as taking a job that could have been given to someone with better or more suitable qualifications. What does seem to be important is that a quota scheme should be backed by sanctions to ensure that minimum requirements are reached.

Even where a job is secured, through the quota scheme or otherwise, people with disabilities can face problems such as lack of promotional opportunities and restricted facility for moving from one job to another. A particularly significant development for those with physical disabilities is the remarkable advances that have been and continue to be made in the area of information and communication technology, which create the potential to open fields of employment for people with a variety of different disabilities. It is vital that those who could benefit in this way gain access to appropriate technology; it is of little benefit if it exists but is not available. This is where the concept of rights (see pp. 145–7 above) again comes to the fore. Emphasis on the barriers which impede people with disabilities will define technology as a basic requirement 'to open up the employment domain and create an environment in which the chance for expression of abilities can be optimised' (Roulstone, 1993: 247). The Commission acknowledged that the impact of technology and telecommunications have the potential to 'play a major role in helping people with disabilities to secure equal status in most areas of life and society' (Commission, 1996: 209).

The Employment Equality Act of 1998 is based on the principle that all individuals are entitled to equal treatment in training and employment opportunities regardless of gender, marital status, family status, sexual orientation, religious, age, disability, race, or membership of the travelling community. Conroy (2003: 51–3) notes that implementation of the Act was delayed by a constitutional challenge against one of its clauses which required employers to provide adequate accommodation for disabled workers at their own expense. This clause was subsequently removed and replaced with one that obliged employers to accommodate disabled workers 'subject to a nominal cost'. The 2002 annual report for the Irish Equality Authority (Equality Authority, 2003) noted that that the number of employment equality claims brought by disabled people discriminated against by the public/semi state sectors at the point of access to employment has been striking. The report notes that the effectiveness of the Employment Equality Act to deter such discriminatory behaviour is hampered by the low maximum financial award that employers found in breach of the Act can be asked to pay. Put simply, employers in public or semi-state organisations may prefer to pay the maximum fine of €12,700 (at 2002 rates) rather than incur the expense of taking on a suitably qualified disabled person as an employee. For more details on issues relating to employment and disability reader are advised to consult Conroy's chapter on employment in *Disability and Social Policy in Ireland* (Quin and Redmond, 2003: 45–56).

Conclusion

We have traced the major changes that have occurred in many aspects of the lives of those with a disability. It has demonstrated the similarity of problems experienced by those with intellectual or physical disability, such as social exclusion, paucity of service provision and an overall lack of planning for future service development. The varying practical needs of those with different types of disability, and the lack of wisdom of perceiving all those with disabilities as one homogeneous group, have been identified. Not only must the particular needs of each category of disability be acknowledged, but also, within these categories, the unique needs of each individual should be articulated in an individual, person-centred plan. It is vital that individuals with disability and their families play central roles in deciding on a care plan for the short and long term and, to this end, that their opinions are not only heard but also listened to. Finding ways of ensuring that they have a chance to say what services they feel they want is crucial in any effective individual planning system (Simons, 1995: 174). Simons points out, however, that 'the empowerment of people with disability will not lead to a quiet life for professionals – sometimes they will tell us things we do not like to hear' (Simons, 1995: 171).

Traditionally, disability has not been high on the policy agenda, lacking the immediacy of such issues as child abuse. In the 1990s, the establishment of the permanent Council for the Status of People with Disabilities and the creation of the National Disability Authority were both significant steps in ensuring that the issues of people with disabilities achieve a greater ongoing public profile. The further development of services to ensure opportunities for full participation in society on the part of people with disabilities depends not just on prevailing economic conditions. It is also determined by how current and future policy makers view the importance of those with disabilities in our society, and how the general public support and uphold the rights of their fellow citizens with disability.

Table 7.1 **Policy developments**

1961	Foundation of National Association of Mental Handicap in Ireland, first nationwide association of parents and friends of those with intellectual disability.
1967	Foundation of National Rehabilitation Board (now called NDA) to advise Minster for Health on disability issues and to offer occupational advice to those with disability.
1981	International Year of Disabled People
1984	Publication of Green Paper on Services for People with Disability, Towards a Full Life.
1991	Report of the Review Group on Mental Handicap Services, Needs and Abilities, recommends changing the term 'mental handicap' to 'intellectual disability'.
1992	Green Paper on Education, Education for a Changing World, recommends integrated educational opportunities for children with both physical and intellectual disabilities.
1995	Establishment, by Department of Health, of a National Intellectual Disability Database, to provide accurate information for planning services.
1996	Publication of A Strategy for Equality, Report of the Commission on the Status of People with Disabilities.
1997	Marie O'Donoghue wins her case in the Supreme Court which acknowledges the right of her 12-year-old son Paul to have an education provided for him by the state, under Article 42 of the Constitution. Paul has both severe physical and intellectual disability.
1998	Establishment of the National Disability Authority by the Minister for Justice, Equality and Law Reform.
	Employment Equality Act.
	Education Act
2001	Disability Bill (withdrawn for redrafting)
2003	Education for Persons with Disabilities Bill
	Special Olympics World Games, Dublin
	European Year of Disabled People
2004	DIsability Bill

Recommended reading

Malin, N. (ed.) (1995) *Services for People with Learning Disability.* London: Routledge.

Mittler, P. and H. Mittler (eds) (1994) I*nnovations in Family Support for People with Learning Disabilities.* Chorley: Lisieux Hall.

Quin, S. and B. Redmond (eds) (2003) *Disability and Social Policy in Ireland.* Dublin: UCD Press.

Quinn, P. (1998) *Understanding Disability: A Lifespan Approach.* London: Sage.

Commission on the Status of People with Disabilities (1996) *A Strategy for Equality.* Dublin: Stationery Office.

Ryan, J and F. Thomas (1987) *The Politics of Mental Handicap.* London: Free Association Press.

Tubridy, J. (1996) *Pegged Down: Experiences of People in Ireland with Significant Physical Disabilities.* Dublin: IPA.

Chapter 8

Children and social policy

Valerie Richardson

The way a society treats children reflects not only its qualities of compassion and protective caring but also its sense of justice, its commitment to the future and its urge to enhance the human condition for coming generations.

Perez de Cuellar, UN Secretary General, Lignano, Italy, September 1987

Definition and scope of policy area

The Child Care Act 1991 (s.2 (1)) defines a child as 'a person under the age of 18 years other than a person who is or has been married'. The 2002 Census of the Population shows that there are 1,013,031 people under the age of 18 years in Ireland. Children therefore make up just over one quarter of the total population of 3.9 m and represent a sizeable proportion of the population for whom national policies are needed (CSO, 2003). As the Task Force on Child Care Services noted: 'children are special in two respects. Firstly, they are persons in the process of formation; secondly they are not independent' (1980: 34). Children are therefore dependent on adults to secure their needs and their welfare. Children share with adults the universal human needs for food, shelter, warmth and security. However, children also have specific needs for love and security, new experiences, praise and recognition and responsibility (Kellmer Pringle, 1974), together with the need to be treated as an individual. It is widely accepted that the family, as the basic unit in society, is the primary source of love and individual care for children and provides the setting in which the child's needs can be met. The welfare of children depends on the stability and effectiveness of the family to which they belong. For children who have the benefit of warm, continuous and intimate relationships with their parent or parents throughout their childhood, there is the opportunity to develop a strong sense of identity, self-worth, trust in others and him or herself, the ability to handle stress and frustration and to develop and maintain relationships. The child's experience in a stable and effective family lays the foundation of his future psychological, physical and cognitive development (see, for example, Bowlby, 1953; Erikson, 1969; Fahlberg, 1981). For some children the opportunity never exists for them to experience family life: some families never exist as a viable unit, some temporarily or permanently break down and some parents are unwilling or unable to care for their children. In these circumstances state intervention in the form of childcare services are needed to ensure that the needs of children are met.

Children, in common with adults, are affected by almost every aspect of social policy and social service provision discussed in other chapters in this book. This chapter addresses social policies which are concerned primarily with the protection and welfare of children in Irish society. It will first present a brief statistical overview in relation to children in need of care and protection, followed by a discussion of the historical development of childcare policy and practice in Ireland before addressing particular issues in contemporary childcare policy.

Statistical overview

The latest available statistics from the Department of Health and Children show that health boards received 8,269 reports of child abuse during 2000 of which 37.3 per cent (3,085) were confirmed. Of the total number, the majority were cases of neglect (1,453) with 548 of physical abuse, 517 sexual abuse and 567 emotional abuse. This is an increase of almost 30 per cent over the previous five years. However, it is difficult to assess whether the increase in cases notified is due to a higher incidence of abuse or whether increased public awareness has led to increased reporting. (Department of Health and Children, 2003c)

The number of children in the care of Health Boards at the end of December 2002 was 4,424 with the largest number being in the Eastern Regional Health Authority area (1,732) and the smallest number in the North Western Health Board (217). Just over three quarters (76.5 per cent) of the children in care were placed in foster care and of that number 18 per cent (797) of children were fostered with relatives. Fourteen per cent (636) of children were in residential care and 139 (13.1 per cent) were at home under the supervision of the Health Boards (Department of Health and Children, 2003) The largest number of children (1,304: 29.5 per cent) were in care because their parents were described as 'parents unable to cope/parental illness', 'neglect' accounted for 1,219 (27.6 per cent) and physical or sexual abuse was the reason for admission of 497 children (11.3 per cent). An important factor arising from *Health Statistics 2000* (Department of Health and Children, 2003) is that the children of lone parents represent 40 per cent of the children in care during 2000 which is far higher than the percentage of lone parents in the general population. These parents are clearly a vulnerable group who require additional supports in parenting their children. There is also evidence that the children of the Travelling community (Task Force on the Travelling Community, 1995), children from deprived backgrounds and those from families where drug use is prevalent are particularly vulnerable to admission to care (McKeown, 1991; Woods, 1994).

The number of children placed for adoption has continued to fall over the past two decades. In 1982 there were 1,191 adoption orders made, compared with 266 Irish adoption orders made in 2002. The majority of these orders were family adoptions (167 orders) of which 156 were made in favour of the child's birth mother and her husband. The drop in the number of Irish children placed for adoption reflects the changing attitudes towards children born outside marriage and the increase in the number of never married women deciding to parent their babies.

Historical origins of child care policy

The process of the social construction of child abuse as a social problem and the emergence and development of the Irish child protection system have been comprehensively chronicled by Ferguson (1993, 1996) and Buckley (1997). Five distinct periods of development can be identified, these being 1889–1908, 1909–69, 1970–90, 1991–9 and 2000 to the present.

Foundations of childcare policy 1889–1908
The first attempts to deal with the protection of children resulted in the passing of the Cruelty to Children Act, 1889, which made child cruelty a criminal act, provided for inspectors to remove children from parental custody and to prosecute parents. The year 1889 also saw the establishment of the National Society for the Prevention of Cruelty to Children (NSPCC) in Ireland. The twin aims of the Society were to investigate cases of suspected cruelty and to work towards changes in the legislation. The NSPCC rapidly developed an inspectorate and by 1908 they were servicing 100 centres throughout the country with annual increases in the number of cases investigated (Ferguson, 1996: 8). In 1908 the Children Act was introduced to provide legislation to protect children against offences and to provide for children who had committed offences (Greene, 1979). It was this Act, regarded as a liberal reform at the time, which became the legislative framework for child protection in Ireland for a further 83 years. Where neglect or abuse was proven, children could be removed from their parents to a 'place of safety' and placed in the care of a 'fit person', either a foster parent or residential institution (Children Act 1908 SS. 20, 24, 58). Children who had committed an offence could be dealt with in a number of ways including being sent to an industrial school or place of detention (Children Act 1908 S107),

Punishment to casework ideology 1909–69

After 1908 there was a shift from the punishment centred ideology involving prosecution of parents to the casework ideology and practice based on the supervision of parent–child relations in their homes (Ferguson, 1996: 9). During this period child protection remained the sole responsibility of voluntary agencies, spearheaded by the NSPCC, with residential facilities provided by the religious in the form of Industrial and Reformatory Schools.

The development of child protection legislation and services was very firmly rooted in the principle of family autonomy, a principle which became enshrined in the 1937 Constitution (Bunreacht na hÉireann, 1937, Article 42), recognising the family as the 'primary and fundamental unit group of society' and ascribing to parents 'inalienable and imprescriptible' rights, that is, rights that cannot be taken away and rights that cannot be given away. Constitutional permission for state intervention was limited under Article 42.5 to 'exceptional cases, where the parents for physical or moral reasons fail in their duty towards their children'. This principle of minimal intervention in family life was endorsed by the social teaching of the Catholic Church which left the family outside the sphere of state intervention (Breen et al., 1990). However, the constitutional support for the rights of parents and families was not matched by similar support for the rights and welfare of children (O'Connor, 1992; Buckley, 1997). During this second period of development of child welfare services there was a growing emphasis on the belief that children could be protected and their welfare promoted through social intervention, together with a confidence in professional expertise, which could manage the risk to children at an individual level. In 1956 the Irish Society for the Prevention of Cruelty to Children (ISPCC) broke away from the NSPCC, providing a casework service covering the 26 counties and providing the foundations for development of 'a truly distinctive Irish child protection system' (Ferguson, 1996: 12).

During this period two important pieces of legislation were implemented which changed the nature of childcare policy. The first was the Adoption Act 1952 which regularised the informal nature of the adoption procedures. Until that time adoptions had been arranged on an informal basis between agencies, third parties or directly by the biological parents and the adopting parents. For the first time the state was intervening directly and regulating relationships between parents and children with the permanent and legal transfer of parental rights from biological to adoptive parents, despite strong and prolonged resistance from the Catholic Church (Whyte, 1980). The second piece of legislation was The Guardianship of Infants Act 1964 which marked a significant attitudinal change in childcare policy. This Act was the first piece of legislation to incorporate a definition of 'welfare' as 'the religious, moral, intellectual, physical and social welfare of the infant' (Section 2) and more importantly it enshrined the principle of 'paramountcy', that is, that in any decisions involving a child's welfare the best interests of the child must be the first and paramount consideration (Section 3). This Act, therefore, marked a change in the state's relationship with the family in any dispute over the welfare of a child and raised for the first time the real possibility of conflict between the rights of the parents and the rights of children.

During this period, casework services continued to develop under the auspices of the ISPCC with growing professionalisation of the child protection system. Increasing numbers of professionals were obtaining social work training in the UK and USA and social science courses were being developed in the universities in Ireland, eventually leading to the establishment of the first professional social work training course in 1968 in University College Dublin and a course for residential childcare in Kilkenny in 1971. In 1968, following considerable pressure, the Minister for Education, set up the Kennedy Committee, which reported in 1970 on the state of the reformatory and industrial schools. The most important recommendation made by the Committee was that:

> the whole aim of the child care system should be geared towards the prevention of family breakdown and the problems consequent on it. The committal or admission of children to residential care should be considered only when there is no satisfactory alternative. (Committee of Enquiry into the Reformatory and Industrial Schools System, 1970: 6)

The Kennedy Report was to become a watershed in terms of childcare policy since it focused service provision on prevention and the support of families in the community rather than the removal of children where families had failed them.

Child abuse and pressure groups, 1970–90

The publication of the Kennedy Report (Committee of Enquiry, 1970) coincided with a reorganisation of the health and social services. The Health Act 1970 decentralised the delivery of these services to the eight regional health boards and the community care programmes became responsible for the delivery of the personal social services which included those of childcare and protection (Curry, 1998). For those working in the field of childcare it became increasingly obvious that the current legislation was inadequate to deal with the welfare of children. An important feature of the early 1970s was the establishment of CARE – a group of professionals and academics whose aim was to pressurise the government to introduce reforms in line with the recommendations of the Kennedy Report. This group produced an influential document *Children Deprived* (CARE, 1972) which set out best practice in the field of child welfare and made strong recommendations for change. Among the many deficiencies in the system, they highlighted as the most notable the lack of one authority at a national level to co-ordinate and take responsibility for childcare policy. Such responsibilities were divided between three government ministers causing both overlaps and gaps to occur (CARE, 1972: 28). Under increasing pressure the government established the Task Force on Child Care Services in 1974, whose mandate was to make recommendations for improved services for deprived children and children at risk, to prepare a new Children's Bill to modernise the law and to make recommendations on the administrative reform necessary to implement these. The final report of the Task Force (1981) highlighted the need for one government department to have overall responsibility for children and re-emphasised that, as far as possible, deprived children should be catered for in a family or community setting with support from social services, rather than in residential care. It recommended neighbourhood resource centres whose function would be

> to mobilise community resources on behalf of children and their families and by combining the resources of the community, voluntary organisations [and the relevant statutory authorities] maximise their impact on the well-being of children and families in the area. (Task Force on Child Care Services, 1981: 145).

However, it was the voluntary rather than the statutory services which responded to the recommendations for community services. The ISPCC developed three family centres in Dublin, Cork and Wexford (Nic Giolla Choille, 1983; 1984; 1985), and Barnardos developed a range of community support services for families.

The family-centred philosophy underlying the Kennedy and Task Force reports was, to a certain extent, reflected in changing policies during the 1970s. Many of the large childcare institutions were closed or re-formed as smaller group homes together with an emphasis on placing children in foster homes or with adoptive parents where possible. The health boards developed community care programmes, employing social workers whose primary focus was to offer child-centred family casework with an emphasis on supporting families to provide for the welfare of their children. The need for updated legislation became increasingly obvious as the child protection discourse became more widespread and the inability to provide adequate protection for children and support for families more blatant. During the late 1960s and early 1970s, there was growing awareness internationally about non-accidental injury to children (Kempe and Helfer, 1968). As Buckley (1997: 104) has stated:

The evolution of the child protection system in Ireland was heavily influenced by international trends and events as well as by its own unique social framework . . . the 'rediscovery' of child abuse in the 1960s in Britain and the USA, with the work of Kempe and Helfer and the repercussions in Britain of the first child abuse 'scandals' started to have an influence on awareness of the problem in Ireland.

In 1975 the Department of Health set up a committee to discuss the issue of non-accidental injury to children which reported in 1976. It received a mixed reception, being criticised for its concentration on physical abuse to the exclusion of emotional, psychological and social neglect. In addition there was too great an emphasis on the management of reported abuse and too little on developing prevention and early intervention (Buckley, 1997: 104). The first child abuse guidelines, known as the Memorandum on Non-Accidental Injury to Children, were published in 1977 and subsequently revised in 1980 and 1983. While the first edition concentrated on physical abuse to the exclusion of sexual abuse, later editions extended the definition of abuse to include neglect, emotional abuse and child sexual abuse reflecting the increasing knowledge of the nature of the harm to which children were subjected (Buckley, 1996: 38). The revisions were informed by the work of the Irish Council for Civil Liberties (Cooney and Torode, 1989). This group highlighted the factors affecting the recognition of child sexual abuse in Ireland as being the patriarchal nature of the Irish family – unresolved moral questions which were too threatening to allow for open debate leading to late disclosure, inadequate legislation, lack of resources and professional awareness. They recommended, *inter alia*, improved funding to voluntary agencies to provide services, mandatory reporting of child abuse, co-ordination of childcare services at a national level and a central register of suspected and confirmed cases of child sexual abuse. In response to the growing awareness of child sexual abuse the Department of Health reissued its Child Abuse Guidelines in 1987, the contents of which reflected a change in the conceptualisation of child abuse. For the first time abuse was defined as consisting of 'physical injuries, severe neglect and sexual or emotional abuse' and the roles and responsibilities of professionals involved in child protection were spelt out. The Law Reform Commission issued a *Report on Child Sexual Abuse* in 1990 which recommended wide-ranging changes in the law in relation to child sexual abuse, including the introduction of mandatory reporting.

The role of pressure groups such as CARE, Children First, the Federation of Services for Unmarried Parents, professional organisations such as the Irish Association of Social Workers and the Residential Care Association, together with groups such as the Irish Foster Parents Association and voluntary agencies working with children, was of considerable importance in the 1980s in putting increasing pressure on governments to update the childcare legislation. Various attempts were made to amend the legislation relating to the protection of children at risk and those in trouble with the law. The first attempt in the form of the Child (Care and Protection) Bill 1985 underwent radical revision to become the Child Care Bill 1988, and finally the Child Care Act 1991. However, the attempts at providing comprehensive legislation to protect children failed to address issues relating to children in trouble with the law. (For a discussion of the Juvenile Justice system see chapter 13, pp. 277–98).

Two pieces of legislation passed during this period were of importance in moving policy towards a recognition of the special needs and rights of particular groups of children. The first, the Status of Children Act 1987, abolished the concept of illegitimacy and was important in its underlying philosophy of equalising the status of children irrespective of the marital status of their parents. The second Adoption Act 1988 was notable in that, for the first time, it provided for the permanent dissolution of the constitutional rights of married parents where it could be proved that the parents had failed in their duty towards the child thus allowing for an adoption order to be made where appropriate. This Act therefore recognised a child's need for a permanent home, guaranteed for the future, rather than a transitory placement in substitute family care. These two pieces of legislation acted as a prelude to the children's rights movement which was to gain momentum after 1990.

Towards a children's rights perspective, 1991–9

The two decades from 1970 laid the foundations for policy developments in the 1990s and the enactment of the Child Care Act 1991. The developing awareness of the extent of child physical and sexual abuse (Ferguson, 1996: 23–5), the increasing body of research on child abuse, the official reports of child neglect and abuse in the UK (Beckford Report, 1985; Carlile Inquiry, 1987; Butler-Sloss, 1988), the increasing role of voluntary bodies in the support of families, strong pressure group activity, the development of health board structures and the professionalisation of social work services all came together to affect policy during this period. The period was characterised by attempts to move towards policies of prevention and support for families in providing for the care and welfare of their children. The overriding responsibility for child welfare became firmly rooted in the health board structures with central government guidelines allowing for regional variations of interpretation (Kenny, 1995: 56). However, Ferguson (1996: 26) has argued that during the late 1980s government policy became much more concerned with influencing what practitioners actually do in relation to suspected cases, putting less emphasis on the prevention and family support aspects. It is this legacy which has carried forward to the present child protection policies.

This period of development in childcare policy was characterised by the implementation of new legislation and dominated by increasing public awareness of physical and sexual abuse as a major factor in Irish society. A growing awareness of children's rights has been significant in the development of a philosophy surrounding children and their needs, together with an increasing understanding of the need to institute measures to educate children and the public about child abuse with a concentration on prevention. The passing of the Child Care Act 1991 brought together many of the strands of childcare policy and marked the beginning of the present era.

The Child Care Act 1991

The passing of the Child Care Act 1991 marked a watershed in childcare policy in Ireland. It clarifies and sets out the functions and duties of the health boards and deals with three areas of childcare: child protection, alternative care for children who cannot remain at home, and family support. The Act is based on the principle that it is generally in the best interests of a child to be brought up in his or her own family (S.3.2c) and that it is the function of the health board to promote the welfare of children in its area who are not receiving adequate care and protection (S.3.1). The underlying principle of the Act is that, while having regard to the rights and duties of parents, whether under the Constitution or otherwise, the welfare of the child is at the centre of any decision-making process (S.3.1.(b) ii), and that, as far as is practicable, due consideration should be given to the wishes of the child having regard to age and understanding (S.3.2b.ii). This, however, provides for a potential conflict with the constitutional rights of the family as set out in Articles 41 and 42 of the Constitution and the personal rights of the individual members of the family as protected under Article 40.3. Thus attachment to both the autonomy of the family and the paramountcy of the child's welfare creates a difficult tension around the appropriate limits of state intervention into family life. Partly in response to this, the emphasis in the legislation has been on prevention and development of services to promote family welfare. The Act therefore places a general duty on health boards to 'provide childcare and family support services' (S.3.3), but does not provide any detail of what is envisaged under this section. In order to monitor such provision the health boards are required to publish an annual report (S.8) setting out their services under this section.

Part III and Part IV of the Act provide measures for the protection of children in emergencies and for care proceedings. They broaden the grounds on which a health board may obtain a Care Order (S. 18) to include both physical and sexual abuse and neglect and under S.18.1.c it allows for a Care Order to be obtained if 'the child's health, development or welfare is likely to be avoidably impaired or neglected'. This anticipatory ground is an important one since it provides protection for a child where he or she is thought to be at risk in the future and may provide an important element of prevention and protection.

In keeping with the principle of support for the family and promoting the welfare of children within the family, the Act provides for a Supervision Order (S.19) which requires the health board to visit a child in his or her own home, on a regular basis, to ensure the child's welfare. This is an important change in policy in relation to children at risk as it allows the child to remain at home while simultaneously receiving protection from the statutory services. (For a detailed discussion of the legal provisions of the Child Care Act 1991, see Ward, 1997.)

The Child Care Act 1991 has the potential to promote children's rights in that it provides for a child's wishes to be taken into account and also allows for the appointment of a solicitor to act independently for a child who is a party to any care proceedings (S.25.1 and 2), or the appointment of a Guardian ad Litem (S. 26(1)) where a child is not party to the dispute but is the individual to whom the proceedings relate.

The Child Care Act 1991, despite being signed into law in 1991, was not fully implemented until December 1996. The sections dealing with protection of children in emergencies, taking care proceedings and regulations for placing children in care were not implemented until October 1995. O'Sullivan (1995) has argued that the long delay was not only due to lack of staff and resources to work the new system but also had its roots in political inertia. It took three child sexual abuse cases: the 'X' case in 1992, the Kilkenny incest case in 1993 and the Kelly Fitzgerald case in 1994 to raise public awareness and to finally motivate the government to implement the Child Care Act 1991 in full.

The Kilkenny Incest Inquiry
The Kilkenny Incest Inquiry centred on a case of incest in which a young woman had been abused by her father over a number of years and during which time the health and social services had had continuous contact with the family. The Minister for Health set up a public inquiry under the chairmanship of a circuit court judge. It was the first enquiry of this nature in Ireland. The Report made a number of far reaching recommendations relating to child protection, professional involvement in such cases and the need for greater inter-agency co-operation. It also highlighted the difficulties for professionals working in a system which is based on the principle of family autonomy supported by the constitutional right of parents which may come into conflict with the duty of the state to intervene in situations of abuse. The Report outlined certain principles which, it argued, should inform policy and practice:

- the rights of children
- parental involvement
- multi-disciplinary involvement
- inter-agency collaboration/co-operation

- the need for proper planning and evaluation of services
- the primacy of prevention
- the provision of treatment services
- the need to provide for a balance between child protection and the rights of parents   (Kilkenny Incest Investigation, 1993: 94)

Among other things the Report recommended changes in the Constitution to take account of the rights of children, revision of the child abuse guidelines to include parameters for best practice, a system of mandatory reporting, the introduction of child abuse registers, an emphasis on case conferences as a method of interdisciplinary contact and decision making and the extension of primary prevention programmes and family support services. However, Buckley (1996: 39; 1997: 110) has argued that it is questionable whether or not an inquiry such as this one is a suitable theoretical foundation for the design of a set of general principles aimed at governing professional practice. As she states

> child protection policy making in Ireland has tended to follow high profile happenings in a political, piecemeal fashion and the Report of the Kilkenny Incest Investigation provided the catalyst needed to progress the child care services.

It certainly galvanised the government to address some of the recommendations. It led to the government expediting the implementation of the remaining sections of the Child Care Act 1991, to pledge considerable financial investment in resourcing new services and personnel, to increase the numbers of places for the training of social workers and to open the debate on mandatory reporting. In addition it raised public awareness of the issues and added to the increasing debate on child protection and children's rights.

Mandatory reporting of child abuse

Both the Law Reform Commission (1990) and the Report of the Kilkenny Incest Investigation (Kilkenny Incest Investigation, 1993) recommended the introduction of mandatory reporting of child abuse. In their discussions they highlighted the advantages of such a system as empowering professionals to report abuse, securing consistency in the management of the disclosure of child abuse, increasing identification of children who are being abused and providing a better basis for statistical evidence and research. However, these were balanced with some disadvantages: the danger of over-reporting of cases, using scarce resources on unsubstantiated cases, and the danger of deterring victims from disclosing abuse and undermining the therapeutic relationship between professionals and their clients. Following extensive discussions with various professional groups, the government decided against introducing mandatory reporting on the basis that it would not be in the best interests of children and would not improve the childcare services (Department of Health, 1997c). At the Irish Government's meeting with the UN Committee on the Rights of the Child in January 1998, the Junior Minister for Foreign Affairs, who represented the government, indicated that Ireland did intend to introduce mandatory reporting (*The Irish Times*, 13 Jan. 1998). However, mandatory reporting was not introduced and the focus changed to the introduction of new regulations governing the reporting of suspected cases of abuse.

Regulations governing implementation of childcare policies

Following the passing of the Child Care Act 1991 there were increasing attempts to regulate and standardise procedures and practice in the area of childcare services. The Report of the Kilkenny Incest Inquiry (Kilkenny Incest Investigation, 1993) had highlighted the fact that the Child Abuse Guidelines (Department of Health, 1987) were not being interpreted in a standardised way and in some instances professionals were unaware of their existence. In addition they particularly noted the lack of co-ordination between the health boards and the Gardaí. Consequently, new guidelines on the *Notification of Suspected Cases of Child Abuse between Health Boards and Gardaí* (Department of Health, 1995c) were issued which laid down standard procedures for the notification of cases between the two agencies. Buckley (1996) offers a valuable critique of child abuse guidelines in Ireland. From her research, she argues that the Gardaí continued to lack information about services and many of them were unaware of child abuse guidelines. In addition, social workers 'responded with apprehension to the expectation that they will report all allegations of child abuse to the Gardaí' (Buckley, 1996: 44). Buckley believes that policies and official guidelines can only form the background to co-operative work between social workers and the Gardaí and that formalising this in child abuse guidelines does not take account of the fragile nature of the negotiations which go on in families and between family members and the social services. She argues that more effective co-operation and collaboration are achieved in the context of specialised services, referral and liaison systems and training to gain better understanding of each other's tasks and roles.

In 1998 the Department of Health began a review of the 1987 Child Abuse Guidelines which resulted in the publication of *Children First: National Guidelines for the Protection and Welfare of Children* (Department of Health and Children, 1999). These guidelines were introduced to assist people in identifying and reporting child abuse and to improve professional practice in both statutory and voluntary agencies. They emphasise that the needs of children and families must be at the centre of child-care and protection activity and that a partnership approach must inform the delivery of the services. They also highlight the importance of consistency between policies and procedures across health boards and other statutory and voluntary agencies and that the welfare of children must be at the centre of all activity. The principles underlying the guidelines are (*inter alia*) that:

1   the welfare of children is paramount
2   a balance must be struck between protecting children and respecting the rights and needs of parents and families but where there is a conflict the child's welfare must come first
3   children have a right to be heard and taken seriously
4   early intervention and support for families must be provided with the child being seen in a family setting rather than in isolation
5   there should be partnership between parents and agencies
6   co-ordination and co-operation based on a multi-disciplinary approach

(1999: 22–3)

The guidelines contained for the first time regulations concerning the setting up of a Child Protection Notification System in each Health Board. This is a record of every child about whom, following a preliminary assessment, there is a child protection concern. An important element of *Children First* (Department of Health and Children, 1999) was the responsibility placed on voluntary agencies to develop effective procedures for the reporting and management of child protection issues and in the selection of their staff and volunteers. In order to encourage individuals and organisations to take responsibility for reporting suspicions of child abuse the Government introduced the Protection for Persons Reporting Child Abuse Act 1998 which provides protection from civil liability of persons who have reported child abuse in good faith.

These guidelines provide a valuable framework for practice and a means by which professionals can be made accountable for the work they undertake. In addition they can standardise practice. However, Buckley (2002) makes a cogent argument warning of the dangers of an over-regulated system which can lose the individual discretion and therapeutic skill of professionals in favour of administrative management and regulation. She also suggested that the formalising of procedures with its increased demand for accountability has the potential to prioritise protection to cover the worker and agency first and the child and family second. There is also a danger that with increased regulation social workers are being forced to focus their attention on children at risk rather than responding to the prevention of crisis by addressing families and children in need through family support services. (Buckley 2002; Ferguson and O'Reilly 2001)

The Social Services Inspectorate was asked to monitor the implementation of the guidelines. This exercise took place over a two-year period and an interim report was issued in October 2001. The SSI concluded that some health boards made greater progress in implementing *Children First* than others. Child protection training and information and advice given to voluntary and community groups were said to be impressive. However, progress in key areas such as Garda/Health Board co-support services has been slow and there is a need for more work at health board and at national level in order to implement these aspects of the guidelines. In particular there was confusion over some aspects of the guidelines, particularly in relation to the Child Protection Notification System (CPNS). The SSI recommended that this aspect of the guidelines could not be brought into operation without clarification and accordingly it was postponed until 2002/early 2003. The SSI and the National Implementation Group recommended that there should be one CPNS rather than ten separate ones which would have undermined the raison d'être of national guidelines. However, the confusion over the role and function of the CPNS and the delay in agreeing the need for further clarification set back progress in the implementation of the Guidelines.

Guidelines for residential homes and foster care

Following a number of investigations into the abuse of children in residential homes and the publication of the Report on the Inquiry into the Operation of Madonna House (Eastern Health Board, 1996b), regulations were issued in relation to both residential care and foster care. The Child Care (Standards in Children's Residential Centres) Regulations 1996 and *Guide to Good Practice in Children's Residential Centres* (Department of Health, 1997b) are the first comprehensive guidelines for this sector. They are based on the principle of respect for a child's dignity and individuality, the need to preserve the child's sense of identity and the child's right to be heard. They are also based on the principle of partnership between the agencies and professionals and both the child and his or her parents. There is, therefore, emphasis on developing a written care plan for each child in residential care which identifies the child's needs and the tasks to be undertaken by named individuals to meet those needs. The plan must be developed with the participation of all parties, including the child and his/her parents and extended family together with the professionals involved. Similarly, the principle of partnership underscores the Child Care (Placement of Children in Foster Care) Regulations 1995. They too require a care plan with review meetings to include the child. The Child Care Act 1991 (S.41) specifically makes provision for the placement of children with relatives as foster-parents (Department of Health, 1996a).

Emerging themes in the policy area
1 *Development of substitute care for children*
Until the establishment of workhouses in Ireland after 1838, attempts to provide alternative care for children who were orphaned, abandoned or

homeless was on an ad hoc basis operated by individuals and religious organisations mainly concerned with the moral and spiritual welfare of the child. Workhouses provided the majority of the care for children until the early part of the twentieth century when there was a general recognition that they were not the most appropriate institutions for the care of children. The continuing concern of the churches about the religious and moral welfare of children reared in workhouses and the government's recognition of the need to make provisions for young delinquents led to the expansion of the work of voluntary and lay organisations for homeless children and to the introduction of a system of reformatory and industrial schools (Robins, 1980). Reformatory schools for young offenders were set up under the Reformatory Schools Act 1854 and industrial schools for homeless children after 1868. However, local authorities were unwilling to finance these schools and as a result various religious orders were requested to undertake the work (Robins, 1980: 292–302). The Children Act 1908 confirmed the position of the reformatory and industrial schools as the major provision for orphaned, homeless and delinquent children. The first enquiry into the organisation of these schools was the Cussen Report published in 1936. This report expressed some reservations about the nature of the education and training, the lack of local authority support and the stigma attached to them but concluded that the system affords the most suitable method of dealing with these children and that schools should remain under the management of the religious orders who have undertaken the work (Committee of Enquiry into the Reformatory and Industrial Schools System, 1936: 49)

In 1966, an independent organisation, Tuairim, published a report on residential childcare which was far more critical of the provisions. In response, the government established the Committee of Enquiry into the Industrial and Reformatory Schools in 1967 to make a detailed examination of the existing system. The report of this committee was of enormous significance on the future structure of the residential care system. It recommended that 'residential care should be considered only where there is no satisfactory alternative' and that the institutions should be replaced by group homes which would mirror normal family units (Committee of Enquiry into the Reformatory and Industrial Schools System, 1970: 6). Following the publication of the report changes did occur with the closure of many of the large institutions and the rebuilding of smaller family units. The Task Force on Child Care Services (1981: 272–3) pointed to the need for improvement in the training, salaries and career prospects of those wishing to work in the residential sector and to move towards professionalising the service. This was becoming a matter of concern with the falling numbers of religious vocations and the need to employ skilled lay people to staff the residential homes. The Committee also recommended that residential care should be considered only where there was no satisfactory alternative. Policy began to focus on the development and use of foster care. The Eastern Health Board, for example, operated a specialised Fostering Resource Group from 1977 (O'Sullivan, 1982; Cunniffe, 1983). This change in emphasis was reflected in the changing ratio of children in residential and foster care. In 1968–9 there were 4,834 children in care with three quarters in residential care. By 1988 there were 2,614 children in care with just over one quarter in residential care (Gilligan, 1991: 185). Despite the fall in the numbers of children in residential care the sector was by no means obsolete. A research study carried out by the Streetwise National Coalition and Resident Managers Association (1991) highlighted the need to develop more specialised services directed at older and more difficult children who had been omitted from the move towards foster care. In addition they identified a very real gap in the provision for homeless young people. A further independent study on residential care (McCarthy et al., 1996) again highlighted the 'incoherent and unplanned' system which still existed. Despite recommendations dating back to 1970, responsibility for the residential care system remained divided between the Departments of Health, Education and Justice, resulting in uneven resourcing and developments across the sector. The division of responsibility made it impossible to plan for the childcare system as a whole. As the Report states:

> the growing sense of professionalism . . . and the serious attempts to rationalise the service that are evident on the ground need to be matched now by a coherent, openly debated policy on residential child care which integrates and coordinates all the government departments involved and ensures that there are suitable care places for all children in need of care (McCarthy et al., 1996: 131).

Once again, two serious gaps in the residential care system were identified: provision for very disturbed children and those categorised as 'homeless'. The use of adult hostels or bed and breakfast establishments to accommodate these children became widespread despite being unsuitable to meet their needs. In 1993, 131 homeless children were placed in bed and breakfast accommodation and 29 in hospitals (Streetwise National Coalition, 1994). Until the Child Care Act 1991 there were no specific statutory provisions for homeless children but the new Act (Section 5) placed an obligation on the health boards to provide accommodation for these children. Despite this requirement, the provision of services to meet the needs of these children was very slow and a number of cases were taken in the Courts to ensure that the Eastern Health Board was fulfilling its obligations under the Act (O'Sullivan, 1995: 84; O'Sullivan, 1996a: 220).

A study carried out by Focus Ireland in 1998 again highlighted defects in the residential care sector. In particular, major failings were noted as:

- misplacement of a large proportion of young people
- lack of access to services
- lack of appropriate accommodation when young people are being discharged
- lack of a follow-up service for care-leavers
- need to assess the numbers in need of care and the provision available
- need to develop guidelines on a range of issues, such as aftercare, care plans and reviews
- urgent need for a range of care placements for adolescents. (Focus Ireland, 1998: 99)

Similarly, Craig et al. (1998), in their review of residential care in Ireland, highlighted the importance of listening to and involving children and their families in the decisions affecting their lives in the care system, the need to recognise the central role of the care worker within a multidisciplinary and multiskilled team and the overriding importance of developing a national strategy based on a needs-led approach, rather than an ad hoc reactive system.

In response to the criticism of the UN Committee on the Rights of the Child the Government set up the Social Services Inspectorate (SSI) in 1999. The SSI drafted standards for residential child care and began a series of inspections of residential centres. Following inspections a number of procedures have been instituted which resulted in children in residential care having greater contact with their parents and others in the community. The centres are now smaller and less institutional in nature. There are also complaints procedures in place in some centres that will enable children to have their concerns investigated. Substantial efforts are being made to ensure there is more integration with the local communities where centres are located and, most importantly, increasing attention is being given to children's rights which enables children to have a greater say in the care they receive and to make them less vulnerable.

The development of substitute care for children has been characterised by a movement away from institutional care to the provision of group homes and to foster-care, based on the increasing awareness of a child's need for family life. There has been a long tradition of foster care in Ireland dating back to the Brehon Laws, although the present system is grounded in the Irish Poor Law Amendment Act 1862 which allowed the boards of guardians to place children with foster parents. The control and regulation of the service was commenced with the appointment of inspectors after the Infant Life Protection Act 1897 (Robins, 1980). The system of foster care was regularised under the Health Act 1953 together with Boarding Out of Children Regulations. These regulations not only set down guidelines for the selection and monitoring of foster homes but also required health boards to place children in foster care in preference to residential care (Boarding Out of Children Regulations, 1983:

Section 5). As a result of this explicit policy the number of places in residential facilities gradually declined (McCarthy et al., 1996: 32) and health boards put additional resources into recruiting and supporting foster parents (Cunniffe, 1983; Gilligan, 1991). The Irish Foster Parent Association, founded in 1982, played its part in the developing professionalisation of the foster care system as a key player in the overall provision of substitute care for children. They emphasised the need for foster parents to be seen as partners with the health boards in meeting the needs of the children for whom they cared resulting in improvements in training and support of the foster parents by the health boards. Relative foster care as distinct from foster care by strangers is a care option now being used increasingly in Ireland which involves 'the formal placement of children unable to live with their parents in their extended family networks' (O'Brien 2001: 69). Under the Child Care Act 1991 relative care was introduced as a viable option. Relative care emerged from the re-examination in research and practice of issues around family and social networks, attachment, identity, separation and loss together with increasing evidence from outcome studies which indicated lower disruption rates and more security for children placed within family networks (O'Brien 2001: 72). The Report of the Working Group on Foster Care (Department of Health and Children 2001f) highlighted concerns about the quality of foster care services. Following its publication a committee was established to develop National Standards on Practices and Procedures on Foster Care which were published in 2003. These National Standards serve as a basis for consistently promoting quality of care in the foster care services. They apply to those services provided under the Child Care (Placement of Children in Foster Care) Regulations 1995 and the Child Care (Placement of Children with Relatives) Regulations 1995. The Standards should provide useful and con-structive guidelines for health boards and foster carers as well as a basis for those in foster care and their families to judge the quality of the services they are receiving.

2   *Prevention and family support*

The concept of family support has been part of childcare provisions since the early 1960s but it was defined mainly in terms of casework with families to prevent children coming into the care of the state. This focus remained during the 1970s with limited discussions on the need to address more fundamental issues of child poverty to prevent child disadvantage. In the 1980s the concept was broadened and neighbourhood resource centres, youth projects and family centres were developed (Murphy, 1996: 75). In general, these were developed by voluntary bodies to incorporate a range of professionals and volunteers widening the concept of family support to include a 'more self-directed and community based approach and one that involves group learning and action' (Murphy, 1996: 76). With the increasing referrals of child abuse in the 1980s the statutory services became primarily child protection agencies providing a system which reacted to events rather than taking a proactive role in prevention. Health boards did begin to develop schemes such as the Community Mothers Programme in the Eastern Health Board and to provide grants to voluntary groups to provide support services. For the first time, the Child Care Act 1991 (S.3) made it a function of the health boards to 'provide childcare and family support services'. Murphy challenges the view inherent in the Act that prevention and family support services are synonymous (1996: 78). She argues that families cannot be seen separately from the existing economic, political and social systems. In addition, family support seems to imply that the family is one unit without conflict of interests among its members. It is necessary, therefore, to disaggregate these concepts and provide policies which touch on each of them separately. Thus policies which develop shared responsibility for childcare between parents, the state and professionals, intergenerational care, and between men and women, have the potential to prevent child disadvantage and abuse. Policies which improve levels of low parental incomes, promote employment, provide educational opportunities and improve the community environment may both prevent neglect and abuse and also promote children's welfare (Gilligan, 1995: 60–78; Murphy, 1996: 95). There was a gradual development within the child protection debate that the specific child protection services needed to be complemented by a more broadly based family support approach.

In June 1998 the government launched *Springboard* an initiative of 15 family support projects and in 1999 the Government also committed itself to establishing 100 family and community centres throughout the country in line with the recommendations of the Commission on the Family (1998: 17) which had highlighted the need for health boards to prioritise family support work at the preventive level and to make resources available to do so. The centres were planned as a social partnership between the statutory and voluntary agencies driven by the communities involved. In particular the Commission on the Family (1998) recommend the extension of the Family Support Workers Scheme (Eastern Health Board, 1996b) and the Community Mothers Programmes (Johnson et al., 1993). In addition, the government proposed developing parenting programmes and 'other supports for vulnerable families' (Department of Health Press Release, 22 June 1998). An evaluation of the *Springboard* projects found that parents and children showed considerable improvement in well-being and it was estimated that the projects had halved the number of children at moderate to high risk of being abused or going into care (McKeown et al., 2001). By the end of the century family support services were at an expansionary phase. The National Development Plan 2000–2006 contained a commitment to the allocation of funds to child care, community and family support and youth services. The importance of family support was also underlined in *Children First* (Department of Health and Children, 1999: 59–63) These initiatives indicated a very important policy change in relation to the prevention and support of families.

A further aspect of prevention has been the development of a national primary school based prevention programme (*Stay Safe Programme*) focusing on educating children to be aware of child abuse issues. (McIntyre, 1993). This programme has been introduced amidst considerable controversy although it appears now to have been accepted as part of national policy (Gilligan, 1996: 64). A similar programme is currently being drawn up for second level schools which will be incorporated into the programme in Relationships and Sexuality Education (First National Report of Ireland, 1996: 53).

This period of development also saw the beginning of a children's rights perspective within childcare policy and practice. Ireland ratified the United Nations Convention on the Rights of the Child in September 1992. Since then the issue of children's rights has been part of the discourse around child welfare. The UN Convention sets out the rights guaranteed to children and young people under 18 years of age in all areas of their lives and it imposes obligations on parents, the family, the community and the state in this regard (Children's Rights Alliance, 1997: ix; Kilmurray and Richardson, 1994). The Convention is based on three underlying principles: non-discrimination insofar as the articles apply to all children equally, whatever their race, sex, religion, disability, opinion or family background; the child's best interests must govern all decisions affecting the child; the child's view must be taken into consideration in any decisions concerning him or her, in accordance with age and maturity. The Convention covers four broad areas of rights: survival, development, protection and participation rights. However, the Convention merely provides a framework in which governments are required to ensure that children's rights are actualised. It places an onus on them to provide the legislative and administrative structures together with adequate resources to implement them.

In the early 1990s it was clear that Ireland had some way to go to fulfil the requirements of the UN Convention (Kilmurray and Richardson, 1994). Cousins (1996) and the Children's Rights Alliance (1997), in its submission to the United Nations Committee on the Rights of the Child, highlighted the deficits. In January 1998, the UN Committee published its concerns about Ireland's performance in relation to its obligations under the UN Convention on the Rights of the Child, having heard both the submission of the Irish government (First National Report of Ireland, 1996) and the responses of the Irish non-governmental organisations (Children's Rights Alliance, 1997). The major areas of concern were:

- the need for a comprehensive national policy on children's rights
- the need for greater emphasis on prevention
- improved statistical base for the formulation of policies
- the need to increase awareness of the UN Convention on the Rights of the Child
- concern over the low age limits in the legislation particularly in the area of juvenile justice and the low age of criminal responsibility
- lack of concern for the views of children
- absence of mandatory reporting of child abuse
- lack of a national policy to ensure the rights of children with disabilities, and in the area of mental health of children and families
- concern over children excluded from schools
- the lack of a Rights' Commissioner/Ombudsman for children (Committee on the Rights of the Child, Geneva, 17th Session CRC/C/15/Add.85 23 Jan. 1998)

Cousins (1996) analysed the existing mechanisms for the promotion and protection of children's rights in Ireland. He concluded that although the Child Care Act 1991 had the potential to promote the rights of children, there were no overall public mechanisms for the promotion of the rights of children generally and this made it difficult for public bodies to recognise the special needs of children. He recommended that the office of a statutory Children's Commissioner should be established to promote and protect children's rights (Cousins, 1996: 72). While such a system would go a long way to promote and protect children's rights, he considered it would be ineffective unless set in the context of co-ordinated government structures and structures within schools, social services and the legal system to enable and encourage children to make their voices heard.

Statutory responsibility for the welfare of children remained divided between the Departments of Health and Children, Education and Science, and Justice, Equality and Law Reform, with responsibility for the welfare of children in need of care and protection and children with disabilities lying with the Department of Health and Children. These departments tended to work in an unco-ordinated fashion in relation to children's affairs. Every report on childcare policy and practice since 1970 had emphasised the need for rationalisation of the administrative systems affecting children. Slow progress has been made since 1974 when the then Department of Health was given the major responsibility for childcare. It was not until 1993 that a Child Care Policy Unit was set up within that Department of Health. The Interim Report of the Commission on the Family (November 1996) once again commented on the inadequate co-ordination between departments with responsibility for children's affairs. However, some of these criticisms have been accepted and the present government has created a Department of Health and Children which has a Child Care Policy Unit within it and a junior Minister for Children. It appears that there is now improved co-ordination between the three departments. This was evidenced during the preparation of the Children Bill 1996. Each health board is required to establish a Child Care Advisory Committee (Child Care Act 1991 S.7) with a membership composed of representatives from both statutory and voluntary agencies whose function is to advise the health board on the provision of child and family support services in its area. In June 1998, it was announced that a new national children's strategy was to be drawn up by the government with the aim of improving the way government departments work together in relation to children, based on a children's rights perspective (Department of Health and Children, Press Release, 22 June 1998). Thus, by the end of the twentieth century a change in the underlying philosophy related to child protection had begun to take shape providing a base on which to move into the twenty-first century.

Child protection in the twenty-first century

A number of important developments marked the beginning of the new millennium. In 2000 the Government published its National Children's Strategy, *Our Children – Their Lives* (Department of Health and Children, 2000b). The publication of the Strategy followed the setting up of an Inter-Departmental Group together with two advisory panels, one of non-governmental service providers and one on research and information. There was also an extensive consultation programme including consultations with children and young people. The development of the Strategy was based on an analysis of the main areas of children's concerns and needs which were identified as:

- health and well-being
- learning and education
- play, leisure and cultural opportunities
- children in crisis
- child poverty and homelessness
- discrimination in children's lives
- supporting children with disabilities
- responding to and harnessing children's concern for the environment

Three national goals were identified: children will have a voice, children's lives will be better understood and children will receive quality supports and services. In order to ensure that the goals and objectives of the National Children's Strategy are met, a plan was set out which involved co-operation between government departments, the statutory and voluntary agencies and the research community. As a part of the implementation a National Children's

Advisory Council was set up together with the National Children's Office in 2002. This office has the lead role in the implementation of the Strategy. Its functions are to advise the Minister on all aspects of children's lives, including the development of child well-being indicators, to advise the Minister on better co-ordination and delivery of services, to undertake and advise on research and to advise on the development of mechanisms to consult with children. In respect of the latter, the National Children's Office has promoted the setting up of Comhairle Aitiul n nOg at local level and the national Dail na nOg and has mounted a campaign on the development of these institutions (NCO, 2003). The ISPCC Children's Consultation Unit has been involved with the National Children's Office in organising and facilitating youth consultations and Radio Telefis Éireann, in partnership with the NCO, has established a children's news programme. In 2003 the NCO prepared a National Play Policy which was published in 2004 and has continued to monitor the Youth Homelessness Strategy.

One of the criticisms made by the UN Committee on the Rights of the Child was the lack of a Children's Ombudsman. In June 2002 legislation was passed to enable the setting up of an office of an Ombudsman for Children. Following consultations, which included involving children, over the functions of such an office, it was finally established in December 2003 and the Ombudsman took up office in March 2004. The appointment of the Ombudsman involved children in the role description, the advertising for and interviewing of candidates. This innovative move caused some discomfort in traditional civil service establishments but ensured that the system was true to the spirit of the National Children's Strategy, to consult with and involve children in matters concerning them.

Juvenile justice: Children Act 2001

The new millennium also saw the introduction of the Children Act 2001. The purpose of the Act was to replace the remaining provisions of the Children's Act 1908 and provide a framework for the development of the juvenile justice system. In order to address one of the criticisms of the UN Committee on the Rights of the Child, the Act raises the age of criminal responsibility to 12 years with a rebuttable presumption that a child between the age of 12 and 14 years is incapable of committing an offence because the child did not have the capacity to know that the act or omission concerned was wrong (Section 52).

The underlying philosophy of the Act is based on the need for children out of control or who have committed offences to be seen within the context of their family and community. The emphasis is on children's needs and welfare rather than on the actions that have brought them before the court. The Act attempts to do this by developing diversionary measures and punishment in the community, introducing victim involvement in decision making and emphasising parental responsibility. Detention is to be the last resort. It provides new measures for dealing with out of control non-offending children with the introduction of Special Care Orders. The Act also introduces a number of community-based orders available to the Courts and strengthens the diversionary programme. Development of partnership with parents is through the introduction of family welfare conferences which involve parents in the decision making process concerning the care and control of their children. Where a child has committed an offence the welfare conferences also provide the possibility of victim involvement in the system thus encompassing an element of 'restorative justice'.

When the Act is fully implemented a number of new community-based orders are to be introduced and the Juvenile Liaison Service is to be put on a statutory basis. The Children Act 2001 therefore provides a new framework for the development of the juvenile justice system and makes provision for addressing the needs of non-offending children in need of special care or protection. The Act also provides a framework for inter-agency co-operation in relation to the provision of services for young offenders and non-offending children in need of special care or protection and it clarifies the respective areas of responsibility of the Departments of Health and Children, Justice, Equality and Law Reform and Education and Science. The National Children's Office was given a lead role in relation to co-ordinating the implementation of the Children Act 2001 and in 2003 commissioned research on the preparation of a guide to the law and procedures relating to young offenders and non-offending children in need of special care or protection. It also instituted a review of the provisions of the Guardian ad Litem system under the Child Care Act 1991.

While the Act is based on the concept of involving parents there is also an element of punishment of parents with the introduction of fines imposed on parents, parental supervision and an order that the parent or guardian be bound over (Section 98). The problem with these orders lies in the lack of support for parents in their parenting role. In addition, the majority of children who appear in the juvenile courts come from areas of deprivation and imposition of fines and other orders on parents may only exacerbate difficult situations which are outside their control. However, the implementation of the Children Act 2001 has been slow and the full effects of changing the system of juvenile justice will need careful monitoring in order to assess whether the needs of children are being met within the new system.

Conclusions: challenges for the future

Much of the development of childcare policy has centred on the conflict between the rights of parents, the rights of children, and the rights of the state to intervene in family life. The concept of 'familialisation' is central in the discussion of children's rights and the rights of the state vis-à-vis the family. The term 'familialisation' refers to the fusion of childhood into the institution of the family defining children only as an extension of their parents. Children's social identity is defined only in relation to their parents' social status, set of values and lifestyles. Children then are absorbed into the family and their individual needs are seen to be met through and by the family (Makrinioti, 1994: 268). Thus the fusion of children into the family unit becomes the main frame of reference when dealing with children, both formally and informally.

The essence of the welfare state is to provide minimum standards of income, nutrition, health, housing and education through the provision of social services and state regulation of private activities that alter the conditions of life of individuals or groups (Offe, 1985: 3–4). Such services are designed to supplement the role of the family in meeting the needs of its members. Within the welfare state the family still prevails as the overriding institution expected to meet the needs of the individual members. In particular, policies take for granted that parents will care for their children and will aspire to meet their needs. This conceptualisation is, however, based on the assumption that the interests of parents and children are identical and inseparable. In the majority of cases parents do act in the best interests of their children. However, Webb and Wistow (1987: 20) have argued that the welfare state also exercises social control by regulating interpersonal relations in situations in which some individuals, such as children, are weaker than others. Thus the dichotomy between the autonomy of the family and the intervention of the state exists in relation to children. One side of this dichotomy is the state adopting a marginal role in its concern for family privacy and the other side is concerned with intervention in order to promote the welfare of children and maintain their rights as individuals. Policies concerning child protection acknowledge the family's failure to ensure adequate care and protection for their children. Thus the social discourse around child protection widens into a discussion of welfare in terms of children's rights and children as citizens. A change from conceptualising children in terms of familialisation to one of citizenship with individual autonomy, the right to participation and consultation on issues affecting their lives, and the possibility of choosing among alternatives will radically alter welfare policies for children.

The Irish Constitution contains no formal recognition of the rights of children. Their rights have been defined as being subsumed within the rights of the family (Article 41 and 42) In the case of *G* v *An Bord Uchtála* (1980, IR 32), J. O'Higgins stated:

> The child also has natural rights. Normally these will be safe under the care and protection of its mother. Having been born the child has the right to be fed and to live, to be reared and educated, to have the opportunity of working and of realising his or her full personality and dignity as a human being. These rights . . . must equally be protected and vindicated by the State.

The Kilkenny Incest Investigation (1993: 31) argued that in taking this view it might well be impossible to regard the welfare of the child as the first and paramount consideration in any dispute as to its upbringing or custody between parents and third parties without first considering the rights of the family. It argued that the emphasis on the rights of the family in the Constitution might be interpreted as giving a higher value to the rights of parents than to the rights of children. The Report therefore recommended amending the Constitution to include a statement of the constitutional rights of children (1993: 96). The Report of the Constitutional Review Group supported this view. It stated that 'if parental rights and children's rights are both being expressly guaranteed it would be desirable that the Constitution make clear which of these rights should take precedence in the event of a conflict between the rights' (Constitution Review Group, 1996: 330). Thus it recommended that the Constitution should include an Article clearly stating the rights of children and in particular 'the express requirement that in all actions concerning children, whether by legislative, judicial or administrative authorities, the best interests of the child shall be the paramount consideration' (1996: 337), which would give a Constitutional guarantee to what already exists in legislation and reduce the potential for a conflict between the rights of parents and the rights of children.

Childcare policy in Ireland has developed in an ad hoc and reactive fashion in response to a number of factors including pressure group activity from a range of interest groups, concerned professionals and researchers, voluntary agencies working in the field and a number of significant enquiries and reports, some initiated by government and others from independent sources. In addition, policy developments have been circumscribed by the Irish Constitution and the reluctance of the state to interfere in family life. Policies have resulted from attempts to balance the rights of parents, the rights of children and the rights of the state. However, until the early 1990s, the focus was firmly on the rights of parents. The full implementation of the Child Care Act 1991 has laid the foundation for policy to focus far more clearly on the rights and needs of children. Constitutional change is needed now to underpin the legislation. Its emphasis on prevention, on partnership between parents, the state and other social service agencies and co-operation and co-ordination between all agencies involved with children provides a framework for policy development. However, it is only a framework. Despite the proactive orientation of the Child Care Act, much of the childcare and protection work remains reactive and partnership with families operates at a low level (Buckley, 1997: 120). Since the beginning of the twenty-first century there has been considerable movement in the commitment by workers and government towards listening to children, involving them and their families in the decision-making process, and striving towards a children's rights perspective.

The growing awareness of child abuse in the 1990s has at last brought the issue of child protection firmly into the political arena. Since the passing of the Child Care Act 1991, the amount of money invested in childcare and social work services has risen annually. Since 1993 the Department of Health and Children has financed the creation of 850 new posts within the childcare services. In its submission to the UN Committee on the Rights of the Child (First National Report of Ireland, 1996: 13), the government stated that it had approved a range of developments designed to ensure that:

- child protection services are strengthened and equipped to respond to the needs of children
- intensive counselling and treatment is available for victims of child abuse
- special therapeutic care is provided for those damaged by abuse and neglect
- adequate accommodation is available to help homeless young people
- children in foster-care and residential care are supervised and monitored on a systematic basis
- locally based services are available to assist families in difficulty

Much of this work has been undertaken and is ongoing. The challenge now is for adequate resources to be made available on a continuous basis in order that the full potential of the frameworks and policies developed can be realised. Policy must now be proactive rather than reactive and driven by a real political commitment to enhancing the position of children in Ireland. The government has given a commitment to undertake a longitudinal study of children in Ireland to be conducted by the Departments of Health and Children and Social and Family Affairs. It is planned that the lives of 18,000 children will be closely monitored over a seven-year period in an effort to find out how effective formal and informal state supports are for them and their families. However, it is imperative that such a study should be instituted as soon as possible in order that the true impact of the child care policies that exist can be measured against the real lived lives of all Irish children.

Table 8.1 **Main policy developments**

1889	Cruelty to Children Act
1889	Establishment in Ireland of the National Society for Prevention of Cruelty to Children
1908	Children Act
1936	Report of the Committee of Enquiry into the Reformatory and Industrial Schools System (The Cussen Report)
1937	Irish Constitution
1952	The Adoption Act
1964	Guardianship of Infants Act
1970	Report on Industrial Schools and Reformatories (Kennedy Report)
1970	Health Act establishing regional health boards
1970	Establishment of the group CARE
1971	Irish Association of Social Workers founded
1972	Publication of the CARE Memorandum
1974	Government sets up the Task Force on Child Care Services
	Children First founded as a pressure group for improvements in adoption and fostering
	Department of Health given the major responsibility for childcare services
1975	Publication of the Interim Report of the Task Force on Child Care Services
1977	Publication of guidelines for professionals dealing with non-accidental injury to children.
1978	Fostering Resource Group established in the Eastern Health Board
1979	Child Care Division established in the Department of Health
1981	Final Report of the Task Force on Child Care Services published
1982	Irish Foster Care Association founded
1983	New Boarding Out of Children Regulations issued
1984	Report of the Review Committee on Adoption published
1985	Child (Care and Protection) Bill published
1987	Department of Health publishes revised Child Abuse Guidelines
	Status of Children Act passed
1988	Child Care Bill replaces the Child (Care and Protection) Bill
	Adoption Act 1988 provides for adoption of children of married parents under particular circumstances
1990	Government commits Ireland to ratifying the UN Convention on the Rights of the Child
1991	Child Care Act signed into law. Its implementation is to be phased in over five years
1992	Ireland ratifies the UN Convention on the Rights of the Child
	Commencement Order signed under Child Care Act 1991 redefining the age of a child as a person under the age of 18 years other than a person who is or has been married
1993	Report of the Kilkenny Incest Investigation published
	Child Care Policy Unit established in the Department of Health
1994	Government appointed a Minister of State to the Department of Health, Education and Justice with special responsibility for children and for coordination of the activities of the three departments.

1995   Publication of new guidelines on the Notification of Suspected Cases of Child Abuse
            between Health Boards and Gardaí
        Publication of Child Care (Placement of Children in Foster Care) Regulations
        Publication of Child Care (Placement of Children in Residential Care) Regulations
        Publication of Child Care (Placement of Children with Relatives) Regulations
        Government establishes the Commission on the Family
        October 1995 Parts III, IV and V of the Child Care Act 1991 implemented
1996   Report of the Constitutional Review Group published
        Publication of the First National Report of Ireland under the UN Convention on the
            Rights of the Child
        All sections of the Child Care Act 1991 finally implemented
        Publication of the Report on the Operation of Madonna House
1997   Department of Health and Children established with Junior Minister responsible
            for children
        Department of Social, Community and Family Affairs established
1998   Final Report of the Family Commission published
        Ireland appears before the UN Committee on the Rights of the Child in Geneva
1999   Publication of *Children First: National Guidelines for the Protection and Welfare
            of Children*
2000   Publication of *Our Children – Their Lives: The National Children's Strategy*
2001   National Children's Advisory Council set up
        Children Act
2002   National Children's Office established
        First meeting of Dail na nOg
        Ombudsman for Children Act 2002
2003   Ombudsman for Children takes up appointment
        National Standards for Foster Care published
2004   National Play Policy published

Recommended reading

Buckley, H. (2002) *Child Protection and Welfare: Innovations and Interventions.* Dublin:
    IPA.
Buckley, H. (2003) *Child Protection: Beyond the Rhetoric.* London: Jessica Kingsley
Children's Rights Alliance (1997) *Small Voices: Vital Rights.* Dublin: Children's Rights
    Alliance.
Ferguson, H. and P. Kenny (1995) *On Behalf of the Child: Child Welfare, Child Protection
    and the Child Care Act 1991.* Dublin: A. & A. Farmar.
Ferguson, H. and O'Reilly, M. (2001) *Keeping Children Safe.* Dublin: A. & A. Farmar.
First National Report of Ireland (1996) *Ireland: United Nations Convention on the Rights
    of the Child.* Dublin: Stationery Office.
Gilligan, R. (1991) *Irish Child Care Services: Policy, Practice and Provision.* Dublin: IPA.
Kilmurray, A. and V. Richardson (1994) *Focus on Children: Blueprint for Action.* Dublin/
    Belfast: Focus on Children.

Chapter 9

Youth policy

Elizabeth Kiely
Patricia Kennedy

Introduction

In this chapter youth work is discussed solely in the context of youth policy. It refers to out of school education, recreation and other activities operated mainly by voluntary youth organisations, administered by Vocational Education Committees (VECs) and supported by the Youth Affairs Section of the Department of Education and Science. The aim of youth work was defined in the Youth Work Act 2001 as:

> a planned programme of education designed for the purpose of aiding and enhancing the personal and social development of young persons through their voluntary participation, and which is complementary to their formal, academic or vocational education and training; and provided primarily by voluntary youth work organisations.

The Costello Report (Department of Labour, 1984) invoked the social change agenda in youth work, which unfortunately has tended to feature less in youth policy discourse in recent years. According to this report (Department of Labour, 1984; 116):

> If youth work is to have any impact on the problems facing young people today then it must concern itself with social change. This implies that youth work must have a key role in enabling young people to analyse society and in motivating and helping them to develop the skills and capacities to become involved in effecting change.

The following key principles are set out below to differentiate youth work from other kinds of social provision for young people:

- It is based on young people's voluntary rather than compulsory participation.

- It involves a transfer of power to young people, prioritising their active participation.
- It is youth centred, placing young people's needs above other issues.
- It seeks to raise young people's awareness of the society in which they live and to assist them to act upon it. (See the Costello Report, Department of Labour, 1984 and Jenkinson, 2000 for a more complete discussion of youth work principles.)

As 37 per cent of the Irish population is under 25 years of age, this represents the highest proportion of young people under 25 in any EU member state (CSO, 2002). There is now more than ever a very large number and array of institutions, structures and processes in Irish society, shaping the contours of young people's lives. Thus it is vital to consider whether there is a well-resourced youth service capable of the level of interpretation and systematic analysis necessary, to really represent the interests of young people in contemporary society.

The concept of youth

Youth has been traditionally conceptualised as an age-related process. However, many commentators (Furlong and Cartmel, 1997; Wyn and White, 1997) have highlighted the problematic constructions of both youth and adulthood in contemporary society where some of the important transitions, or key life events, are becoming increasingly less age related and less clear cut. Defining youth with reference to age is important in terms of recognising the common status of this stage of the lifecycle and acknowledging the universality of the experience of youth. Some commentators (Wyn and White, 1997) favour a more *relational* concept of youth, based on the appreciation that, apart from age, young people may have very little else in common; this acknowledges the heterogeneity that characterises the category of youth as well as its homogeneity. It recognises that young people negotiate the experience of growing up and that this negotiation takes place at a particular time, in a particular socio-economic, cultural and political context through which young people are also being actively constructed and differentiated from each other. This universality and difference are also reflected in youth work where young people are recognised as constituting a universal group, but at the same time they are differentiated and demarcated in terms of the levels and kinds of interventions they are perceived to need.

The foundations of youth work

The foundations of youth work are usually connected with the industrial revolution in Britain and developments in provision there occurred soon after in Ireland. Sociological and psychological theories of the instability of youth began to appear around the time of industrialisation. It was believed that adolescents who were left too much to themselves tended to become disordered (Davies and Gibson, 1967; Tobias, 1967). There was an emphasis on the increase of juvenile mental disorders, misspent leisure and rising crime rates as evidence of increasing delinquency among the young. The origin of youth work was closely related to and depended on broader and deeper processes in nineteenth-century society, such as industrialisation, urbanisation and the desire to maintain social order. In studying the development of youth work in Ireland, it is necessary to look at Britain where many of our youth organisations developed in the years 1870–1910. Youth work in Ireland thus has its roots in nineteenth-century Britain where the earliest youth organisations emerged.

Youth organisations

Voluntarism

Early youth work initiatives were entirely dependent on voluntary endeavour. Though lack of records prevents a thorough assessment of the motivations for volunteering, Davies and Gibson (1967) have suggested that fear, compassion, social conscience and religious conviction would have been key factors. In 1844 in Britain, the Young Men's Christian Association (YMCA) was founded. The first boys' clubs and girls' clubs were established in the 1880s and the early uniformed organisations began to emerge also at this time. What took place in the period between 1870 and 1910 tended to shape youth work and give it its most distinguished features. Though Davies (1999a) has acknowledged that the informal mode of working with young people was not unique to the particular organisations identified in this chapter, they were the ones granted official status and credited as models for other youth clubs and centres.

Uniformed youth organisations

Uniformed youth organisations such as the Boys' Brigade and the Girls' Guildry, directed at both boys and girls grew out of the Victorian age. Almost totally British in origin, they soon appeared in urban areas in Ireland. Most early youth groups were concerned with Christianity, patriotism and militarism. They depended on a spirit of altruism and voluntarism. They emphasised a need for social control and moral education. Youth organisations attempted to develop the model adolescent – the organised youth, secure from temptation – while the independent and precocious youth was stigmatised as delinquent (Gillis, 1975: 97).

The Boys' Brigade, established in Glasgow in 1883, was one of the most influential of the early uniformed groups. By 1899 there were 66 companies in

Ireland with almost 3,000 members. These figures had more than doubled by 1941. In 1900 the Girls' Guildry was founded. The Boy Scouts Association was established in 1907 by Baden-Powell; it was non-denominational, encouraged efficiency and controlled independence (Springhall, 1977). After the establishment of the Irish Free State, a separate Catholic Boy Scout Movement was established in Ireland (Hurley, 1992). The Scout movement encouraged romantic notions of scoutcraft, resourcefulness, chivalry, trustworthiness and courage rather than the drill of the Boys' Brigade. The Girl Guides Association, founded in Britain in 1909, spread to Ireland in 1911. The Catholic Girl Guides movement was established in Ireland in the 1930s (Hurley, 1992). In writing of the Catholic Girl Guides in France, Marguerite de Perroy (1927: 313) gives an indication of the model of adolescent girl desired by the Girl Guide movement:

> A guide is proud of her faith and subordinates all her life to it . . . the fundamental duties of the guide are within her home . . . the practice of the daily good deed undertaken by the guide combats egotism against which all mothers strive – too often in vain – and which often poisons the peace of the home.

Non-uniformed youth organisations

Uniformed organisations, because of geographical and monetary constraints, did not reach all of Irish youth. To fill this void, rural and other youth movements of mostly Catholic ethos developed in Ireland. Richardson (1886: 158) referred to 'the necessity of a good religious organisation to keep all our youth to the Sacraments and to find them Catholic work to do on Sundays and then wherever they go during the week they will not go far, stray and must remain good Catholics'. He recommended a good lending library, and penny banks to encourage thrift. The idea behind such clubs was to offer young people a place to spend their leisure time, which had a strong Catholic ethos and would offer close supervision, and thus keep them out of trouble (Kennedy, 1984).

Revolutionary nationalism

As nationalism became a more dominant force in nineteenth-century Ireland, it was reflected in the development of youth movements. From 1880 to 1890, there was what has been described as a great 'cultural revolution' (Tierney, 1978: 88), which emphasised every characteristic that contributed a unique and distinct quality to Irish life. Many new organisations developed, some of which were directed at young people. One such organisation, Inghinidhe na hÉireann (Daughters of Ireland), was established in 1900 by Maud Gonne. This was a revolutionary nationalist organisation which supported Irish nationalism and the 'Irish Irish' movement (a term which referred to cultural nationalism). It was absorbed into Cumann na mBan in 1913. Under this guise it continued its activities through the troubled years of the 1920s and 1930s. The average age of its members was 20 to 25 years (Ward, 1980), which would be the upper end of the age cohort with which youth services were concerned.

A similar group for boys was Na Fianna Éireann (Sons of Ireland), which was an alternative to the Boy Scouts, formed in 1909 by Bulmer Hobson (a pioneer of the Sinn Féin Movement) and Countess Markievicz (an active Republican and follower of Sinn Féin). Its objective was to establish the independence of Ireland by training young people, both mentally and physically, by teaching scouting and military exercises, Irish history and Irish language, as indicated in their pledge 'I promise to work for the independence of Ireland, never to join England's armed forces, to obey my superior officers' (*Na Fianna Éireann Handbook*). Na Fianna acted as a recruiting ground for the Irish Republican Brotherhood (IRB) which aimed to overthrow British rule in Ireland and to create an Irish Republic. The organisation spread rapidly with a membership of over 20,000 by the early 1920s (O'Driscoll, 1964: 32).

Another important uniformed youth organisation of this period was the Young Ireland Association, founded in 1932. It evolved from the Fascist Army Comrades Association (the Blueshirts). Members of the organisation auto-matically became members of Fine Gael. The movement was organised in local sections and its members marched in uniform to meetings. Girls' sections ran dances, while boys' sections were more involved in military-style drill. Thornley (1967: 48) refers to 'proud six-year-olds [who] displayed themselves in uniform'. By 1934 the enthusiasm of members was beginning to decline and this was hastened when the government took steps to ban the wearing of uniforms in public.

Other groups less obviously revolutionary in character, but nevertheless with a strong nationalist ideology, included the Gaelic Athletic Association (GAA). Founded by Michael Cusack in 1884, it was not directed solely at young people but by its very nature it attracted young men as members. It acted as a de-Anglicising force, determined to encourage native Irish games enabling people to assert their Irish identity. It banned two groups from its membership: members of the Royal Irish Constabulary (RIC) and those who played English games. The GAA aimed to build a strong active manhood and its training closely mirrored military drill. As Tierney (1978: 91) indicates: 'In 1891 two thousand hurlers formed a guard of honour at [Charles Stewart] Parnell's funeral, shouldering their hurleys like rifles and marching in military formation through Dublin.'

Political youth movements were thus a particular feature of Irish society in the early decades of the twentieth century originating because of the political climate of the time. They were established by those who wanted to shape young people, to use their strength for political reasons, to mould their minds, to instil in them a love of Ireland, a love so great that they were prepared to fight for it. These values were passed on because young people were recognised as a strong force, an asset to be used to fuel the forces seeking an Irish free state.

Rural youth movements

A distinctive feature of the 1920–50 period in Ireland was the concern with rural youth. In 1931, Muintir na Tíre (People of the Land), was founded by Father John Hayes. Starting as an economic organisation, it later changed its focus to community development. Writing in its 1943 official handbook, O'Barry Walsh (Muintir na Tíre, 1943: 21) promoted the idea of a rural youth movement, which he claimed would lead to laying the 'foundation for better farming and better citizenship'.

In 1943, the Hospital Guild (a regional branch based in County Limerick) inaugurated a youth section which adopted as its model the 4H Movement, a rural club movement in the US which acquired its name from its pledge: 'I pledge my head to clearer thinking, my heart to greater loyalty, my hands to larger service, my health to better living for my club, my community and my country'. Its activities of a practical nature were concerned with training for agriculture, including the construction of beehives and the rearing of calves for sale.

Another rural youth group, Macra na Feirme (Sons of the Farms), was established in 1944, concerned again with social, cultural, personal and community development. It was instrumental in setting up the *Farmers' Journal,* Macra na Tuaithe (now Foróige), the Irish Farmers Association (IFA), the Irish Creamery Milk Suppliers Association (ICMSA), the Agricultural Institute and the Farm Apprenticeship Board. At present its membership is 8,000 and it provides eight programmes: adult education, travel, young farmers, sports and social, competitions, art and culture and rural development (www.Macra.ie). Formerly Macra Na Tuaithe, the Foróige organisation today operates 450 clubs and is actively involved in mainline and special youth service provision in both urban and rural Ireland (www.Foroige.ie).

Statutory involvement

The beginnings

Responsibility for statutory involvement in youth policy and youth services has tended to shift between two government departments: the Department of Education (since 1998 the Department of Education and Science) and the Department of Labour, depending on the social emphasis at a particular time, which is largely dictated by economic factors. In times of economic depression and stagnation as in the 1980s, emphasis tended to be on labour, concern with unemployment and training for young people, preparing them as workers, as potential members of the labour force. At other times, there has been a stronger emphasis on social education, and on young people as potential social citizens.

The state became involved with youth provision for the first time in 1930. In the wake of a very turbulent period in Irish history, which included the 1916 Rising, the establishment of Dáil Éireann, the struggle for Independence, the Civil War, and the economic war with Britain, there was an increasing concern with the perceived decline in moral standards. Church and state were increasingly focused on temperance and sexual morality. They became pre-occupied with dance halls, cinemas and literature, as is evident from a 1925 statement issued by the Irish Roman Catholic hierarchy: 'The surroundings of the dance hall, withdrawal from the hall for intervals and the back way home have been the destruction of virtue in every part of Ireland' (quoted in Whyte, 1980: 26). Writing in the *Irish Ecclesiastical Record* of 1930, the Rev. R. S. Devane blamed the state for the perceived increasing immorality: 'This country so backward in youth organisations may have done nothing by way of real scientific study of youth' (1930: 23). Considering these viewpoints, it is no surprise that the state became involved in youth provision during the 1930s.

Continuation education
In 1930 the Vocational Education Act placed responsibility for 'continuation education' in the hands of the Vocational Education Committee (VEC). By continuation education, it meant:

> Education to continue and supplement education provided in secondary schools and includes general and practical training in preparation for employment in trades, manufacture, agriculture, commerce, and other industrial pursuits and also general and practical training for the improvement of persons in the early stages of such employment.

The 1930 Act empowered the VEC to subscribe to any organisation which included among its functions the collection and communication of information with respect to employment of people under 18 years. This was the first attempt at state involvement in youth provision. No direct action was taken until the 1940s, however, after much pressure had been brought to bear on the state to intervene in youth affairs. The *Annual Report* of the Department of Education for 1941–2 outlined the beginnings of a statutory youth service. The Dublin VEC in 1942 set up youth training schemes and a statutory committee, known as Comhairle le Leas Óige, was established with wide powers. It made provision for the training of youth leaders who were volunteers from the Society of St Vincent de Paul and the Legion of Mary to receive training in physical education, arts and crafts and youth leadership. By

1942 there were 14 such youth centres established, catering for 200 boys. These had a nationalist and Catholic ideology, with Irish language and ballads featuring as an important part of the curriculum together with trades such as boot repair and woodwork. The importance of the role of the chaplain was emphasised. Boys were taught a trade which would be beneficial both socially and individually. Comhairle le Leas Óige also supported clubs and societies, which satisfied certain conditions. By 1943 there were 23 affiliated clubs with 1,400 members.

In analysing youth policy in Ireland from a historical perspective, it is useful to refer to Kennedy's classification of the Irish social services (1975) where she outlines the objectives of social policy in Ireland from the Second World War until the mid-1970s. Kennedy outlines three distinct phases, which were closely linked to the prevailing economic climate. Firstly, the 1947–51 period was an expansionary phase during which public social expenditure doubled. The period 1952–62 was a regressive phase when social expenditure fell from 14.9 per cent to 13.7 per cent of GNP. Thirdly, 1963 to 1974 was a period of social as well as economic growth and development. The first phase coincided with the 1951 Commission on Youth Unemployment.

The Commission on Youth Unemployment

In 1943, the Minister for Industry and Commerce, Seán Lemass, set up the Commission on Youth Unemployment. This was during 'The Emergency' or Second World War, when there was high unemployment in Ireland and high emigration, partly as a response to the demand for Irish labour in Britain. The report was commissioned in the same year in which a British report, *The Youth Service after the War* was commissioned. The British report promoted integration, stating that 'we do not want to see young people segregated . . . from the community as a whole' (Board of Education, Youth Advisory Council, 1943). These views were echoed in the Irish report which viewed young people not as a separate entity but as members of the wider economy to be encouraged to play a useful part in the economic life of the country (Department of Industry and Commerce, 1951: 1). It saw the problem of youth unemployment as a reflection of general unemployment; its remedies included the expansion of industry, raising the school leaving age, retirement of over-age workers, the introduction of special schemes designed to provide employment for young people and special measures to deal with 'unoccupied youth'.

The 1951 report attempted to look at 'the problem of youth' in a methodical way. This included looking at its extent and causes, with a view to submitting recommendations which were 'designed to afford the boys and girls of this country a better opportunity of becoming useful citizens of a

Christian state, adequately instructed in the teaching of religion, healthy in mind and body, willing and able to work for their own benefit and that of their country' (Department of Industry and Commerce, 1951: 1), in the context of a Nationalist and Christian ideology. It touched on many issues other than unemployment, such as the physical development, education, training and welfare of young people, and juvenile delinquency.

The report, in referring to the link between youth unemployment and adult unemployment, stressed that the solution of one 'is bound up inextricably with the solution of the other' (Department of Industry and Commerce, 1951: 8). The Government was beginning to adopt a Keynesian approach. It was actively encouraging economic growth by establishing two new semi-state bodies, encouraging agricultural development and entering into a new trade agreement with Britain. The report claimed that 'the backbone of industry is skilled tradesmen' (Department of Industry and Commerce, 1951: 21). It was very much concerned with developing a skilled and healthy workforce (sentiments which were often echoed in Ireland in the 1990s). Thus it emphasised the importance of good physique, health and intelligence. It called for increased thrift, criticising the individual who was 'turning more and more to the state to look after him in illness, unemployment and old age' (Department of Industry and Commerce, 1951: 19). This was in line with Catholic social teaching and the principle of subsidiarity.[1] It is striking that Revd John Charles McQuaid, Archbishop of Dublin, chaired the Committee. The report indicates: 'we deal first with the question of promoting the religious development of young persons and controlling conditions of employment for the purpose of controlling their spiritual development' (Department of Industry and Commerce, 1951: 14).

A notable aspect of the 1951 report was its attitude towards sex roles. It spoke of the need to train a girl for her natural vocation – 'the care and management of a home and children', while for boys 'manual instruction is an asset'. Louie Bennett, a committee member and trade union activist, refused to sign the document, claiming:

> I am obliged to assert that the report shows little understanding of the modern girl. Nor does it draw attention to the very serious national problem raised by the exodus of girls to seek employment in other countries. It is futile to cling to domestic occupations as the main employment outlet for girls (Department of Industry and Commerce, 1951: 51).

---

1   The principle of subsidiarity refers to a principle, endorsed by Pope Pius XI in Quadragesimo Anno, that in the case of education the state should not assume its control if it can be adequately managed by a less comprehensive agency, such as the local community of parents or of citizens (Clarke, 1984).

Expansion

Returning to Kennedy's classification of the Irish social services (1975), she refers to the period between 1963 and 1974 as a period of social as well as economic growth and development. With the 1960s came a period of growth in education. The publication of *Investment in Education* (Department of Education, 1965) in this period ushered in free post-primary education, the establishment of comprehensive and community schools and Regional Technical Colleges. There was a parallel expansion of the youth service. The National Federation of Youth Clubs (now called the National Youth Federation) emerged after a conference held in 1961 and it acts as a co-ordinating body for its affiliated youth services. From 1963 onwards the state became increasingly involved in youth provision, in part due to the increasing youth population, but also to the publication in Britain of the Albermarle Report (1960), the first of many influential British reports on youth provision.

The early years of the decade were marked by many negotiations between the National Federation of Youth Clubs (NFYC) and the Departments of Education, Justice and Finance. This led to the payment in 1967–8 of the first state grant of £450, which was increased to £2,220 a year later and to £7,000 by 1970 (Kennedy, 1984). As the state became increasingly involved in financing youth provision it also became involved in youth policy. In 1967, the National Youth Council (NYC) was established with the objectives of bringing together youth-serving organisations and agencies in Ireland, the advancement of education and learning of young people and the promotion of the common interests of young people. The NYC soon became the main consultative link between the state and the voluntary sector. The NYC (now NYCI) is still in existence, and it is at present an important co-ordinating body for voluntary youth organisations and services in Ireland.

The evolution of a national youth policy

In the 1970s, the state became more involved in formulating youth policy, producing a series of youth policy documents, which made many recommendations that for the most part were never implemented. In 1974, John Bruton, TD, Parliamentary Secretary to the Minister for Education, initiated a study entitled *The Development of Youth Services*, which was the first in a series of such reports to be written over the following twenty years. It encouraged increased VEC involvement. It acknowledged the importance of monitoring and evaluation, called for the grant aid scheme to be expanded and encouraged local agency networking.

In 1977, another report, *A Policy for Youth and Sport*, was published by the Department of Education. It acknowledged that while youth work alone could not remedy the physical and economic causes of social deprivation, it could nevertheless uncover the potential of young people and encourage optimism and ambition, while at the same time provide skills for 'commercial self-help and self-government'. It claimed 'the fulfilment of five objectives of education, recreation, counselling, voluntary service and community development has significance' (Department of Education, 1977: 41) for the development of youth services.

In 1978, a National Youth Council report, *A Policy on Youth Work Services*, looked at the educational contribution of youth work, the role of professional youth workers, statutory funding, evaluation and assessment, the role of VECs, and training for full-time workers – issues still being addressed more than twenty years later (Government of Ireland, 1995b). In the following year, a second document entitled *The Development of Youth Work Services* was commissioned by James Tunney, TD, Minister of State at the Department of Education. It dealt with youth work and the needs of young people and addressed such issues as the nature and effectiveness of youth programmes, the voluntary sector, youth unemployment and the statutory sector, especially the role of the Department of Education (NYC, 1980).

The *Task Force Report on Child Care Services* (Department of Health, 1980b) claimed there was a lack of co-ordination of services for children and young people. It recommended that the Department of Health exercise responsibility for young people as part of the childcare system. It recommended the establishment of Neighbourhood Youth Projects (NYPs) and Youth Encounter Projects (YEPs) targeting children and young people at risk of being taken into care or custody. The introduction of a small number of these projects in cities throughout Ireland reflected the move away from institutional care for children towards community-based alternatives.

Despite the recommendation that responsibility for youth provision be handed over to the Department of Health in 1980, some time later it was the Department of Labour that took responsibility for youth provision. This undoubtedly reflected the preoccupation with the unemployment crisis of the 1980s and the corresponding need to keep young unemployed people who might pose a threat to social order gainfully occupied. In that year, the Youth Policy Committee was officially launched by Dr Garret FitzGerald and George Bermingham, Minister of State for Youth Affairs, and was chaired by Justice Declan Costello. It was asked to draw up policy recommendations. The launch coincided with the publication of a discussion document, which was in the words of George Bermingham, 'a major stimulant for a major Irish debate on the role of young people in modern Irish Society and on the problems and challenges which they face' (government statement on the launching of the Youth Policy Committee, September 1983). Entitled *Shaping the Future: Towards a National Youth Policy, A Discussion Document* (Department of Labour, 1983), it addressed such issues as participation, transition from school to work, disadvantaged young people and the development of youth organisations.

The Report of the Costello Committee (Department of Labour, 1984) was particularly significant as it recommended that a National Youth Service be established. This was the first time that a need for such a service was officially recognised in Ireland. It envisaged a Youth Service that would be distinct and independent, while at the same time having links with other services for youth. The target group for the youth service would be 12–21 years, with priority given to the older teenage group and with special services for those with particular needs. It recognised the need for training, including in-service training, and it recommended that a Department of Youth and Community Studies should be developed within a third-level institution. However, it also stated that it did not recognise the need for full-time professional training. This implied that the Committee did not view youth workers as professionals to the same extent as, for example, teachers. It also recommended the establishment of a National Advisory Committee to advise the Minister generally on youth affairs.

The Costello Committee made explicit the philosophy informing its recommendations. In formulating a youth policy the committee sought to address the question of what kind of society was desired, acknowledging that a youth policy would inevitably reflect this vision. It aimed to enable all young people to become 'self-reliant, responsible and active participants in society' (government statement on the launching of the Youth Policy Committee, Sept. 1983). It argued that this would involve a democratic philosophy, which it viewed as:

> The best ideal for government . . . it most assuredly promotes the moral, social economic, political, cultural and intellectual development of the people and it permits the maximum freedom consistent with social order. It should also inculcate a spirit of mutual co-operation, informed by a strong sense of social justice. To approach this ideal the concept of the 'active' citizen, of participation in social and political life, of the growth of a responsible public spirit, as tending to elevate the life of the community as a whole, is of fundamental importance (Department of Labour, 1984: 15).

The promotion of the concept of social education in the Costello Report (Department of Labour, 1984) offered a more daring perspective for youth work in a society where young people's heterogeneity was clearly marked by divisions along class, gender and other lines. The section of the Costello Report entitled 'Disadvantaged Young' highlighted the distinctive needs of homeless young people, young Travellers, young people with disabilities, young people experiencing problematic drug use and young offenders. *In*

Partnership with Youth was the Government's modest response published in December 1985. It pledged to make funds available for the establishment of its proposed co-ordinating structures called Local Youth Service Boards.

Jenkinson (1997) indicates how, in 1987, a new Fianna Fáil government recommended a re-examination of youth policy. This was presented as an insignificant part of the Green Paper on education, *Education for a Changing World* (Department of Education, 1992), which examined Irish education as a whole. A Committee representing youth work agencies prepared a response to the Green Paper in 1993 entitled *Report of the Consultative Group on the Development of Youth Work*. This made recommendations on issues central to the future development of a youth policy. These were incorporated two years later into the White Paper on Education, *Charting our Education Future* (Government of Ireland, 1995b) which included among its recommendations:

• The establishment of Regional Education Boards with statutory responsibility for youth work services and policy
• The establishment of a single body to represent all voluntary youth organisations
• The establishment of a National Youth Advisory Committe
• A system of monitoring and evaluating youth services, as well as research
• A Youth Service Act

Following the White Paper on Education (1995), a Youth Services Bill was prepared and subsequently enacted in 1997. This established for the very first time a legislative base for youth work in Ireland. However, the Fianna Fáil/PD coalition which came into government after the election declared the Act inoperable on the grounds that the proposed local education boards were an unnecessary bureaucracy and would only duplicate the work already being undertaken by the VECs. The Fianna Fáil /PD government set about drafting new legislation.

Recent legislative/youth policy developments
A new bill emerged after a considerably long time, passed its final stage in the Oireachtas in November 2001 and became law. The Youth Work Act 2001 involves the devolution of a number of statutory powers and responsibilities to local Vocational Education Committees. The role of the Assessor of Youth Work, as proposed in the Act, is to carry out a number of Ministerial functions, mainly involved in ensuring accountability for funding allocated for service provision. The Act introduced the long awaited National Youth Work Advisory Committee (of no fewer than 31 and no more than 33 persons) whose role it is to advise and consult the Minister in relation to the development of youth work. Each local VEC has an appointed Youth Work

Committee for its particular area, which is to include representatives of the relevant statutory agencies as well as a number of local voluntary youth council nominees. This constitutes the partnership structure at local level where representatives of local organisations sit at the same table as representatives of statutory agencies working together on matters of local policy and provision. The voluntary youth council provides the forum for voluntary youth organisations in each area to get together, co-ordinate their efforts, share resources and discuss issues relating to youth service provision in the relevant area.

At national level, the Act conveniently legitimated only one voice to represent young people's interests and the entire youth sector generally in Irish society. This voice is the NYCI. It receives its core funding from the state and is one of the social partners involved in negotiating national partnership agreements. It is also represented on the National Economic and Social Council (NESC), the National Economic and Social Forum (NESF) and FÁS (Foras Áiseanna Saothar). It represents youth interests at European level through the Council of European Youth Committees, the European Youth Forum and the Youth Directorate of the Council of Europe. At the time of its introduction into law, it was recognised that considerable additional resources were needed to implement the Act, particularly to fill the gaps that existed in local service provision. However, it appears that the implementation of the Act is practically at a standstill owing to inadequate funding and it has been estimated that it may take up to three years before some of the practical structures are in place for the act to have effect (Kearney, 2003). The main achievement of the Youth Work Act 2001 might yet be the establishment of a very elaborate bureaucratic structure giving more specific shape to the youth services' programmes and forms of delivery in line with government aims. However, if funding for service stays at its current inadequate level this will have to be done within the constraints of a very modest budget.

In November 2001, a European Commission White Paper *A New Impetus For European Youth* (Commission of the European Community, 2001) was published which was judged overall as a disappointment in the Irish context. It was strongly criticised by the NYCI and the 20 young Irish young people involved in the extensive consultative process that took place prior to its publication. They challenged the 'Open Method of Co-ordination' or OMC framework[2] proposed in the White Paper on the grounds that no explicit mention was made of the role of youth organisations in such a framework.

---

2 The open method of co-ordination (OMC) is an approach developed by the EU. It refers to enhanced co-operation at European level between member states so that guidelines, goals and timetables are agreed collectively and translated into national and regional policies by setting specific targets and adopting particular measures (see Devlin, 2002).

Some key areas of dissatisfaction included the failure to emphasise the importance of youth input at different levels of policy making, the discouragement
of youth protest as a means of expression and the indicated intention to 'head
off' the involvement of young people in the anti-globalisation movement
(NYCI, 2001). Devlin (2002) also outlined a number of flaws and limitations
in the depth and scope of the White Paper, acknowledging as a major problem
the inadequacy of the legislative basis that currently exists for EU-level action
where young people are concerned. On a positive note, however, he claimed
that the White Paper could be of important symbolic value at European level
and possibly also at national level, if it provides the necessary impetus for the
implementation of the Youth Work Act and the National Youth Work
Development Plan.

The first National Youth Work Development Plan (2003–7) was finally
published in Autumn 2003. The following areas were prioritised for action:

1   The appointment of a National Assessor of Youth Work under the terms
    of the Youth Work Act 2001.
2   The expansion of the existing Local Youth Clubs Grant Scheme.
3   The introduction of a Funding Review Body.
4   The creation of a Development Unit.
5   The establishment of a validation body for youth work training.

A much more enhanced infrastructure for the development, support and
co-ordination of youth work at national and local levels was envisaged in the
plan (Department of Education and Science, 2003c). At an estimated cost of
€35 million, it was reported in *The Irish Times* that Síle de Valera, the Minister
of State for Youth Affairs, acknowledged that the sum of €120,000 provided
for the operation of the first year of the plan would allow her to implement
only two of the recommendations made: to establish a child protection
training programme and to appoint a National Assessor of Youth Work
(Dooley, 2003).

Overview of contemporary youth work provision in Ireland
Traditionally youth work tended to be divided into mainline youth provision
and special youth services. Mainline youth provision largely consists of youth
clubs in local areas staffed by voluntary adult youth leaders and supported by
a small number of full-time staff in the local youth organisation to which the
club is affiliated. The uniformed youth movements (Scouting Ireland and
Girl Guides) are also very active throughout the country. Youth work also
manifests itself in outdoor pursuits, summer programmes, after-school
activities, exchange programmes as well as arts and other cultural activities. A
number of Youth Information Centres exist around the country providing

information and advice to young people on a wide range of youth-related issues. What tends to be the defining characteristic of this kind of mainline provision is its universal 'open to all' feature, rather than its selective targeting of certain groups of young people for more intense intervention.

It has always been a traditional feature of youth work to reach out to the groups of young people who do not, for whatever reason, participate or survive in universal provision. These young people tend to be identified as the 'unclubbables', or the more challenging groups of young people who are often labelled as being 'at risk'. They may have come to the attention of other social agencies because of the perceived threat they pose to social order. More specialised youth interventions designed to meet the needs of this particular cohort have been introduced by voluntary youth work agencies, supported by VECs. These specialised projects, arguably because of their target groups, tend to receive a significant share of the youth work budget. They tend to be staffed by professionally trained full-time youth workers, supported by part-time personnel or volunteers. They vary in terms of their target groups (early school leavers, school non-attenders, teenage parents, young offenders, young homeless, drug users) and in terms of the programmes on offer. At times these projects have an outreach / detached dimension, which is designed to meet the needs of the particularly marginalised or socially excluded young people in local communities.

In recent years there has also been a growing number of independently managed community based youth projects, not affiliated to any national voluntary youth organisations and funded by government departments other than the Youth Affairs Section of the Department of Education and Science. They also employ professional youth workers, community workers or related professionals. Garda special projects provide one such example. They are local youth based crime prevention projects that started to come into existence from 1981 onwards. They are managed locally either by a youth service or a local management committee and they are funded by the Department of Justice, Equality and Law Reform.

Despite the ratification of the UN Convention on the Rights of the Child in Ireland in 1992, a UN Committee on the Rights of the Child concluded from its observations in 1998 that Irish policies and practices were not reflecting the child rights based approach enshrined in the Convention (Smyth, 1998). The National Children's Strategy (Department of Health and Children, 1999) has thus resulted in the introduction of a number of specific interventions designed to afford more opportunities to children to discuss issues of importance to them and to ensure that due regard is given to their views. These include Dáil na nOg (the National Children's Parliament) at national level as well as other national and local fora where planning decisions about services are being made.

It is also important to point out that many statutory or voluntary services have work with young people as a significant part of their brief though they are not classified as youth work organisations.[3] They may indeed borrow some youth work methodologies, but they do not necessarily espouse key youth work principles, owing to their legal/statutory obligations, the modes of practice they engage in, or the quality of the relationships they have with the young people with whom they work.

The voluntary youth work sector is thus only one part of an increasingly complicated landscape of services directly or indirectly experienced by children and young people in Irish society. This means that a number of government departments, including Education and Science, Health and Children, Enterprise, Trade and Employment, Justice, Equality and Law Reform are all to some extent concerned with this labyrinth of youth provision. Youth policy is thus not an isolated aspect of social policy. It has the unenviable task of preventing or responding to any damage caused by policies across the range of areas of government, as young people's lives are never completely disconnected from their families, peer groups and local communities.

Contemporary Irish youth policy – issues and dilemmas

As a very small percentage of the education budget is dedicated to the voluntary youth service, funding continues to be an ongoing problem impacting on the development of the youth service in Ireland. Funding tends to be short-term and what is generally allocated to any one project usually has to be supplemented from other funding sources. In 1997, a Young People's Facilities and Services Fund (YPSFS) of £30 million was provided for youth provision over a three-year period. The sum of £20 million was designated to support projects in drugs task force areas and the remaining £10 million was provided to support projects in other areas of the country. Adams (1998: 3) describes the evolution of the Young People's Facilities and Services Fund stating: 'Like all things in life, the £30m fund did not come easy'. A second round of funding for the Young People's Services and Facilities has since been postponed and the increase in funding for youth provision in 2002 was so minimal that it proved negligible in the context of the rate of inflation (NYCI, 2002). Other policy and funding decisions made by the recent Fine Fáil/PD government have also negatively impacted on the youth service indirectly, for example in

---

3   Responsibility for child welfare and protection rests with community care social work. Second chance education initiatives, such as community training workshops and youthreach programmes, respond to the educational needs of early school leavers or unqualified young people. The Juvenile Liaison Officer scheme/Garda Diversion Programme is operated by the Garda Síochána and targets first- and second-time young offenders. The Probation and Welfare Service would also have a significant number of young offenders making up its caseload (for a further discussion, see Jenkinson, 2000).

reduced access to the Community Employment Scheme, the cutting back of funding for arts and development education as well as for community/youth projects resourced through partnership companies.

Connected with the funding problem and a major source of dissatisfaction are the insecure and inadequate employment conditions experienced by people employed in the youth work sector. Voluntary adult youth leaders still exist in significant numbers to make a huge contribution to the service. However, the myriad of difficulties already documented (Ruddle and Mulvihill, 1994; 1999) that have beset volunteering in recent years have also been experienced in the youth work sector (Hurley, 1993).

In March 2003 the NYCI, the social partner organisation representing young people after balloting its 45 member organisations, voted to accept the most recent national agreement *Sustaining Progress* (Government of Ireland, 2003a). The Director of the NYCI accepted that ratifying the agreement constituted 'a significant leap of faith' by its members particularly when commitments made under the previous national agreement had not been honoured (NYCI, 2003). Indeed, successive governments have failed to resource and support the Irish youth service sufficiently over the years. There is evidence of a persistent problem of poverty among children and young people despite a period of unforeseen economic growth.[4] There has been a lack of progress on key NYCI demands made on behalf of young people over the years.[5] Assessing this evidence, a strong case could, in particular, be made that Irish social partnership is stymieing rather than assisting many groups of young people in Irish society from reaping their fair share in a more prosperous Ireland.

Conclusion

There is now a very active youth service in Ireland, with over 50 organisations, a membership of 500,000 young people, supported by 40,0000 volunteer youth leaders and 1,000 full-time paid staff (NYCI, 2003a). It is evident that

4   In 1998, one in eight children were in severe or consistent poverty (i.e. households both below 60 per cent of average household income and experiencing basic deprivation). Ireland has one of the highest rates of child poverty (16.8 per cent) in the EU and rates sixth highest on the list of OECD countries (See Nolan, 2000; UNICEF, 2000).

5   Key NYCI demands relate to taking very low paid workers (often young people) out of the tax net, the extension of the medical card scheme to include all young people under the age of 18 and full time students up to the age of 21; more substantial increases in child benefit to ameliorate child poverty; additional inspectors to properly enforce the Protection of Young Persons Employment Act and reductions in the cost of motor insurance premiums for young drivers. There has been very little and in some cases no action taken in relation to implementing these measures.

the existing service has been very much shaped by the context from which it emerged. It is very difficult, however, to be optimistic about the future of the service in Ireland, particularly when one examines the long drawn out, erratic development of policy in the area. The biggest setback is the inadequate financial resources dedicated to the implementation of the Youth Work Act and the National Youth Work Development Plan. Indeed, on the basis of past performance, it would not be unreasonable to assume that the Youth Work Act 2001 and the National Youth Work Development Plan (2003–7) may well exceed their sell by date, without having made any significant impact. Now, more than ever, a social change agenda may need to be reactivated at all levels of youth work, if this distinctive service is to survive into the future.

Figure 9.1 **Chronology of developments of youth work services and policy in Ireland**

1880s to 1910   The early uniformed and non-uniformed organisations emerged
1930   Vocational Education Act
1942   Comhairle le Leas Oige established
1943   Commission on Youth Unemployment established
1951   Report of Commission on Youth Unemployment
1967   National Youth Council established
1974   Department of Education, *Development of Youth Work Services*
1977   Department of Education, *A Policy on Youth and Sport*
1978   National Youth Council, *A Policy on Youth Work Service*
1980   National Youth Council, *The Development of Youth Work Services*
          Task Force Report on Childcare Services
1984   Department of Labour, Shaping the Future
1985   National Youth Policy (Costello) Committee Final Report, *In Partnership with Youth*
1992   Green Paper on Education, *Education for a Changing World*
1993   Report of the Consultative Group on the Development of Youth Work
1995   White Paper on Education, *Charting our Education Future*
1997   Youth Services Act
1998   Young People's Facilities and Services Fund (YPFSF)
2001   Youth Work Act
          European Commission White Paper, *A New Impetus For European Youth*
2003   National Youth Work Development Plan (2003–2007)

Recommended reading

Burgess, P. (ed.) (1977) *Youth and Community Work.* Cork: UCC Centre for Adult and Continuing Education.

Davies, B. (1999a) *From Voluntarism to Welfare State: A History of the Youth Service in England. Vol. I, 1939–1979.* Leicester: National Youth Agency.

Davies, B. (1999b) *From Thatcherism to New Labour: A History of the Youth Service in England. Vol. 2, 1979–1999*. Leicester: National Youth Agency.

Forde, W. (1995) *Growing Up in Ireland: The Development of Irish Youth Services*. Wexford: Cara Publications.

Furlong, A. and F. Cartmel (1997) *Young People and Social Change*. Buckingham: Open University Press.

Jenkinson, H. (2000) 'Youth work in Ireland: the struggle for identity', *Irish Journal of Applied Social Studies* 2 (2) 2000: 106–24.

National Youth Council of Ireland (1996) *The State of Youth Report: Putting Youth on the Agenda*. Dublin: NYCI.

O'Connor, P. (1998) Young women: just other young people', pp. 161–87 in P. O'Connor (ed.), *Emerging Voices: Women in Contemporary Irish Society*. Dublin: IPA.

Roche J. and S. Tucker (eds) (1997) *Youth in Society*. London: Sage.

Journals / Serials

Irish YouthWork Scene: A Journal for Youth Workers, published by the National Federation of Youth Clubs.

Youth and Policy, Journal of Critical Analysis. London: Sage.

Chapter 10

Social policy and older people

Anne O'Loughlin

Introduction

Directing policy towards older people carries with it the risk of perceiving them as a single population. Elderly people have always been an important group in relation to social policy. Current ideas about ageing and old age have a long history. The conception and measurement of age and old age in the past have a close connection to the form of social oppression we now know as ageism (Bytheway, 1995). Social policy making is often based, at least in part, on a set of assumptions and attitudes, which can influence and shape older people's lives. A more critical appreciation of the role of the social policies in this chapter requires consideration of the significance of old age in the past, the social and personal process of ageing and the potential power of ageism.

Old age in history

A degree of scepticism is necessary when looking at historical accounts of old age, as they are coloured by the authors' experiences of the ageism of their own society, and an uncritical adoption of popular assumptions (Bytheway, 1995: 17). De Beauvoir (1977: 44–99) reviewed the ethnological data and found that few made any organised synthesis of their observations on the subject of old age. While urging caution against oversimplification, the survey highlighted the link between the condition of the aged and their social context in primitive societies. The picture of the condition of old people in history is 'blurred, uncertain and contradictory' (De Beauvoir, 1977: 99). In particular, the history of the aged poor is passed over. In so far as old age is revealed, it refers to the privileged classes and to the personal experiences of men. The attitudes and images of historical societies towards older people give little support to the images of a 'golden age' of ageing, whether the focus is classical Rome (Haynes, 1963), pre-industrial Britain (Thomas, 1976) or the United States (Haber, 1983).

Ageism

Bytheway (1995) reviews the complex phenomenon of ageism. This concept was introduced in the 1960s through Butler (1975) and gradually became established in the popular consciousness with a number of other publications (Hendricks and Hendricks, 1977; Comfort, 1977). The 'working definition' of Bytheway and Johnson (1990, cited in Bytheway, 1995: 14) is a useful framework for this chapter:

- Ageism is a set of beliefs originating in the biological variation between people and relating to the ageing process.
- It is in the actions of corporate bodies, what is said and done by their representatives, and the resulting views that are held by ordinary ageing people, that ageism is made manifest.

In consequence of this, it follows that:

- Ageism generates and reinforces a fear and denigration of the ageing process and stereotyping assumptions regarding competence and the need for protection.
- In particular, ageism legitimates the use of chronological age to mark out classes of people who are systematically denied resources and opportunities that others enjoy, and who suffer the consequences of such denigration, ranging from well-meaning patronage to unambiguous vilification.

In this definition the emphasis is on expanding the popular conception of ageism as discrimination against older people to include the fact that young people can also suffer from ageist prejudice. It also highlights that ageism puts forward a biological basis for discrimination with the dangers of the ultimate oppression of euthanasia and 'chronological cleansing' (Bytheway, 1995: 27). Ageism is more than individual prejudice. The idea of old age is a powerful element in making distinctions and imposing expectations upon individuals in those categories. Ageism can be manifested in individual actions but organisations and institutions can also be intrinsically ageist.

A focus on social policy and older people must also take into account the role of images. Featherstone and Hepworth (1990: 250–75) highlight the tension between the ways of seeing and defining ageing, which are in public circulation, and 'the private and unspoken thoughts of individuals'. Images of ageing help to simplify and categorise but they do not do justice to the highly individual process of ageing. The tension between social categories and the actual experience of ageing is an increasingly important issue for policy makers.

Ageing, then, is not reducible to biological processes of physical decline which take place in some vacuum sealed off from social life, but is shaped or constructed in terms of the symbolic imagery available to us at any given time (Featherstone and Hepworth, 1990: 253).

There are many ways in which ageism is evident, and how 'important and pervasive age has become in the relationship between the individual and society' should be recognised (Bytheway, 1995: 8). There is a certain lack of understanding about the status of older people in Irish society. Some recent insights into the concept of ageism have implications for policy making. Progress may be achieved by a broader conception of age discrimination, which considers its harmful consequences for older people, for children and young people. The characterisation of childhood as a time of 'innocence' and old age as a time of 'serenity' are both manifestations of an ageist ideology (Bytheway, 1995; Thompson, 1997: 59–65). Acknowledging the commonalities across forms of age discrimination and developing links between those who are attempting to combat it are possible ways forward.

Historical overview

Historically there are records of a form of hospital service in Ireland dating as far back as 300 BC with the foundation of *Broin Berg* or the 'house of sorrow' near Armagh. Under Brehon Law the ruler of every territory had to provide hospital facilities known as *briugu*. A fragmentary text in early Irish law, *Do brethaib gaire* (appendix 1, nr 28) deals with the kin's obligation to care for its members who were insane, aged or suffering from physical disability (Kelly, 1988; O'Connor 1995). The advent of Christianity in the late fourth and early fifth centuries led to the development and expansion of the monasteries, which provided care for the sick, the poor and the aged. The suppression of the monasteries, which began with the Reformation in 1535, 'meant that the poor, the sick and the elderly had now no avenue of escape from the harsh reality of deprivation' (O'Connor, 1995: 25). The Poor Relief Act of 1601 instituted England's first statutory social service, but this did not extend to Ireland. The rapidly growing population in Ireland compounded the widespread poverty. In 1703 the Irish Parliament enacted legislation for the building of a 'House of Industry' in Dublin. The old and infirm were among those provided for but the record of provision was very limited. The care of older people who were mentally ill was not considered before the eighteenth century. The Dublin House of Industry, set up in 1773 for the shelter of the poor, found that it soon had to contend also with the mentally ill. The conditions of overcrowding, with the ill treatment of patients and the lack of segregation have been graphically described (Reynolds, 1992: 9–14). A separate institution named the Richmond Lunatic Asylum was officially opened in 1815. However, care of the aged and infirm continued at the House of Industry, with their numbers reaching 610 out of 2,900 in 1817 (Reynolds, 1992: 32). Squalid conditions endured by old and incontinent patients in the Richmond Asylum were also evident in 1830 (Reynolds 1992: 44).

The existence of the lunatic asylums, voluntary and state-aided hospitals, workhouses and houses of industry, voluntary dispensaries and relief-giving charities and public works schemes provided the background into which the Irish Poor Law of 1838 was introduced. These services 'made no real impression on Ireland's vast social problems in the early nineteenth century' (Burke, 1987: 14). O'Connor describes older people as being totally reliant on charity in the absence of legal provision (1995: 47). After numerous Royal Commissions and special Committees of Enquiry set up to report on conditions of the poor in Ireland between 1800 and 1840, the Act of 1838 for the more Effectual Relief of the Destitute Poor in Ireland passed into law.

The workhouse was a central feature of Poor Law relief and included among its inmates 'such destitute poor persons as by reason of old age, infirmity or defect may be unable to support themselves' (O'Connor, 1995: 69). They were accommodated in segregated quarters; workhouse plans show wards for aged women and aged men on opposite sides of the entrance block. The Great Famine in 1845 resulted in the system of workhouses being completely overwhelmed, leading to appalling conditions and high mortality. From the end of the Famine, conditions began to improve. The Poor Relief (Ireland) Act 1862 led to the appointment of the Sisters of Mercy as qualified nurses and the improvement of the care of the sick. The workhouse became more and more an institution for the old and sick. However, for many older people the stigma still remains, the memory of the workhouse deep in folk consciousness (O'Connor, 1995: 181).

The formation of the Irish Workhouse Association in 1896 was a sign of increasing public awareness of the need for reform. The Commissions on Poor Law Reform of 1903 and 1909 recommended that the infirm and the aged be removed from workhouses and placed in separate institutions. These recommendations were not implemented, and in 1921 there were still 127 workhouses in Ireland. A Commission on Poor Relief in 1927 recommended that the County Homes, which were converted workhouses, be reserved for the aged and infirm poor and chronic invalids. In 1949 an Inter-Departmental Committee recommended the reconstruction of the County Homes to house the aged and chronic sick (Inter-Departmental Committee, 1949). A White Paper issued in 1951 accepted these recommendations and grant-aided the work. This continued until the Inter-Departmental Committee on the Care of the Aged reported to the Minister for Health in 1968. This report has been described as 'a major catalyst for change' (Ruddle et al., 1997: 38).

Before moving on to the 1968 Report, a number of significant developments will be discussed. The establishment of a structured system of social
welfare payments began in 1847 when 'outdoor' relief was authorised for
Ireland. This scheme was abolished by the establishment of a national means-
tested supplementary welfare allowance scheme in 1975, which was generally
applied to older people for additional payments for rent, heating, diet etc.
The non-contributory old age pension was introduced in 1908 and it established 'for the first time in the British Isles the important principle of regular
cash payments being made available to a specified group of citizens from
monies provided by parliament' (Carney, 1985: 486). This was a highly controversial scheme initially that gradually became a central component of
government income maintenance strategies.

In the early years of the Irish social welfare system, means-tested payments
dominated. The establishment of the Department of Social Welfare in 1947
and the passing of the Social Welfare Act 1952 led to expansion of the social
insurance scheme. A contributory old age pension was introduced in 1961 and
pension age was reduced from 70 to 66 by 1977. A retirement pension at age
65 began in 1970. The structure and development of social welfare payments
for care in Ireland will be addressed later in this chapter (pp. 231–2). These
payments developed in the context of a growing emphasis on community care
in the 1960s which is made evident in the report on the care of the aged (Inter-
Departmental Committee on Care of the Aged, 1968).

The Care of the Aged Report

An Inter-Departmental Committee was appointed in 1965 by the Minister for
Health in consultation with the Ministers for Local Government and Social
Welfare to 'examine and report on the general problem of the care of the aged
and to make recommendations regarding the improvement and extension of
services' (Inter-Departmental Committee, 1968: 22). The major shift in policy
evident in this report is outlined in the recommendations of the committee
'based on the belief that it is better, and probably much cheaper, to help the
aged to live in the community than to provide for them in hospitals or other
institutions' (1968: 13). The policy is outlined in the aims of services as follows:

(*a*) to enable the aged who can do so to continue to live in their own homes;
(*b*) to enable the aged who cannot live in their own homes to live in other similar
   accommodation;
(*c*) to provide substitutes for normal homes for those who cannot be dealt with as
   at (*a*) and (*b*);
(*d*) to provide hospital services for those who cannot be dealt with as at (*a*), (*b*) or
   (*c*).

(1968: 49)

To achieve these aims, the Committee recommended planning, co-ordination and the integration of housing services, schemes of financial assistance and health services. Emphasis was placed on the concept of 'partnership', between the family and public and voluntary organisations. In total, the Care of the Aged Report made 94 recommendations. The Report has been described as having 'dominated policy towards services for the elderly' for 20 years after its publication (Working Party on Services for the Elderly, 1988: 15). Improvements in income maintenance schemes resulted in a general improvement in the income position of older people with a minority of older people still remaining economically vulnerable – those dependent on social welfare pensions and those living alone (Blackwell, 1984). Some significant developments also took place in housing policy. The majority of sheltered housing schemes dated from the mid-1970s. A later research study on the role of sheltered housing identified wide regional variation and inadequacy of provision (O'Connor et al., 1989). Housing policy for the elderly also focused on home improvement schemes for the adaptation and repair of existing dwellings. The recommendations of the Care of the Aged Report (Inter-Departmental Committee, 1968) in relation to community services covered a broad range including the provision of domiciliary nursing, medical care, specialist advice, provision of appliances, ophthalmic services, dental services, paramedical and social work services, home helps, home visiting and meals. In reviewing the progress of implementing these recommendations, the Working Party on Services for the Elderly established in 1986 noted 'substantial progress' and 'a rapid expansion in health services' (Working Party on Services for the Elderly, 1988: 21). However, 'shortcomings in services' and 'many gaps in service provision' were also documented. Direct quotation from this Report provides a sobering reflection on social policy in relation to older people up to 1988.

> It is clear to us that housing, health and welfare services are not sufficiently targeted at assisting the most vulnerable elderly people. Existing domiciliary health and welfare services are inadequate in most parts of the country to maintain the elderly at home when ill or infirm. Persons caring for their elderly relatives at home receive insufficient support from statutory bodies. The shortcomings in domiciliary support services lead to a continuing bias towards long-term institutional care. This is aggravated by the absence of adequate assessment and rehabilitation facilities. There is a major gap in the provision of facilities for the demented elderly, a need to which little attention has been given up to now. Where the administration of services is concerned, there is a lack of coordination. The care of the elderly in the professional training courses is accorded a low priority. (Working Party on Services for the Elderly, 1988: 28)

Current policy

The Working Party on Services for the Elderly was appointed by the Minister for Health in 1986. Acknowledging that they were standing 'on the shoulders of the Care of the Aged Report' of twenty years earlier (Working Party on Services for the Elderly, 1988: 26), the committee published *The Years Ahead: A Policy for the Elderly.* This Report is the basis of official policy for older people in Ireland. Its terms of reference, clearly related to the policy of the Care of the Aged Report, accepted that the aims of services for the elderly were:

(*a*) to enable the elderly person to live at home, where possible, at an optimum level of health and independence;

(*b*) to enable those who cannot live at home to receive treatment, rehabilitation and care in accommodation and in an environment as near as possible to home.   (Working Party on Services for the Elderly, 1988: ix)

Detailed recommendations were made for an appropriate framework for co-ordination of services: the development and expansion of community care services; the provision of support, information and advice for carers; improved care of older people in general hospitals; development of community hospitals; care of elderly mentally infirm; development of the psychiatry of old age; housing policy; health promotion and education.

The Care of the Aged Report (Inter-Departmental Committee, 1968) had emphasised the encouragement of voluntary activity in the provision of services, viewing their role as 'complementary' to the health authorities (Par. 6.24). The voluntary nature of the work was heavily emphasised and seen to represent a considerable saving to the public authorities (Par. 6.24). The setting up of Social Service Councils and a National Council for the Aged was proposed to co-ordinate activities at local and national level, motivated by the view that 'the field of voluntary effort is almost unlimited' (Par 6.24).

The stimulation provided by the Care of the Aged Report was further enhanced by the Health Act 1970, which established health boards and a structure for community care (Department of Health, 1970). The Health Act 1953 contributed to the current operation of voluntary bodies by the power given in Section 65 to 'give assistance' to any organisation 'which provides or proposes to provide a service similar or ancillary to a service which the health authority may provide' (Department of Health, 1953).

The Years Ahead (Working Party on Services for the Elderly, 1988) proposed that voluntary organisations are 'major partners' along with 'families' and 'professionals working for statutory agencies'. The recommendations in *The Years Ahead* in relation to voluntary organisations were as follows:

'encouragement by all possible means the involvement of voluntary organisations in caring for the elderly' (Par. 11.17); formal contracts setting out services to be provided for a period of two or three years (Par. 11.17); establishment of a development fund (Par 11.18); development of a mechanism to co-ordinate voluntary activity locally (Par. 11.18); a formal review of the relationship of statutory and voluntary sectors; and the development of national guidelines (Par. 11.19).

The Years Ahead outlined the objectives of public policy. Services were to be guided by these underlying principles: comprehensiveness, equity, accessibility, responsiveness, flexibility, co-ordination, planning and cost effectiveness. The objectives proposed in this report and in the Care of the Aged Report (Inter-Departmental Committee, 1968) are very similar. The later document adds an emphasis on rehabilitation and on the values of 'dignity and independence' (Working Party on Services for the Elderly, 1988: 38). The objectives of public policy were put forward as: to maintain elderly people in dignity and independence in their own home; to restore those elderly people who become ill or dependent to independence at home; to encourage and support the care of the elderly in their own community by family, neighbours and voluntary bodies in every way possible; to provide a high quality of hospital and residential care for the elderly people when they can no longer be maintained in dignity and independence at home (1988: 38).

The main advances in the recommendations between the Care of the Aged Report (Inter-Departmental Committee, 1968) and *The Years Ahead* (Working Party on Services for the Elderly, 1988) were in co-ordination of services, the development of the community hospital to provide a wide range of services in each district, and specific recommendations about the financial implications of implementation. *The Years Ahead* focused most of its recommendations on a normative approach to service provision based on projected changes in the demographic situation up to the early years of the twenty-first century. Some of the underlying assumptions have been questioned (Ruddle et al., 1997: 43–8). In particular the estimation of the demand for services and the actual growth in population aged over 75 were underestimated. The assumption that there would be an opportunity to redeploy resources from child care have been offset by the urgency of implementing the Child Care Act 1990. *The Years Ahead* also tended towards a service delivery model that relied on service providers and administrators rather than user involvement in planning and evaluation.

Policy for health services: the health strategies of 1994 and 2001

Shaping a Healthier Future: A Strategy for Effective Healthcare in the 1990s (Department of Health, 1994) (hereafter referred to as *Shaping a Healthier Future*) outlined a comprehensive health strategy, whose main theme was 'the reorientation or reshaping of our health services' (1994: 3). The dimensions of this reorientation were in the following areas:

- *service provision* – an increased emphasis on the provision of the most appropriate care;
- *management and organisational structures* – more decision making and accountability allied to better methods of performance measurement;
- *the participants* – greater sensitivity to the right of the consumer to a service which responds to his or her needs in an equitable and quality driven manner and greater recognition to service providers (Department of Health, 1994: 8).

The key principles underpinning the health strategy were equity, quality of service and accountability. A four-year action plan for the implementation of the health strategy was set out. One aspect of this plan focused on 'ill and dependent elderly'. While acknowledging that 'much remains to be done' before the objectives of *The Years Ahead* (Working Party on Services for the Elderly, 1988) are achieved, the plan reiterated the objectives of the 1988 report and prioritised: promoting healthy ageing; increasing specialist departments of medicine of old age; funding the Health (Nursing Homes) Act 1990; providing additional convalescent care and small-scale nursing units. The support of older people who live at home is designed 'to ensure that not less than 90 per cent of those over 75 years of age continue to live at home' (Department of Health, 1994: 67). Enhancement of services for the care of people with mental illness or infirmity is also included in the action plan (Department of Health, 1994: 70).

   Quality and Fairness: A Health System for You (hereafter referred to as *Quality and Fairness*) was developed as a 'blueprint to guide policy makers and service providers in achieving the vision of a future health system' guided by the principles of equity, people-centredness, quality and accountability (Department of Health and Children, 2001c: 17). Four national goals encompass the many proposed developments:

- Better health for everyone
- Fair access
- Responsive and appropriate care delivery
- High performance (Department of Health and Children, 2001c: 59)

The needs of older people received 'particular prominence during the consultation process' (Department of Health and Children, 2001c: 52). Among the specific objectives and actions to achieve these goals relevant to older people are: a National Injury Prevention Strategy; a co-ordinated action plan to meet the needs of ageing and older people; funding of community groups to facilitate volunteers in providing support services; implementation of the Health Promotion Strategy for Older People, *Adding Years to Life and Life to Years* (Department of Health and Children, 1998); implementation of an action plan for dementia; an action plan for rehabilitation services; development of a national palliative care service to include access to palliative care for those with non-malignant disease and measures to prevent domestic violence and support victims. Legislation regarding the framework for entitlement to services is to be reviewed. This is particularly relevant to the eligibility of older people for long-term residential care and financing of this care. (See further discussion of this issue on pp. 219–21 below). The development of care management and appointment of key workers for dependent older people are part of the actions to be taken to develop appropriate care delivery. Investment in increasing capacity of services includes services specifically targeted at older people, such as recruitment of a multi-disciplinary range of staff, provision of day care places and a new scheme of subvention for home based care. National standards for community and long term care of older people are to be drawn up. The Social Services Inspectorate (SSI) is to be established on a statutory basis and its remit extended to include residential care for people with disabilities and older people (Department of Health and Children, 2001c: 59–91).

In July 2001, the Health (Miscellaneous Provisions) Act 2001 was enacted. This amended the Health Act 1970, S.45 by changing the criteria for "full eligibility" for services. This was a controversial amendment, which gave medical cards to all persons over the age of 70 years on the basis of their age, removing the means test, which had governed the scheme for over thirty years. The main controversies surrounding this were: that the cost ran way ahead of Department of Health and Children estimates; that GPs negotiated a higher fee for these patients; and the inequity caused by the failure to increase eligibility levels for those on low incomes, while giving medical cards to the 'wealthy' older people.

A recent report of the Human Rights Commission states that many of the commitments of *The Years Ahead*, the health strategy 1994, and the health strategy 2001 have not been delivered or implemented. These include improved community services, the provision of publicly funded long term care, clarification on the entitlement to long term care, the establishment of an independent inspectorate, the establishment of a statutory independent complaints and appeals procedure within health boards and putting community care services on a statutory basis (Mangan, 2003: 3–5).

Policy developments in mental health
In 1992 a Green Paper on Mental Health was published to review progress in the development of a new psychiatric service as recommended in the report *Planning for the Future* (Department of Health, 1984a). It was also concerned

with new legislation to replace the Mental Treatment Act 1945. Public comment on the proposals in the Green Paper led to the publication in 1995 of the White Paper, *A New Mental Health Act* (Department of Health, 1995d). The most significant proposals of the White Paper relevant to older people included: changing criteria for involuntary admission to an approved centre; defining 'mental disorder' to include the term 'severe dementia' associated with severe behavioural disturbance; broadening the category of centres where involuntary admission is possible e.g. a centre specialising in the care of persons with dementia; setting up a Mental Health Review Board to review decisions to detain patients in psychiatric hospitals and developing the Inspectorate of Mental Hospitals; introduction of an adult care order which could be used to protect mentally disordered persons (including those with mental infirmity) from abuse; considerably narrowing the grounds for detention of a person with dementia (currently classified as a person of unsound mind, who might be detained for an indefinite period); and the development of specialised centres for the care of those with severe dementia.

The Mental Health Act 2001 (Department of Health and Children, 2001a) was signed into law in 2001 and is the most significant legislative provision in the area of mental health services since the enactment of the Mental Treatment Act 1945. The Act defines 'mental disorder' as mental illness, severe dementia or significant intellectual disability (2001, Par. 3). The Act concentrates on providing for the involuntary admission to approved centres of persons suffering from mental disorders. It is a milestone towards bringing legislation into line with international obligations for the protection of the rights of individuals, who require compulsory admission and treatment. Some sections of the Act, relating to the establishment of the Mental Health Commission to promote best practice and high standards of care, the appointment of the Inspector of Mental Health Services and the Director of Mental Health Tribunals, the independent review system for patients involuntarily detained (mainly Part 3), were implemented in April 2002. Important aspects of the new legislation, which still await implementation, are those dealing with the procedures for involuntary admission (Part 2), the registration and regulation of approved centres (Part 4) and guidance on restraint (Part 6). In an annual report of the Mental Health Commission, mid-2004 was targeted for the commencement of Part 2 of the Act, 'contingent on the availability of adequate resources' (Mental Health Commission, 2002: 4).

The Mental Health Act, when implemented fully, will alleviate many of the problems associated with existing legislation. Its focus is not, however, sufficient to deal with the many aspects of mental health of older persons, in particular those suffering from dementia, who do not meet the definition of 'severe dementia' as outlined in the Act:

Severe dementia means a deterioration of the brain of a person, which significantly impairs the intellectual function of the person, thereby affecting thought, comprehension and memory and which includes some psychiatric or behavioural symptoms such as physical aggression (Department of Health and Children, 2001a, par. 3, subsection 2).

It is also significant that the Act does not include the proposals for an adult care order as outlined in the White Paper. This issue will be addressed later in this chapter in discussion of the proposals of the Law Reform Commission on law and older people.

Quality and Fairness (Department of Health and Children, 2001c: 150) includes a commitment to implementing an action plan for dementia based on the recommendations of the National Council on Ageing Report, *An Action Plan for Dementia* (O'Shea and O'Reilly, 1999). This report outlines an action plan towards the development of accessible, high quality services, incorporating the views of all major stakeholders and placing 'the individual with dementia at the centre of the planning process' (1999: 6). The authors acknowledge that the gap in services for the care of people with dementia as outlined in *The Years Ahead* (Working Party on Services for the Elderly, 1998) remains. 'Unfortunately, this gap has not been significantly bridged in the last ten years and services remain under-developed' (O'Shea and O'Reilly, 1999: 8). The implementation of the recommendations of the Action Plan for Dementia involved additional resources for the development of services as a key element, with costing spread over three years (O'Shea and O'Reilly 1999: 125). Readers are referred to the Report for an elaboration of its thirty-three recommendations (O'Shea and O'Reilly, 1999: 22–4). The commitment in *Quality and Fairness* to implementation is crucial in the light of the 'weakness of existing dementia-specific services in both community and residential care settings' (O'Shea and O'Reilly, 1999: 124).

The Law Reform Commission
The Law Reform Commission is an independent statutory body whose main aim is to keep the law under review. One of the priority areas of the Commission's Second Programme for Law Reform was reform of the law in relation to older people. The Consultation Paper, *Law and the Elderly* was published in June 2003 as a basis for discussion before making final recommendations on this topic (Law Reform Commission, 2003). While the main provisional recommendations are outlined in this chapter, readers are recommended to consult the report for excellent overview of the whole area of legal capacity, the historical background of substitute decision-making system in Ireland and review of international systems. The Consultation Paper is concerned with the legal mechanisms for the protection of older

people from abuse or the appointment of a substitute decision maker. The Commission recommends that both aspects 'should be dealt with in an integrated way' (Law Reform Commission, 2003: 4). The report sets out proposals for a new system, trying to address the inadequacies of the current Irish system. In summary, the new system involves:

- A substitute decision-making system and/or protection system, which it is proposed to call Guardianship. This would involve application for a Guardianship Order and the appointment of a Personal Guardian, who could make some of the required decisions on behalf of those who do not have legal capacity (Par. 6.07).
- A system of orders to be known as intervention orders, service orders and adult care orders. These orders would apply to those without legal capacity, who do not need Guardianship or to those who have legal capacity but are unable to obtain protection from abuse for themselves (Par. 6.07).
- An Adult Care Order is an order that an adult be removed from their residence which could only be made by the Tribunal (Par. 6.88)
- Establishment of a new independent Office of the Public Guardian with specific decision-making powers and an overall supervisory role over Personal Guardians as well as a 'wide ranging advice, support and advocacy role for vulnerable elderly people' (Par. 6.34).
- The establishment of a Tribunal to make decisions about the general legal capacity of an individual. This is a significant change for Ireland, as at present decisions on general legal capacity is made by the High Court (Par. 6.49).
- A legal obligation on the Health Boards to monitor the care being given to the Protected Adult (Par. 6.31).

In the light of other discussion in this chapter, it is important to note the following comment from the report of the Law Reform Commission:

> While this Consultation Paper is primarily concerned with the legal mechanisms and responses which are required to protect the elderly, these must be seen in the context of health and social care services because the protection of vulnerable elderly people cannot be guaranteed by legal mechanisms alone, and the need for protection would be considerably reduced if adequate health and social care services were available. (2003: 5)

Development of social welfare payment for care

The development of payments for care must be seen in the context of the policy of 'community care' outlined in this chapter. The first payment for care in Ireland was introduced in 1968, and was known as the Prescribed Relative's Allowance. It was payable to older people aged over 70, who required full-time care and attention. The payment, a supplement to the pension, was paid in return for the provision of full-time care by a co-residing female relative (initially only daughter or step-daughter). Gradually the restrictiveness of the payment lessened. The rules on social insurance contributions of the prescribed relative were abolished and the range of female relatives extended in 1969. By 1972 the scheme extended to male relatives and social welfare contributions were credited to those who gave up employment to provide care.

The Social Welfare Act 1989 paid the Prescribed Relative's Allowance directly to the carer. The Prescribed Relative's Allowance was restrictive and very small financially. The Social Welfare Act 1990 introduced a means-tested Carer's Allowance. The Carer's Allowance is a social assistance payment payable to someone providing care to a person in receipt of a range of social welfare payments and needing 'full-time care and attention'. The payment is very much constructed as an earnings substitution, prohibiting the carer from engaging in employment. The means-testing procedure has been changed gradually and includes a disregard of the first €500 of earnings for a married or cohabiting couple and €250 in the case of a single carer (April 2004). However, spouses or partners who receive a social welfare payment must forfeit the adult dependent allowance if the claim is successful, thus greatly reducing the net gain to the household. This has led to a situation where, in 1996, '36 per cent of applicants were not transferred to the Carer's Allowance, even though they were eligible because they would actually have been worse off' (Yeates, 1997: 35).

Recent developments in criteria of eligibility for Carer's Allowance include the possibility for the carer to attend a course of education or training, take up voluntary or community work for up to ten hours per week or work part-time as a home help for a health board for around ten hours per week, or engage in limited self-employment within the home or outside the home for up to ten hours (from which income will be assessed). This is subject to 'adequate care being arranged for the care recipient' and work outside the home 'must be cleared with the Department'. This change represents an alteration of the conditions for the allowance, which up to now focused on the dependence of the care-recipient. Introducing some 'monitoring' in the caring situation may change the payment from an allowance to 'quasi-wage payment' with conditions attached to evidence that the caring has been carried out.

Long-term care

The policy planning report *The Years Ahead* (Working Party on Services for the Elderly, 1988) points the way towards the objective of 'community care' for older people but also the provision of 'high quality hospital and residential care'. Prior to *The Years Ahead*, nursing homes were regulated under the Health (Homes for Incapacitated Persons) Act 1964. The Health (Nursing Homes) Act 1990 introduced regulation in relation to subvention arrangements, regulation and inspection of private and voluntary homes and stricter enforcement of care and welfare regulations. The legislation, which became operational in 1993, led to debate on policy issues such as the underprovision of resources for community care, the large increase in spending on private nursing home care by the Department of Health and Children, inspection and regulation, and financing options.

The rising cost of institutional care is a major issue and the existing division between public and private provision requires a more integrated approach. One of the most controversial aspects of the Health (Nursing Homes) Act 1990 was that of family responsibility for financing long-term care. This was enshrined in the legislation in the process of assessment of applicants for the subvention. The subvention regulations (Statutory Instrument 227 of 1993) required an assessment of 'means' and 'circumstances' of applicants. 'Means' were defined as income and imputed value of assets. 'Circumstances' were defined as 'the capacity of a son and/or daughter aged 21 years and over residing in the jurisdiction of a person who has qualified for a subvention to contribute towards the cost of nursing home care of his or her parent.' This definition of 'circumstances' and the ensuing de facto obligation of support between children and parents is a glaring example of the use of delegated or secondary legislation to introduce restrictions not specifically provided for in primary legislation, i.e. the Act itself.

As a public policy measure, the regulation introduced very difficult issues and within a few months of the commencement of the 1990 Act, complaints in relation to family assessments were made to the Ombudsman's Office. This was addressed in the report, *An Investigation by the Ombudsman of Complaints Regarding Payment of Nursing Home Subventions by Health Boards* (Office of the Ombudsman, 2001). Following this investigation, the provisions in the Regulations which dealt with family assessment were deleted (SI no. 498, 1998). The health boards received approval to pay arrears in those cases where family assessment operated. The Ombudsman concluded that:

- The family assessment provisions were almost certainly legally invalid.
- Health Boards generally misled families into believing that they had an obligation to contribute.
- The Department knew from the outset that the family assessment arrangements were legally invalid (Office of the Ombudsman, 2001: 33)

A second issue addressed in the Ombudsman's report is known as 'the Pocket Money Issue'. This dealt with the assessment of the means of applicants for the Nursing Home Subvention and the possibility of older people retaining a minimum level of their income as 'pocket money'. The conclusion reached by the Ombudsman on this issue was:

- That the Department was aware from the outset that its interpretation of Article 8.2 was incorrect.
- That it gave incorrect advice to the health boards.
- That it was dilatory in withdrawing its incorrect advice. (Office of the Ombudsman, 2001: 42)

An allocation was paid to health boards to pay arrears to claimants adversely affected by this practice. Readers are referred to O' Loughlin (2002) for an analysis of this issue as a form of elder abuse.

A Review of the Nursing Home Subvention Scheme was conducted by the Department of Health and Children and a new model of Subvention for Long Stay Care proposed (O'Shea, 2002). The reforms include: national guidelines for the measurement of dependency; the establishment of independent external audit of quality of care; state funding of 'care costs' in private long stay care i.e. 70 per cent of costs; residents in both public and private long stay care 'co-financing' at the equivalent of 90 per cent of the Non-Contributory Old Age Pension 'to cover hotel costs'; a time limit on public funding of long-term care with private insurance to take over from the state 'cut off point'; an alternative possibility of drawing on the assets of older people after their death to recoup costs. The latter proposal is acknowledged in the report to be 'controversial' (O'Shea, 2002: 98–107). The proposal that 'a subvention for nursing home care would never be granted unless it was clear that a community based subvention would not have succeeded in maintaining the elderly person in their own home' is also contingent on an expansion of community care services. One of the debates in this proposal is about the payment of cash with the possibility of using the money to pay family carers (O'Shea, 2002: 108).

A second report, commissioned by the Department of Social and Family Affairs, reviews long-term care financing and makes similar detailed proposals for a new social insurance scheme for long-term care, including home care (Department of Social and Family Affairs, 2002b).

The National Council on Ageing and Older People
The Care of the Aged Report in 1968 first suggested the formation of a National Council for the Aged 'to promote in every way possible the general welfare of the aged' (Inter-Departmental Committee, 1968: 122). The National Council for the Aged was set up in 1981. Its terms of reference were to advise the Minister for Health on all aspects of the welfare of the aged, on methods of ensuring co-ordination in planning and provision of services, on ways of meeting the needs of the most vulnerable elderly, on ways of encouraging positive attitudes to ageing, on encouraging greater participation by elderly people, on promoting models of good practice and research. It was set up for

a three-year term, followed by a second council's five-year term of office. It was succeeded by the National Council for the Elderly in January 1990, which added to the terms of reference the responsibility to advise the Minister for Health on 'the implementation of the recommendations of the report, *The Years Ahead: A Policy for the Elderly*' (Working Party on Services for the Elderly, 1988).

In March 1997, the National Council on Ageing and Older People succeeded the National Council for the Elderly, adding to the terms of reference 'measures to promote the social inclusion of older people' and 'to assist in the development of national and regional policies and strategies designed to produce health and social gain for older people'. The National Council on Ageing and Older People (and its forerunners) has, through analysis and research conducted on its behalf, identified for policy makers the emerging issues which require policy change, e.g. the home-help service, mental disorders in older people, financing long-term care, elder abuse and case management. In each study, the Council makes detailed recommendations for changes in policy and practice and has held consultative seminars on the subject of each study. While the implementation of policy changes can be very slow, there is no doubt that the Council is very influential as a specialist advisory body.

Implementation of current policy

The National Council on Ageing and Older People, in accordance with its terms of reference, commissioned the Policy Research Centre of the National College of Industrial Relations to carry out a review of the implementation of *The Years Ahead* Report (Working Party on Services for the Elderly, 1988). The reader is referred to the detailed and painstaking research for a complete evaluation of the current situation (Ruddle et al., 1997). However, a summary of some key findings will point the way forward to the final section of this chapter on challenges for the future. The review found: 'significant gaps in the care options for older people' (1997: 306); significant steps in health promotion in the development of a Healthy Ageing Programme by the National Council on Ageing and Older People but 'little evidence of interdepartmental cooperation' (1997: 306); a number of deficits in the provision of effective support services in the community (1997: 300); slow development of community hospitals, assessment and rehabilitation facilities (1997: 310); poorly developed services for psychiatry of old age (1997: 311); 'major needs of carers are not being adequately addressed' (1997: 312); no legislation underpinning the provision of services (1997: 313); and that the co-ordination of services 'requires a much greater commitment of personnel and financial resources' (1997: 318).

Policy documents on the overall health services, *Shaping a Healthier Future* (Department of Health, 1994) and *Quality and Fairness: A Health System for You* (Department of Health and Children, 2001) added some changes in policy orientation and emphasis, notably the importance of evaluation, greater consumer orientation and user responsiveness. The obstacles to policy implementation – such as ambivalence at management level, lack of information on the part of some agencies outside the health boards about recommendations, the absence of a legislative framework and failure to provide funding – highlight the challenges ahead in responding to key issues for future policy. Many of the issues involved radical questioning about the assumptions on which current policy is based.

Challenges for the future

In this section some of the major issues that confront policy makers will be addressed. Space allows merely the highlighting of issues, with references for further reading rather than detailed analysis.

Ageism
The challenge for policy makers is the need to rethink the concept of ageism. A report of the Equality Authority has highlighted a widespread ageism in Irish society and maps out a new future for older people in Ireland as a result of the implementation of the Employment Equality Act 1998 and the Equal Status Act 2000. This legislation places Ireland at the forefront across the European Union in working to eliminate discrimination (Equality Authority, 2003). Bytheway (1995), in the concluding chapter of his study of ageism, proposes that the assumption that old people exist as a group must be questioned and that the us/them question must be resolved. He argues that we must critically examine the creation of a category of people called the elderly:

> Where ageism comes in is, in our pathetic attempts to be certain about the changes that come with age, in the assumptions that they are all universal, in our efforts to distance ourselves from those who appear different, in our negative interpretations and in the consequential regulations of the social order (Bytheway, 1995: 125).

Challenging the power of ageism will require facing the reality that it is a shared experience and seeing ourselves in terms of the broader context of the whole of our lives.

Demography
There are many academic controversies concerning the relationships between mortality, morbidity and disability and how to make projections, which will define the demand for medical care and social services. In Ireland, the trend is

towards population ageing, which 'is not exceptional by the standards of the last 20 to 30 years' (Fahey, 1995: 37). In absolute terms the increase among the old elderly occurs more among women than men. The growth in the population aged eighty years and over is the largest both in absolute and relative terms and represents the most dramatic change (Fahey, 1995: 43). A full discussion of demography as an influence on health and social care provision is undertaken in Fahey's (1995) report for the National Council on Ageing and Older People. While the report outlines the reasons for 'the puzzling absence of a relationship between population ageing and health expenditure', it makes a very significant point in relation to 'social care'. The role of demographic factors could be very significant on the size of the population pool in need of social care services, such as personal care, home help and surveillance. This must be incorporated into policy analysis.

A theory that is particularly appealing to policy makers was put forward by Fries (1980: 130–5). Referred to as 'the compression of morbidity', the theory suggests that illness and death will be progressively confined to a few months and occupy a smaller proportion of the typical lifespan (1980: 130). Evidence however shows that increased longevity may be accompanied by an extension of the period of dependency (Guralnik, 1990; Kaplan, 1991). In the light of these findings lies one of the most difficult challenges – that of 'constructing a positive image of deep old age which will help us detach ourselves from the emotional response of aversion and disgust' (Featherstone and Hepworth, 1990: 273).

Family responsibility
The Years Ahead (Working Party on Services for the Elderly, 1988) identified the family as making by far the greatest contribution to the care of dependent older people. The review of its implementation in relation to support states that 'several substantial studies have demonstrated clearly that little has been done' (Ruddle et al., 1997: 291). Policy makers hold many assumptions about family obligations, which may or may not be accurate. There is a need for a greater understanding of patterns of support for older people and the kind of factors that bring this about.

The assumption that elderly people would prefer family care also needs a more detailed understanding. Qureshi (1996: 100–19) discusses the issue of obligations and support within families, highlighting the need for nationally representative data about care providers. Important questions face policy makers: What networks of care can respond to high levels of dependency? On what basis is care provided? Is there agreement about the responsibility of kin? The complex negotiations about caring for kin in the context of social and demographic changes will continue to be a major challenge for services (Finch, 1989; Finch and Mason, 1993).

Family obligation and its treatment in law and social policy are important issues and may for historical and cultural reasons vary from society to society. The contrasting conceptions of family obligation in France and England are explored by Twigg and Grand (1998). In a detailed discussion of the laws on family obligation and inheritance in both countries, the conclusion that the financial contribution of relatives comes into play mainly in the context of means-tested benefits at the point of transition into institutional care is similar to the controversial aspects of the Irish Health (Nursing Homes) Act 1990 as discussed earlier. The provision of care is an area in which the issue of family obligation is not legally 'enforced'. How much it is enforced through 'an absence of alternatives' is a key question (Twigg and Grand, 1998: 146). The problem of financial responsibility of spouses and children to support older people requires consideration of the moral and administrative issues involved and 'entails finding solutions to agonisingly difficult legal issues in embarrassing, sometimes even tragic, factual contexts' (Levy, 1989: 257).

Concepts of care
Much Irish research on caring has involved studies focusing on the 'costs' of caring (O'Connor and Ruddle, 1988; Blackwell et al., 1992; Ruddle and O'Connor, 1993). An analytical framework, which introduces a broader picture of caring has been developed by Thomas (1993: 649–69). She identified seven dimensions that are common to all concepts of care. These dimensions are: the social identity of the carer; the social identity of the care recipient; the interpersonal relationship between the carer and the care-recipient; the nature of the care; the social domain within which the caring relationship is located; the economic character of the care relationship; and the institutional setting in which the care is delivered.

O'Donovan (1997) uses this framework to explore the concept of care used by the health boards in relation to the home-help service. The home-help service was established under Section 61 of the Health Act 1970 (Department of Health, 1970) and has greatly expanded since its establishment. It consists predominantly of female workers employed on a part-time basis with low rates of pay and a lack of investment in training. The service is mainly provided by the health boards with some voluntary sector involvement. Its development has been constrained by the absence of an adequate legal basis. If the service is to have an impact on the more dependent elderly person at home, considerable additional resources are required. The concept of care identified – one which focuses on care provided by women, whose primary motivation is philanthropic and whose work is a form of paid volunteering – exposes the policy agenda of the health boards as 'promoting care of older people in the "community", but not resourcing this care' and 'the gender ideology that informs this policy' (O'Donovan, 1997: 153).

Payments for care

Payments for care systems are likely to be developed further and this poses many dilemmas in the current social and economic climate. The Carer's Allowance is a payment, made directly to carers, which is relatively rare and occurs only in Britain and Ireland. Other forms of payment are those paid directly to the person who is disabled and 'symbolic payments' made to volunteers. (The term 'symbolic payments' is used by O'Donovan (1997) to describe payment to home helps in Ireland.)

It is increasingly important to understand the classification of payments for care as 'quasi-wages payments' (those made to 'volunteers' or to caregivers by care recipients using benefits) or 'carer-allowance payments for care' (benefits paid to carers). These are leading to 'a politics of payments and allowances for care' (Ungerson, 1995: 31–52). The ways in which such payments impact on the public/private dichotomy, the gender issues involved in the disproportionate number of women receiving such payments and the threat of an informal labour market of 'unregulated caring labour' are issues that need to be seriously considered. The challenge is summarised by Yeates (1997):

> Any attempt to overhaul the Carer's Allowance to more effectively support care giving across the population must explicitly address the relationship between the state and the family on the one hand and the expectation of women as providers of care on the other (1997: 22).

This issue is also relevant to the proposals discussed earlier, to subvent community care in the form of cash transfers to family carers (Department of Social and Family Affairs, 2002b: 94, O'Shea, 2002: 108). It is clear that the challenge is not confined to the Carer's Allowance or to gender alone, but may also broaden to issues of race and nationality (Ungerson, 1995: 48).

Elder abuse

The abuse of older people in Ireland – both in the domestic and the institutional setting – is slowly making its way onto the political agenda. Raising awareness about the reality of elder abuse and the dissemination of information are important activities for members of the public and for professionals. From the early attention to the phenomenon in the United Kingdom in the early 1970s (Burston, 1975: 592), elder abuse has become an issue in many countries with much debate about definition, causation, appropriate forms of legislation, intervention and a growing research base. In Ireland, the recognition of elder abuse is taking place in the context of the 'discovery' of many other forms of abuse, both in the domestic and institutional setting. The publication by the National Council on Ageing and Older People of a report on elder abuse, with recommendations of a way forward for addressing the issue within a clear and satisfactory policy framework was a significant step in the legitimation of this social problem (O'Loughlin and Duggan, 1998). The major recommendation of this study was:

> The establishment of a Working Party at Government level to co-ordinate the development of policy in elder abuse, and to give national guidance on procedures and guidelines. (O'Loughlin and Duggan, 1998: 104)

In October 1999, the Minister of State at the Department of Health and Children, with special responsibility for older people, established the Working Group on Elder Abuse. The Group developed draft policies and procedures and these were piloted over six months in two community care areas, following a training programme for staff. Following an evaluation of the pilot projects, the Working Group submitted its report, *Protecting Our Future* (Working Group on Elder Abuse, 2002). The recommendations included:

- Development and implementation of policy on elder abuse by health boards
- Minimum staff structure in each Health Board area, including a Steering Group, Officer with responsibility for Elder Abuse and a Senior Case Worker
- Legislative reform (much of which is addressed in the Report of the Law Reform Commission (2003) as discussed earlier)
- A nationwide publicity campaign to raise awareness
- Training programmes and inclusion of elder abuse in professional curricula
- Establishment of a National Implementation Group to guide implementation of recommendations and a National Centre on Elder Abuse to promote research and education (Working Group on Elder Abuse, 2002: 17–23)

The National Implementation Group was established in December 2003. Regional Steering Groups have been established in some health boards but only one (North Eastern Health Board) have officially launched a policy on elder abuse (June 2004). The restructuring of the Health Service and the replacement of the health board structure in January 2005 will undoubtedly have an impact on the implementation of the Working Group recommendations. The Working Group on Elder Abuse notes the importance of fully implementing existing government policy and the availability of adequate resources.

Conclusion

This chapter has offered an overview of some of the social policy developments in relation to older people in Ireland. A future strategy outlined by Ruddle et al. (1997: 325) addresses the importance of the perspective of older people themselves. The language pertaining to 'the old' is an example of a categorisation used to 'bring a sense of order to an otherwise unfathomable experience' (Hazan, 1994: 1). So much knowledge about older people and the professional literature relies on professional expertise and is interested in the state of the elderly as objects. Perhaps the most demanding task for social policy development is that of deciphering the world of older people as subjects and understanding the ways in which knowledge about ageing is produced.

Table 10.1 **Chronology of leading policy developments**

1703	Act providing for the erection of a 'House of Industry' in Dublin
1773	Dublin House of Industry set up
1815	Richmond Lunatic Asylum officially opened
1838	Act 'for the more effectual relief of the Destitute Poor in Ireland'
1847	'Outdoor relief' authorised
1862	Poor Relief (Ireland) Act (qualified nursing in workhouses)
1896	Irish Workhouse Association formed
1903, 1909	Commission on Poor Law Reform
1908	Old Age Pension Act (non-contributory old age pension)
1927	Commission of Poor Relief (development of County Homes for Aged)
1953	Health Act (grants to voluntary bodies)
1961	Contributory Old Age Pension
1965	Inter-Departmental Committee on Care of the Aged appointed
1968	Report of Inter-Departmental Committee Care of the Aged
	Prescribed Relatives' Allowance
1970	Health Act (community care structures)
	Retirement Pension
1975	Supplementary Welfare Allowance Scheme (remnants of Poor Law abolished)
1977	Pension age reduced to 66 years
1981	National Council for the Aged appointed
1986	Appointment of Working Party on Services for the Elderly
1988	Report of Working Party on Services for the Elderly, *The Years Ahead – A Policy for the Elderly*
1990	Carer's Allowance introduced
	Health (Nursing Homes) Act passed
	National Council for the Elderly established
1992	Green Paper on Mental Health

1993	Health (Nursing Homes) Act implemented
1994	*Shaping a Healthier Future: A Strategy for Effective Healthcare in the 1990s*
1995	White Paper – A New Mental Health Act
1996	Domestic Violence Act
1997	National Council on Ageing and Older People appointed
	Report of the Task Force on Violence Against Women
	Review of the implementation of *The Years Ahead*
1998	Publication of report of the National Council on Ageing and Older People: *Abuse, Neglect and Mistreatment of Older People: An Exploratory Study*
	Employment Equality Act
1999	Equality Authority established
	Establishment of the Working Group on Elder Abuse
2000	Equal Status Act
	Human Rights Commission Act
2001	Health Strategy, *Quality and Fairness: A Health System for You*
	Mental Health Act signed into law
	Report of an investigation by the Ombudsman of complaints regarding payment of nursing home subventions by health boards
	Health (Miscellaneous Provisions) Act 2001 enacted abolishing medical card means test for the over 70s
2002	Report of the Working Group on Elder Abuse, Protecting Our Future.
	Implementation of Part 3 of the Mental Health Act 2001– establishment of the Mental Health Commission
	Report of Department of Health and Children: Review of the Nursing Home Subvention Scheme
	Report of the Department of Social and Family Affairs: Study to Examine the Future Financing of Long-Term Care in Ireland
2003	Report of the Law Reform Commission, Law and the Elderly
	Report of the Human Rights Commission, Older People in Long Stay Care
	National Implementation Group for Elder Abuse Policy established
2004	Health (Amendment) Bill No. 2 referred to Supreme Court

Recommended reading

Bytheway, B. (1995) *Ageism*. Buckingham: Open University Press.

Estes, C. L., S. Biggs and C. Phillipson (2003) *Social Theory, Social Policy and Ageing: A Critical Introduction* (Milton Keynes: Open University Press).

Inter-Departmental Committee on the Care of the Aged (1968) *Report*. Dublin: Stationery Office.

Law Reform Commission (2003) *Law and the Elderly*. Dublin: Law Reform Commission.

Office of the Ombudsman (2001) *Nursing Home Subventions*. Dublin: Stationery Office.

Ruddle, H., F. Donoghue and R. Mulvihill (1997) *The Years Ahead Report: A Review of the Implementation of Its Recommendations*. Dublin: National Council on Ageing and Older People.

Working Group on Elder Abuse (2002) *Protecting Our Future*. Dublin: Stationery Office.
Working Party on Services for the Elderly (1988) *The Years Ahead: A Policy for the Elderly*.
    Dublin: Stationery Office.
Publications of the National Council on Ageing and Older People.

Chapter 11

Travellers and social policy

Niall Crowley

Introduction

In 1960, the then Parliamentary Secretary to the Minister for Justice, Charles Haughey, addressed the inaugural meeting of the Commission on Itinerancy. Referring to their terms of reference, he said that they 'acknowledge the fact that there can be no final solution to the problems created by itinerants until they are absorbed into the general community' (Commission on Itinerancy, 1963: 111). In 1991, Charles Haughey, now Taoiseach, stated in his address to the Fianna Fáil Ard Fheis that

> Local authorities throughout the country will be called upon to take special urgent action in this anniversary year to meet the needs of all Travellers within their area. And we should respect the culture of our Travelling community and develop a better public understanding of their time-honoured way of life.

The contrast between the two statements illustrates the distance travelled by policy and policy makers in seeking to address the situation of Travellers. However, social policy in relation to Travellers is still very much an unfinished and contested business. The two quotations above also illustrate the importance of a broad focus in relation to social policy that encompasses the thinking which informs policy, policy making and policy implementation. That 'urgent action' was still considered necessary 28 years after the Commission Report of 1963 raises questions as to the quality of thinking informing policy and to the ability of public sector systems to implement new policy.

The National Economic and Social Forum (NESF) in their review of social partnership, *A Framework for Partnership* (NESF, 1997c), addressed the need for this broad focus in highlighting the frustration of the social partners in translating agreed policy into real change. A need to focus on the concept of 'policy design' was suggested, which was defined as the 'fusion of policy making, implementation and monitoring' (NESF, 1997c: 47). Reform of the public sector system through the Strategic Management Initiative was recommended, and also a more active engagement by the social partners with policy implementation and monitoring if the challenges of 'policy design' were to be met.

This chapter explores how social policy is addressing the situation of Travellers in Ireland. It sets out current policy and the influences that have contributed to it and concludes by discussing policy implementation and monitoring.

The Travellers

Travellers are a minority ethnic group with a nomadic tradition. They identify themselves as a distinct community and are seen by others as such. They share common cultural characteristics, traditions and values which are evident in their organisation of family, social and economic life. Nomadism, in a range of forms, has been central to the development and expression of these characteristics, traditions and values. Travellers have a long shared history which, though undocumented, can be traced back before the twelfth century through mention of Travellers in the law and through analysis of their language, the Cant. They have a distinct oral tradition and largely marry within their own community. These elements have all been identified as defining an ethnic group. Ethnicity focuses on the importance of identity and cultural difference. It is defined as 'a symbolic meaning system, a way of a "people" to organise social reality in terms of their cultural similarities and differences' (Tovey, 1989: 8).

Traveller ethnicity has been contested by the majority settled community. It has been a focus for struggle by Travellers and Traveller organisations. Travellers have been defined as deviants or misfits. This definition perceives Travellers as failed settled people in need of rehabilitation and assimilation. It denies Travellers their history, their language and their cultural contribution. Travellers have been defined as a subculture of poverty. This definition perceives Travellers' economic circumstances as defining their identity and culture. Welfare, education and anti-poverty strategies would therefore aim to remove their differences and secure their reintegration. However, this definition incorrectly suggests that Travellers are economically homogeneous and ignores the fact that the wealthiest Travellers tend to be the more nomadic.

The contest over Traveller ethnicity highlights their minority status in relation to a dominant settled community. Tovey (1989) has described these power relations:

> Dominant ethnicity contrasts sharply with subordinate ethnicity. The one enjoys both political and economic power, as well as cultural presumption, while the

other, in extreme cases, may be so marginal as to be at the centre of nothing in the larger system but its own ethnic world. (Tovey, 1989: 8)

This process and relationship pose the Traveller situation in terms of racism. Racism involves discrimination against groups on the basis of physical or cultural difference. It occurs at both the level of the individual and of a society's institutions. Racism at the individual level tends to be more overt, often involving verbal and physical abuse. However, it is racism at the level of the institution which creates the conditions for individual-level racism and which perpetuates this from one generation to another. At this institutional level, racism can be invisible and is all too often ignored. Yet it is at this level that the outcomes of inequitable power relations are at their most damaging. Racism at the institutional level is most visible in the outcomes of policy and provision for minority ethnic groups, where these outcomes are significantly worse than those for the dominant group. Institutional racism rarely involves intent. Institutions where people pursue routine practices, often with the best of intentions, produce these outcomes. Specific account is not taken of the particular needs and aspirations of minority ethnic groups.

It should be noted that accurate up-to-date data on Travellers are not available. Data gathering systems do not include a focus on Travellers. However, the data available indicate significant disadvantage experienced by the Traveller community in comparison with the settled community. The outcomes do evidence institutional racism as a core issue. The 2002 count of Traveller families, for example, provides such evidence. It identified 939 families as living on the side of the road without basic facilities and subject to the constant threat of eviction. This figure is out of a total of 5,461 families identified in the count.

In this brief description of Travellers, it is important to acknowledge the specific experience of Traveller women and Travellers with a disability. While Traveller women experience discrimination as Travellers together with the rest of their community, they also experience discrimination as women within the Traveller community and the wider society. While there has been significant work done by Traveller organisations with Traveller women, there remains a lack of information about the specificity of Traveller women's experience of racism. Travellers with a disability also live out of a twofold identity. They have been a particularly invisible subgroup within the Traveller community. In care, Travellers with a disability have been isolated from their community and their Traveller identity has not been recognised and resourced. Within their own community, services specific to Travellers have not addressed the need to be accessible to Travellers with a disability. A recent study by the Equality Authority has explored the particular situation, experience and identity of minority ethnic people with disabilities (Pierce, 2003a) and is an important initiative in seeking to contribute to a situation where the multiple identities held by people are acknowledged, valued and accommodated.

Policy thinking

The ideas and analysis that have informed policy making are neatly encapsulated in the three major reports on Travellers:

- Report of the Commission on Itinerancy (1963)
- Report of the Travelling People Review Body (1983)
- Report of the Task Force on the Travelling Community (1995)

The Commission on Itinerancy (1963)

The policy thinking encapsulated in the Report of the Commission on Itinerancy (Commission on Itinerancy, 1963) was set out in the central objective identified by the Commission:

> While it is appreciated that difficulties and objections will be met in the early years from many members of the settled population, it is not considered that there is any alternative to a positive drive for housing itinerants if a permanent solution of the problem of itinerancy, based on absorption and integration is to be achieved. (1963: 62)

Housing and education were seen as the key to addressing the problem, which was defined as itinerancy or nomadism:

> The immediate objective should be to provide dwellings as soon as possible for all itinerant families who desire to settle. Eventually, the example given by those who successfully settle should encourage the remainder to leave the road. (1963: 61)

The Commission stated the purpose of education:

> It is urgently necessary, both as a means of providing opportunities for a better way of life and of promoting their absorption into the settled community, to make such arrangements which, in the light of the following paragraphs (14–21), may be practicable to ensure that as many itinerant children as possible may from now on receive an adequate elementary education. (1963: 67)

The objectives and strategies for policy that flowed from this thinking focused on rehabilitation and assimilation. What was defined as Travellers' failure to live according to the norms of the dominant groups was to be corrected.

Report of the Travelling People Review Body (1983)

The Review Body (Travelling People Review Body, 1983), although flawed, was a major advance on the policy thinking in the Report of the Commission on Itinerancy (1963). The significant evolution of this thinking over 20 years can be seen by comparing the policy thinking in the two reports.

The Review Body put forward a valuable definition of Travellers:

> They are an identifiable group of people, identified both by themselves and by other members of the community (referred to for convenience as the 'settled community') as people with their own distinctive lifestyle, traditionally of a nomadic nature but not now habitual wanderers. They have needs, wants and values which are different in some ways from those of the settled community. (1983: 6)

This would suggest an ethnic status for Travellers. However, the Review Body failed to develop this, partly because they saw cultural difference as a focus for individual choice rather than collective rights. It suggested that 'as far as Travellers are concerned the extent to which they will integrate with the settled community will depend on individual decisions by them and not on decisions by Travellers as a whole or of any grouping of them' (1983: 6).

The Review Body also limited their focus on culture as being about what people do. This approach is evident in the recommendation that 'the traditional self-employed occupations of Travellers should be encouraged. Even though many of the skills involved belong to another era, consideration should be given to the adaptation of such skills for use in modern light industrial employment' (1983: 82). By focusing on the tangible – the economic activity – the Review Body missed the point of how that activity is organised. While the skills used might have suggested a future in modern light industry, the manner in which they were deployed does not. Despite significant investment, few Travellers are found employed in 'modern light industrial employment'.

The thinking of the Review Body encompassed a range of perspectives. The dominant view, however, was one of a community in need of reintegration whose difference was a product of disadvantage and poverty. This was neatly suggested in the recommendation: 'Newly wed couples who have to occupy caravans following their marriage should be considered extra sympathetically for housing to lessen the risks of regression to a Travelling way of life' (1983: 45). The objectives and strategies suggested were focused on integration, with policy designed to support Travellers adapting to the settled 'norm' and provision included for targeting Travellers for this purpose. No particular provision was identified as necessary to resource nomadism.

Task Force on the Travelling Community (1995)

The Report of the Task Force on the Travelling Community (Task Force, 1995) established current policy thinking in its chapter on culture which was central to the whole report. It recommended that the distinct culture and identity of Travellers should be taken into account. It defined culture in the following terms:

> Everybody has a culture. It is the package of customs, traditions, symbols, values, phrases and other forms of communication by which we can belong to a community. The belonging is in understanding the meanings of these culture forms and in sharing values and identity. Culture is the way we learn to think, behave and do things (Task Force, 1995: 71).

This definition is valuable in its acknowledgement of culture as both tangible and intangible. The understanding of culture is often limited to doing or making or behaving in a particular way. However, at its most profound, culture is about thinking, about how the world is seen and understood, about values and about what is defined as important. The Report of the Task Force applied its own recommendation and understanding to the fields of discrimination, accommodation, health, education and training, and the Traveller economy.

This thinking has been further consolidated. The National Economic and Social Forum, in their report *Equality Proofing Issues* (NESF, 1996c), recommended that 'the proposed Equal Status Legislation will provide a unique opportunity to validate and accept the ethnic identity of the Travellers'. The Irish National Coordinating Committee for the European Year against Racism (1997), set up by the then Department of Equality and Law Reform to develop a programme of action, found that 'one of the more visible forms of racism is that experienced by the Traveller community, based on their distinct culture and identity which is rooted in a tradition of nomadism' (1997: 5). It has been a considerable achievement for a small minority to overcome the challenge to its ethnic status made by the dominant group. It provides a new basis for policy making with significant potential to change the situation of Travellers. The policy focus that flows from this is one of mainstreaming. 'Mainstreaming' involves a dual strategy of making special provision, targeting the distinct needs and aspirations specific to Travellers as well as adapting standard provision to ensure that it is accessible and relevant to Travellers. Nomadism becomes a central concern within policy.

While policy making is currently informed by the Task Force Report (Task Force on the Travelling Community, 1995), evidence would suggest that policy implementation continues to be informed by the thinking encapsulated by the Travelling People Review Body Report (1983), and even by the Report of the Commission on Itinerancy (Commission on Itinerancy, 1963).

Policy making

A wide range of national-level policy making in relation to Travellers now seeks to advance the recommendations of the Task Force on the Travelling Community (1995). New policy reflects the new thinking encapsulated in the *Task Force Report*. This is a 'mainstreaming approach' to policy making which should involve:

- Naming Travellers within mainstream legislation and policy documentation.
- Developing Traveller-specific approaches within policy where these are required by distinct aspirations, values and cultural characteristics or by the need to address a history of discrimination.
- Changing policy delivery systems to secure an equality of outcomes for Travellers.
- Setting targets and timescales to address a backlog of inequitable outcomes for Travellers.

Accommodation

The Dáil has enacted the Housing (Traveller Accommodation) Act 1998, which was published by the Department of the Environment and Local Government. This is the first piece of legislation specifically dedicated to addressing Traveller accommodation. It requires local authorities to:

- Make an assessment of the need for halting sites in their functional area.
- Prepare and adopt an accommodation programme specifying the accommodation needs of Travellers and the provision of accommodation to be made to meet those needs over a five-year period. This is a reserved function, but where councillors fail to adopt such a programme in the specified timescale, the manager is required to adopt it by order.
- Take any necessary reasonable steps to implement the programme and to report annually on progress.

The legislation puts increased pressure on local authorities to address Traveller accommodation needs – a responsibility they had failed to live up to. The legislation acknowledges Traveller nomadism, which breaks important new ground. Local accommodation programmes now have to have regard to 'the provision of sites to address the accommodation needs of Travellers other than as their normal place of residence and having regard to the annual patterns of movement by Travellers' (Housing (Traveller Accommodation) Act 1998: 10). The new Act amends the 1988 Housing Act which itself broke new ground as the first piece of legislation to specifically name Travellers. Section 13 of that Act is applied to 'persons belonging to the class of persons who traditionally pursue or have pursued a nomadic way of life'. This section enabled local authorities to 'provide, improve, manage and control' halting sites.

To date, Traveller accommodation provision has included a mix of standard houses, group housing schemes for Travellers, Traveller halting sites and temporary sites. This provision has been criticised for:

- Inadequate provision with nearly one fifth of families living on the side of the road without access to basic facilities
- Inappropriate provision with accommodation provided not allowing for Traveller economic activities traditionally organised about a home and family basis
- Absence of provision for Travellers transient through or within a local authority area
- Conditions on overcrowded and under-serviced temporary sites over long time periods

In 2000 the First Progress Report of the Committee to Monitor and Co-ordinate the Implementation of the Recommendations of the Task Force on the Travelling Community was published. This highlighted progress in putting in place 'the administrative, legislative and financial framework for the provision of Traveller accommodation' but found that 'the accommodation situation has disimproved [*sic*] over the past five years'. This is a disturbing conclusion and raises questions about the effectiveness of the new legislation and its implementation.

Education

The Department of Education published a White Paper on education in 1995. This set important targets and timescales for Traveller participation in education. It stated that: 'The policy objective is that all Traveller children in primary school age be enrolled and participate fully in primary education, according to their individual abilities and potential within five years' (*Charting Our Education Future*, White Paper on Education (Government of Ireland, 1995b: 26)).

> The overall policy object is that, within ten years, all Traveller children of second level, school-going age will complete junior cycle education and 50 per cent will complete the senior cycle (1995b: 58).

The White Paper highlighted that progress will be made only if Traveller children 'are encouraged to enjoy a full and integrated education within the schools system' (1995b: 26), and if this participation involves 'retaining respect and value for their individual culture' (1995b: 57).

The challenge remains to develop a detailed strategy to achieve these important targets within the defined timescales.

The Education Act 1998 further develops the focus on equality in education provision. It imposes obligations on Boards of Management to publish an admissions policy and requires Boards of Management to ensure that this respects principles of equality. Boards of Managements must also prepare a school plan to state the objectives of the school regarding equality of access to and participation in the school and the measures which the school proposes to take to achieve them. A further requirement on Boards of Management is to prepare a code of behaviour setting standards to be observed by students.

The Equal Status Act 2000 which prohibits discrimination in the provision of goods and services, accommodation and education has an important contribution to make to this focus on equality in education provision. It has specific provision relating to educational establishments prohibiting discrimination in

- the admission or the terms or conditions of admission of a person as a student
- access of a student to any course, facility or benefit provided by the establishment
- any other term or condition of participation in the establishment by a student
- the expulsion of a student or any other sanction

This covers nine grounds including a specific focus on the Traveller community. Policy within the Department of Education and Science has witnessed a valuable shift towards inter-cultural education, which has been described by the Irish Traveller Movement as involving 'an education that promotes inter-action and understanding among and between different cultures and ethnic groups on the assumption that ethnic diversity can enrich society' (Irish Traveller Movement, 1993: 19). The Report of the Task Force on the Travelling Community proposed a number of principles to be reflected in an inter-cultural curriculum: the experiences of minority groups such as Travellers should be presented accurately and sensitively; texts should be monitored to avoid ethnocentric and racist interpretations; information about Travellers and other minority groups should be integrated into the total curriculum; and a focus should be introduced on broader equality and human rights issues, including anti-racism, rather than on exotic customs and practices of Travellers. The Report also considered that a study of minority and majority ethnic groups was needed to help students acquire the knowledge, values and skills to contribute to social change in a multi-cultural context. Current Traveller-specific education provision includes:

- 52 Traveller pre-schools with an estimated enrolment of 537 children (in 2000)
- Three special schools catering for Traveller children at primary level
- 443 Resource Teachers for Travellers serving 404 primary schools (in 2000)
- Junior Training Centres catering for about 120 children in the 12 to 15 age group
- A Visiting Teacher Service (established in 1980) to identify the educational needs of Traveller children in their region, assist in planning and establishment of education provision and ensure optimal use of existing educational facilities by Travellers. Visiting teachers provide an important liaison between schools and Traveller families. In 2000 there were 40 visiting Teachers and a National Education Officer for Travellers.
- 26 Senior Traveller Training Centres which cater for about 600 Traveller trainees over the age of 15.

Current provision has been criticised for several reasons. High levels of early school leaving and underachievement among Travellers have not been prevented. An inter-cultural curriculum to affirm the Traveller identity and to challenge racism is lacking. The absence of guidelines and support hinders a common quality standard across pre-school provision. Access to education remains a major problem for many Traveller children, owing to discrimination or a failure to facilitate constantly nomadic families. A support infrastructure to sustain Travellers in second-level education remains limited. Junior Training Centres should be phased out as the Task Force recommended. There is a danger that Senior Traveller Training Centres serve as an alternative system drawing Travellers out of the mainstream second-level provision. School planning with an equality focus has been slow to emerge.

Health
In April 1994, the Department of Health published a national health strategy, which established equity as one of three underlying principles: 'the pursuit of equity must extend beyond the question of access to treatment and care, and must examine variations in the health status of different groups in society and how these might be addressed' (Department of Health, 1994: 10). This was of a particular relevance to Travellers. The National Health Strategy focused on Traveller health and promised to publish a policy on Travellers' health on the basis of the Task Force recommendations. It highlighted the importance of targeted health education programmes and models of Traveller participation in health promotion, the need for special arrangements to encourage and permit Traveller access to primary healthcare services, and proposed simplifying services under the GMS (General Medical Services) scheme.

The Report of the Task Force on the Travelling Community (Task Force, 1995) focused on strategies to enhance Traveller access to the health system and to improve channels of communication between Travellers and service providers. The Task Force highlighted the need for change in:

- The gathering of data on Traveller take-up of health services and improved systems to transfer medical records within and between health board regions.
- Developing systems of personal communication between Traveller patients and the health service.
- Developing a range of Traveller-specific services which should be designed to complement mainstream services and to improve Traveller access to them.
- Simplifying the renewal of medical cards and extending their validity.
- Providing health education to Travellers.
- Providing training to all health professionals on the circumstances and culture of Travellers, and the discrimination practised against them.

A Plan for Women's Health (Department of Health, 1997a) lists Traveller women among those particularly disadvantaged in relation to health care. It pointed to the significant difference in life expectancy between Traveller women and women from the settled community.

Traveller Health: A National Strategy 2002–2005 was published, with the assistance of a Traveller Health Advisory Committee, by the Department of Health and Children (2002a). This establishes equity in health service provision as a core value and sets out underlying principles that include a commitment to:

- take account of the particular needs, culture and way of life of Travellers
- equality of outcomes for Travellers
- a dual strategy of mainstreaming and targeting Travellers
- Traveller participation
- data gathering
- Traveller proofing
- training health providers on Traveller culture and on racism

It makes a range of specific commitments in relation to health promotion, primary health care, general practioner services, public health nurses, dental services, other community services and general hospital services.

Traveller health status data have provided graphic evidence of the exclusion and institutional racism experienced by Travellers. The last major study was published in 1989, *The Travellers Health Status Study* (Barry et al.,

1989). This found that the 'infant mortality rate for Travellers in 1987 was 18.1 per 100 live births compared to the national figure of 7.4' (1989: 14). It also found that 'male Travellers have over twice the risk of dying in a given year than settled males, whereas for female Travellers the risk is increased more than threefold' (Barry et al., 1989: 15). Work is currently under way on a new national study on Traveller health status. This will provide important evidence as to whether progress has been made as a result of new policy.

Economic development

The naming of Travellers in economic development policy is both recent and rare, but it is central to the achievement of equality for Travellers. Social policy objectives and strategies need to be integrated with economic policy objectives and strategies, if the Traveller community is to secure its future as an ethnic group in Irish society with a capacity for self-determination. *Partnership 2000* contained an important commitment:

> Action will be taken to endorse labour force participation by the Traveller com-
> munity and the viability of the Traveller economy on foot of the recommendations
> of the Task Force and in the context of the National Anti-Poverty Strategy
> (Government of Ireland, 1996d: 35).

Action has been limited particularly with regard to stimulating and supporting the Traveller economy.

The Report of the Task Force on the Travelling Community set out a two-pronged strategy:

- To support the Traveller economy: this refers to those economic activities engaged in by Travellers and organised in a manner traditional to that community. The Task Force explored recycling, trading and horse dealing as key activities pursued within the Traveller economy and identified obstacles to be removed and supports to be provided so that the activity, and the manner in which it is organised, could be sustained and used as a foundation for further development.
- To support Traveller access to the mainstream labour market: two strategies of potential are identified. The first is through providing support to Travellers and Traveller organisations in setting up Traveller enter-
prises, particularly within the social economy. The second is through positive-action measures to secure employment, particularly within the public sector, for Travellers in providing services to their own community.

Three important policy developments have been the identification of special access criteria for Travellers to community employment, the naming of

Travellers as a target group in local development strategies and an initiative to support Traveller recruitment into the civil service. Community employment is an important labour market scheme. Traveller take-up had been poor but has improved since criteria for access to it were relaxed for Travellers. Local development strategies target funds at designated areas of disadvantage through area-based partnerships. The funds support locally defined area-based action plans of integrated socio-economic development. Pavee Point, a national Traveller organisation, is funded as a positive action flanking measure to support and advocate appropriate inclusion of Travellers in these local plans. The civil service and Local Appointments Commission are working with Traveller organisations and the Department of Finance in developing an initiative to support the recruitment of Travellers into the civil service.

Discrimination

Anti discrimination legislation has been introduced that makes specific mention of the Traveller community. The Employment Equality Act 1998 prohibits discrimination in the workplace. The Equal Status Act 2000 prohibits discrimination in the provision of goods and services, accommodation and education and makes specific provision in relation to registered clubs. Both Acts cover the nine grounds of gender, marital status, family status, age, sexual orientation, disability, race, religion and membership of the Traveller community, prohibit sexual harassment and harassment and allow positive action on grounds including Traveller community ground. The legislation established the Equality Authority with a mandate to combat discrimination and to promote equality of opportunity in the areas covered by the legislation and the ODEI – Equality Tribunal to investigate and hear cases under the legislation.

The Equality Authority case files show a significant take up by Travellers of the potential in this legislation. In 2002 Travellers accounted for 54 per cent of all case files under the Equal Status Act. These case files included complaints of persistent and widespread discrimination by public houses and complaints of discrimination in seeking access to schools, shops, accommodation and insurance. In the same year Travellers accounted for two per cent of all case files under the Employment Equality Act. This figure reflects the low participation by Travellers in the mainstream labour market. These case files included complaints in relation to discrimination in access to employment and in dismissal from employment once the person's Traveller identity was uncovered.

In earlier legislation, Travellers had been named in the 1993 Unfair Dismissals Act and the 1989 Prohibition of Incitement to Hatred Act. This 1989 Act has been found to be ineffective, owing to the difficulty of proving that actual hatred was incited. The commitment to equality legislation also found expression in the 'Agreement reached in the Multi-Party Negotiations' on the future of Northern Ireland. The Agreement introduced a new focus on human rights that have a particular relevance to Travellers, with commitments to establish a Human Rights Commission and to ratify the Council of Europe Framework Convention on National Minorities. Both these commitments have been realised.

Previous legislation

The naming of Travellers as a specific concern for social policy is a relatively recent and still emerging phenomenon. Formerly, legislation and policy were undifferentiated and were assumed to cover all citizens equally, which often resulted in unintended consequences for Travellers. At the same time, undifferentiated legislation and policies have failed to have an impact on Travellers even where it appeared that it would have the potential to do so.

A body of legislation emerged prior to the 1990s that served as a basis for Traveller evictions and for action to block the construction of Traveller-specific accommodation. This included the:

- Local Government (Sanitary Services) Act 1948 which gave powers to local authorities to regulate and control land used for camping and temporary dwellings and to use prohibition orders to this end.
- Road Safety Act 1961 which regulated the distance from the roadside that a tent or caravan might be placed.
- Third section of the Local Government (Planning and Development) Act 1963 which sets out certain categories of objectives to be catered for in the development plan. None of these categories relate specifically to the Traveller community. Planning legislation has been used by residents' associations to legally challenge the construction of Travellers' accommodation.

Policy implementation and monitoring

Participation

The participation of Travellers and Traveller organisations has emerged as a key element of policy making, implementation and monitoring. The following important developments can be identified:

- The three national Traveller organisations (Irish Traveller Movement, National Traveller Women's Forum, and Pavee Point) are represented on the National Traveller Consultative Committee set up to advise the Minister for the Environment and Local Government in relation to any general matter concerning accommodation for Travellers. This committee was given a legislative basis in the Housing (Travellers Accommodation) Act 1998.

- The same representation participates in the Travellers' Health Advisory Committee which is advising the Minister for Health and Children on Traveller health policy.
- The Department of Education convenes a liaison committee for Traveller organisations and an internal committee established to develop the national policy framework for Traveller education.
- Local authorities have set up Traveller Accommodation Consultative Committees, with Traveller organisations, councillors and officials as members, to advise on the preparation of local accommodation programmes.
- Health boards have set up Traveller health units with representation from Traveller organisations to provide a regional focus on Traveller health status and service provision to Travellers.
- Travellers are among the interests represented on the Equality Authority created under equality legislation to combat discrimination and to promote equality of opportunity.

These developments enhance the potential fusion of policy thinking, policy making and policy implementation and increase the possibility of national policy being transformed into local action. However, one area of concern that has been identified is the advisory and consultative nature of these bodies. The resistance at local level to securing change in the situation of Travellers has proved durable and effective. It is this resistance that the new structures have to overcome and their status and powers need to be adequate to this challenge.

Strategic Management Initiative
Policy implementation could be significantly influenced by the Strategic Management Initiative. This initiative is focused on modernising the public sector. It aims to deliver better government through improved service delivery, better quality regulation and more effective management of major national issues, and to give improved performance and a clear focus on achieving objectives.

Six working groups were established to progress key areas of the Strategic Management Initiative. The Irish National Coordinating Committee for the European Year against Racism identified quality service and human resources as being of particular relevance: 'quality of service requires an anti-racist dimension. Such a dimension in turn, requires appropriate human resource management strategies' (Irish National Coordinating Committee for the European Year against Racism, 1997: 6).

In July 2000 the government revised the quality customer service principles for the civil service. The revised principles include a focus on equality/diversity in committing civil service departments and public service offices to

Ensure the rights to equal treatment established by equality legislation and accommodate diversity, so as to contribute to equality for the groups covered by equality legislation (under the grounds of gender, marital status, family status, age, disability, race, religious belief and membership of the Traveller community). (Department of the Taoiseach 2001b:1)

A 'Support Pack on the Equality Diversity Aspects of Quality Customer Service for Civil and Public Service' was published by the Quality Customer Service working group of the Strategic Management Initiative in partnership with the Equality Authority. This highlights an accessibility checklist, the need for equal status policies and strategies for accommodating diversity.

Overall, the equality dimension to the Strategic Management Initiative could be further enhanced. This was emphasised when the National Economic and Social Forum found it necessary to recommend that 'equality should be an explicit principle underlying the Strategic Management Initiative as a whole' (NESF, 1997c: 29).

National Anti-Poverty Strategy

Another key policy initiative with the potential to impact on policy implementation is the National Anti-Poverty Strategy (NAPS) which was launched in 1997. It has been described as 'a major cross-departmental policy initiative by the government designed to place the needs of the poor and the socially excluded among the issues at the top of the national agenda in terms of government policy development and action' (Government of Ireland, 1997: 2). The Strategy requires government departments, state agencies, local and regional bodies to address the question of poverty in their statements of strategy under the Strategic Management Initiative. They are also required to report annually on progress.

Five theme areas were identified to be progressed under the NAPS – educational disadvantage, unemployment (particularly long-term unemployment), income adequacy, disadvantaged urban areas and rural poverty. Travellers were identified as a target group for the NAPS and received specific mention in relation to educational disadvantage, where the commitments of the education White Paper were reiterated, and in relation to unemployment where there was a commitment to address the 'double discrimination' experienced by Travellers in accessing employment (NAPS, 1997: 12).

The NAPS also identified a number of over-arching principles which have relevance to Traveller inclusion. They include 'ensuring equal access and encouraging participation for all', and 'guaranteeing the rights of minorities especially through anti-discrimination measures' (NAPS, 1997: 7).

The National Anti Poverty Strategy was reviewed in consultation with the social partners as a result of a commitment in the Programme for Prosperity and Fairness. The revised strategy was published in February 2002, *Building an Inclusive Society* (Government of Ireland, 2002a). This focused on the thematic areas of consistent poverty, income adequacy, employment and unemployment, education, health, and housing and accommodation. It maintained a targeting of Travellers with a focus on the gap in life expectancy between the Traveller community and the whole population, the transfer rate of Travellers to post-primary schools, age appropriate placement of Travellers in primary schools, participation of Travellers in third-level education and Traveller accommodation. Targets and timescales are set for each of these areas.

The National Anti Poverty Strategy was also a focus for the most recent national agreement – *Sustaining Progress* (Government of Ireland, 2003a) where the focus was on ensuring real and significant progress in relation to implementation. This process has also been further developed through the European Union 'open method of co-ordination' in seeking to make a decisive impact on the eradication of poverty and social exclusion. Member states are required to draw up National Action Plans against Poverty and Social Exclusion every two years. These should set out the strategies, specific measures and institutional arrangements to progress the objective of eliminating poverty and social exclusion. They are prepared to agreed objectives and to a common outline.

The Irish government submitted its first plan in 2001 and its second and current plan in 2003. The current plan reflects *Building an Inclusive Society*. It introduces a valuable understanding in stating:

> Equality is a key goal which must underpin activity in all policy areas to ensure a fair and inclusive society with equal opportunity. Anti Poverty Strategies need, therefore, to be able to accommodate the diversity of people living in poverty in terms of identity, situation and experience across the nine grounds of the equality legislation. Policy responses will aim to address the poverty/inequality link by emphasising non-discrimination, equality and the accommodation of diversity (Government of Ireland, 2003a:22).

Key targets are established in relation to Travellers including reducing the gap in life expectancy between Travellers and whole population by 10 per cent by 2007, increasing the transfer rate of Travellers to post primary schools to 95 per cent by 2004, and appropriately accommodating all Traveller families identified in the local authority five-year Traveller Accommodation Plan by the end of 2004.

The National Anti-Poverty Strategy has also created a valuable foundation for poverty proofing. The 1997 strategy stated that:

> The question of the impact of poverty will also be a key consideration when decisions are being made about spending priorities in the context of the national

budgetary process and the allocation of EU Structural Funds (Government of Ireland, 1997: 21).

Poverty proofing is about testing out policies and programmes at design stage for their potential impact on poverty. Guidelines were developed to assist government departments, state agencies and local authorities to assess the impact on poverty of substantive policy initiatives. These included an important focus on inequalities likely to lead to poverty which specifically identified Travellers in this regard.

These guidelines provide a valuable foundation for the development of approaches to poverty and equality proofing. These have been assisted by commitments to equality proofing in the three most recent national agreements – *Partnership 2000*, *Programme for Prosperity and Fairness*, and *Sustaining Progress*. A working group of the social partners was established on this issue and continues to develop a long term vision of an integrated approach to poverty and equality proofing that would cover poverty and the nine grounds identified in the equality legislation and that would have a legal basis in the form of a statutory duty on the public sector to have due regard to poverty and equality in carrying out its functions. This work has been assisted by the NESC which carried out a review of poverty proofing, the gender equality unit of the Department of Justice, Equality and Law Reform responsible for supporting gender mainstreaming in the National Development Plan and the work of the Equality Authority on nine ground approaches to equality proofing and equality impact assessments. Poverty and equality proofing, where it is effective and properly resourced, has a key contribution to make to the institutional change central to the mainstreaming approach for Traveller inclusion.

Monitoring
The Department of Justice, Equality and Law Reform has established a committee to monitor the implementation of the recommendations of the Task Force on the Travelling Community, made up of government departments, Travellers and Traveller organisations and representatives of the social partners. Previous experience of monitoring committees would suggest that they have little to offer in terms of promoting and supporting progress. A monitoring committee established after the Report of the Review Body (Travelling People Review Body, 1983) was widely criticised for its powerlessness in influencing government policy and provision and for being reduced to presenting annual lists of actions taken by government departments, with little analysis or critique.

The monitoring committee for the Task Force on the Travelling Community produced its first report in 2000. This highlighted the steps taken to implement the recommendations of the Task Force. A second report is now in preparation.

Monitoring should be a key element in a process of policy design, providing space for review and reflection that would serve where necessary to reformulate policy and provision. The National Economic and Social Forum sought the realisation of this potential in recommending that:

> A more active role for the monitoring committees be encouraged. This would mean going beyond monitoring to evaluating the implementation process and identifying inaction and constraints as well as good practice. It would also involve the committees in taking a more proactive role in addressing issues relating to inaction and constraints as well as identifying new priorities for action. (NESF, 1997c: 34)

Such a role requires adequate terms of reference for, provision of resources to, and attribution of status to the monitoring committee. It remains to be seen if this challenge will be met in a manner that will allow monitoring to make its full contribution to the policy design process.

Backlash and implementation

Two new issues are emerging centre stage in relation to social policy development and Travellers: backlash and implementation. As they emerge they demand new reflection and new creativity in policy making, and they shape a very different environment within which to seek change in the situation and experience of Travellers.

Backlash is evident in an apparent growing public hostility to Travellers. It can be seen in constant, negative media reports. A perception can be created that the Travellers have cornered the market on state resources, which can feed the backlash.

Backlash is evident at a policy level in responses to illegal parking of Traveller families and to the huge take up by Travellers of provisions in the Equal Status Act prohibiting discrimination in access to services in licensed premises. The Housing (Miscellaneous Provisions) Act 2002 makes it a criminal offence to trespass on and occupy public or private property. The punishment involves immediate eviction, a month in prison and/or €3,000 fine, and the confiscation of property. When the legislation came into operation it was emphasised that it was to be used for large-scale illegal encampments, yet its implementation has not been confined in that way. The Intoxicating Liquor Act 2003 transferred jurisdiction for discrimination claims against licensed premises under the Equal Status Act from the ODEI – Equality Tribunal to the District Court. The Equality Authority has highlighted the advantages of a tribunal setting for discrimination claims from the point of view of accessibility given its investigative role, its ability to offer mediation as an alternative dispute resolution, the simpler procedures and less formal atmosphere, the particular expertise of specialised tribunals, and the fact that it is a low cost venue. New barriers could thus emerge for Travellers seeking redress for discrimination on licensed premises.

The difficulty of implementation occurs when the design cycle of policy thinking, policy making and policy implementation is broken at the point of implementation. The past decade has seen widespread and innovative policy thinking and policy making in relation to Travellers. This is not reflected in the level of change experienced by Travellers in their situation and experiences. Barriers have not yet been overcome at policy implementation stage. Emphasis now needs to be given to the identification and elimination of such barriers. Practice needs to be a key focus for work and attention alongside policy.

Policy influencing
Traveller organisations
Traveller organisations have played a key role in creating conditions for, establishing the need for, and informing the content of new policy making. The Task Force on the Travelling Community usefully established three identifying features of Traveller organisations: they are non-governmental; they involve effective Traveller participation; they are in solidarity with Traveller interests. The Task Force also highlighted the growth in number and the changing nature and role of Traveller organisations over the previous decade. It described a shift in focus 'from a welfare approach inspired by charity to a more rights-based approach', an increase in Traveller participation, a redefinition 'of the Traveller situation in terms of cultural rights, as opposed to simply being a poverty issue', and

> the emergence of a range of more conflictual relationships with statutory bodies is evident. These relationships were preceded by earlier consensus around a welfare agenda. The present thrust is now towards a new partnership based on a common understanding of the cultural rights of Travellers and of the urgent need to respond to the situation of Travellers (Task Force, 1995: 63).

The strategies pursued by Traveller organisations evolved over the decade. A number of central elements can be identified:

* Securing national and European funding to develop new responses in education, training, capacity building, youth and community work, health and economic development to the situation of Travellers.
* Linking analysis and policy development to this local action to create a body of knowledge and a political agenda to inform change.

- Generating a new and extensive media coverage of Travellers focusing on issues of ethnicity and racism over those of poverty and deprivation.
- Targeting Travellers and settled people within their work programmes.
- Extensive networking between Traveller organisations, particularly within the Irish Traveller Movement and the National Traveller Women's Forum, and between Traveller organisations and the wider community sector.
- Engaging in negotiations within the statutory sector on the basis of partnership.

Social Partnership Arenas

This period of change has coincided with the achievement of social partnership status by the community sector. This was realised in the Partnership 2000 national agreement 1996, where the sector was identified as one of the four pillars to the partnership process. Traveller groups, such as the Irish Traveller Movement and Pavee Point, made a contribution to the development of the Community Platform as a mechanism for the sector to organise its representation in the arenas of social partnership. This involvement of the sector has supported an enhanced focus within social partnership arenas for Traveller issues. This is evident in:

- *Partnership 2000 for Inclusion, Employment and Competitiveness* (Government of Ireland, 1996d), which identified Travellers as a particular focus in its equality agenda. A section on Travellers made important commitments to Traveller accommodation, education, health, employment, participation and anti-discrimination measures.
- *Programme for Prosperity and Fairness* (Government of Ireland, 2000e) which made commitments in relation to a national Traveller health strategy, monitoring local authority Traveller accommodation programmes, enactment of equality legislation, the need for improved relations between the Traveller community and the settled community and monitoring implementation of the Task Force Report.
- *Sustaining Progress* (Government of Ireland, 2003a), a commitment to an integrated strategy to improve the participation and achievement of Travellers at every level of education; new approaches to promoting tolerance and understanding between the Traveller and settled community and a more focused approach to implementing the Task Force recommendations. Housing and accommodation is a particular focus for attention and Travellers are named as part of this focus.
- The National Economic and Social Council report *An Investment in Quality: Services, Inclusion and Enterprise* which shaped the negotiations for 'Sustaining Progress' identifies Travellers as experiencing an unacceptable incidence of social risks and levels of need, and suggests that key

determinants of progress towards equality will be the strength and reputation of the institutions charged with promotion of equality and, across a wide range of policies, the ability to recast national frameworks and institutions in the light of local innovations.
- The National Economic and Social Forum has included a Traveller dimension across the full body of its broad-ranging work. There are Traveller dimensions to equality issues, rural renewal, delivery of social services, job creation and unemployment, among other topics. The NESF has also contributed to new policy thinking in relation to equality. This is reflected in key reports on *Equality Proofing Issues* (NESF, 1996c) and *A Strategic Framework for Equality Issues* (NESF, 2002c).

A significant development in relation to the social partnership process occurred during the ratification process of *Sustaining Progress*. The Community Platform, which includes the national Traveller organisations, decided the commitments made were inadequate and chose not to ratify the agreement. This placed the national Traveller organisations outside the core social partnership arenas and created a new social partnership context in which the Traveller voice is not articulated.

The courts

Travellers and Traveller organisations have used the courts for advancing policy making and the interpretation of policy. A number of key cases can be identified:

- *McDonald* vs *Feeley and Dublin County Council* (1980). This case established that Traveller evictions by local authorities from areas deemed unsuitable required the local authority to provide reasonable alternative accommodation.
- *O'Reilly and Others vs. Limerick Corporation* (1989). This case established that if a need for halting sites was established, then the local authority had to include proposals to meet those needs in their building programme. It also established that services could be provided to Travellers on unofficial sites.
- *University of Limerick vs. Ryan, McCarthy and Limerick County Council Third Party High Court* (1991). This case established that Section 13 of the 1988 Housing Act imposed a duty on the local authority to provide halting sites for Travellers living permanently in an area.

A number of Traveller families have pursued legal challenges to the implementation of the Housing (Miscellaneous Provisions) Act 2002. High Court cases on these issues are pending.

The European Union
One early initiative of the European Union, the EC Resolution (89K/53/02) on School Provision for Travellers, has been influential in establishing a focus on inter-cultural approaches within the education system. The European Commission published *An Action Plan against Racism* (1998) which consisted of four strands:

- Introducing legislation to combat racism
- Mainstreaming a focus on racism into Community policies
- Piloting new initiatives
- Information work

The European Union also co-ordinated a European Year Against Racism in 1997. The Irish government responded to the work of the Irish National Co-ordinating Committee for the European Year against Racism by forming a longer-term National Consultative Committee on Racism and Inter-culturalism. This has representation from Traveller organisations.

The European Commission has also established a European Union Monitoring Centre on Racism and Xenophobia which is based in Vienna. 'The main remit of the Centre is to study the extent of and trends in racism, xenophobia and anti-Semitism in the European Union and to analyse under-lying causes, consequences and effects.' (European Commission, 1998: 7) A European Union Directive on discrimination on grounds of race was agreed under Article 13 of the Amsterdam treaty. This Article accords new functions to the European Union in stating:

> without prejudice to the other provisions of this Treaty and within the limits of the powers conferred by it upon the community, the Council, acting unanimously on a proposal from the Commission and after consulting the European Parliament may take appropriate action to combat discrimination based on sex, racial or ethnic origin, religion or belief, disability, age or sexual orientation.

The Race directive when transposed into Irish equality legislation (the deadline was July 2003) will further strengthen this legislation in areas such as redress, burden of proof, definitions of indirect discrimination, positive action, the definition of services, and in reducing the number of exemptions.

International agreements
A range of international agreements in the human rights field have begun to exert an influence on Irish policy making in a manner that has the potential to benefit Travellers including:

- The International Covenant on Economic, Social and Cultural Rights: the Irish government has to report on its performance in relation to these rights to the UN Human Rights Committee.
- The International Covenant on Civil and Political Rights: the Irish government reported in 1992 to the UN Human Rights Committee. The Committee's published response included a focus on the need to improve the situation for Travellers.
- International Covenant on the Elimination of All Forms of Racial Discrimination: the Irish government ratified this covenant with the introduction of equality legislation. It is currently preparing its first report to the UN on its implementation.

Conclusion

The study of Travellers and social policy indicates the present period as one of significant policy making alongside major challenges of policy implementation. Emerging policy at national level reflects new thinking in terms of its understanding and response to the Traveller community. A significant gap between policy making and policy implementation remains to be bridged before the potential of this new policy context can be realised in a definitive improvement in the experience and situation of the Traveller community.

Table 11.1 **Policy developments**

1948	Local Government (Sanitary Services) Act
1961	Road Safety Act
1963	Report of the Commission on Itinerancy
	Local Government (Planning and Development) Act
1966	Housing Act
1983	Report of the Travelling People Review Body
1988	Housing Act
1989	Prohibition of Incitement to Hatred Act
1990	Unfair Dismissals Act
1994	National Health Strategy Shaping a Healthier Future
1995	Report of the Task Force on the Travelling Community
	White Paper on Education, Charting Our Education Future
1996	Partnership 2000 for Inclusion, Employment and Competitiveness
1997	Sharing in Progress, National Anti-Poverty Strategy
1998	Employment Equality Act
	Housing (Traveller Accommodation) Bill
	Education Act

2000 Programme for Prosperity and Fairness
      Equal Status Act
      First Progress Report of the Committee to Monitor and Co-ordinate the
      Implementation of the Recommendations of the Task Force on the Travelling
          Community.
2002 Building an Inclusive Society (Government of Ireland, 2002)
      Housing (Miscellaneous Provisions) Act
      Traveller Health: A National Strategy 2002–2005 (Department of Health, 2002a)
2003 Sustaining Progress (Government of Ireland, 2003a)
      Intoxicating Liquor Act

Recommended reading

DTEDG File: Irish Travellers: New Analysis and New Initiatives (1992) Dublin: Pavee
    Point.
McCann, M., S. Ó Siocháin and J. Ruane (1994) *Irish Travellers: Culture and Ethnicity.*
    Belfast: Institute of Irish Studies, Queen's University of Belfast.
Task Force on the Travelling Community (1995) *Report.* Dublin: Stationery Office.

Chapter 12

Refugees and social policy

Joe Moran

Introduction

Until recently when Irish commentators wrote of refugees and public policy it was only in terms of legal policies concerning asylum determination and associated procedures. Even on these terms, the discourse on refugees and public policy is relatively new in this country; as only since the mid-1990s have asylum seekers in increasing numbers chosen Ireland as their preferred country of protection.

To understand the policy context and the developments that have taken place in recent years it is important to distinguish between the different broad categories of 'refugees' – asylum seeker, refugee/Convention refugee, programme refugee, and person given leave to remain. These are defined in figure 12.1. These distinctions are very important, as each category title confers a different status upon those to whom it refers in legal terms. Furthermore, the nature of the status permits or limits access to services normally discussed under social policy. Thus the social policy objectives are different for those on one side, those with refugee or subsidiary status (Convention refugee/leave to remain/ programme refugee) as against asylum seekers on the other. Throughout this chapter, when the generic term refugee is used its application includes all groups of refugees (Convention, programme, and persons with leave to remain).

Figure 12.1 **Categories of Refugee**

Asylum seeker – A person who seeks to be recognised as a refugee in accordance with the terms of the 1951 Geneva Convention Relating to the Status of Refugees.

Refugee/Convention refugee – A person who fulfils the requirements of the definition of a refugee under the 1951 Geneva Convention and is granted refugee status.

Programme refugee – A person who has been invited to Ireland as a result of a government decision in response to humanitarian requests from bodies such as the United Nations High Commissioner for Refugees (UNHCR).

Person with leave to remain – A person who has been granted permission to remain in the State at the discretion of the Minister for Justice, Equality and Law Reform. Leave to remain may, for example, be granted to a person who does not fully meet the requirements of the definition of a refugee under the 1951 Convention, but who the Minister decides should be allowed to remain in the state for humanitarian reasons.

Current policy

Within the past six years there has been an enormous shift in how the Irish state relates to asylum seekers and refugees that live within its borders and for whom it has responsibility. Six years ago Ireland's approach to refugees, asylum seekers and those with leave to remain was relatively benign, even if there were few services in place for any of these groups. One commentator noted about Ireland's asylum policies in the late 1990s – 'Ireland appears to have comparatively open social security, settlement and asylum-related rulings' (Roberts and Bolderson, 1999: 209). Only those who came to Ireland as pro-gramme refugees were provided with supports by a government agency established specifically to carry out this work, while refugees, persons given leave to remain and asylum seekers were left to look after themselves. Six years on, Ireland's public policy has changed dramatically as it moves towards containment, restriction and emotional distance from these socially and economically vulnerable groups.

Asylum seekers
In April 2000 the government introduced its dispersal and direct provision programme thus changing fundamentally the nature of the Irish reception policy for asylum seekers. The number of asylum seekers arriving in the country reached 10,000 plus per annum by the end of the 1990s. The sourcing of accommodation, formerly obtained almost exclusively in Dublin by asylum seekers themselves in the private rented sector, was brought under state control and sought throughout the entire country to accommodate the increasing number of new arrivals. This accommodation included hostels, large bed and breakfasts, hotels, convents, a holiday camp and an army barracks. Purpose built accommodation was provided in a number of centres around the country.

Under dispersal and direct provision asylum seekers on arrival in the state stay in a reception centre in the Dublin region for a brief period so that their initial claims, health screening, documentation and other matters are put in order. After their stay in the reception centre, officials from the Reception and Integration Agency (RIA), the Department of Justice agency established to oversee the reception of asylum seekers and the integration of refugees, allocate asylum seekers to an accommodation centre in another part of the country. Asylum seekers must remain in this accommodation centre until their claim for asylum has been decided. Under direct provision asylum seekers receive full board and income maintenance of €19.10 per week for adults and €9.60 for children and child benefit. They are also entitled to emergency needs payments from the community welfare service. Asylum seekers are entitled to health care on the same basis as Irish nationals, and are given a medical card. They are also provided with voluntary health screening which they are encouraged to take up on public health grounds.

Adults are not entitled to education, vocational training or to apply for work. Vocational Educational Committees may provide English classes in line with the White Paper on Adult Education, where it was proposed that adult asylum seekers would be given 'free access to adult literacy, English language and mother culture supports' (Government of Ireland, 2000b: 174). Children of schoolgoing age are obliged to attend school just as Irish children are. Access to third-level education is restricted because these young people are treated as non-EU nationals for the purposes of tertiary education and are therefore required to pay full economic fees.

Separated children (unaccompanied minors)

Most separated children arrive and stay in the Dublin area where the local health board must provide care for them. Under the Refugee Act 1996 as amended health boards have a responsibility for separated children as part of their obligation to children under the Child Care Act 1991. In the eastern region this responsibility falls to the East Coast Area Health Board where a special team of social workers and project workers was appointed in 2000 to provide a service for separated asylum seeking children or unaccompanied minors. Providing suitable accommodation for these children is a constant challenge for the social work service, and a range of options are used, such as fostering, residential and hostel. The Southern and Mid-Western Health Boards have also developed specific social work services and have in place their own arrangements to care for the very small number of separated children in their administrative areas (Christie, 2003). In a recent research report, Veale et al. (2003), state that significant progress has been made in the provision of services and developing procedures for separated children but that identified gaps remain in 'guardianship, accommodation and interim care, access to and support in participating in education, and the identification and implementation of durable solutions' (Veale et al., 2003: 7).

O'Mahoney (2003) points out that separated children face many difficulties – physical, emotional and psychological – having been thrust into independent life at a premature age. These difficulties are added to by having to enter into a complex asylum procedure which they may find difficult to understand. In his view, Irish asylum authorities have responded very well to these young people by providing specially trained staff to work with separated children (O'Mahoney, 2003).

Refugees, programme refugees and persons given leave to remain
Those with refugee status, programme refugees or those with leave to remain can make use of all public services which fall within the social policy arena on the same terms as Irish citizens. In other words, those with these forms of status can avail themselves of housing, health and social services, income maintenance, education, and vocational training. They may also take up employment. In a number of social policy areas some developments have taken place in the statutory sector, which have made a positive impact on refugees and people with leave to remain, as well as for asylum seekers in certain circumstances.

* Integrate Ireland Language and Training (IILT) was established to provide English language support for refugees and people with leave to remain. This is a Dublin-based agency funded by the Department of Education and Science and operates under the auspices of Trinity College. As well as organising the provision of English language classes IILT also develops training materials and provides training for teachers at primary and post-primary level.
* The Department of Education and Science makes available extra supports for schools at both primary and post-primary level for non-national children including refugees and asylum seekers who have significant English language deficits.
* There is a psychological service for refugees and asylum seekers located within the Northern Area Health Board. This service has developed from a service originally established for the Bosnian programme refugees in the mid-1990s. It provides for refugees and asylum seekers living in the greater Dublin area.
* All health boards have provided community welfare officers to meet the increasing demands on the community welfare service with the introduction of the government's dispersal policy.

Apart from a small number of initiatives such as the examples outlined above, many of the policy responses in education, health, housing, employment and income maintenance are met within the existing service provision for Irish nationals. There have been some improvements in the availability and use of interpreters and some state agencies deploy staff to co-ordinate responses to the needs of refuges and asylum seekers – such as to develop agency protocols and to provide training and information for staff.

Reception and Integration Agency
In April 2001 the Minister for Justice, Equality and Law Reform established the Reception and Integration Agency (RIA). This new agency, established on a non-statutory basis, was formerly known as the Directorate for Asylum Support Services (DASS), a Department of Justice, Equality and Law Reform agency, and now incorporated the Refugee Agency, formerly an agency of the Department of Foreign Affairs. The RIA has a number of functions:

- planning and co-ordinating the provision of services to both asylum seekers and refugees;
- co-ordinating and implementing integration policy for all refugees and persons who, though not refugees, are granted leave to remain in the state; and
- responding to crisis situations which result in relatively large numbers of refugees arriving in the state within a short period of time. (Reception and Integration Agency, 2001: 4)

As can be seen from its remit, the RIA holds the central role in the provision of services for asylum seekers, refugees, programme refugees and those given leave to remain. The influence of the RIA and its parent department is therefore enormous in the development of all policies, social and other, for those with a refugee or subsidiary status and asylum seekers.

Historical origins

It is important to examine the historical context of Irish refugee policy to allow the observer an overview and an understanding of some of the peculiarly Irish circumstances which preceded policies developed since the late 1990s. It must be pointed out that the limited literature available on this subject is almost entirely critical of Ireland's attitude and response to refugees since the foundation of the state. For example, Fanning argues that Irish responses to asylum seekers 'have been shaped by a legacy of exclusionary state practices and racism' (Fanning, 2002: 87).

Refugee policies from the foundation of the state until the 1990s
At the foundation of the state and for many years afterwards, Ireland was not an attractive location for those fleeing from persecution, given its own impoverishment and its geographical position, a 'monocultural island on the fringe of Europe' (McGovern, 1990: 126). It was not solely a problem of place or of poverty, however; it was also, according to Ward (1996), due to reluctance by the Irish state to offer protection to those from beyond its shores who needed it. Ward, in her review of Ireland's response to the Hungarian refugee

crisis in 1956, documents how this reluctance manifested itself. She describes how 'from the early years of the state, it was clear that Ireland never saw itself as offering a protective mantle to stateless persons' (Ward, 1996: 132). She also shows how certain groups were specifically discouraged and discriminated against, such as Jews and refugees from the Spanish Civil War, and quotes a secretary of the Department of External Affairs saying about the latter group 'that Ireland's unemployment problems excluded extending the hand of mercy to non-nationals in need – most particularly to "Spanish reds"' (Ward, 1996: 133). On the former, Ward quotes from a 1945 Department of Justice Memorandum:

> it was said that because Jews 'do not become assimilated with the native population like other immigrants, there is a danger that any big increase in their numbers might create a social problem' (1996: 133).

Ireland acceded to the 1951 Geneva Convention Relating to the Status of Refugees in 1956 and announced in its maiden speech to the United Nations in that same year its intention to participate in the international response to the Hungarian refugee crisis. An Interdepartmental Conference on Hungarian Refugees was set up to prepare the way for the arrival of a group of 539 refugees, the first group of 'programme' refugees accepted by the state for resettlement. The agreed criteria for the acceptance of the refugees had a resonance in the attitude towards other groups who might have sought asylum in Ireland in the 1930s and 1940s. The criteria required amongst other things that 'they would be suitable on grounds of race and religion, to ensure assimilation' (Ward, 1996: 136). McGovern describes how no resettlement strategy was put in place for the Hungarian refugees. Instead they were 'literally dumped in disued army huts' in the middle of the Irish countryside (McGovern, 1990: 127). Ward recounts in some detail the experience of the Hungarian refugees in Ireland, which turned out to be a very unhappy one for them and for the Irish authorities. She observes that:

> [t]he key problem that emerged during the Hungarian situation . . . was the absence of domestic legislation and the unwillingness of the state to provide adequate housing, accommodation, work and schooling for the refugees (Ward, 1996: 140).

Some have argued that the next two large groups of refugees accepted for resettlement by the Irish government, the 120 Chileans who arrived in 1973 and 1974, and the 212 Vietnamese who arrived in 1979, fared little better. The difficulties the Chileans encountered were due to the absence of any resettlement strategy by the government (McGovern, 1990; Collins, 1993). Regarding the Vietnamese, McGovern has argued that the state decided to maintain a 'peripheral' involvement and 'devolved' its responsibilities for the resettlement of the Vietnamese on to church organisations and non-governmental organisations (McGovern, 1990: 185). She concludes that

> the reason for the Irish Government's failure to respond positively to the challenge of resettling the Vietnamese can be attributed to a fear that the Government would not be able to accomplish their resettlement successfully in a society which was predominantly monocultural (McGovern, 1990: 244).

Refugee and asylum policies from the 1990s

In the 1990s the Irish refugee landscape began to change dramatically, paving the way for the current policies. There were three key elements in this changing landscape, one of which appears to have been transient and two that have impacted at the core of policies towards all those who have come as asylum seekers and programme refugees to seek protection from the Irish state in the twenty-first century. The first of these was the change in the state's own attitude towards programme refugees, which began in 1991 with the establishment of the Refugee Agency by the Department of Foreign Affairs to provide support for programme refugees. In the 1990s, firstly with the Bosnians and then with the Kosovars, the state became a more willing participant in providing supports for refugees. During that period the state gave more resources to the Refugee Agency than had been provided to its predecessor the Refugee Resettlement Committee. This new government agency was encouraged to develop more appropriate strategies for the reception and settlement of programme refugees. Ward acknowledges the improvements, which came with the Bosnian resettlement programme and suggests that it 'symbolises a long-awaited coming of age of the Irish state in its responsibilities . . . it also provides a model of good practice that can be replicated and built upon in the future' (Ward, 1998: 47). The positive developments in the state's response to refugees were recognised by other writers commenting on the Irish government's Kosovar programme (Ni Chiosan, 2001; Faughnn et al., 2002). However, these developments appear to have been transient and were subsequently virtually abandoned. Fanning sums up the retreat as follows: 'this emphasis upon good practice was sidelined within the histrionic response to the arrival of the increased numbers of asylum seekers from the late 1990s' (Fanning, 2002: 98).

The second key element in the changing landscape has been the increase in asylum claims which began in the mid-1990s and has continued into this century. For a country which a decade ago had fewer than 100 asylum claims annually to one which has over 10,000 claims a year, the increase has been dramatic. For the first time in the state's history Ireland had become a place of choice for protection. According to Bloch and Schuster the reasons for making such a choice emerge from a complex interaction of variables at three levels – micro, meso and macro:

> micro factors include the desires and expectancies of an individual migrant; meso level variables relate to collectives and social networks; macro level factors are concerned with nation state (i.e. sending and receiving countries) as well as transnational relations (Bloch and Schuster, 2002, 402).

Whatever the motivations and circumstances that influenced their decisions to come to Ireland, the Irish state was ill prepared for the large numbers of people who came here seeking asylum towards the end of the 1990s. It struggled on legislative and administrative fronts to deal with the challenges of this new phenomenon. Existing state services had great difficulties meeting the needs of the new arrivals in a policy vacuum. This began to change with the establishment of the Directorate for Asylum Seeker Supports in 1999 and the enactment of legislation.

Legislative development was the third key element in the dramatic overhaul of Ireland's approach to asylum seekers that occurred during the last ten years. In the early to mid-1990s a number of attempts were made to bring refugee legislation through the Oireachtas. This culminated in the passing of the Refugee Act 1996 with all party support and welcomed by the non-governmental organisations that had campaigned for the introduction of such legislation. Sections of this piece of legislation distinguished it 'as one of the most progressive models of refugee legislation in the region' (Byrne, 1997: 109). However, the passing of the Refugee Act 1996 coincided with the beginning of increased numbers of people claiming asylum, and it was never fully implemented. As a result, the 1996 Act has been amended in subsequent legislation. The development of asylum legislation was long overdue but the impetus to introduce it in the form that it has taken is partly because of the increase in numbers but mainly as a result of Ireland's membership of the EU with its commitment to a common policy on refugees and asylum seekers which was set out in the Treaty of Amsterdam.

For a time the state struggled to respond to the increased numbers of asylum seekers entering the country, but has recovered that ground over the past four years having introduced asylum legislation, developed a reception policy, and sped up the asylum process. The consequences of this have been a more streamlined and regulated approach to those who seek asylum in Ireland. With the state concentrating on the control of asylum seekers, it has placed less emphasis on the integration needs of those who have been given refugee status or the right to remain in the country or those invited as programme refugees. The Department of Justice, Equality and Law Reform published a document, 'Integration: A two way process' in 2000. This report from the Interdepartmental Working Group on the Integration of Refugees in Ireland was an important first step in setting out a policy on integration, even if it is at times vague and short on specific policy targets. The then Minister for Justice at the launch of the report said 'the government agreed that the report should form the framework for government policy on integration' (O'Donoghue, 2000). However, little of significance has been done since then to follow up on that policy.

The development of specific social policy for refugees is a relatively new departure in Ireland. In the early years of refugee arrivals, which were mainly through government programmes, the apparent reluctance by the state to accept people for resettlement was reflected in an assimilationist approach, where people were expected to avail themselves of the services provided generally for the native population. The more recent approach to the reception and resettlement of Bosnian and Kosovar refugees demonstrated a shift in this policy where services specifically aimed at assisting these groups were introduced. It was hoped that with the establishment of the Reception and Integration Agency that this approach would be extended to Convention refugees and those given leave to remain. There is little evidence that this is happening and the policy approach appears to have drifted back to the familiar non-interventionist model used in the past. For asylum seekers social policy developments are restricted to meeting need through the provision of basic accommodation, income maintenance at less than the norm, education for children up to the end of second level, and health care. There are no indications that these minimalist policy interventions will change for the foreseeable future.

Principal actors in the development of policy

The principal actors in this sphere consist of the government itself, the various government departments within whose remit lies a particular aspect of policy, government agencies which have direct dealings with refugees through the provision of general public services, the Reception and Integration Agency, political parties, faith-based organisations, social partners, and non-governmental organisations – both Irish-led and refugee-led.

The government's decisions on matters of public policy are supported and informed by the civil service. It is stated frequently that it is within this combination that the power over matters of policy remains; that the Oireachtas, political parties and interest groups have limited say in the development of public policy (Chubb, 1992). In the area of immigration where refugee issues reside, the Minister for Justice has enormous powers (Costello, 1994;

Marshall, 2000). The most important and most powerful influence on asylum and refugee policy therefore comes from the Minister for Justice and the Department of Justice, Equality and Law Reform (DJELR). The Minister for Foreign Affairs and his department had played the lead role in government policy towards programme refugees until the establishment of the Reception and Integration Agency under the DJELR. While other government departments develop policy in this area, the passing of time appears to show that they have less and less of a say in any decisions regarding asylum seekers, as the influence of the Minister for Justice and the DJELR is almost total in this area of policy.

State agencies may and do develop social policy responses to particular areas of need in their role as providers of services. However, there is no doubt that DJELR's own agency, the RIA, is the most influential state agency in the area of service provision for asylum seekers and refugees given its central role in the overall implementation and management of the state's policies towards refugees and asylum seekers.

Political parties and individual politicians have contributed to the policy debate on refugees. There was a commitment in 1993 by the newly formed Fianna Fáil–Labour coalition government to the highest international standards for dealing with refugees. In 1996 a White Paper on Foreign Policy contained within it a commitment to best international practice in resettling refugees (Government of Ireland, 1996a). The Oireachtas debates in the lead up to the passing of the Refugee Act 1996 were in general well informed, with the eventual coming together of opinion across both houses over the years of the debate providing all-party support for the final passing of the legislation. The politicians and political parties have since then watched governments initially baulk at implementing the legislation in full and then restructuring it in subsequent years.

The social partners and faith-based organisations are all broadly supportive of progressive policies towards refugees and asylum seekers, if not always for the same reasons. In one of the more controversial policy areas, the right to work for asylum seekers, these groups, including ICTU, IBEC and the Catholic Church, joined with NGOs to lead an unsuccessful campaign to give asylum seekers the right to work after six months if their case for asylum has not been heard. Most of the main social partners and faith-based organisations have been involved in developing responses to the needs of immigrants, refugees and asylum seekers at a practical and policy level.

Within the NGO sector the biggest contribution to policy development during the past ten years was without doubt the development and passing of the Refugee Act 1996. Two NGOs in particular were to the forefront in making this contribution – Amnesty International and the Irish Refugee Council. I have argued previously that these two organisations contributed substantially to getting this legislation passed after five years of campaigning (Moran, 1998). It is a fundamental part of Amnesty International's human rights brief to influence public policy to protect those at risk of persecution, including refugees. The Irish Refugee Council, on the other hand, has a broader brief which spans issues such as legislation on asylum determination and the welfare of refugees.

Well established organisations such as the Irish Red Cross Society, Irish Council for Civil Liberties and Barnardos, amongst others, have all developed an interest in refugee issues in Ireland, either as campaigning organisations and/or as providers of services to refugees and asylum seekers. Another NGO, Comhlamh established Integrating Ireland as its response to the needs of those who work with refugee organisations. Integrating Ireland is the national network of the large number of groups and organisations throughout Ireland that have been established in recent years to work with refugees, asylum seekers and immigrants. Area partnership companies, community development projects and local development organisations have dedicated staff, resources, and/or set aside funding to support refugees and asylum seekers. Some of the new organisations have their base in church or already established organisations, such as SPIRASI (the Spiritan Asylum Seekers Initiative of the Holy Ghost Fathers), the Vincentian Refugee Project, Access Ireland (the Irish Refugee Council), and the Refugee Information Service (the Irish Refugee Council and the Community Information Centres). The development of projects has not been limited to Dublin, as there are support groups and organisations in most areas of the country, such as Doras Luimni (Limerick), Trasnet (Tralee), Nasc (Cork), and the Galway Refugee Support Group. There are also some refugee-led groups, and these include ARASI (Association of Refugees and Asylum Seekers in Ireland), the African Refugee Network, ARAK (Association of Refugees and Asylum Seekers in Kilkenny), Roma Support Group, AKIDWA (African women's group) and Waterford Refugee and Asylum Seekers Council (WRAC). All of these groups, and the many more not mentioned, provide supports in one form or other to asylum seekers and refugees.

As for their influence on refugee policy, there is little evidence to show that the NGO sector has made any real impact on national policy development in this area. A small number of NGOs pursue policy development and influence as their primary objective. The majority of the organisations in the NGO sector are mostly concerned with the provision of badly needed supports at local level; influencing national policy is for many only a marginal activity. Furthermore, many of the new organisations and groups that work exclusively with these new minority communities do not have the resources (Faughnan and O'Donovan, 2002). However, the NGO sector, with its lesser resources, is not alone in its failure to influence refugee policy. The more powerful social partners and the churches, where they have taken up issues relating to asylum seekers and refugees, have been equally unsuccessful in impacting on the state's refugee and asylum policies.

Evaluation of current policy

The 1990s saw the EU move ever closer towards economic integration through the creation of a single European market. Economic integration requires removal of all internal barriers and free movement of people within the EU. At the same time the EU is attempting to harmonise its asylum and refugee policies. This is not an easy task as Duvell and Jordan point out, 'the attempt to bring together issues of economic migration and those of asylum, within a single framework, represents a delicate balancing act' (Duvell and Jordan, 2002: 498). Yet owing to shortages of skilled and unskilled labour within the EU there is a need to accept 'that immigration will continue and should be properly regulated' (European Commission, 2001). Refugees do not fit comfortably within this framework – spontaneous migration cannot be controlled – and hence the move towards harmonisation of asylum policies to avoid making any one state appear more attractive than another (Duvell and Jordan, 2002). However, harmonisation of asylum policies has a tendency to mean more restrictive policies (Joly with Nettleton and Poulton, 1992).

> The new, restrictive policies introduced in Western Europe, which were aimed at combating illegal immigration and abuse of asylum systems, shifted the balance between refugee protection and immigration control. The term 'fortress Europe' became a shorthand for this phenomenon (UNHCR, 2000: 161).

This 'fortress Europe' phenomenon and the measures taken to tackle the flows of immigrants into the territories of the EU have had an indiscriminate affect on asylum seekers 'making it more difficult for people seeking protection to reach a country where they could ask for it', according to the UNHCR (2000: 161). UNHCR states that much of the development of the EU's immigration and asylum policies in the 1990s 'focused on coordinating and tightening member states' admission policies' (UNHCR, 2000:162).

UNHCR identifies a number of ways in which these policies have been developed. First, the EU states sought to adopt 'non-arrival' policies, which were aimed at preventing aliens, including potential asylum seekers, without proper documentation from reaching Europe. This has been done by making it more difficult for nationals from certain countries to get visas and by introducing carrier sanctions. Secondly, for those asylum seekers who did breach the first barrier and reached European territory, 'diversion' policies were designed, shifting to other countries responsibility for assessing asylum claims and providing protection. This burden has been devolved to former East European Soviet Bloc countries where their capacity to cope with asylum seekers and refugees has been increased – and provide 'safe third countries'. Third, the governments of the EU have increasingly 'opted for restrictive applications of the 1951 Geneva Convention in an effort to exclude certain categories of claimants from the scope of the refugee definition' (UNHCR, 2000: 162). These developments have led to an increase in secondary or lesser forms of protection. Fourth, was the introduction of a range of 'deterrent' measures, including the increased use of detention, denial of social assistance, and restriction to access to employment (UNHCR, 2000).

Ireland's asylum and refugee policies have mirrored the general developments that have taken place in the EU. Since 1999, restrictive legislation and measures in keeping with what has been described above in the wider European context have been introduced by the Irish government. The Refugee Act 1996 has been amended in each piece of related legislation introduced since 1999 – Immigration Act 1999, Illegal Immigrants (Trafficking Act) 2000 and most recently, the Immigration Act 2003. In so doing the state has pulled back on its original commitments to asylum seekers and refugees as outlined in the 1996 legislation and the spirit in which it was passed. The state's challenge and subsequent victory in the Supreme Court in January 2003 on the automatic right of non-national parents of Irish born children to remain in the state after the birth of their child further underlines the deterrent measures being used. Add to this the introduction of a section in the Social Welfare (Miscellaneous Provisions) Act 2003 to prevent asylum seekers from taking up supplementary rent allowance to force them to stay in accommodation centres, one can only form the opinion that the state is determined to use whatever powers it has to make Ireland as unattractive as possible for asylum seekers. The assumption being that these measures will deter asylum seekers from entering Ireland (and Europe) and cut down on their numbers (Bloch and Schuster, 2002).

Asylum seekers
Policies in Ireland towards asylum seekers were relatively benign up to the late 1990s, and while they were not allowed work or access to public housing, asylum seekers were entitled to supplementary welfare payments and could apply for rent supplement to live in the private rented sector. Access to health and education (for children) services remain the same for asylum seekers, but the introduction of dispersal and direct provision and the consequent reduction in income support as well as the withdrawal of housing benefits mark a major shift in policy towards this group. These restrictions on welfare and freedom of movement add a new dimension to control where the state is not only attempting to limit access to its territories at its borders. It is also attempting

to implement internal controls on those asylum seekers who have gained access to the state by restricting the availability of welfare and accommodation as well as the freedom to move and live where they wish. It is argued by both Geddes (2000) and Bank (2000) that there are two reasons for welfare restrictions for asylum seekers. One is that depriving them of full welfare entitlements will discourage asylum seekers who, it is argued by governments, are not genuine in the first place, from trying to enter European states and live off their generous welfare provision. The second reason for this restrictive and exclusionary measure is to keep asylum seekers from integrating into the local community because

> by excluding asylum seekers as far as possible from participation in the normal life of the host society, states attempt to ensure that law enforcement against rejected asylum seekers is not impaired by the developments of strong social ties (Bank, 2000: 149).

Social policy has thus become a weapon in the armoury of the Irish state to deter and control asylum seekers. As a result asylum seekers will be 'generally provided with inferior provisions' and will continue to be 'negatively discriminated against' (Roberts and Bolderson, 1999: 211). Roberts and Bolderson (1999) point out that unlike refugees who have the principle of the right to non-discrimination accepted in the 1951 Geneva Convention, asylum seekers have no such rights, and are tolerated only conditionally by host countries. Although Ireland does not participate in the common European policy on 'Minimum standards on the reception of asylum seekers in Member States' (2003) arising from the Amsterdam Treaty in 1999, Irish asylum reception practices fall within the wide discretion allowed in interpreting that directive's provisions. These practices have brought Ireland into the mainstream of European asylum policies, which tend towards the 'lowest common denominator' of social provision and inter-governmental processes (UNHCR, 2000; Papademetriou, 1996).

Refugees and persons given leave to remain

The rapidity and thoroughness with which Irish government policies towards asylum seekers have been developed since 1999 are in contrast to the lethargy and inertia associated with the development of integration policies and practices for refugees and others with a subsidiary status. There is no national integration policy, with the result that those who have been excluded from Irish society in the asylum process and newly invited programme refugees have little assistance to help them settle in this country.

One of the consequences of the accommodation-led dispersal programme and its exclusionary practices is the lack of a comprehensive approach to the long-term needs of those who are allowed to stay in the state. Bloch and Schuster (2002) claim that the exclusion of asylum seekers delays the process of their integration. The lack of a basic income, inappropriate accommodation, not being allowed to cook, no access to adult education, very limited access to language training, no access to vocational training or work, and having most of one's needs met in an accommodation centre, develop a dependency mentality, which requires unlearning at the end of whatever time is spent in such centres. Faughnan et al., in their study of the community welfare service and asylum seekers, report that 'direct provision was seen as continuing its negative impact on the lives of asylum seekers even when they move into the private rented sector' (Faughnan et al., 2002: 31). They continue by stating that close to two thirds of the community welfare officers interviewed in their study claimed that 'asylum seekers experience difficulties on moving on from accommodation centres with many highlighting budgeting problems, dependency and institutionalisation' (Faughnan, Humphries and Whelan, 2002: 31) The lack of any formal settlement and integration services, for those who obtain a status, to assist with their adjustment to a new independent life adds to an already difficult experience.

These groups are allowed to avail themselves of state supports and participate in Irish society on the same basis as nationals. However, this has been shown in the past not to suffice (Collins 1993; McGovern 1990). Even where supports have been provided the task of settlement and integration is such that many struggle to attain the economic, social and cultural benefits enjoyed by the majority of the Irish population, which must surely be the measurement against which success is tested (O'Regan, 1998; Bradley and Humphries 1999).

Challenges for the future

The current asylum and refugee policies in place throughout Europe and replicated in Ireland do not augur well for the development of progressive social policies for refugees and asylum seekers. Within the Irish context there are a number of potential challenges to be faced now and into the future, two of which are racism, and poverty and social exclusion.

Racism

Setting asylum seekers apart from the rest of the community is to sow the seed of racism and xenophobia in our society (European Race Bulletin, 2000). The introduction of compulsory dispersal to, at times, remote accommodation in different parts of the country without attendant social provision and supports and preparation of local communities adds to the separation of asylum seekers from mainstream society. This structural distancing of asylum seekers does little to discourage negative attitudes towards them, which flies in the face of government funded anti-racism programmes. Even during the time of more open welfare policies towards asylum seekers in the second half of the 1990s racism was a frequent experience for asylum seekers and refugees (Begley at al., 1999). The social distancing of asylum seekers through dispersal and direct provision suggests that they are different and potentially a threat to society (Westin, 1999; Chimni, 2000). Furthermore, this distancing leads to objectifying and dehumanising asylum seekers so that it becomes easier to ignore their rights as human beings and in turn colludes with racism and xenophobia. This process sets out the basic components of what West refers to in the African American experience as 'invisibility and namelessness', where black people are seen as problems rather than people with problems, where they become abstractions and objects rather than individuals (West, 1999: 103).

A number of authors suggest that there is an inextricable link between racism and social policy and that this link is further enmeshed in the social policy approach to asylum seekers (Bloch and Schuster, 2002; Cohen, 2002, Duvell and Jordan, 2002; Penketh and Ali, 1997; Williams, 1999). Combating racism in social policy, such as in income support or housing, will prove near impossible given the premise on which asylum policy in Ireland appears to be based – that the majority of those seeking asylum are bogus and economic migrants. Such publicly rehearsed positions by politicians and the media foment the public's negative and hostile image of asylum seekers and refugees and further embed racist beliefs. Into the future the dispersal and direct provision policy will become even more obviously racialised when in the coming years most of those who currently claim asylum from Eastern European states will no longer be in a position to do so, as they will be members of the EU. By 2007, based on current trends, there will only be a small number of white Europeans from the former Soviet bloc countries applying for asylum. In such circumstances black people from African countries will make up the overwhelming majority of asylum seekers in Ireland before the end of this decade. Careful consideration of how these asylum seekers are treated will be required as punitive asylum policies will only serve to reinforce racism in this country.

Poverty and social exclusion

A number of commentators and studies point to poverty and social exclusion as a normal part of the asylum and refugee experience in Ireland (Begley et al., 1999; Fanning et al., 2001; Fanning, 2002; Faughnan and Woods, 2000; Murphy-Lawless and Kennedy, 2002). Irish anti-poverty and social inclusion policies offer little comfort for refugees and asylum seekers. In recent policy documents, which inform and guide the corporatist nature of Irish public policy decision making, such as the Review of the National Anti-Poverty

Strategy (NAPS), and *Sustaining Progress: Social Partnership Agreement 2003–2005*, the cause of asylum seekers and refugees barely receive a mention. The NAPS review includes refugees and asylum seekers under the umbrella term 'ethnic minority groups' about which it has little to say. It has the general aim of ensuring that people from these groups living in the state are not more likely to experience poverty than the majority group members. However, the NAPS says that because of the lack of quantitative information about the socio-economic situation of foreign born residents in Ireland it is not possible to define specific targets for this group. The overall policy approach of NAPS is to 'tackle barriers to integration', which include tackling racism, developing new immigrant legislative framework, make available resources to improve asylum procedures, and a commitment by the state and social partners to ensuring equality (Department of Social, Community and Family Affairs, 2002).

In *Sustaining Progress* there is the 'challenge of delivering a fair and inclusive society' (Government of Ireland, 2003a: 60), but this apparently refers to Irish and EU citizens, as the only reference to those from outside the territories is to migrant workers and this in a context of immigration and labour market co-ordination. There is acknowledgement that 'preventing racism in the workplace is extremely important' and IBEC and ICTU are to agree on a code of practice against racism in the workplace (Government of Ireland, 2003a: 87). However, 'asylum seekers are excluded . . . from the key provisions of the partnership agreement Sustaining Progress' (O'Mahoney, 2003: 135).

The National Economic and Social Council (NESC) 2002 strategy report, *An Investment in Quality: Services, Inclusion and Enterprise*, is the third policy document and especially important as NESC sets the agenda for all others. In the NESC's chapter on poverty, exclusion and inequality there is a section on new population flows and cultural diversity, which includes sub-sections on asylum seekers and people with refugee status or leave to remain, as well as migrant workers. In contrast to the previous two policy documents, refugees and asylum seekers receive greater attention in the NESC Strategy Report. It identifies asylum seekers as the 'most vulnerable' among non-EEA nationals living in Ireland (NESC, 2002: 409) and gives a number of reasons for this including

> once in Ireland they find themselves under suspicion of being economic migrants seeking to evade immigration controls; their differential treatment by the Irish state (direct provision, fingerprinting, denial of the right to work, liability to deportation, etc.) mark them out as special groups and can lower their status in the eyes of some people (NESC, 2002: 410).

NESC declares its impartial concern for civil liberties and says 'arrangements governing asylum seekers should be exceptional only in so far as they are strictly necessary, and should be kept under review' (NESC, 2002: 212). It suggests that 'the single best way to bring asylum seekers to enjoy the same treatment and rights as others in the state' is through ensuring an improved asylum determination process (NESC, 2002: 413). This sub-section of the Report concludes by saying that 'that the arrangements in place are generally fair and reasonable' (NESC, 2002: 413). On people who are granted refugee status or leave to remain the NESC Report makes a general observation on the importance of facilitating their full participation in society. It also recommends the 'relevant' authorities should ensure that the different elements of this participation, such as conditions of employment, comply with national standards. While the NESC Report gives more space to asylum seekers and refugees than the other two documents referred to, and at times is precise and to the point on what the problems of asylum seekers are, it offers no substantial analysis or responses to the issues of poverty, exclusion and inequality for these groups. Just as with the NAPS, the NESC refers to the need for more quantitative information on the socio-economic circumstances of ethnic minorities in Ireland and, furthermore, that Ireland should learn from the experiences of other EU states.

The overall lack of substance in these key policy-making arenas reflects the prevailing government influence in this area of social policy where 'the goal of discouraging applications for asylum has superseded those of addressing social exclusion' (Faughnan et al., 2002: 87). It also shows the lack of influence and weakness of the groups that work in the refugee and asylum sector and the low priority of this issue for the main social partners. The physical marginality of asylum seekers from Irish society and the lack of integration strategies for refugees and those with leave to remain have yet to be fully included in the policy debate on poverty, social exclusion and inequality. As a result these groups will remain at the margins of Irish society into the future with the possibility of long-term structural exclusion for many families and individuals, as is the case in other Western countries with black and ethnic minority populations.

The fundamental philosophical approach by the Irish state to social policy for asylum seekers is based on a different premise to that of citizens. This approach challenges the belief of supporting all members of our society on the basis of common needs and replaces it with a policy of differentiation of need between citizens, whose basic needs are judged to be at a higher level than those of the asylum seeker – the 'deserving' citizen and the 'undeserving' asylum seeker (Sales, 2002). Fanning suggests that this differentiation breaks down even further as 'the Irish state stratifies groups of non-citizens on the basis of decisions about their entitlements' (Fanning, 2004: 203).

Conclusion

Ward (1998) characterises Irish refugee policy historically in terms of 'closure' towards the plight of refugees and asylum seekers up to the mid-1990s. With the passing of the 1996 Refugee Act and the more progressive approach adopted by the state towards programme refugees, through the Department of Foreign Affairs' Refugee Agency, there was a period of openness and grounds for some optimism about a new emerging Irish refugee policy. This optimism was short lived, however, as successive governments dragged their heels in implementing the 1996 Refugee Act before it was changed beyond recognition and the Refugee Agency disappeared into a bigger and more controlling Reception and Integration Agency under the Department of Justice, Equality and Law Reform. The legislative changes were justified because increasing numbers of asylum seekers came to Ireland during the late 1990s and into this century. Furthermore, the earlier optimism clearly did not take into account the developments already under way in EU asylum policies, which indicated that the move towards a common asylum policy would almost inevitably mean achieving policies of the 'lowest common denominator'.

The manner in which asylum and refugee policies are arrived at and the content of these policies when compared to other important national policies show enormous gaps in both the consultation processes used and the declared outcomes of policies. In other policy areas inclusive consultation processes are used extensively, but with refugees and asylum seekers they barely exist. For the Irish population the declared outcomes of policies as expressed in our political discourse include terms like social inclusion, the elimination of poverty, full employment and equality. For refugees and asylum seekers such language is generally not used and where it is used it is almost meaningless in the context of existing contradictory policies and practices.

And yet at local level in Ireland there are many groups and individuals who support refugees and asylum seekers in different ways, by providing advice, friendship, support and direct services. Many individuals within state agencies likewise push their organisations to improve their services to refugees and asylum seekers. Refugees and asylum seekers themselves also play a huge part, against the odds, in supporting each other and, where they can, in pushing the agenda for a more tolerant and inclusive society. Historically in Ireland the involvement and commitment of a few has often proved the catalyst to change government social policies and the development of services. Influences such as these have often taken years of struggle to achieve their desired outcomes. This may have to be the way forward for those working in the refugee and asylum sector, for at the moment the state is not for turning. In the meantime Ireland will continue a policy of exclusion of people who might have expected more from a nation with its own long and painful history of forced migration.

Table 12.1 **Main policy developments**

1935   Aliens Act

1946   Aliens Order

1956   Ireland signs 1951 UN Convention on Status Relating to Refugees and agrees to
       accept a quota of Hungarian refugees.

1979   Government decision to accept a quota of Vietnamese refugees; to request Irish
       Red Cross to set up and manage reception centre; and, to establish ad hoc group
       under Department of Defence to formulate and administer a refugee
       resettlement programme.

1985   Government decision to establish a policy Advisory Committee and Refugee
       Resettlement Committee under the Department of Foreign Affairs.
       Letter from Department of Justice to UNHCR setting out procedure (Von Arnim
       Procedure) for the determination of refugee status in Ireland.

1991   Government decision to merge the Policy Advisory Committee and Refugee
       Resettlement Committee to establish the Refugee Agency under the Department
       of Foreign Affairs.

1992   First of a number of government decisions about the admittance of refugees from
       the former Yugoslavia.

1993   High Court found that December 1985 letter on determination of status was
       binding against the government.
       Alan Shatter TD introduced Refugee Protection Bill.
       Interdepartmental Committee on Non-Irish Nationals established, published
       report in November 1993.

1996   Refugee Act passed by the Oireachtas.

1997   Implementation of six sections of Refugee Act 1996, including Dublin Convention
       Introduction of new administrative procedures for processing asylum claims –
       Hope Hanlan Procedures to replace 1985 Von Arnim procedures
       Eastern Health Board established refugee unit for asylum seekers.

1998   Establishment of 'one-stop-shop' for asylum seekers in Dublin.
       Government decision on accepting a quota of ten refugees and their immediate
       families for resettlement annually.

1999   1,032 Kosovars given temporary protection by the state and accommodated in
       ten reception centres in the southern and eastern parts of the country
       Government decision on introduction of dispersal and direct provision
       Establishment of the Directorate for Asylum Support Services.
       Immigration Act passed by the Oireachtas

2000   Dispersal and direct provision policy begins.
       Illegal Immigrants (Trafficking Act) 2000 passed by the Oireachtas
       Implementation of Refugee Act 1996 as amended by Immigration Act 1999 –
       establishment of the Office of the Refugee Applications Commissioner and the
       Refugee Appeals Tribunal

2001   Establishment of the Reception and Integration Agency, incorporating the
            Directorate for Asylum Support Services and the Refugee Agency.
        Establishment of the Interim Advisory Board of the Reception and Integration
            Agency.
2002   Interim Advisory Board of the Reception and Integration Agency disbanded after
            18 months.
2003   Supreme Court judgement – Irish born children no longer have an automatic right
            to have their non-national parents bring them up in Ireland.
        Social Welfare (Miscellaneous Provisions Act) 2003 passed by the Dáil – section 13
            prevents persons from getting rent allowance if they have made an application to
            the Minister for Justice, Equality and Law Reform for a declaration of refugee.
        Immigration Act 2003 passed by the Oireachtas

Recommended reading

Bradley, S. and N. Humphries (1999) *From Bosnia to Ireland's Private Rented Sector: A Study of Bosnian Housing Needs in Ireland.* Dublin: Clann Housing Association.

Fanning, B. (2002) *Racism and Social Change in the Republic of Ireland.* Manchester: Manchester University Press.

Faughnan, P., N. Humphries and S. Whelan (2002) *Patching up the System: The Community Welfare Service and Asylum Seekers.* Dublin: Social Science Research Centre, UCD.

Fraser, U and C. Harvey (eds) (2003) *Sanctuary in Ireland: Perspectives on Asylum Law and Policy.* Dublin: IPA

O'Regan, C. (1998) *Report of a Survey of the Vietnamese and Bosnian Refugee Communities in Ireland.* Dublin: Refugee Agency/Department of Psychology, Eastern Health Board.

Veale, A., L. Palaudaries and C. Gibbons (2003) *Separated Children Seeking Asylum in Ireland.* Dublin: Irish Refugee Council.

Ward, E. (1996) 'Ireland's refugee policies and the case of the Hungarians', *Irish Studies in International Affairs* 7: 131–41.

Chapter 13

The criminal justice system

Anthony Cotter

This chapter examines the Irish criminal justice system. It explains the various agencies which are central to the system and it discusses the major issues which are key to understanding offending behaviour and how the treatment of offenders in Ireland has evolved since the beginning of the state.

The criminal justice system

The criminal justice system is a complex and multilayered structure, which provides the framework for the operation of many distinct but interrelated agencies and institutions. These include the Courts of Justice, the Garda Síochána, the prison system, and the Probation and Welfare Service, all co-ordinated by the Department of Justice, Equality and Law Reform. Other state agencies which play a central role in the operation of the system are the offices of the Director of Public Prosecutions (DPP) which is totally independent in the performance of its duties from all other agencies, including the government and the Attorney General, the legal adviser to the government, and the Chief State Solicitor.

The Courts of Justice
The Irish Constitution (1937) determines that justice shall be administered publicly, in courts established by law and by an independent judiciary comprised of judges appointed by the President of Ireland on the advice of the government, having itself been advised since 1995 by the Judicial Appointments Board. The structure of the court system comprises: the Supreme Court (final appeal); the High Court, with full jurisdiction in all criminal and civil matters; the Circuit Court and District Court with distinctive limited jurisdiction.

The courts are the pivotal institution in the criminal justice system. They determine guilt or innocence, circumscribing the defendant's future contact with the system. Rothman (1984) highlights the main sequential decisions involved in court proceedings as being: arrest and summons; initiation of court proceedings, which includes the involvement of the DPP in serious cases; determination of charges and court jurisdiction; verdict; and sentencing.

The defendant appears before the District Court, which is the court of first hearing in all cases. A preliminary examination of the facts of the case is conducted, unless the defendant waives his or her right and opts to have the case heard before the court without a jury. If the court decides there is a prima facie case to answer, the case goes forward to the Circuit Criminal Court, or to the Central Criminal Court in cases of rape, murder, and treason. The prosecution must put together, in written form, all the evidence to be used against the accused. This is presented in what is called a Book of Evidence. The accused and his or her legal representatives are legally entitled to a copy of the evidence to allow them to prepare their defence strategy. The case is then heard by a judge and jury to determine guilt or innocence.

The court system functions on the basis of a due process philosophy whereby justice is administered within a framework of legal rules and procedures which are generally known, totally fair, and perceived as being just. Over the centuries the court system has been perceived to be distant, uncaring, out of touch – even when it functions competently within the context of due process. The court system itself has not helped this viewpoint by communicating in archaic language, by moving slowly and in apparently mysterious ways. The Constitution (1937) guarantees 'due process' under section 38.1, which states that 'no person shall be tried on any criminal charge save in due course of law'. The term 'due process' means that a defendant in the courts is entitled to a decision-making process subject to, and open to, public scrutiny, an unalienable right to defend his or her position, and an independence and impartiality on the part of the decision makers.

The establishment of the Irish courts service in 1999 was the most revolutionary and historic change in the administration of the court system since the foundation of the state. Its formation was recommended by the Working Group on a Courts Commission (established in 1996, chaired by Justice Susan Denham, Judge of the Supreme Court). It was enacted into law by the Courts Service Act 1998. Section 5 of the Act outlines the main functions of the new Service:

- To manage the courts
- To provide support services for the judges
- To provide information on the courts system to the public
- To provide, manage and maintain court buildings
- To provide facilities for users of the courts

The service is managed by its own board, chaired by the Chief Justice and has its own Chief Executive. One of a number of projects initiated by the service was the establishment (2001) of a pilot drug court in the Dublin Metropolitan District Court for people convicted of non-violent drug offences.

The Law Reform Commission was established in 1975 to provide a constant review of legislation and procedures. The Commission, comprising six members, is presided over by a senior judge of the High or Supreme Court. Its task is to discuss and evaluate aspects of the law before submitting detailed proposals to Government. These proposals frequently form the basis for subsequent legislative changes, which have had considerable implications for the operation of the criminal justice system.

The Garda Síochána

With the establishment of the Irish Free State in 1922, the new government adopted the British policing system already in place. The structures and administration remained largely intact with the only significant change being that of personnel. Subsequent developments in policing reflected what was happening throughout Europe, where 'police organisations tended to be structured militarily, and to be nationally organised and centrally controlled' (O'Reilly, 1986: 34).

Such a development has meant that the Garda Síochána is very much a centralised organisation, controlled, apart from operational matters, by the Department of Justice, Equality and Law Reform and, as a consequence, directly answerable to the Minister of the day. The Garda Commissioner heads what is uniquely a largely unarmed force. In an article on policing in Ireland, O'Reilly (1986: 38) states that the Gardaí have two central areas of operation: the detection and prevention of crime. While these may be primary functions of the Gardaí, in common with other police forces a considerable amount of time is devoted to what might be called service works, whereby Gardaí respond to people seeking assistance and advice not directly associated with criminal or illegal activity. The five key areas of Gardaí work in contemporary Ireland are: crime prevention and detection; traffic control and related matters; community relations and dealing with community problems; answering and responding to calls for assistance; public reassurance and public order maintenance.

The role of the Gardaí has expanded considerably over the past twenty years. This has increased the complexity of their work, necessitating new skills of operation and demanding an increased sophistication in their relations with the community. Commissioner Byrne recognised the importance of mutual co-operation and respect between the force and the community it serves:

> the community itself must be seen as an equal part of the equation. Without the participation and the support of the community any police service will falter. Public support must not be taken for granted. An Garda Síochána must continue

to work ever more closely with members of the community in helping to build a society in which we can all take pride (Byrne 2002: 440/441).

The Neighbourhood Watch and Community Alert (rural) strategies were initiated to involve the community in preventing and reporting criminal activity.

In 1963, in a radical development for a police force at the time, the Garda Juvenile Diversion Programme (Juvenile Liaison Scheme) was established. Its aim was wherever possible to divert juvenile offenders from the criminal justice system by way of caution rather than prosecution. In 2002 the programme was put on a statutory basis as part of the Children Act, 2001. The Garda Youth Diversion Projects (Garda Special Projects) aim to actively involve young people 'at risk' in programmes or activities which would give them the opportunity to develop themselves personally and socially, and away from criminal activity. The profile of the young people attending these projects was examined in the *Study of Participants in Garda Special Projects* commissioned by the Department of Justice, Equality and Law Reform which found that:

> the extent to which the majority of areas in which the young people grow up and reside are homogenous . . . they share many of the same characteristics and associated social problems . . . A clear cycle of disadvantage exists with regard to the types of social problems faced by this group of young people within their communities (Centre for Social and Educational Research, DIT, 2001:7).

Other important recent developments include: the PULSE (Police Using Leading Systems Effectively) information technology system; the use of CCTV systems in major urban areas; the Garda Dog Unit; the Mounted Unit based in Dublin; the National Drugs Unit and the Bureau of Fraud Investigation. In 1996 the Criminal Assets Bureau (CAB) was established to freeze or confiscate, through the Civil Courts, the assets of offenders. The Garda Complaints Board, established in 1996, investigates complaints against individual Garda members. In February 2004, the Minister for Justice, Equality and Law Reform announced the replacement of the Board by an Ombudsman Committee of three.

The role of the Garda Síochána has expanded considerably over the past twenty years. This has increased the complexity of their work, necessitating new operational strategies and demanding an increased sophistication in their relations with the community. Policing has consequently become so laden with expectations that whether it can deliver in terms of detection, prosecution and the reduction of crime levels is a continuing source of debate and ideological conflict.

The prison system

Imprisonment is clearly, as in other jurisdictions, central to the functioning of the Criminal Justice System in Ireland. Its primary function is exclusion. It is the most severe sanction that society, through the courts, can impose on those who fail to comply with the criminal law. The philosophy of imprisonment is elucidated by Cesare Beccaria.

> Anyone who disturbs the public peace, who does not obey the laws, that is, the conditions under which men agree to support one another, must be excluded from society – he must be banished from it (1996 [1764]: 11).

In the prison system, exclusion from the mainstream of society is reinforced by a structured and regimented organisation in which control and independence of movement is totally removed from the prisoner. The smooth running of the prison is based on compliance with the prevailing rules and regulations. Prisoners are categorised as either compliant or non-compliant, the latter being perceived as doubly deviant and appropriate subjects for further correction. The philosophical and political motivation for the establishment, maintenance and expansion of imprisonment is beyond the scope of this chapter. However, it is important to mention that many theorists see the prison not solely as a means of punishing transgressors of the criminal law, but as part of a wider strategy of social control which seeks to develop a new kind of individual, 'subject to habits, rules, orders, an authority that is exercised continually around him and upon him and which he must allow to function automatically in him' (Foucault, 1977: 198).

Since the establishment of the prison system in the thirteenth century, the purpose of imprisonment has changed depending on the prevailing criminal philosophy. Today imprisonment is seen as serving a number of different and seemingly contradictory functions:

> Imprisonment is aimed at: retribution, the rebalancing of the benefits an offender might have gained from crime by the application of a quantifiable disbenefit; the reform and rehabilitation of the offender; a publicly visible form of punishment; deterrence both of the punished individual and the public at large; the exclusion of offenders from open society; direct prevention of crime by incapacitation of the offender for the period of imprisonment; the expression of community values and social disapproval (O'Mahony, 1993: 548).

The Irish prison system has expanded hugely over the last twenty years in terms of prisoner numbers, prison personnel and the number of prisons. The daily average number of prisoners in custody in 1973 was 963; in 1993 it was 2,171 (Department of Justice, 1993); in 2002 it was 2,463, an increase of 1.7 per cent on 2001 (Irish Prison Service, 2003a). At the end of 2003 there were 16 different prisons in the country. These comprise a women's prison, Dochas, part of the Mountjoy complex, two open prisons, a juvenile prison, 11 closed prisons of various sizes for adult male offenders and a remand prison, Cloverhill Prison in Dublin which has a specially built District Court within the Complex. In 2004 the Government began a process of reorganising the prison system with the closure of the Curragh Place of Detention, Fort Mitchell Place of Detention (Spike Island) with the possibility of further major changes including the closure of Mountjoy Prison, which was established in 1850, and its replacement with a large new prison reflecting best planning in modern penology.

The Prison Board
In 1985 the *Whitaker Report* (Committee of Inquiry into the Penal System) indicated the need for change in the infrastructure administration and organisation of the prison system which had remained unchanged since Independence. This was reiterated a decade later in *The Management of Offenders – A Five Year Plan*, which indicated that there was a need 'to change the management structure of prisons, and to involve other interests in the general direction of the prison service' (Department of Justice, 1994). In 1996, the government decided to establish a Prisons Board, which would be responsible for an independent agency with responsibility for running the prison system. The Expert Group in its report *Towards an Independent Prison Agency*, published in 1997, supported the establishment of an independent prison agency with an independent board to ensure its operational functions complied with sound and prudent management principles. In 1998, the Minister for Justice, Equality and Law Reform established an Interim Prisons Board and sanctioned the appointment of a Secretary General to manage the operation of what is now called the Irish Prison Service. Its mission statement is:

> To provide safe, secure and humane custody for people who are sent to prison and to manage custodial sentences in a manner which encourages and supports prisoners in their endeavouring to live law abiding and purposeful lives (Irish Prison Service, 2003b).

The Parole Board
Under the Prison Rules 1947 all sentenced prisoners have a statutory right to one-quarter remission of their full prison sentence. In addition, prisoners may be released on supervised or unsupervised Temporary Release, under the Criminal Justice Acts 1960 and 2003, at the discretion of the Irish Prison Service and the Minister for Justice, Equality and Law Reform. From 1989, the Minister of Justice was advised on the temporary release of prisoners

serving long sentences by the Sentence Review Group, a non-statutory body. In 1997, the Report of the Expert Group, *Towards an Independent Prisons Agency* stated that:

> As a corollary to the establishment of an independent Prisons Agency, we consider that it would now be logical to establish a Parole Board, which was referred to in the Programme for Government, on a statutory basis" (Department of Justice, 1997b: Sec.7.3).

In April 2001, the Minister for Justice, Equality and Law Reform established the Parole Board on an interim administrative basis pending the enactment of the necessary legislation whose primary function is:

> to inform and advise the Minister on: 'the administration of the sentences of persons whose cases have been referred to the Board by the Minister: Where temporary release is recommended, the conditions which should attach to any such release' (Parole Board Annual Report 2002).

Eligible prisoners sentenced to more than seven years' imprisonment are reviewed by the Board which is a voluntary process.

Inspector of Prisons and Places of Detention
The Whitaker Report (Committee of Inquiry into the Penal System, 1985), *The Management of Offenders – a Five-Year Plan* (Department of Justice, 1994) and *Towards an Independent Prisons Agency* (Department of Justice, 1997b) all recommended the appointment of an Inspector of Prisons. The Committee for the Prevention of Torture and Inhuman or Degrading Treatment or Punishment (CPT), an international body which published two reports in 1995 and 1999 on their observational visits to examine the Irish penal system, recommended the appointment of an independent person to inspect all prisons. In April 2002, a Ministerial Order confirmed the appointment of Mr Justice Dermot Kinlan, a retired High Court Judge as the first Inspector of Prisons since the foundation of the state for a five-year period. The First Annual Report of the Inspector of Prisons and Places of Detention was published in 2003.

The Probation and Welfare Service
Probation, involving an informal system of supervision of offenders brought before the courts was initially provided by philanthropic societies in the latter part of the nineteenth century. It was not until the enactment of the Probation of Offenders Act 1907 that the practice achieved a formal legal status. In 1969, after an external review of the work of the Service, three

Senior Probation and Welfare Officers and 27 Probation and Welfare Officers were appointed. This expansion marked the beginning of the modern Probation and Welfare Service which in March 2004 has 208 Probation and Welfare Officers, 48 Senior Probation and Welfare Officers, 14 Assistant Principal Probation and Welfare Officers, one Principal Probation and Welfare Officer, 36 offices nationwide and an annual budget in 2004 of approximately €40,000,000. There are 46 full time Community Service Supervisors nationwide.

The provision of a probation service to the courts became more structured and formal during the 1960s and 1970s under the aegis of the Department of Justice. At this time it became known as the Probation and Welfare Service. In essence it is the social work service attached to the courts, prisons, places of detention, special schools, hostels, probation workshops and various ancillary community inter-agency projects. Its primary role is that of providing an advisory service on offending behaviour to the courts; writing pre-sentence reports for the courts; supervising offenders in the community; organising community service orders; providing a welfare service to offenders in prisons, places of detention and special schools; providing assessments to the Family Law Courts (pilot project 2003–4); and directed by the Probation of Offenders Act 1907 to advise, assist and befriend all those entrusted to its care by the courts.

The present service has continued, maintained and developed on a formal basis its historic links with voluntary and community groups, and in 2004 financially supports 74 projects nationwide. An example is the Cornmarket Project, an initiative of the Wexford Area Partnership under its Social Inclusion Plan 2000–6 which is funded by the Probation and Welfare Service. Its aim is 'to ensure that the voice of the community is heard in the development and provision of appropriate treatment, education and prevention services and responses' (Cornmarket Project Annual Report 2002).

The Probation and Welfare Service is organised on a national basis, with offices in all major centres of population. It is a professional agency within the Department of Justice, Equality and Law Reform. It has a centralised and hierarchical bureaucratic structure similar to that pertaining in all civil service departments. Since its development into a formal professional organisation, its work has increased not only in the courts but in its involvement in over seventy community-based projects nationally which address the twin problems of marginalisation and problematic social behaviour.

The Probation and Welfare Service has four principal community-based court orders available to it:

1   Probation Order – a statutory period of supervision, from one to three years, imposed by the District Court, under which the offender must enter into a recognisance. Conditions regarding behaviour, treatment, domicile

may be attached to the Order (Probation of Offenders Act, 1907). A Probation Order is not a criminal conviction; the facts are proved but the court does not proceed to convict.

2 Community Service Order – this Order is in lieu of a prison sentence after a finding of guilt. The duration of the Order is a minimum of 40 hours and a maximum of 240 hours. Under the Act (1983) an offender cannot be assigned to the Community Service Scheme unless a Probation and Welfare Officer's report deems him/her suitable and the offender agrees.

3 Supervision during deferment of sentence – this Order has no basis in legislation. It is used by all courts but especially by the Circuit Criminal Court. During the deferred period the offender is supervised by a Probation and Welfare Officer. On completion of the Order the offender returns to court where an assessment report presented to the judge outlines progress made and other relevant information.

4 Post Release Supervision Order – Under the Sex Offenders Act 2001 the court can make an Order where, on release from prison, the offender is subject to a determinate period of statutory supervision by a Probation and Welfare Officer. The period of imprisonment and the period of supervision must not exceed the maximum sentence the court can impose for any particular offence.

The considerable increase in the number of Community Orders, made by courts (Probation and Welfare Service Reports, 1995 and 1998) would seem to indicate a major move by the courts in the direction of imposing non-custodial sentences. However, according to O'Mahony (1993: 81), there is no definitive evidence that these cases 'represent the substitution of a non-custodial sentence for what would otherwise have been a custodial sentence'.

In 1983, the enactment of the Criminal Justice (Community Service) Act, 1983 marked the first major change in the Probation and Welfare Service's intervention with offenders since the enactment of the Probation of Offenders Act 1907. Under the Act offenders do community work in lieu of a prison sentence, the underlying philosophy being that the offenders should make restitution to society for their wrongdoing. It has proved to be a very successful development, having the confidence of both the judiciary and the public. An analysis of the operation of Community Service as a non-custodial disposal by the courts was carried out by Walsh and Sexton (1999).

The changing nature of criminal or offending behaviour has motivated the service to adapt new intervention strategies to respond to such changes. Intensive Probation Programmes were established in Dublin and Cork in 1991 with the aim of providing a community based group intervention strategy as an alternative to imprisonment for recidivist, high risk offenders. In 2002 Gerard Philips, a former Probation Officer published his research

An Empirical Study of the Intensive Probation Scheme in Cork. The research incorporated a qualitative and longitudinal analysis and concluded that 'the findings of this report suggest the following core elements of the IPS were beneficial to participants and led to lasting change in offending behaviour in some cases' (2002: 208).

Restorative justice and the concept of certain offenders meeting victims in supervised formal settings has become part of innovative practice in addressing offending behaviour. It can take the form of sentencing circles, family group or community conferencing, and victim-offender mediation. Restorative justice 'concentrates on restoring and repairing the relationship between the offender, victim and the community at large' (Lockhart, 2002: 747). Two Court based restorative justice projects, funded by the Probation and Welfare Service and overseen by community management committees, have been established in Tallaght/Dublin (Victim/Offender Mediation Service) and in Nenagh, County Tipperary (Nenagh Community Reparation Project). Both 'are based on models of best restorative justice practice' (Probation and Welfare Service Annual Report 1998: 6).

In November 1997, an Expert Group was established by the Government to examine the Probation and Welfare Service and to make recommendations. The first report was published in October 1998. The final report of the Expert Group which ran to 128 pages was published in 1999. The group made 30 recommendations which included: a significant shift in policy to facilitate the increased use of a much greater range of non-custodial sanctions; the repeal of the Probation of Offenders Act 1907 and new legislation enacted; non-custodial sanctions should be sanctions in their own right and not described as alternatives to imprisonment; the role of (Probation) Officers should be enhanced in such areas as addictions and other behaviours which might contribute to criminal activity. It also recommended the establishment of a statutory Probation and Welfare Agency.

Social policy and crime

As crime is a complex and contested issue it is inevitable that the social policy response will also be both complex and contested. The National Crime Council publication *Tackling the Underlying Causes of Crime* (2002) addressed many of the central issues pertinent to the 'crime problem' and made, among others, the following recommendations:

• Government policy, in the area of crime prevention must involve a range of policy initiatives in the short, medium and long term to address the complexity of the factors that give rise to crime and anti-social behaviour.

- A comprehensive crime prevention strategy must dovetail with the work of all government departments
- The important role of early intervention and diversion from the criminal justice system, as provided in the Children Act 2001, should be adopted in all public policy legislation.
- There is a need for ongoing independent evaluation of existing initiatives before bringing forward a new initiative. (National Crime Council, 2002: 16)

Since 1985 the basis of virtually all discussion on the Criminal Justice System has been the *Report of the Committee of Inquiry into the Penal System*, known as the Whitaker Report (Committee of Inquiry into the Penal System, 1985). This was the first independent government-sponsored investigation into the penal system in the history of the state. Its contents provided controversy, argument, and no little opposition on its publication and for a long time subsequently. While the report is not beyond criticism, it was and remains a humane, enlightened and progressive analysis of the Irish penal system. While much lip service and many laudatory remarks from both commentators and politicians followed the publication of the Whitaker Report, for many years there was no strategy to implement its recommendations as part of any overall plan to change and reform a system already strained by the persistent increase in the number of offenders. However, the wisdom and perspicacity of the Report can be seen in the gradual implementation of a number of its recommendations as outlined in this chapter.

Over the past 15 years, the importance of addressing the needs and rights of victims of crime has become more recognised as having a major relevance to the development of crime policies. In 1985, Victim Support was established in Ireland. It is reliant on Government funding which in 2003 amounted to just over €1m, a reduction of four per cent on the previous year. Based on a belief in the centrality of community and its role in supporting victims of crime, it is a national organisation with trained volunteers who offer a confidential, non-judgmental service to victims of crime. Victims can either refer themselves or be referred by the Garda investigating a particular crime. In addition to its core activity of a generic service to victims, it has developed specialist programmes for victims/families of murder or violence, tourists who have been victimised in different ways and, in 1998, a 24-hour freephone helpline was established.

Juvenile crime

The Whitaker Report indicates that about 'one third of all offences are attributable to young persons under 17 years of age' (Committee of Inquiry into the Penal System, 1985: 31). Ireland has had a tendency, in comparison with other European countries, to imprison a high proportion of its juvenile offenders. In its 2002 Annual Report, the Irish Prison Service stated that St Patrick's Institution, the main place of detention for males aged 16 to 21 years of age, had 1,158 prisoners committed during the year and that the average daily custody population was 179. The underlying causes of juvenile crime have been identified by a variety of research studies and include poverty, poor housing, low intelligence, inadequate (inconsistent) parental control, criminogenic living environment and age at commencement of offending. However, how these factors interact in an individual young person and contribute to offending behaviour is more complex and less transparent.

Juvenile justice policy with responsibility dissipated between the Departments of Justice, Equality and Law Reform; Health and Children; and Education and Science has been reflected in a lack of long term planning and a disjointed and unco-ordinated strategy for managing juvenile crime and its consequences. However, in the recent past there has been a marked increase in the quality of the discourse on the strategy needed to adequately address juvenile crime leading Quinn to observe that:

> In response to a growing awareness of the seriousness of the problems of juvenile crime and inadequacy of the official Irish reaction over many years, the Irish Juvenile Justice System has in the last few years experienced a unique period of debate and discussion (2002: 678).

In 1999, the Probation and Welfare Service published a research project on 150 young offenders in custody (Geiran et al., 1999). Examining the young offenders' experience of community sanctions prior to a custodial sentence, the research found that: two out of three (66 per cent) of the sample had been on supervision by the Probation and Welfare Service prior to receiving their first sentence; three out of four (78 per cent) had some contact with the Service; three out of ten (30 per cent) of the supervision orders were completed successfully; (25 per cent) were terminated by a new custodial sentence and the balance of 45 per cent were breached in court by the supervising officer because of non-compliance by the offender of the court order.

The culmination of the energetic and perceptive discussion over the past decade on the needs of 'troublesome' children was the major legislative change brought about by the Children Act 2001. The Act, which has major and far reaching implications, administrative, organisational and structural – for the Department of Health and Children, the Garda Síochána, the Probation and Welfare Service, the education system, and the courts – shifts the emphasis away from the idea of punishment and detention and proposes a comprehensive range of community-based sanctions. Some of its main provisions include:

- Increasing the age of responsibility to 12 years of age
- Person to be regarded as a child up to 18 years of age
- The Garda Diversionary Scheme (TLO) placed on a statutory footing (Section 9)
- Responsibility for under-age children where parental care is not present transferred to health boards
- Providing for the abolition of reformatory and industrial schools, renaming them children's detention schools
- Increased powers given to health boards to provide special care for non-offending out-of-control children (S. 216–18)
- Introducing family group conferencing
- Detention to be an absolute 'last resort'
- Rights and interests of victims highlighted
- Role and responsibilities of parents explicitly outlined

The Act, which is complex, far reaching and resource intensive has been positively welcomed by all professionals working in the area of child protection and juvenile justice. As Tutt states:

> The proposals in the Children Bill for diverting young people from crime are a serious attempt to implement the principles of restorative justice, which invites and enables victims, offenders and the community to repair some of the injustices resulting from crime (1996: 8).

The expected outcomes from the Act when fully implemented include: a reduction in re-offending; increased use of community sanctions; detention as a last resort; better co-ordination of services to young offenders; a reduction of victimisation and improved community safety.

There are, however, other perspectives on the objectives of juvenile justice. O'Sullivan (1998a) sees the move from industrial schools to community sanctions as being underlined by the same ideology. For him the 'new technologies of regulation' have the same purpose as the institutional confinement of old which was:

> to contain the risk that these children exhibit through technologies of normalisation, socialisation, and prevention. For those that fail to adapt or conform to the new technologies of prevention, the carceral archipelagos of Lusk, Clonmel and the North Circular Road retain their central role in the disciplining of the poor (1998a: 91).

Women and crime

Criminal behaviour is largely perceived as being male dominated, with women contributing to a relatively insignificant percentage of crimes. In 2002, a total of 8,673 males and 1,043 females were committed to prison. Males accounted for approximately 90 per cent of all committals. As a consequence, women tend to be disadvantaged by comparison with their male counterparts when it comes to facilities and resources. James (1998, 2004) shows that the institutions of the Irish criminal justice system are predominantly patriarchal in nature and that there is a dearth of research on the subject of female offending and appropriate services. Although the Irish prison system is broadly a humane regime, women have been traditionally confined in what were shameful conditions. The old refurbished women's prison in the Mountjoy complex was thus described:

> a proliferation of new metal, cage-like barriers and steel meshing in the passage-ways and landings of the women's prison fails to disguise the gloomy Victorian penitentiary but rather adds dramatically to the brutal, demoralising spirit of the place (O'Mahony, 1996: 101).

In its Strategy Statement 1998–2000 the Department of Justice, Equality and Law Reform (1998b) committed itself to building a new female prison for 80 prisoners. In 1999 that undertaking was realised when the Dochas Centre, part of the Mountjoy Complex was opened at a cost of 20 million pounds. It is a closed, medium security prison, which accommodates 80 women in seven separate houses, providing modern prison accommodation and facilities including a gymnasium and a crèche in a user-friendly milieu. In 2002, the average daily number imprisoned was 88 with a maximum of 102. In February 2004 the Minister for Justice, Equality and Law Reform announced the closing of the Mountjoy Complex possibly including the Dochas Centre. The Minister indicated that a new modern complex would be built on a greenfield site.

With the exception of James's groundbreaking studies (1998, 2004), there is a paucity of research, documentation and academic discourse in Ireland relating to female prisoners. Carmody and McEvoy's study (1996) makes grim reading. One hundred women committed to prison over a six-week period were interviewed. The general conclusion from the study is that women prisoners are a very vulnerable and disadvantaged group in our community. Most were in their mid-20s and came from Dublin's inner city. Many had drug or alcohol problems, a sizeable minority were HIV-positive and half the sample had previous psychiatric treatment. Most had a previous history of being in prison. Offence categories tended to be minor, with larceny and robbery being the most usual categories.

Notwithstanding the improvement in the quality of prison accommodation for women, there is a lack of post-release supports for women who
have a multiplicity of problems including drug use. Considering the issues
associated with female offenders, an open, more 'therapeutic community'
style prison would appear much more appropriate and provide a greater
possibility of reducing re-offending. The *Whitaker Report* (Committee of
Inquiry into the Penal System, 1985) realised this when it proposed an open
centre to accommodate most women offenders and a secure probation hostel
as an alternative to prison for some juvenile (female) offenders. The National
Economic and Social Forum (NESF) Report *Reintegration of Prisoners* also
recommends the development of an open prison for women (2002b: 12).

Sex offending

Sexual assaults against adults and children are now recognised as a major
social and criminal problem in Ireland. The perpetrators of sexual assault,
contrary to the stereotype frequently portrayed in the media are not generally
sex starved, insane and readily identifiable as different. It is important that
the image of the perpetrator as being a 'pervert' and beyond redemption is
corrected. Sexual assault is a multi-layered, complex, multi-dimensional
phenomenon. We must be mindful of the fact that when we talk about sex
offenders we are identifying mostly men who have been found guilty of an
identifiable assault in a Criminal Court and within the context of a specific
statute. What generally identifies the convicted sex offender from others is the
level of violence involved in committing crime.

While the number of sexual assaults reported to rape crisis centres and
the Garda Síochána have increased over the past two decades, there is no
empirical evidence to determine whether the rate of increase is due to an
increase in the incidence of sexual assault or an increase in the level of reporting.
In 1986 there were 400 sexual crimes reported to the police. In 1994 they had
risen to 600 and in 1999 this had further increased to 975 (Murphy, 2002: 707).
The position for 2002–3 was that 2,463 sex offences were reported to the police.

In 1993 there were 159 sex offenders in our prisons (Irish Prison Service
Annual Report). In 1997 there were 279 (Annual Report of the Inspector of
Prisons) and in March 2004 there were approximately 340, comprising
approximately 12 per cent of the total prison population. It is important to
remember that the number of sex offenders convicted and imprisoned for
their crimes is a small proportion of the number of offences reported to the
police. The implication of this is that 'reducing sexual victimisation in society
will require a lot more in terms of social policy than simply focusing on
imprisoned or indeed convicted sex offenders' (Murphy, 2002: 708).

In 1998, the Department of Justice, Equality and Law Reform published
its discussion paper *The Law on Sexual Offences* which represented a new

departure in stimulating discussion on the complex problem that is sexual offending. This was preceded in 1996 by the report *Victims of Sexual and Other Crimes of Violence Against Women and Children* (National Women's Council of Ireland) which made 50 recommendations in relation to rape, sexual assault and child sexual abuse. The National Steering Committee on Violence Against Women published its first report in 1999. The groundbreaking *SAVI (Sexual Abuse and Violence in Ireland) Report* (McGee et al., 2002) was published in 2002. The Report details the views, beliefs, concerns and other attitudes concerning sexual violence of 3,118 randomly selected people from the general population. On the basis of the study, the researchers determined that 80,000 adult women and 37,000 adult men had been exposed to sexual abuse as children.

In 1993, the Department of Justice published a discussion document, *A Proposal for a Structured Psychological Treatment Programme for Sex Offenders.* In 1994, the first prison-based sex offender programme was established in Arbour Hill Prison. Delivered by the Probation and Welfare Service and the Prison Psychology Service it is a demanding therapeutic programme lasting approximately one year. A similar programme commenced in the Curragh Prison in 2000. All sex offenders throughout the prison system are invited to apply for both courses. The programmes are voluntary and in this context the Curragh programmes did not begin in 2003 due to a paucity of applications from offenders.

A community-based sex offender programme began in Dublin in 2003. Funded by the Probation and Welfare Service, it is run on a partnership basis by the Service and the Granada Institute. A similar programme has been run by the Probation and Welfare Service and the North Western Health Board in the north-west for over a decade.

The two most recent pieces of legislation governing the prosecution of sexual offences are The Child Trafficking and Pornography Act 1998 which protects children from being trafficked in, out and through Ireland for the purpose of sexual exploitation. The Act also criminalises the creation, distribution and possession of child pornography.

The Sex Offenders Act 2001 introduces many new provisions not covered in previous legislation, which include:

- A notification system (frequently referred to as the sex offender register), which requires sex offenders to notify the police where they are living within seven days of their conviction or on their release from prison.
- A requirement by the offender to notify any prospective employer of their conviction if the position involves *any* unsupervised access to children.
- A post release supervision order whereby the offender is subject to a period of statutory supervision by the Probation and Welfare Service on release from prison for a specific length of time.

For many years and until the present the policy of the Department of Justice, Equality and Law Reform and of successive Ministers has been clear and unequivocal. No sex offenders are released from jail prior to the expiry of their full sentence. They are not considered for temporary release, supervised or otherwise, under the Criminal Justice (Temporary Release) Act 1960 or the Criminal Justice (Temporary Release of Prisoners) Act 2003.

Conclusion

Any examination of the criminal justice system highlights the complexity of crime, criminal behaviour and society's often-inadequate response to violent crime in particular. Policies, strategies, legislation and possible solutions are strongly influenced by the ideology prevailing at any particular time. In its Strategy Statement 2003–2005 the Department of Justice, Equality and Law Reform states:

> The need for balance and proportionality. A key task for the Department is to find the right balance between the competing rights of the accused, the prosecutor, the victims of crime and society generally. An essential prerequisite to finding this balance is ensuring protection of fundamental human rights and freedoms consistent with constitutional obligations and international commitments. (2003: 47)

At the policing level, a new pragmatism is evident in the strategy being implemented. This includes high-profile Garda operations against 'hard core' criminals i.e. *Operation Dochas* (1997), *Operation Cleanstreet* (1998) and, in terms of child pornography, *Operation Amethyst* (2003). This has been accompanied by a parallel legislative programme with more wide-ranging penalties, i.e. the Criminal Justice (Drug Trafficking) Acts of 1996 and 1999 provide for mandatory minimum sentences for certain drug offences. Another innovative strategy for addressing particular offences has been the pilot Drug Court in the Dublin Metropolitan District Court area. The Criminal Assets Bureau (CAB) established in 1996 has been highly successful in freezing or confiscating (having processed the cases through the courts), the assets of people accumulated through criminal exploits.

In this context it is important to remember the argument put forward in the National Economic and Social Council's report, *The Criminal Justice System: Policy and Performance*, 'There is, and will remain, a core of law breaking activity that cannot be reduced by any policy option available, either the most severe crime control measures or the most extensive programme to combat inequality' (NESC, 1984: 30). The celebrated sociologist Emile Durkheim went even further, making the point that crime is present in all societies. Accepting that crime is an ephemeral concept and that the criminality of particular acts changes over time (with society periodically re-examining what constitutes criminal behaviour), he argues that:

> crime is necessary, it is bound up with the fundamental conditions of all social life and by that very fact it is useful, because these conditions of which it is a part are themselves indispensable to the normal evaluation of morality and law (Durkheim, 1895: 70).

It is now generally accepted that, in itself, prison is an ineffective means of rehabilitating those incarcerated. That is not to say that particular focused rehabilitative programmes within prison cannot have an effect on some offenders' behaviour, such as violence and sexual assault. However, imprisonment is going to remain a central factor in our efforts to control crime. If it is to serve its purpose adequately, i.e. a combination of incapacitation, deterrence and rehabilitation, then it has to be used more judiciously and more selectively.

The National Economic and Social Forum in its report, *The Re-integration of Prisoners*, makes a number of recommendations to enhance and develop the way the criminal justice system deals with offenders and criminal behaviour (NESF, 2002b: 5)

- increase the use of non-custodial options
- increase emphasis on reintegration throughout the prison system
- introduce positive sentence management and involve all stakeholders
- develop more planned and integrated after-care for prisoners on release
- end discrimination on the basis of a criminal record, bar exceptional circumstances
- increase data gathering, monitoring and independent evaluation to better inform policy development

Custody dominates all discussion about the penal system and acts as a reference point for everything else. As we grapple intellectually and emotionally with the concepts surrounding the crime problem, it is clear that the importance of what could be termed community-based sanctions or penalties are gaining some ground, particularly as the financial cost of imprisonment soars. However, progress in expanding community sanctions has been slow. The use of the term 'alternatives to custody' has contributed to this. These terms suggest the centrality of custody as the norm, with alternatives competing with it rather than being part of a range of sentencing options (Pratt, 1987). While there has been a reasonably clear conceptualisation by successive governments in Ireland about the objectives for reducing the use of custody, there has not been a parallel emphasis on how community-based penalties might be promoted or on outlining the circumstances in which such penalties might be applied. In Ireland, probation, intensive supervision and community service have been the central pillars of the community approach. Latterly, multi-agency community strategies are being implemented, such as the Bridge Project, BOND and the Cornmarket Project. As part of this developing strategy the following issues should be examined: fines (with failure to pay being dealt with through community sanctions rather than prison); suspended sentences with a supervisory condition, as advocated by Whitaker (Committee of Inquiry, 1985); electronic monitoring – when combined with mandatory supervision as operated by the Probation Directorate in the Home Office in Britain can be used with great effect for particular offenders (Whitfield, 1997).

A major hindrance to the development of a cohesive and comprehensive analysis of crime in Ireland, and to the implementation of the most appropriate intervention strategies, is the absence of a single unified source of research data. There is an urgent need for a proactive co-ordinated plan with adequate resources to be developed, in which research and data analysis become an integral part of the overall strategic management of the Department of Justice, Equality and Law Reform. As long ago as 1974, the Henchy Committee recommended that the Minister for Justice establish a 'suitably staffed research and statistics unit as a matter of urgency'.

When we think of crime we visualise courts, offenders, police, prison, prosecution, defence. However, crime also concerns victims. The complaints about the criminal process from agencies like Victim Support and rape crisis centres are that victims are marginalised and their suffering is not adequately addressed. Two initiatives addressing this deficiency should be noted. The Criminal Justice Act 1993 introduced the concept of the victim impact statement in criminal cases. This statement, which can only be given after a finding of guilt, is intended to allow the victims / victims' family members, to address the court on the impact the offence had on them physically, emotionally, psychologically, socially, financially. The court itself can look for a victim impact report to be presented outlining the victims' circumstances, the pain and suffering endured and the negative impact of the crime on their personal integrity. The Charter of Victims Rights in the Criminal Justice System (Department of Justice, Equality and Law Reform, 1999) outlines what victims can expect from a number of different agencies involved in the system, including victim support.

Over the past decade, Ireland has become a multi-racial and a multi-cultural society. Since 1998 approximately 128,000 immigrants have arrived in the country from a variety of ethnic backgrounds (*Sunday Independent,* 11 March 2004). Inevitably such a development is reflected in the composition of the prison population. 'Over 160 foreign nationals in Irish prisons from 20 different countries reveals the reality of the growing complexity of the problems which must be addressed by the Criminal Justice System including the possible escalation of organised crime' (*Sunday Independent,* 11 March 2004). Such a development will put considerable pressure on the capacity of the Gardai to deal adequately with such a challenge and will necessitate a force with a more diverse cultural and ethnic composition.

Bacik and O'Connell state that 'crime is best understood primarily as a social problem arising from particular economic conditions' (1998: vi). O'Donnell, discussing begging, a crime under the Vagrancy Act 1847, for which the only penalty available is imprisonment, states that 'it is a cause of some concern that the criminal law is used in this way to penalise poverty and social inadequacy. This is hardly the hallmark of an enlightened society' (1998: 36). In the same publication, O'Mahony exhorts us to stop believing in the comfortable certainty that the offender is the only one responsible for criminal behaviour. We need to look at the influence of the functioning of society on the existence and persistence of crime. Such an analysis might lead to the uncomfortable conclusion that the changes needed are broader that that of the Criminal Justice system itself, raising 'fundamental issues of social justice which cannot be solved simply by ensuring that the penal system is run in a just and decent manner' (O'Mahony, 1998: 65). A complex problem needs and demands complex solutions. Our current concept of crime implies a unity to what is essentially a vast array of diverse behaviours, events and legal sanctions. Crime, while being a major problem, is also one of the most enduring factors in modern society. A significant proportion of crime is avoidable if, through policies in areas like education and unemployment, all individuals, particularly the young, are enabled to participate fully in their community and society. If such a commitment is unforthcoming, it is foolish to expect the Criminal Justice System by itself to limit crime to an irreducible minimum.

Table 13.1 **Chronology of developments in the criminal justice system in Ireland**

1847	Vagrancy Act
1907	Probation of Offenders Act
1937	Bunreacht na hÉireann (Constitution of Ireland)
1939	Office of Attorney General
1947	Prison Rules (still operational)
1960	Criminal Justice (Temporary Release) Act
1963	Garda Juvenile Liaison Scheme
1974	Director of Public Prosecutions
	Henchy Committee
1975	Law Reform Commission

1983   Criminal Justice (Community Service) Act
1985   Report of the Committee of Inquiry into the Penal System (Whitaker Report)
       Victim Support established
1989   Sentence Review Group
1993   Criminal Justice Act (Victim Impact Statement)
       A Proposal for a Structural Psychological Treatment Programme for Sex Offenders
            (Report)
1994   *The Management of Offenders – A Five Year Plan* (Report)
       Irish Penal Reform Trust
       Sex Offender Treatment Programme (Prisons)
1995   Committee (EU) for the Prevention of Torture and Inhuman or Degrading Treatment
            or Punishment (Report)
       Transfer of Sentenced Persons Act 1995
1996   Garda Síochána (Complaints) Act
       Garda Complaints Board
       Working Group on a Courts Commission
       Sexual Offences (Jurisdiction) Act
       Criminal Assets Bureau (CAB)
1997   Criminal Justice Act
       Department of Justice, Equality and Law Reform Annual Report
       Towards an Independent Prisons Agency (Report)
1998   Courts Service Act
       Interim Prisons Board
       Child Trafficking and Pornography Act
1999   Irish Courts Service
       Report of the Expert Group on the Probation and Welfare Service (final)
       Dochas, new women's prison
       Victim's Charter (Department of Justice, Equality and Law Reform)
       Committee (EU) for the Prevention of Torture and Inhuman or Degrading Treatment
            or Punishment (Report)
2001   Children's Act
       Drugs Court
       Interim Parole Board
       Sex Offenders Act
2002   Inspector of Prisons
2003   Criminal Justice (Temporary Release of Prisoners) Act 2003

Recommended reading

Bacik, I. and M. O'Connell (eds) (1998) *Crime and Poverty in Ireland*. Dublin: Round
    Hall Sweet and Maxwell.
Department of Justice, Equality and Law Reform (2003) *Strategy Statement 2003–2005,
    Community Security and Equality*. Dublin: Department of Justice, Equality and Law
    Reform.

Geiran, V., M. McCarthy, M. Morahan and V. O'Connell (1999) *Young Offenders in Penal Custody*. Dublin: Brunswick Press.

McCullogh, C. (1996) *Crime in Ireland: A Sociological Introduction*. Cork: Cork University Press.

NESF (2002) *Re-integration of Prisoners: Forum Report No. 22*. Dublin: Stationery Office.

O'Mahony, P. (2002) *Criminal Justice in Ireland*. Dublin: IPA.

Young, P., I. O'Donnell and E. Clare (2001) *Crime in Ireland*. Dublin: Stationery Office.

Chapter 14

Drugs policy

Hilda Loughran

Introduction

Drug use continues to be a major concern in Ireland in the new millennium. The problems related to drug use impact not just on those who actually take drugs but also on the general population. Drugs issues span several areas relevant to social policy studies. Perhaps the most widely discussed of these is that of crime. Criminal activity is associated with drugs at different levels. Firstly, it is associated with users who have to commit crimes in order to support their drug habits. Perhaps more attention is currently being paid to the second level of activity, organised crime. A sophisticated, organised crime network has been a prerequisite for the establishment and expansion of the drugs problem. The drugs problem has medical aspects as well, of course, which have perhaps been highlighted by the emergence of HIV and AIDS in the 1980s. However, the medical questions go beyond transmission of HIV and AIDS to the broader definition of health care which incorporates the immediate and long-term effects of drug use on the user's general health status and the need for health promotion as an integral part of drugs policy. Other areas linked to the drugs issue are social welfare, local development and housing, education and youth services. This chapter will explore and evaluate the complex nature of the drugs problem in Ireland as it has developed through the 1990s and into the new millennium. Government policies and initiatives designed to address the problem will be outlined. The sometimes conflicting needs of drug users and the communities they live in will also be discussed.

Definition and scope of this policy area

A discussion about drugs policy must first define the parameters of the term drug. In most countries, as in Ireland, a distinction is made between drugs which are legal and those which have been designated as illegal. The distinction may, in fact, be unhelpful in that it may offer some air of safety to legal drugs and focus attention almost exclusively on illegal drugs. In reality, the health, social and economic costs of both legal and illegal drugs are a major cause for concern in our society today. The term legal drugs is generally used in relation to alcohol, tobacco and prescription drugs. In the present context, the term illegal drugs refers to 'street drugs'; this includes opiates (predominantly heroin), stimulants (including cocaine, crack and ecstasy), cannabis, LSD and various tranquillisers (which can be acquired both legally and illegally). For the purposes of policy formulation and treatment provision in Ireland, the legal and illegal substances are treated completely separately. With regard to policy developments, the two areas remain relatively segregated. The main policy document dealing with policy developments for alcohol is the National Alcohol Policy of 1996. The policy could be criticised for being conservative in its goals and methods. The policy has, however, been reviewed and the *Strategic Task Force on Alcohol Interim Report* 2002 has done much to highlight the need for more positive action. The equivalent policy agenda for illegal substances is laid out in the Government Strategy to Prevent Drug Misuse, 1991, the two Task Force Reports of 1996, 1997 and the National Drugs Strategy 2001–8. While the separation of the two aspects of the drugs issue is a fact of life in the Irish scene, it may be misleading in that this separation might suggest that the problems with legal drugs are somehow less significant. Problems relating to alcohol accounted in 1992 for up to 23 per cent of admissions to psychiatric hospitals, 22,482 prosecutions for all types of offences involving alcohol, as well as road traffic accidents (Corrigan, 1994: 22–3). By 2002 (Department of Health and Children, 2002b: 8–11) it was evident that delays in tackling the drinks issue had had serious adverse consequences. Alcohol policy and other drug policy have developed in quite a diverse manner and so the alcohol aspect deserves a discussion in its own right. However, this chapter will focus on policy strategies that relate to illegal drugs.

Several questions emerge in a discussion of illegal drugs. What constitutes a problem in relation to the use of drugs? Is use alone definitive of a problem, or is it necessary that some medical, social or economic damage is incurred because of the drug use? What level or nature of problem is evidence of abuse or addiction? In Irish policy the use of illegal drugs is, in and of itself, considered problematic. This is inevitable, of course, in a situation where the very possession of such drugs constitutes an illegal activity – hence the possessor is already 'in trouble'. While all drug use is therefore covered in the ambit of drug policy, it is fair to say that the central focus of concern is on those who could be classified as problem drug users:

> A problem drug taker would be any person who experiences social, psychological, physical or legal problems related to intoxication and/or regular excessive consumption and/or dependence as a consequence of his own use of drugs or other

chemical substances (excluding alcohol and tobacco). (Report of the Advisory Council on the Misuse of Drugs, 1982: 34)

Historical overview of drugs policy in Ireland

Government drugs policy in Ireland has been greatly influenced historically by the temperance movement in the USA and the UK. The movement, initiated by Benjamin Rush in 1784, identified addiction as a disease and clearly recommended that the only course of action to resolve the problem was total abstinence. While this model for dealing with addiction clearly fitted with a view that combined the medical concerns about the disease with the moral concern about the evils of addiction, it did little to assist in the development of inclusive and tolerant policy strategies. Rather, the history of both legislation and social policy in Ireland in relation to drug use would be typified by its exclusionist nature. The result of this construction of drug addiction as primarily an issue of medical concern was to deny the socio-cultural and socio-economic nature of the predominance of drug problems in economically deprived communities. The dual concerns of tackling the supply and the demand for drugs formed the central rationale for policy in the 1990s. It has remained a core aspect of policy framework to date. It is also from these early influences that the emphasis on the individual as the target of policy and treatment has its roots. The supply-and-demand reduction factors, along with the individual focus, will form the basis of a paradigm for understanding drug policy presented later in this chapter.

The history of the development of Irish drugs policy is comprehensively analysed by Butler (1991). He points out that, as far back as 1983, there was clear evidence of the connection between developing drug problems, poverty and the powerlessness of a small number of working-class neighbourhoods (Butler, 1991: 19). However, recommendations of the 1983 Task Force were never endorsed in policy and it was not until the 1990s that any attempt was made to follow through on this earlier suggestion to identify Community Priority Areas. The failure to identify and acknowledge the marginalising effects of the drug problem itself and governmental attempts to control that problem are evident in activities in the drugs arena today. In Ireland, evidence confirms that the problems relating to drug use are concentrated in the Greater Dublin area (Task Force, 1996). This is especially the case for opiate use. Cork, however, has a serious cannabis problem, twice the rate of other areas for lifetime use (Jackson, 1998: 31). Dublin has both a cannabis and an opiate problem (Task Force, 1996).

The 1990s saw more activity in policy development than previously. Of course, the presence of policy documents does not ensure the resolution of the drugs problem. The move to tackle the drugs issue may have lost its momentum in succeeding years. This could be attributed to the 'high' of the Celtic Tiger on the one hand followed by attempts to moderate government spending across the board. One has to examine the rash of policy initiatives in the 1990s in the light of past experiences. In particular, it is important to question whether traditional interpretations of what 'addiction' actually means and the subsequent legislative avenues for addressing the problem have in fact altered at all since the early days of the drug problem in the 1960s.

It could be argued that in spite of a pressure to act on the drug problem because of growing social concern, fuelled by increased drug related crime and the establishment of ecstasy use as a young middle-class activity, successive governments have been unable to transcend the strictures of what Murphy (1996) refers to as a deterrence perspective. Perhaps current policy is yet another attempt to condemn drug users to the margins of society while attempting to safeguard the rest of society from the evils of drug use. This concern was echoed in an article by Loughran (1996), in which Fergus McCabe, a member of the Inner City Organisations Network (ICON), suggested that 'we either address the major economic and social issues that underpin the problems of crime and drug abuse or we go the route of other countries and attempt to build a ring of steel around areas – keep a lid on it – contain it' (Loughran, 1996: 13).

The 1990s was one of the most active phases in the Irish government's attempts to tackle the drugs issue, in contrast to the early years where political responses to the problem were at best reactive and at worst restrictive. The struggle to understand the drugs issue in Ireland has been hampered by the importation of ideas about the nature of drug addiction and the political and, indeed, philosophical commitment to prohibitions perspectives (predominantly from the USA). These perspectives propound the view that drugs are bad and that they must be stamped out: the goal is to remove the problem of drug abuse from society. This viewpoint has its merits, although many in the treatment and policy field would probably support the view that, from a social policy perspective, it is not enough to consider ideals. Social policy must also address the reality of the situation and in doing so recognise that previous attempts at prohibition have failed (Murphy, 1996). Social policy must address the needs of the socially excluded, in this case drug users and often their families. Policy must also concern itself with effectiveness and fairness. Forder (1974), in his classic work on need, drew attention not only to need as defined by society at large, but also to the validity of the felt needs of service users and marginalised groups.

Murphy (1996) contends that prohibitionist policies promoted the 'war-on-drugs' paradigm. The central tenet of such a policy is the implementation of legislation which criminalises drug use and the manufacturing, distribution and supply of drugs. This also supports the promotion of abstinence as *the* treatment response. These approaches have proved unsuccessful (Murphy, 1996). This lack of success needs no further evidence than the combined escalation of the drug problem as documented by O'Hare and O'Brien (1993), O'Higgins (1996), and Moran et al. (1997). The futility of dealing with all illegal drugs in the same manner is exemplified by moves in the United Kingdom to differentiate between classes of illegal drugs. This move will culminate in the change in status of cannabis from a class B to a class C drug in the near future (www.drugs.gov.uk/nationalStragegy/CannabisReclassification).

Butler (1991) identifies three phases in the development of the drugs problem and government responses to them over a 25-year period from 1966–90. The first stage was from 1966–79, which he refers to as the early years (Butler, 1991: 212–18). Drugs were considered within the ambit of mental health policy. This era witnessed the establishment of the Drugs Squad, the publication of the *Report of the Working Party on Drug Abuse* (1971), and the establishment of the first treatment facilities in the form of Coolmine Therapeutic Community and the National Drug Treatment Centre. The second stage Butler refers to was from 1980 to 1985, which he calls the opiate epidemic (1991: 218–25). He documents the escalating heroin problems in Dublin and various attempts to address the 'epidemic'.

> No effort was made to establish clear conceptual and practical distinctions between drug control policies, which are the responsibility of the criminal justice system, and health and welfare policies which operate on a radically different value system and are the responsibility of the health and welfare institutions. (Butler, 1991: 224)

The third stage discussed is 1986–91, the AIDS connection (Butler, 1991: 225–9). The impact of the emergence of HIV and AIDS is outlined and government reaction is critically analysed. In concluding his review of 25 years of drugs policy, Butler suggests that

> the consensus which has been a feature of Irish drug policy making has been superficial, that it has been achieved and maintained by ignoring many real policy dilemmas, and that such consensus-seeking may in the long run be of less societal value than an open acknowledgement of institutional and cultural ambivalence. (1991: 230)

Table 14.1 gives details of developments since the late 1960s. Prior to that time, legislation regarding drugs was predominately vested in customs legislation, including the Dangerous Drugs Act 1934, the Customs Act 1956, and the Customs Consolidation Act 1976.

Table 14.1 **Paradigm for analysis of drug policy (demand–reduction/supply–reduction forming one axis and an individual/communities focus forming the second)**

INDIVIDUAL	
education and prevention	(offer of alternative supply)
abstinence treatment	methadone maintenance
harm reduction treatment	needle exchange
rehabilitation	targetting of individual dealers
DEMAND REDUCTION	**SUPPLY REDUCTION**
education and prevention	Drugs Squad
youth services and employment	Europol
diversionary strategies (e.g. sport)	increased number of judges and gardai
community-based services	improved legislation
development of community awareness	supported community action
estate management	
structural change[1]	
COMMUNITIES	

1 Structural change is currently aspirational rather than evident in policy.

Before looking more critically at policy developments in the 1990s and beyond, it might be useful to summarise policy-led activities prior to that time (see table 14.2, p. 320). These reflect a policy commitment to control drug problems by tackling supply and criminalising drug use and were the underlying reason for the development of the generally one-dimensional services to drug users. That is, the emphasis was on assisting those drug users who were prepared to attempt total withdrawal from drug use. The biggest shift in policy was inevitably the need to address the broader public health issues which emanated from the emergence of HIV and AIDS. At that time, the task of attracting all drug users to services, even if they had no interest in total abstinence, was clearly of paramount importance. That is because it was only by attracting such users to services that there is any hope, first, of estimating the extent of drug use and second of reducing the risk of harm to both users and the non-using population. The phase identified in Butler as the AIDS connection inevitably set the context for a change of direction in policy. This phase clearly marked the transition of the drugs problem from the confines of the 'marginalised' in society to the centre of general public health concerns. Crossing this boundary has highlighted both concern and commitment to tackling the drug problem in a meaningful and effective manner. However, one might pessimistically suggest that the shift away from abstinence models to harm reduction models may also reflect a further attempt to cordon off the drug problem and protect the general public by keeping drug users under control, if not by criminalising their activity, then more subtly endorsing their drug use by choosing to offer a substitute drug to diminish if not eliminate criminal behaviour associated with drug use.

Drugs policy from 1990 to 1998

The 1990s represent another phase in the ongoing story of drugs in Ireland. During the 1990s attempts were made to move on from the early restrictive responses to drug policy and to allow more creative and inclusive initiatives to develop.

By the time the government strategy for the prevention of drug misuse arrived in 1991, it was clear that 'all evidence here points to a concentration of the problem in specific areas of Dublin with poor housing and high levels of employment' (Department of Health, 1991: 8). The social marginalisation of sectors of society, of communities and neighbourhoods was acknowledged but unchallenged by the strategy document.

1991: Government strategy for the prevention of drug misuse
The main thrust of the 1991 Strategy was to establish and formalise co-operation between various interested parties. Specifically mentioned were the links between voluntary and statutory services, education, treatment services, local communities, prison services and customs and international drug agencies. The overall goal of the new policy was to 'set out to implement realistic and achievable objectives in the areas of supply reduction, demand reduction and increased access to treatment and methadone programmes coupled with a comprehensive structure geared toward their effective implementation' (Department of Health, 1991: 2).

Perhaps the most innovative moves at this time were the attempt to develop community-based services and the official backing for harm reduction approaches to treatment. The community-based services were envisaged as being community drug teams which incorporated a major role for General Practitioners (GPs). Paradoxically, the strategy document specifically highlighted a plan to deal with GPs who might be engaged in 'irresponsible prescribing' (1991: 2).

Apart from GPs, one of the other features of this strategy was the recommendation for legislation to enable the proceeds of drug trafficking to be confiscated. This strategy, perhaps more than the others, offered a new approach to dealing with the supply of drugs as it was directed at the rewards accruing to dealers from their illegal activities. As with many other recommendations of this strategy, it would take the further impetus of the 1996

Task Force to have its potential realised. Details of the drug situation in Ireland were clearly laid out in the strategy document (Department of Health, 1991). The report confirmed that the main focus of the problem was in the Greater Dublin area. The prevalence of drug problems in Limerick, Cork and Galway appeared to refer specifically to use of cannabis, not heroin.

In reading the strategy document, the attention given to the soft drug cannabis is striking (Department of Health, 1991: 6–7). For example, the report notes that in 1989, 70 per cent of charges for drug offences related to cannabis, and the increase in seizures related mainly to cannabis (1991: 7). As already suggested, the definition of what a drug problem is has been influenced by the prohibitionist philosophy of total abstinence from all drugs classified as illegal. The debate about where cannabis should be situated in this drug problem paradigm is strongly debated. It could be argued that the resources used to police the use of cannabis might be better directed to dealing with harder drugs, specifically heroin. However, such a position has never been clearly stated in government policy. (Of course, by the mid-1990s, the extent of concern for the heroin problem far outweighed that of the cannabis issue.) Murphy (1996) suggests a continuum of illegality where cannabis would be situated at one end, with fewer resources being used to police its use, and more diverted to a more exclusive pursuit of hard drugs.

The concern that 'soft drugs' act as 'gateway drugs' (Department of Health, 1991: 26) to the use of hard drugs has contributed to the evolution of drug responses that bind the two categories of drugs inextricably together. Yet there is growing evidence that the use of heroin as the initial drug of choice is on the increase. A report by Keogh (1997: ix) confirms that 30 per cent of known drug users started on heroin. This raises the concern that heroin is becoming more acceptable and accessible as a 'start-up' drug. The implication of this development is that there will be more younger users who potentially will engage in risky behaviour through inexperience and immaturity. Health and safety issues about safe injecting, understanding the strength and the quality of the drug used, and taking precautions in relation to HIV and AIDS may be neglected by this group of users because of their relative immaturity and inexperience. This aspect of the problem was not discussed in the government strategy document of 1991. Because of the problem of compiling accurate statistics on the prevalence of drug use, particularly heroin use and specifically intravenous heroin use, it is difficult to develop strategies to effectively plan services or monitor progress. Some of the most fruitful sources of information are the Health Research Board reports which relate to treated drug misuse only (O'Hare and O'Brien, 1992, 1993; O'Higgins and O'Brien, 1994; O'Higgins, 1996; Moran et al., 1997).

Plans for a more co-ordinated and structured co-operation between all parties involved in working with the drugs issue contained within the 1991 strategy were of course welcomed, as were the suggestions regarding the development of community-based structures. Disappointing, however, was the failure to address the concerns identified by the 1983 committee regarding the real nature of the drug problems, as established and nurtured by social deprivation. This was in spite of the recognition that specific areas of the city of Dublin were clearly drug black spots (Department of Health, 1991). The fact that these correlated with areas of social and economic disadvantage could not really be misinterpreted, but perhaps it was again sidestepped. Policy commitments to decentralise services, specifically in developing the role of the GP, were a major step toward developing services which would be more easily accessible to potential clients. The community-based aspects of this strategy did not meet with universal acclaim. Issues such as the stigmatising of specific communities and labelling of areas as 'drug areas', while attempting to focus services where required, had the effect of alienating those communities and escalating fears that communities with special services would in fact attract more drug misusers. This unforeseen response had ongoing implications for the implementation of some aspects of the 1991 government strategy.

The supply reduction approach, combined with a greater emphasis on demand reduction measures, was established in the 1991 drugs strategy as the central framework for future policy developments. This happened in a climate where a core aspect of such a framework, in the form of education for prevention, was being seriously criticised by researchers (Cripps, 1997: 18). The development of community-based responses appeared to hold more promise.

Tracking the drugs problem through a series of Health Research Board reports from 1991 to 1996 does nothing to instil confidence that the 1991 strategy worked. There was evidence that the percentage treated for heroin had doubled from 1990 to 1996. This indicates that services were more successful in reaching drug users, but it does not support the theory that the drugs problem was under control, as the figures for those receiving treatment can be regarded only as a percentage of those using drugs. The proliferation of services in community-based settings is documented in Moran et al. (1997: Appendix D). The move towards providing community-based, not centralised, services seems to be supported by these results. The concept of outreach intrinsic to the 1991 Strategy demonstrated some success. The fact that in 1996 policy making was still dependent on data derived only from those already in contact with services was disappointing. If one looks at how those drug users gain access to the services, it is of further concern, in that the 1991 strategy seeking to engage a broad range of professionals in the task of working with drug users had shown only limited success. According to O'Higgins (1996: 43), almost 55 per cent of those treated were self- or family-referred, while only

15.5 per cent came through a combination of GPs, hospital, medical settings and social services, with a further 11.3 per cent arriving through the court/probation system.

In its five-year review (O'Higgins, 1996: 8), the Health Research Board noted the decreasing age of users attending for treatment. The Report stated that 'evidence was found of the increase, both proportionate and numerical, in the specific citing of heroin as their drug of misuse by clients who were in treatment' (1996: 11). Again, since data sources are limited to those in treatment, it is difficult to interpret these facts. Perhaps it is a good thing that the age of users in treatment is down, if it indicates that users are getting to services earlier. However, it may also indicate younger people getting into more serious difficulties earlier in their drug use. The information about the levels of heroin as primary drug of choice is again open to interpretation. One possibility is that services are viewed as predominantly services for heroin users and are seen as unacceptable by other drug users. Alternatively the facts might reflect the relative social acceptability of other drug use, specifically cannabis, and therefore use of the drug is less likely to lead to admission to treatment. The push towards harm reduction strategies such as needle exchange and methadone maintenance would clearly indicate concern for heroin users rather than cannabis users. Some positive effects on the treatment/outreach front are indicated by O'Higgins (1996) and Moran et al. (1997).

There is no evidence, however, that the strategy instigated in 1991 has had any impact on the major social issues underlying the drugs problem in Dublin. Eighty to ninety per cent (O'Higgins, 1996: 26) of those counted in the statistics are still unemployed and the same socially and economically deprived areas are over-represented in the statistics (O'Higgins and O'Brien, 1994: 25; Moran et al., 1997: 34). School-leaving age has levelled-off (O'Higgins and O'Brien, 1994: 4), but it still shows 35 per cent leaving before the age of 15. The good news was that the HIV and AIDS education programme as a harm reduction strategy in relation to needle sharing and needle use seems in general to be having an effect. This is apparent in the reduction in numbers of those injecting and sharing (Moran et al., 1997: 2–25). The fact that this is part of a greater health promotion strategy should not be overlooked. The total numbers receiving treatment for drug misuse in 1996 were 4,865. Most were resident in the Eastern Health Board region (Moran et al., 1997: 5); 2,821 of these were in contact with treatment prior to 1996. This means that over 50 per cent of those included in the statistics of the Report had been in contact with services for some time.

Any analysis of the data indicates reasons for concern. The 1991 strategy had not reaped the hoped-for results. It placed confidence in the drug supply and demand reduction tactics, had overestimated the possibilities of curtailing supply and ignored at least some of the factors contributing to demand.

Ministerial committee to review drug policy

In the mid-1990s, Pat Rabbitte, the then Minister of State at the Department of Trade, Enterprise and Employment, chaired a ministerial committee to review drug policy. The committee produced two reports, in 1996 and 1997. Once again, policy development was designed along the dual axes of supply-and-demand reduction. The Committee's reports dealt with demand reduction and refer to complementary efforts when outlining the issues relating to supply reduction. Did these efforts so clearly based on a long-established formulation offer anything new for drugs policy initiatives? Concepts such as 'war on drugs' (Murphy, 1996) and 'zero tolerance' continue to underpin Irish drugs policy. This supply/demand dichotomy will be further analysed later in this chapter.

Table 14.3 (see p. 320) presents a brief summary of developments in policy and services relevant to the drugs field since 1991. The legislative changes are summarised in table 14.5 (p. 321). There was no comprehensive evaluation of the 1991 strategy. The Eastern Health Board commissioned an evaluation of their services in 1995 (Farrell and Buning, 1996).

The first Task Force Report (1996) again contextualised the drug problem, looking at underlying causes, and the nature and extent of the problem. The report presents a summary of current and proposed services in a variety of areas. A major effect of the first Task Force was to validate earlier concerns about the relationship between drug use and social and economic deprivation. The earlier call for the identification of priority areas, where issues of drug use and social deprivation clearly coincide, may have been controversial. However, it did allow for the targeting of those areas as areas of special need. Eleven areas were so identified – ten in the greater Dublin Area and one in Cork (Task Force, 1996: 59–61). Interestingly, the designation of the area in Cork was later criticised, following the publication of a report on drug use in the Southern region (Jackson, 1998). The second major development from the first Task Force Report (1996) was the setting-up of structures to encourage a more integrated approach across government departments. The membership of the Task Force comprised the Minister of State to the Government, the Minister of State to the Departments of Education, the Environment, Health, Justice, Social Welfare, and the Minister of State to the Taoiseach and Foreign Affairs (Task Force, 1996: 23). These departments were to devise a structure for interdepartmental co-operation (table 14.4, p. 321) and work in conjunction with community partnerships.

The first Task Force Report was mainly concerned with the heroin problem. Issues such as misuse of non-opiates (ecstasy and cannabis), prevention and development of youth services, drug use in prisons and the role of therapeutic communities are examined in the second Task Force Report (1997). An evaluation of the effectiveness of these Task Force policies was published in

2002 (National Drugs Strategy Team, 2002). The review highlighted some of the successful interventions facilitated through the Task Force structures. This is a critical aspect of policy development, perhaps more crucial since £12.7 million was allocated to the Task Force since their inception and a further £25.4 million has been assigned to Youth Services developments.

The National Drugs Strategy 2001–8 (Department of Tourism, Sport and Recreation, 2001) was built on the framework established through the Task Force Reports (1996, 1997). Some significant developments had occurred. There were 14 drug task force areas (National Drugs Strategy Team 2002: 70). The Strategy for 2001–8 (Department of Tourism, Sport and Recreation, 2001) set out an action plan to expand the focus of attention from the Greater Dublin area to the country as a whole and to establish a number of regional Drugs Task Forces. The objective of the strategy was to address drug use and the associated harm to individuals and society through focusing on the four pillars: supply reduction, prevention (including education and awareness), treatment (including rehabilitation and risk reduction) and research, which was central to the strategy. The strategy clearly placed tackling the drugs problem in the context of the Government's overall social inclusion strategy.

Principal actors involved in policy development

Political
Interests in the area of drug policy are diverse and often conflicting. The main actors in the field, by virtue of their power and authority, are perhaps inevitably the relevant government departments. However, this central group is strongly influenced, on the one hand, by the medical profession and, on the other, by law enforcement agencies. These two parties have managed to bring to bear their respective concerns and beliefs to shape current political responses to drug policy as designed and supported through government departments.

At the time of writing in 2004, the government department with special responsibility for drugs issues is the newly formulated Department of Community, Rural Development and Gaeltacht Affairs. One of the core functions of the department with responsibility for drugs is to provide an integrative structure for the other departments with interests in the drugs problem. According to the Task Force 1996, these departments include Education and Science, Environment, Health and Children, Justice, Foreign Affairs, Social Welfare, and, more directly, Employment and Enterprise.

From a political perspective, however, a difficult balance must be struck between responding to the demands of voters at large to control the drugs problem, while attempting to respond responsibly to the needs of drug users and their families. This balance has at times given rise to intense controversy.

The interests of political parties are apparently united in attempts to tackle the drugs problem. This is perhaps evident in the continuity of policy across rival political parties, as they succeed to government.

Community

Apart from the key government departments and the influence of political parties, various interest groups attempt to have a voice in policy. The most significant of these has been the various attempts by local communities – specifically community action against drugs, and by inner-city organisations – to draw attention to the plight of their communities. Communities are now finally being recognised as having a key role both in the provision of services at community level, and also in the development of policies and anti-drug strategies. This is reflected in the partnership and task force response to drugs issues that was adopted from 1996, and still supported despite the changes in government.

Service providers

Other significant players are the service providers, particularly the area health boards of the Eastern Regional Health Authority (ERHA) formerly the Eastern Health Board. Covering the region with the biggest problem in relation to drugs, the ERHA must inevitably be at the forefront of responses to the drugs problem. Their policy development strategy has been referred to earlier in this chapter (Eastern Health Board, 1996). Decisions about funding from direct government funds or through the health board are critical in shaping responses to the drug issues at all levels, from prevention initiatives through direct service provisions to rehabilitation and support.

The Eastern Regional Health Authority, while responsible for the majority of services, does not have an exclusive role. Since the early days of the drugs problem, voluntary bodies have been a very important aspect of the service choices for drug users, their families and communities. Some of the voluntary services were established by religious organisations (for example, Merchants Quay Project, Mater Dei), while others were initially developed by a variety of organisations having independent funds, e.g. Anna Liffey, and Talbot Day Centre. Many of the services initiated by voluntary bodies have since become partly or solely state-funded. The presence of voluntary service providers offers a flexible and wider range of services for those with drug-related problems. Their philosophical influences on services are therefore diverse and this is more likely to be a positive feature of services as it ensures real choice for service users.

Consumers

Like many of those who utilise government services, the consumers of drug services are not in general either well organised or articulate in voicing their demands. It could be said that the consumer must fit the service, rather than the service being made to fit the clients. This is not a condemnation of services, but more accurately a reflection of the major gap in our knowledge about drug users. This is an inevitable result of the criminalisation of drug use which sends those affected under cover, giving a clear indication that they have no right to service, or to making demands on the system. Consumers must rely on the relationships they develop with professional helpers and on their community organisations to provide a voice on their behalf, where it can make a difference. Families of consumers are equally marginalised in the process. At times the more strident, well-organised voice of communities who are concerned about the macro picture can drown out the voices of those focused on the more personal micro experiences. An attempt is being made to organise drug users in the form of a drug users forum. This idea is being developed in conjunction with one of the service providers, Merchants Quay (Merchants Quay, 1998: 8–9).

Since the two Task Force reports in 1996 and 1997, there has been a growing emphasis on the need for youth and sports services to develop preventative initiatives at community level. The allocation of £20m in 1998 for this purpose emphasises the investment in this area and offered the promise that these sectors would have some say in how to respond to the needs of young people in general. While the work on expanding drug treatment services has been successful, the drug problem continues to develop. This serves as a sharp reminder that this funding has not resolved the drugs problem.

The media

No discussion of the players that affect this area of policy development would be complete without some comment on the role of the media. Media coverage of issues relating to drugs has been an important aspect of keeping the public informed. They can also serve as a catalyst for marshalling public opinion and creating pressure for particular action. Reports on the arrival of ecstasy and subsequent fatalities were influential in formulating public opinion on the potential problems of ecstasy use. Of potential difficulty in this regard is, of course, the power of the media to sensationalise specific events and create an environment where there is pressure for policy to respond to specific cases, rather than to overall patterns. Media coverage in relation to criminal activities has also been very important in Ireland. This covers both the reporting of drug-related crime on a smaller scale and large-scale drug-dealing activities and organised crime. The murder of Veronica Guerin in June 1996, an Irish investigative journalist who had been persistently reporting on various elements of the 'drugs mafia', might indeed be considered a turning point. Her reports and the public outcry following her death resulted in a palpable increase in the determination to deal with the criminal activities of major drug-barons. For example, the introduction of powerful legislation to allow the confiscation of assets from drug-dealers coincided with the backlash from Ms Guerin's death. From 1996 onwards the legal back up for law enforcement was strengthened and extended.

It is perhaps interesting to note that in attempting to create, rationalise and effect policy and political responses, the outcome of research and the experiences of other countries have had little impact in Ireland. Some examples of this lack of integrating research with policy are shown in the delay in formulating policy strategy to target socioeconomic factors which had long been identified as central to the development of the drugs problem. Further examples relate to the awareness of the usefulness of harm-reduction strategies as part of a comprehensive drugs service. The concept of harm reduction, for example, was developed in the late 1970s (Buning and van Brussel, 1995: 93), yet it did not become part of Irish policy for another decade. Indeed, education as a preventative measure – strongly endorsed by government policy – is not strongly supported in research findings (Cripps, 1997).

Delays in incorporating new ideas and an apparent determination to learn by our own mistakes hamper the development of the most effective policies and limit the flexibility and creativity required to tackle the problem which is clearly still a major concern.

Evaluating current policy

As already discussed, drug policy can be epitomised by reference to two main categories of activity: demand reduction and supply reduction. (See table 14.1, p. 304 for an analysis of the demand/supply reduction and individual/community focused policy paradigm.)

Supply reduction

Taking a look at supply reduction, the aspects of policy directed at achieving this goal fall principally into the domain of the criminal justice and customs and excise systems. Murphy (1996), in an excellent review of prohibitionist policies, concludes that such measures have failed to have a substantial impact on overall drugs supply. Murphy cites information relating to the relative profitability of drug dealing, vis-à-vis the costs of detection and confiscation by law-enforcement agencies, as a factor in the failure of prohibition (Murphy, 1996: 51). He also quotes superintendent John McGroarty, former Garda Drugs Liaison Officer, who suggested that, while 'cannabis seizures in

Europe in 1993 amounted to £170 million, . . . A mere 10% of the quantities available were seized.' (Murphy: 1996: 51). He therefore concludes that 'the occasional drug seizures which are sensationalised by the media, in other words, are merely the tip of an iceberg'. (Murphy, 1996: 50)

The Garda Report of 1997 gave a profile of the drug-related crime situation. It suggested that of the indictable crimes detected during that year, 91 per cent were larceny-type crimes. A reasonable estimate is offered that 43 per cent of these crimes are committed by drug users (Keogh, 1997: xi).

In detailing the profile of known drug users, it becomes evident that strategies which have attempted to address demand reduction have been ineffective in reaching the drug-user population indicted for crimes, 91 per cent were identified as using heroin, with two per cent using methadone. This figure suggests that those drug users who are accessing methadone services are less likely to appear in criminal justice statistics, a finding confirmed in many reports on the effectiveness of methadone maintenance programmes (Ball and Ross, 1991: 1). This research may indicate a need to redress the balance away from the punishment of drug users who commit crimes to feed their habits, and to the expansion of methadone programmes which are consistently proving successful in reducing criminal activity among drug users (Ball and Ross, 1991). Increasing methadone programmes could only be viable with the intro-duction of clearly defined guidelines and protocols. In 1996 the Methadone Protocol Scheme was piloted. This was expanded in 1998 and a review of methadone treatment services was published in 2000.

While this is a logical conclusion to draw, a cautionary note must be struck. If policy becomes exclusively concerned with minimising the negative effect of drug problems on the general public, i.e. crimes against the public committed by drug users, their unrestricted access to methadone is clearly an option. However, there is a danger that this could distract attention away from the structural inequalities that underpin the drugs problem and therefore further ostracise and marginalise those with drug-related difficulties.

The imprisonment of drug users has also been a cause for concern. Anecdotal evidence indicates that a prison sentence may, in fact, mark the beginning of a drug career for some offenders. The continued development of alternatives to custodial sentences is clearly indicated. Projects such as intensive supervision by the probation service, in conjunction with the Bridge Project, appear to offer a more effective response. The development of the Drug Courts has met with mixed reviews. Loughran (2001) voices concerns that once again we are importing a system of dealing with our problems that is not culturally appropriate. The evaluation of the Drug Courts (Farrell Grant Sparks, 2002) was also disappointing. The 'graduation' of only one participant from the drug courts programme, 18 months after its initiation, raised some questions in the media. In spite of such reservations the pilot

Drug Courts programme has been extended. The Drug Courts system, while part of the judicial system, is probably targeted more at demand reduction since serious dealers are not included in the remit of the programme.

In summary, the emphasis on supply reduction has not yet proved itself as a cost-effective tenet of an effective drugs policy. Attention needs to be paid to what aspects of supply-reduction strategies are legitimate and an efficient use of resources.

Demand reduction

Like its related axis of supply reduction, demand reduction comprises a multidimensional set of activities. These include prevention and education, treatment and rehabilitation and also a variety of community-based initiatives. The framework is outlined in table 14.1 (p. 304).

The current policy strategies are dependent on the successful development of inter-departmental structural initiatives and an extensive partnership model. The primary statutory service provider is the Area Health Boards. The boards have restructured areas of administrative responsibilities in the late 1990s. Initially, the Eastern Health Board introduced a special programme to deal with the drugs issue. In the subsequent reorganisation, the current programme was established. The programme manager with responsibility for drugs services holds the position of Manager of the Social Inclusion Programme. This programme, as well as dealing with drugs services, also covers mental health, mental handicap, social inclusion, refugees and health promotion.

The current trend to incorporate drugs issues under the broad umbrella of social inclusion or social development is a welcome advance. Certainly recognition of the social nature – as distinct from the individual pathology – of drug addiction is significant. However, given the struggle to get drugs usage a higher profile in policy formulation, it is important that the issues relating to it do not get sidelined by other social inclusion concerns.

As discussed earlier, most activity until the 1990s was centred in the community/supply reduction quadrant and the individual/demand reduction quadrant. In the 1990s, and specifically since 1996, the need to expand on the community/demand reduction dimension has been emphasised. While this paradigm is in fact too restrictive to depict clearly the need for overlap in these areas, it is important to note that all strategies and policy developments must be of an integrated and co-ordinated nature. This analysis poses some important questions which will serve to stimulate responses which it is hoped will transcend the confines of these limited parameters.

The paradigm in table 14.1 raises the question of where individual and supply/demand reduction strategies fit into the policy equation. In fact, the paradigm challenges us to review the function of such measures as methadone maintenance and harm reduction, which may be misrepresented if they are viewed only as targeting individual demand reduction. Perhaps they should be viewed as offering an alternative supply to individual drug users. If this move is analysed within the more complex nature of the drugs market, then the presence of alternative sources of supply would serve to undermine the dominant suppliers and therefore might be considered a legitimate supply-reduction approach. This alternative interpretation of methadone maintenance and harm reduction measures provides a clearer rationale for the expansion of such services than does an attempt simply to reduce demand. This analysis also raises the question of the desirability of offering a more attractive option than methadone. Experiments of heroin programmes in the UK should be monitored with interest. One suggestion is that drugs should be viewed not only as a social, legal and medical concern but also as a business problem. Moving beyond the confines of the four quadrant paradigm, it may be useful to explore the incentives, motivation and rewards that pertain to drug dealing as a business, albeit an illegal business. Some organisational analysis from the field of business and marketing might help to establish a more informed picture of what, in essence, we are attempting to dismantle when we tackle the issue of supply reduction. It seems evident that although drug dealing is a high-risk enterprise, the potential rewards encourage involvement. If not the financial reward, then the need to access a personal supply may be the greatest incentive to expand the market-base and encourage new purchasers. The familiar marketing strategy of offering free samples is also a widespread practice in engaging new customers in the illegal drugs market. The employment of a highly motivated sales force in the form of user/dealers is perhaps not unique to the illegal drugs market. This perspective suggests that the drugs policy field must look beyond the confines of already tried strategies to find more effective ways to tackle the problem.

The complexities inherent in dealing with the Irish drug problem can best be illustrated by a case example. Since the early days of community responses to drugs in the 1970s, concern was voiced about the impact on specific areas of the city of a developing concentration of drug-related problems. Communities began to feel abandoned by the law enforcement agencies. The resultant frustration and anger culminated in the Community Action against Drugs movement (CADs). The initial intent of this movement, to mobilise communities to respond more effectively to the drugs problems in their own communities was commendable. However, over time, a vigilante element grew and was involved in such acts as compulsory evictions and the apparent harassment of persons considered to be users or dealers. Following promises to police these areas and develop community responses, the CADs disbanded. In the 1990s no real progress had been made in these vulnerable communities. Their continued erosion led to the re-emergence of the perceived needs for Community Action against Drugs (Loughran: 1996: 12–13). This revival of community initiatives was supported by organisations such as Inner City Organisations Network which sympathised with their plight.

The Task Force concept of community involvement was conceived in concert with the partnership movement as developed in other policy areas. The Task Force ideal was designed to formalise relationships and organise voluntary agencies, community action groups and local partnerships with statutory interests. This recognition of the contribution of local communities to their own welfare represented a shift in government drugs strategies. Collaboration and integration became key features of policy.

In the midst of these developments, one issue continued to highlight the inherent difficulties in attempts to address conflicting needs. This was the question of how housing policy could complement and support the work of the Task Forces and enhance community development. The Task Force Reports of 1996 and 1997 affirm the need for estate management. Inevitably, communities had identified that the presence of drug users and, more particularly, drug dealers in their areas was aggravating the situation. Any move to 'clear up' this anti-social behaviour would be welcome. The Task Forces' recommendations regarding estate management incorporated plans to empower local communities in 'greater control of their environment' (Task Force, 1996: 46). The initiatives introduced included:

- Tenant development and information to tenants on the duties and responsibilities of both local authorities and tenants.
- Various steps to ensure improvements in housing management, remedial work schemes and projects to improve run down estates and their immediate environment.
- Legislative proposals to combat anti-social behaviours in local authority housing.

(Task Force, 1996: 31)

These initiatives culminated in the Housing (Miscellaneous Provision) Act 1997, which provides for an excluding-order procedure against individual occupants of a local authority house who are involved in anti-social behaviour, including drug dealing. The Act also supports attempts to promote estate management, particularly in the area of partnership and the authority of tenants (Department of Justice correspondence, 1998).

These moves to empower communities to deal with anti-social behaviour and drug dealing, in co-operation with the local housing authority, are certainly progressive. However, the impact of these developments on some drug users should be considered. At a conference held in June 1998, professionals working in the field of drug use claimed that the most difficult problem now being experienced by drug users attempting to come off drugs or to stabilise their lifestyles was homelessness (Conference on Pilot Drug Project, Community Care Area 5, Dublin, 1998). This escalation in their housing problems was reiterated at the launch of the Merchants Quay Annual Report in July 1998. Removing drug users from communities is an attractive measure, but in the overall resolution of the problem it will in fact create serious difficulties for users attempting to address their problems and also for services trying to attract current users. If users become homeless it exacerbates the chaos in their lives and at a fundamental level makes it even more difficult to keep track of, or to estimate, the numbers involved.

Drugs policy questions for the twenty-first century

While the 1990s witnessed some major progress in the attitude towards and commitment to the dilemmas of drug users, many concerns remain. There is little evidence to support an optimistic view that the drugs problem is abating. The Drug Misuse Research Division of the HRB (2003) reported a consistent increase in numbers of drug users reported to the National Drug Treatment Reporting System from 4,865 in 1996 to 6,994 in 2000. The European Monitoring Centre for Drugs and Drug Addiction (EMCDDA) Annual Report (2003) further substantiates this trend. It is difficult to get accurate figures on the number of drug users since statistics are generally based on treated drug users. This group represent only a portion of all users. The increase in the numbers of treated users is also a reflection of increased and more accessible service provisions. The focus of treatment provision in the government strategies to date has been related to harm reduction approaches to heroin use, policy has not addressed changing trends in drug use. The reported increases in levels of cocaine and crack use and also polydrug use (Drug Misuse Research Division, 2003; European Monitoring Centre, 2003; National Advisory Council on Drugs, 2003), for example, are not tackled within the current framework. Other problems continue to raise concerns for policy makers, including:

• The continued development of community responses to the drugs problem is likely to be a central tenet of future policy. However, a cautionary note must be struck. Focus on local community task forces may distract from the need to address structural inequalities which must be tackled at national level. This may be a factor in the disappointing impact of the task force structures on overall figures for drug use. Community empowerment is helpful only if it is viewed in the context of overall change and not as a mechanism for dispersing responsibility from central government.

- The implementation of Task Force recommendations must be continuously monitored and evaluated. The question of whether the funding available has been spent disproportionately on the more acceptable aspects of drug prevention and education and not on more contentious areas such as locally based harm minimisation services must be examined.
- The continued confidence in the effectiveness of increased legislation as a policy strategy in the area of supply reduction must be a cause for concern. The climate in Ireland is a long way away from radical legal reforms in relation to drug offences. But other countries have acted on these principles, for example the move in the UK to reclassify cannabis. With limited resources and competing demands for services from all areas, the question of the cost effectiveness of legal sanctions and law enforcement strategies will have to be closely scrutinised. The question is whether or not we can afford to continue to create legal sanctions and whether this will ultimately undermine the whole judicial system. Another concern is the impact of legal sanctions and 'drug-busting' operations on the availability of hard drugs on the streets.
- There is a need to target clearly specific categories of the population in relation to the drugs issue. The various levels of drug-related problems demand specifically designed approaches. While the demand and supply reduction paradigm may serve as an appropriate overriding ideal, there may be a case for compartmentalising the problem. This may demand the provision of more flexible and liberal policies for those already caught up in drugs in order to undermine the fabric of the 'drugs industry' per se.
- The apparent neglect in relation to addressing alcohol issues has lead to a marked increase in alcohol use and abuse (Strategic Task Force on Alcohol Interim Report, 2002). This has been noted more specifically in terms of public order issues. Alcohol use can no longer be divorced from the problems related to other drug use and urgent attention must be paid to the development of both a co-ordinated policy response and a co-ordinated, accessible and comprehensive treatment and prevention response.
- More comprehensive information is needed about the structure and organisation of the drugs 'industry'. The appeal of the high gain for high-risk incentives continues to encourage involvement in this illegal activity. This is not just at the level of 'drugs barons' but, just as importantly, at street level with small-time dealers and dealers/users. This aspect must be clearly acknowledged before it can be tackled. The financial gains, whether to feed a habit or simply to make a profit, are incredibly motivating factors in the continued survival and expansion of the drugs market.

The 1990s marked the first time in the history of the drugs problem in Ireland that substantial resources were channelled into resolving the problem.

This was one of the most active phases in the field of drugs policy initiatives. There continues to be a united political will to tackle the problem but the development of a partnership approach which held such promise has not borne the results anticipated. Apportioning money to the problem is not enough. A radical rethinking of the philosophical, political, social, economic and commercial underpinning of the problem is required.

Table 14.2 **Developments in drug-policy strategy in Ireland: summary of policy initiatives, 1968–85**

1968   Establishment of Garda Drug Squad
1968   Establishment of Working Party on Drug Abuse
1969   Establishment of National Drug Treatment Centre
1971   *Report of Working Party on Drug Abuse*
1977   Misuse of Drugs Act
1983   Special Governmental Task Force on Drug Abuse
         (Report not published, aspects of it were leaked)
1984   Misuse of Drugs Act
1984   Criminal Justice Act
1985   National Co-ordinating Committee on Drug Abuse

Table 14.3 **Summary of government reports, 1990–2004**

1991   *Government Strategy for the Prevention of Drug Use*
1994   *Shaping a Healthier Future*
1994   Criminal Justice Act
1995   *A Health Promotion Strategy*
1996   *EHB Drug Services Review of 1995 and Development Plans for 1996. Treated Drug Misuse in the Greater Dublin Area a Review of Five Years, 1990–94.*
1996   *First Report of the Ministerial Task Force on Measures to Reduce the Demand for Drugs*
1997   *Second Report of the Ministerial Task Force on Measures to Reduce the Demand for Drugs*
1997   *Report on Illicit Drug Use and Related Criminal Activity in the Dublin Metropolitan Area (Keogh)*
1997   *Smoking, Alcohol and Drug Use in Cork and Kerry.*
         Department of Justice and Law Reform Strategy Statement 1998–2000 Community Security and Equality
1998   *Report of the Methadone Treatment Services Review Scheme*
2001   *Building on Experience, National Drugs Strategy 2001–2008*
2002   *Review of the Local Drug Task Forces, National Drugs Strategy Team*

Table 14.4 **Current framework for drugs policy monitoring and development**

Cabinet Committee on Social Inclusion (expanded from Drugs Committee in original Task Force Report 1996) chaired by An Taoiseach.

National Drugs Strategy Team
Co-ordinated through Department of Community, Rural and Gaeltacht Affairs
and reporting to Cabinet Committee.

Local Drugs Task Forces
Including members from relevant health board, gardaí, probation service, welfare, relevant local authority, local youth services, voluntary drug agencies, community representatives and chairperson proposed by local Partnership Board and co-ordination provided by the relevant health board.

Source: Adapted from Task Force, 1996, to include 1998 structures

Table 14.5. **Drug-related legislation, 1996–2004**

The Criminal Assets Bureau Act 1996
The Proceeds of Crime Act 1996
The Criminal Justice (Drug Trafficking) Act 1996
The Disclosure of Certain Information for Taxation and Other Purposes Act 1996
Housing (Miscellaneous Provisions) Act 1997
The Criminal Justice (Miscellaneous Provisions) Act 1997
Licensing (Combating Drug Abuse) Act 1997
Bail Act 1997
The Non-Fatal Offences against the Person Act 1997
The Europol Act 1997
Criminal Justice Bill 1997

Source: Compiled from Department of Justice, Equality and Law Reform Memo, 1998

Recommended reading

Butler, S. (1991) 'Drug problems and drug policies in ireland: a quarter of a century reviewed', *Administration* 39 (3): 210–33.

Department of Tourism, Sport and Recreation (2001), *Building on Experience: National Drugs Strategy 2001–2008*, Dublin: Stationery Office.

Department of Health (1991) *Government Strategy to Prevent Drug Misuse*. Dublin: Stationery Office.

Murphy, T. (1996) *Rethinking the War on Drugs in Ireland*. Cork: Cork University Press.

O'Higgins, K. (1996) *Treated Drug Misuse in the Greater Dublin Area: A Review of Five Years, 1990–1994*. Dublin: Health Research Board.

Task Force (1996) *First Report of the Ministerial Task Force on Measures to Reduce the Demand for Drugs.* Dublin: Stationery Office.

Task Force (1997) *Second Report of the Ministerial Task Force on Measures to Reduce the Demand for Drugs.* Dublin: Stationery Office.

References

Action Group on Access to Third Level Education (2001) *Report.* Dublin: Stationery Office.

Adams, J. (1998) '£30 Million young people's facilities and services fund – how it was won/ how it will be used', *Irish Youth Work Scene,* Issue 21, p. 3. Dublin: NYF.

Advisory Council on the Misuse of Drugs (1982) *Report.* London: HMSO.

Advisory Committee on Third Level Student Support (1993) *Third-Level Student Support.* Dublin: Stationery Office.

Aires, P. (1987) *The Hour of Our Death.* London: Peregrine.

Akenson, D.H. (1970) *The Irish Educational Experiment.* London: Routledge & Kegan Paul.

Albemarle Report (1960) *The Youth Service in England and Wales.* London: HMSO.

Allen, M. (1998) *The Bitter Word.* Dublin: Poolbeg.

Area Development Management (1994) *Report on Area-based Responses to Long-term Unemployment.* Dublin: ADM.

Audit Commission (1995) 'A short cut to better services: day surgery in England and Wales', pp. 298–309 in B. Davey, A. Gray and C. Seale (eds), *Health and Disease: A Reader.* Milton Keynes: Open University Press.

Bacik, I. (2002) 'The practice of sentencing in the Irish courts', pp. 348–70 in P. O'Mahony (ed.), *Criminal Justice in Ireland.* Dublin: IPA.

Bacik I. and M. O'Connell (eds) (1998) *Crime and Poverty in Ireland.* Dublin: Round Hall, Sweet & Maxwell.

Bacon, P. and F. MacCabe (1999) *The Housing Market: An Economic Review and Assessment.* Dublin: Stationery Office.

Bacon, P. and F. MacCabe (2000) *The Housing Market in Ireland: An Economic Evaluation of Trends and Prospects.* Dublin: Stationery Office.

Bacon, P., F. MacCabe and A. Murphy (1998) *An Economic Assessment of Recent House Price Developments.* Dublin: Stationery Office.

Bailey, D. (1984) 'The challenge of economic utility', in J. Ahier, B. Cosin and M. Holes (eds), *Beyond the Present and the Particular.* London: Routledge & Kegan Paul.

Baker, T. J. and L. M. O'Brien (1997) *The Irish Housing System: A Critical Overview.* Dublin: ESRI.

Balanda, K. (2001) *Inequalities in Mortality: A Report on All-Ireland Mortality Data 1989–1999.* Dublin: Institute of Public Health in Ireland.

Ball, J. and A. Ross (1991) *The Effectiveness of Methadone Maintenance Treatment, Patients, Programs, Services and Outcome.* New York: Springer-Verlag.

Bank, R. (2000) 'Europeanising the reception of asylum seekers: the opposite of welfare state politics', pp. 148–69 in M. Bommes and A. Geddes (eds), *Immigration and Welfare: Challenging the Borders of the Welfare State.* London: Routledge.

Barrington, R. (1987) *Health, Medicine and Politics in Ireland 1900–1970.* Dublin: IPA.

Barry, D. (1989) 'The involvement and impact of a professional interest group', in D. G. Malachy and D. O'Sullivan (eds), *Irish Educational Policy: Process and Substance.* Dublin: IPA.

Barry, F. and J. Bradley (1991) 'On the causes of Ireland's unemployment', *Economic and Social Review* 22 (4): 253–86.

Barry, J., H. Sinclaire, A. Kelly, R. O'Loughlin, D. Handy and T. O'Dowd (2001) *Inequalities in Health in Ireland: Hard Facts.* Dublin: Department of Community Health and General Practice, TCD.

Barry, J., B. Herity and J. Solan (1989) *The Travellers' Health Status Study: Vital Statistics of Travelling People.* Dublin: Health Research Board.

Bauby, J-D. (1997) *The Diving Bell and the Butterfly.* London: Fourth Estate.

Beccaria, C. (1996 [1764]) 'On Crimes and punishments', pp. 4–13 in J. Muncie, E. McLaughlin and M. Langan (eds), *Criminological Perspectives.* London: Sage.

Beckford Report (1985) *A Child in Trust: Report of the Panel of Inquiry into the Death of Jasmine Beckford.* London: London Borough of Brent.

Begley, M., C. Garavan, M. Condon, I. Kelly, K. Holland and A. Staines (1999) *Asylum in Ireland: A Public Health Perspective.* Dublin: Department of Public Health Medicine and Epidemiology, UCD.

Blackwell, J. (1984) *Incomes of the Elderly in Ireland: An Analysis of the State's Contribution.* Dublin: National Council for the Aged.

Blackwell, J. (1988) *Towards an Efficient and Effective Housing Policy: Special Issue, Administration* 36 (4).

Blackwell, J., G. Moane, P. Murray and E. O'Shea (1992) *Care Provision and Cost Management: Dependent Elderly People at Home and in Geriatric Hospitals.* Dublin: ESRI.

Blanchard, O. (1997) *Macroeconomics.* London: Prentice Hall.

Blaxter, M. (1989) 'A comparison of measures of inequality in morbidity', pp. 199–227 in J. Fox (ed.), *Health Inequalities in European Countries.* Aldershot: Gower.

Bloch, A. and L. Schuster (2002) 'Asylum and welfare: contemporary debates', *Critical Social Policy* 22 (3): 393–414.

Board of Education, Youth Advisory Council (1943) *The Youth Service after the War* (1943) London: HMSO.

An Bord Uchtála. *Reports.* Dublin: Stationery Office.

Bowlby, J. (1953) *Child Care and the Growth of Love.* Harmondsworth: Penguin.

Bradley, S., and N. Humphries (1999) *From Bosnia to Ireland's Private Rented Sector: A Study of Bosnian Housing Needs in Ireland.* Dublin: Clann Housing Association.

Breen, R. (1991) *Education, Employment and Training in the Youth Labour Market.* Dublin: ESRI.

Breen, R. and B. Halpin (1988) *Self-employment and the Unemployed.* Dublin: ESRI paper 140.

Breen, R. and B. Halpin (1989) *Subsidised Jobs: An Evaluation of the Employment Incentive Scheme.* Dublin: ESRI.

Breen, R., D. Hannan, D. Rottman and T. Whelan (1990) *Understanding Contemporary Ireland: State, Class and Development in the Republic of Ireland.* Dublin: Gill & Macmillan.

Breen, R. and S. Shortall (1992) 'The Exchequer costs of unemployment', in J. Bradley, J. FitzGerald and I. Kearney (eds), *The Role of the Structural Funds.* Dublin: ESRI.

Brenner, H. and E. Shelly (1998) *Adding Years to Life and Life to Years: A Health Promotion Strategy for Older People in Ireland.* Dublin: Department of Health and Children.

Brooke, S. (2001) *Social Housing for the Future: Can Housing Associations Meet the Challenge?* Studies in Public Policy No. 8. Dublin: Policy Institute in association with the Combat Poverty Agency.

Brown, A. and J. Fairley (1993) *Restructuring Education in Ireland.* Dublin: Irish Vocational Education Association.

Brown, C. (1887) 'The future of the educated imbecile', *Proceedings of the Association of Medical Officers of American Institutions for Idiotic and Feeble-Minded Persons, 1886*: 401–6.

Brown, P. and G. Chadwick (1997) 'Management and the health professional', pp. 189–209 in J. Robins (ed.), *Reflections on Health, Commemorating Fifty Years of The Department of Health 1947–1997*. Dublin: Department of Health.

Brown, P. and H. Lauder (1996) 'Education, globalisation and economic development', *Journal of Educational Policy* 11: 1–24.

Browne, F. and D. McGettigan (1993) 'The evolution of Irish unemployment: some explanations and lessons', *Labour Market Review* 4 (2): 15–49.

Bruce, I. (1991) 'Employment of people with disabilities', pp. 263–49 in G. Dalley (ed.), *Disability and Social Policy*. London: Policy Studies Institute.

Buckley, H. (1996) 'Child abuse guidelines in Ireland: for whose protection?', in H. Ferguson and T. McNamara (eds), *Protecting Irish Children: Investigation, Protection and Welfare Administration* 44 (2): 37–56.

Buckley, H. (1997) 'Child protection in Ireland', pp. 101–26 in M. Harder and K. Pringle (eds), *Protecting Children in Europe: Towards a New Millennium*. Denmark: Aalborg University Press.

Buckley, H. (2002) *Child Protection and Welfare: Innovations and Interventions*. Dublin: IPA.

Buckley, H. (2003) *Child Protection: Beyond the Rhetoric* London: Jessica Kingsley.

Buning, E. and E. van Brussel (1995) 'The effects of harm reduction in Amsterdam', *European Addiction Research* 1: 92–8.

Bunreacht na hÉireann (1937) *Constitution of Ireland*. Dublin: Stationery Office.

Burgess, P. (ed.) (1997) *Youth and Community Work*. Cork: UCC Centre for Adult and Continuing Education.

Burke, A. (1992) 'Teaching: retrospect and prospect', *Oideas* 39.

Burke, H. (1987) *The People and the Poor Law in Nineteenth Century Ireland*. Littlehampton: WEB.

Burke, S., C. Keenaghan, D. O'Donovan and B. Quirke, B. (2004) *Health in Ireland: An Unequal State*. Dublin: Public Health Alliance Ireland.

Burston, G. (1975) 'Granny battering', *British Medical Journal,* 6 Sept., p. 592

Burtless, G. (1985) 'Are targeted wage subsidies harmful?' *Industrial and Labour Relations Review* 39 (1): 105–14.

Butler, R. N. (1975) *Why Survive? Being Old in America*. New York: Harper & Row.

Butler, S. (1991) 'Drug problems and drug policies in Ireland: a quarter of a century reviewed', *Administration* 39 (3): 210–33.

Butler, S (1994) 'Alcohol and drug education in Ireland: aims, methods and difficulties', *Oideas* Samhradh: 137

Butler-Sloss, Lord Justice E. (1988) *Report of the Inquiry into Child Abuse in Cleveland in 1987*. London: HMSO.

Byrne, P. (2002) 'Challenges facing An Garda Síochána', pp. 431–46 in P. O'Mahony (ed.), *Criminal Justice in Ireland*. Dublin: IPA.

Byrne, R (1997) 'On the sliding scales of justice: the status of asylum seekers and refugees in Ireland', pp. 107–17 in R. Byrne and W. Duncan (eds), *Developments in Discrimination Law in Ireland and Europe*. Dublin: Irish Centre for European Law.

Bytheway, B. (1995) *Ageism*. Buckingham: Open University Press.

Bytheway, B. and J. Johnson (1990) 'On defining ageism', *Critical Social Policy* 27: 27–39.

Callan, T. (1992) *Who Benefits from Public Expenditure in Education?* ESRI Working Paper, no. 32.

Callan, T. and C. P. Harmon (1997) *The Economic Returns to Education in Ireland,* Working Paper 97/23. Dublin: UCD Centre for Economic Research.

Callan, T., M. Keeney and J. Walsh (2003) 'Budget 2004: impact on income distribution and relative income poverty', *Quarterly Economic Review,* Winter, Dublin: ESRI.

Callan, T., B. Nolan, B. J. Whelan, C. T. Whelan and J. Williams (1996a) *Poverty in the 1990s: Evidence from the 1994 Living in Ireland Survey.* Dublin: Oak Tree.

Callan, T., B. Nolan and C. T. Whelan (1996b) *A Review of the Commission on Social Welfare's Minimum Adequate Income.* Dublin: ESRI, Policy Research Series Paper 29.

Callan, T., C. O'Donoghue and C. O'Neill (1994) *Analysis of Basic Income Schemes for Ireland.* Dublin: ESRI.

Caplan, A. (1995) 'An improved future?', *Scientific American,* Sept. 1995: 110–11.

CARE (1972) *Children Deprived: The CARE Memorandum on Deprived Children and Children's Services in Ireland.* Dublin: CARE.

Carlile Inquiry (1987) *A Child in Mind: Protection of Children in a Responsible Society: Report of the Commission of Inquiry into the Circumstances surrounding the Death of Kimberly Carlile.* London: London Borough of Greenwich.

Carmody, P. and M. McEvoy (1996) *A Study of Irish Female Prisoners.* Dublin: Stationery Office.

Carney, C. (1985) 'A case study in social policy: the non-contributory old age pension', *Administration* 33 (4): 483–525.

Centre for Social and Educational Research, DIT (2001) *Study of Participants in Garda Special Projects.* Dublin: Department of Justice, Equality and Law Reform.

Child Care Policy Unit (1996) Dublin: Department of Health.

Children's Rights Alliance (1997) *Small Voices: Vital Rights.* Dublin: Children's Rights Alliance.

Chimni, B.S. (2000) *Globalisation, Humanitarianism and the Erosion of Refugee Protection.* Refugee Studies Centre Working Paper no. 3. Oxford: Refugee Studies Centre.

Christie, A. (2003) 'Unsettling the "social" in social work: responses to asylum seeking children in Ireland', *Child and Family Social Work* 8 (3): 223–31.

Chubb, B. (1992) *The Government and Politics of Ireland.* 3rd edn, London: Longman.

Chubb, J. E. and T. M. Moe (1988) 'Politics, markets and the organisation of schools', *American Political Science Review* 82: 1065–87.

CIRCA Group Europe (1996) *A Comparative Assessment of the Organisation, Management and Funding of University Research in Ireland.* Dublin: HEA.

Clancy, P. (1982) *Participation in Higher Education.* Dublin: HEA.

Clancy, P. (1988) *Who Goes to College?* Dublin: HEA.

Clancy, P. (1991) 'Numerical expansion and contracting autonomy in Irish higher education', *Higher Education Policy* 4 (1): 30–6.

Clancy, P. (1993) 'Goal enlargement and diversification: the evolution of the binary system in Ireland', in C. Gellert (ed.), *Higher Education in Europe.* London: Jessica Kingsley.

Clancy, P. (1995a) 'Education in the Republic of Ireland: the project of modernity?', in P. Clancy, S. Drudy, K. Lynch and L. O'Dowd (eds), *Irish Society: Sociological Perspectives.* Dublin: IPA.

Clancy, P. (1995b) 'Access courses as an aid to addressing socio-economic disparities in higher education', in *Access Courses for Higher Education: Proceedings of Conference at Mary Immaculate College, Limerick.* Dublin: HEA.

Clancy, P. (1995c) *Access to College: Patterns of Continuity and Change*. Dublin: HEA.

Clancy, P. (2001) *College Entry in Focus: A Fourth National Study of Access to Higher Education*. Dublin: HEA.

Clark, C. M. A. and J. Healy (1997) *Pathways to a Basic Income*. Dublin: CORI.

Clarke, D. M. (1984) *Church and State: Essays in Political Philosophy*. Cork: Cork University Press.

Cleary, A. (1997) 'Gender differences in mental health in Ireland', pp. 193–207 in A. Cleary and M. P. Treacy (eds), *The Sociology of Health and Illness in Ireland*. Dublin: UCD Press.

Clements, L and Read, J. (2003) *Disabled People and European Human Rights*. Bristol: Policy Press.

Cohen, S. (2002) 'The local state of immigration controls', *Critical Social Policy* 22 (3): 518–43.

Colgan, A. (1997) 'People with disabilities and the health services', pp. 111–25 in J. Robins (ed.), *Reflections on Health, Commemorating Fifty Years of the Department of Health, 1947–1997*. Dublin: Department of Health.

Collins, A. (1993) 'Inequality in treatment of asylum seekers in Ireland'. Unpublished MA thesis, NUI, Dublin.

Collins, C. and E. Shelley (1997) 'Social class differences in lifestyle and health characteristics in Ireland', pp. 87–98 in A. Cleary and M. P. Treacy (eds), *The Sociology of Health and Illness in Ireland*. Dublin: UCD Press.

Combat Poverty Agency (1988) *Poverty and the Social Welfare System in Ireland*. Dublin: Combat Poverty Agency.

Comfort, A. (1977) *A Good Age*. London: Mitchell Beazley.

Comhairle (2003) *Relate* 30 (8): 1–12.

Comhairle/Threshold (2002) *Rent Supplement in the Private Rented Sector: Issues for Policy and Practice*. Dublin: Comhairle and Threshold.

Commission of the European Community (2001) *European Commission White Paper, A New Impetus for European Youth*.

Commission on the Family (1996) *Strengthening Families for Life: Interim Report to the Minister for Social Welfare*. Dublin: Stationery Office.

Commission on the Family (1998) *Strengthening Families for Life: Final Report to the Minister for Social, Community and Family Affairs, Executive Summary*. Dublin: Stationery Office.

Commission on the Financial Management and Control Systems in the Health Service Report (2003) (Brennan Report). Dublin: Stationery Office.

Commission on Health Funding (1989) *Report*. Dublin: Stationery Office.

Commission of Inquiry on Mental Handicap (1965). *Report*. Dublin: Stationery Office.

Commission on Itinerancy (1963) *Report of the Commission on Itinerancy*. Dublin: Stationery Office.

Commission on the Points System (1999) *Final Report and Recommendations*. Dublin: Stationery office.

Commission on Social Welfare (1986) *Report*. Dublin: Stationery Office.

Commission on the Status of People with Disabilities (1996) *A Strategy for Equality*. Dublin: Stationery Office.

Committee on Access and Participation of Students with Disabilities in Higher Education (1995). *Report to HEA*. Dublin: HEA.

Committee of Enquiry into the Reformatory and Industrial Schools System (1936) *Report* (The Cussen Report). Dublin: Stationery Office.

Committee of Enquiry into the Reformatory and Industrial Schools System (1970) *Report.* (Kennedy Report). Dublin: Stationery Office.

Committee of Inquiry into the Penal System (1985) *Report* (The Whitaker Report). Dublin: Stationery Office.

Committee to Monitor and Co-ordinate the Implementation of the Recommendations of the Task Force on the Travelling Community (2000) *First Progress Report.* Dublin: Department of Justice, Equality and Law Reform.

Conaty, C. (2002) *Including All: Home, School and Community United in Education.* Dublin: Veritas.

Conroy, P. (2003) 'Employment policy', pp. 45–56 in Quin, S. and Redmond, B. (eds), *Disability and Social Policy in Ireland.* Dublin: UCD Press.

Constitution of Ireland (1937). Dublin: Stationery Office.

Constitution Review Group (1996). *Report.* Dublin: Stationery Office.

Consultative Group on the Development of Youth Work (1993) *Report* (Nov.). Dublin: Stationery Office.

Cook, G. (1990) 'Health and social inequalities in Ireland', *Social Science and Medicine* 31 (3): 285–90.

Coolahan, J. (1981) *Irish Education: Its History and Structure.* Dublin: IPA.

Coolahan, J. (1997) 'Third-level education in Ireland: change and development', in F. Ó Muircheartaigh (ed.), *Ireland in the Coming Times: Essays to Celebrate T. K. Whitaker's 80 Years.* Dublin: IPA.

Coolahan, J. and S. McGuinness (1994) *Report on the Roundtable Discussions in Dublin Castle on the Minister for Education's Position Paper 'Regional Education Councils'.* Dublin: Department of Education.

Cooney, T. and R. Torode (1989) *Report of the Irish Council for Civil Liberties Working Party on Child Sexual Abuse.* Dublin: ICCL.

Corcoran, Terry (2002) *Retrospective Analysis of Referral Under the Employment Action Plan (EAP),* FÁS, 2002.

CORI (1994) *Towards an Adequate Income for all.* Dublin: CORI.

CORI (1995) *An Adequate Income Guarantee for All.* Dublin: CORI.

CORI (1996) *Progress, Values and Social Policy.* Dublin: CORI.

CORI (1997a) *Planning for Progress – Socio-Economic Review.* Dublin: CORI.

CORI (1997b) *Religious Congregations in Irish Education: A Role for the Future?* Dublin: CORI.

Cornmarket Project Annual Report (2002). Wexford: Wexford Area Partnership.

Corrigan, D. (1994) *Facts about Drug Abuse in Ireland.* Dublin: Health Promotion Unit, Department of Health.

Costello, K. (1994) 'Some issues in the control of immigration in Irish law', pp. 354–65 in L. Heffernan (ed.), *Human Rights: A European Perspective.* Dublin: Round Hall.

Council of Education (1954) *Report of Council of Education on Function and Curriculum of the Primary School.* Dublin: Stationery Office.

Cousins, M. (1995) *The Irish Social Welfare System: Law and Social Policy.* Dublin: Round Hall.

Cousins, M. (1996) *Seen and Heard: Promoting and Protecting Children's Rights in Ireland.* Dublin: Children's Rights Alliance.

Cousins, M. and B. Charleton (1991) *Benefit Take-up.* Dublin: Free Legal Advice Centres.

Cousins, Mel (1997) *Participation of Long-term Unemployed Men in Education and Training.* Dublin: Connolly Information Centre for the Unemployed.

CPT (Committee for the Prevention of Torture and Inhuman or Degrading Treatment or Punishment) (1995, 1999) *Irish Places of Detention.* Strasbourg: Council of Europe.

Craft, A. (1983) 'Sexuality in mental retardation: a review of the literature', pp. 1–37 in A. Craft and M. Craft (eds), *Sex Education and Counselling for Mentally Handicapped People.* Tunbridge Wells: Costello.

Craft, A. (1987) 'Mental handicap and sexuality: issues for individuals with a mental handicap, the parents and professionals', pp. 13–34 in A. Craft (ed.), *Mental Handicap and Sexuality: Issues and Perspectives.* Tunbridge Wells: Costello.

Craft, A. (1994) *Practical Issues in Sexuality and Learning Disabilities.* London: Routledge.

Craft, A and M. Craft (eds) (1985) *Sex Education and Counselling for Mentally Handicapped People.* Tunbridge Wells: Costello.

Craig, S. (1994) *Progress through Partnership: A Final Evaluation Report on the PESP Initiative on Long-term Unemployment.* Dublin: Combat Poverty Agency.

Craig, S., M. Donnellan, G. Graham and A. Warren (1998) *Learn to Listen: Irish Report of a European Study on Residential Child Care.* Dublin: Centre for Social and Educational Research, DIT.

Cripps, C. (1997) *Drugs: Losing the War.* Cheltenham: New Clarion.

Cromien Report (2000) *Review of Department's Operations, Systems and Staffing Needs.* Dublin: Department of Education and Science.

CSO (annually 1983–1997) *Labour Force Survey.* Dublin: Stationery Office.

CSO (1986) *Census of Population of Ireland 1981*, vol. 8: Housing. Dublin: Stationery Office.

CSO (1996a) *Unemployment Statistics: A Study of the Differences between the Labour Force Survey Estimates of Unemployment and the Live Register.* Cork: CSO.

CSO (1996b) *Census of Population of Ireland.* Dublin: Stationery Office.

CSO (1997a) *Census 91*, vol. 10: Housing. Dublin: Stationery Office.

CSO (1997b) *Census 96: Planning for the Ireland of Tomorrow.* Dublin: Stationery Office.

CSO (1997c) *Household Budget Survey 1994–5.* Dublin: Stationery Office.

CSO (quarterly, from 1998) *Quarterly National Household Survey.* Dublin: Stationery Office.

CSO (2000) *Quarterly National Household Survey: Housing and Households Third Quarter 1998.* Dublin: CSO.

CSO (2002) *Census of Population.*

CSO (2003) *Census 2002: Principal Demographic Results.* Dublin: Stationery Office.

CSO (2004a) *Quarterly National Household Survey: Housing and Households Third Quarter 2003.* Dublin: Stationery Office.

CSO (2004b) *Census 2002*, vol. 13: Housing. Dublin: Stationery Office.

Culliton Report (1992) *A Time for Change: Industrial Policy in the 1990s.* Dublin: Stationery Office.

Cunniffe, R. (1983) *Recruiting Foster Parents.* Dublin: Eastern Health Board.

Curry, J. (1998) *Irish Social Services*, 3rd edn. Dublin: IPA.

Curry, J. (2003) *Irish Social Services*, 4th edn. Dublin: IPA.

Cusack, D. (1997) 'Medico-legal and ethical issues', pp. 159–73 in *Reflections on Health, Commemorating Fifty Years of The Department of Health 1947–1997.* Dublin: Department of Health.

Dale, N. (1996) *Working with Families of Children with Special Needs: Partnership and Practice.* London: Routledge.

Dalley, G. (1988) *Ideologies of Caring: Rethinking Community Collectivism.* London: Macmillan.

Daly, M. (1981) *Social and Economic History of Ireland since 1800.* Dublin: Education Company.

Davies, B. (1999a) *From Voluntarism to Welfare State, A History of the Youth Service in England.* Vol. 1, *1939–1979.* Leicester: National Youth Agency.

Davies, B. (1999b) *From Thatcherism to New Labour: A History of the Youth Service in England.*Vol. 2, *1979–99.* Leicester: National Youth Agency.

Davies, B. and Gibson, A. (1967) *The Social Education of the Adolescent.* London: University of London Press.

Davitt, P. (1998) *Relevant and Quality Training as a Tool for Integration,* Paper for INOU Conference on Active Labour Market Policy, Apr. 1998. Dublin: Ballymun Job Centre.

De Beauvoir, S. (1977) *Old Age.* Harmondsworth: Penguin.

De Perroy, M. (1927) 'Catholic Girl Guides in France', *Irish Monthly* LIV: 313 (transl. by Bowers).

Deloitte and Touche (1998) *Review of Community Employment Programme.* Dublin: Stationery Office.

Department of Education (1941–2) *Annual Report.* Dublin: Stationery Office.

Department of Education (1943) *Annual Report.* Dublin: Stationery Office.

Department of Education (1965) *Investment in Education.* Dublin: Stationery Office.

Department of Education (1974) *The Development of Youth Work Services.* Dublin: Stationery Office.

Department of Education (1977) *A Policy for Youth and Sport.* Dublin: Stationery Office.

Department of Education (1978) *The Development of Youth Work Services.* Dublin: Stationery Office.

Department of Education (1992) *Education for a Changing World,* Green Paper on Education. Dublin: Stationery Office.

Department of Education (1993) *Report of the Special Education Review Committee.* Dublin: Stationery Office.

Department of Education (1996a) *Implementing the Agenda for Change.* Dublin: Stationery Office.

Department of Education (1996b) *Information Note on Youth Services Bill.* Youth Affairs Section.

Department of Education and Science (2001) *Statistical Report 1999/2000.* Dublin: Stationery Office.

Department of Education and Science (2003a) *Summary of All Initiatives Funded by the Department to help Alleviate Educational Disadvantage.* Dublin: Stationery Office.

Department of Education and Science (2003b) *Supporting Equity in Higher Education: A Report to the Minister for Education and Science.* Dublin: Department of Education and Science.

Department of Education and Science (2003c) *National Youth Work Development Plan 2003–2007.* Dublin: Stationery Office.

Department of Education Consultative Group (1993) *Report of the Consultative Group on the Development of Youth Work.* Dublin: SNSL.

Department of Education Working Group on Post-Primary Education for Traveller Children (1992) *Report of the Department of Education Working Group on Post-Primary Education for Traveller Children.* Dublin: Department of Education.

Department of Enterprise and Employment (1996) *Growing and Sharing our Employment: Strategy Paper on the Labour Market.* Dublin: Stationery Office.

Department of Enterprise and Employment (1997) *White Paper: Human Resource Development.* Dublin: Stationery Office.

Department of Enterprise, Trade and Employment (1998a) *Ireland: Employment Action Plan.* Dublin: Stationery Office.

Department of Enterprise, Trade and Employment (1998b) *Management Information Report,* May 1998.

Department of the Environment (1991a) *A Plan for Social Housing.* Dublin: Stationery Office.

Department of the Environment (1991b) *Building Regulations.* Dublin: Stationery Office.

Department of the Environment (1995) *Social Housing: The Way Ahead.* Dublin: Stationery Office.

Department of the Environment (1996) *Better Local Government: A Programme for Change.* Dublin: Stationery Office.

Department of the Environment and Local Government (1997) *Annual Housing Statistics Bulletin 1997.* Dublin: Stationery Office.

Department of the Environment and Local Government (1998) *Action on House Prices.* Dublin: Stationery Office.

Department of the Environment and Local Government (1999) *Action on the Housing Market.* Dublin: Stationery Office.

Department of the Environment and Local Government (2000a) *Homelessness: An Integrated Strategy.* Dublin: Stationery Office.

Department of the Environment and Local Government (2000b) *Action on Housing.* Dublin: Stationery Office.

Department of the Environment and Local Government (2000c) *Part M Technical Guidance Document to the Building Regulations.* Dublin: Stationery Office.

Department of the Environment and Local Government (2002a) *Capital Funding Schemes for the Provision of Rental Accommodation by Approved Housing Bodies.* Memorandum VHU: 2/02 Dublin.

Department of the Environment and Local Government (2002b) *Housing Statistics Bulletin: Sept. Quarter 2002.* Dublin: Stationery Office.

Department of the Environment and Local Government (2002c) *Homelessness Preventative Strategy.* Dublin: Stationery Office.

Department of the Environment and Local Government (2002d) *National Spatial Strategy 2002–2020: People, Places and Potential.* Dublin: Stationery Office.

Department of the Environment and Local Government (2003a) *Housing Statistics Bulletin Dec. Quarter 2002.* Dublin: Stationery Office.

Department of the Environment and Local Government (2003b) *Statement of Strategy 2003–2005.* Dublin: Stationery Office.

Department of the Environment, Heritage and Local Government (2004) *Annual Housing Statistics Bulletin 2003.* Dublin: Stationery Office.

Department of Health (1945) *Mental Treatment Act 1945.* Dublin: Stationery Office.

Department of Health (1953) *Health Act 1953.* Dublin: Stationery Office.

Department of Health (1964) *Health (Homes for Incapacitated Persons) Act 1964.* Dublin: Stationery Office.

Department of Health (1966) *White Paper: The Health Services and Their Future Development.* Dublin: Stationery Office.

Department of Health (1970) *Health Act 1970.* Dublin: Stationery Office.

Department of Health (1977) *Memorandum on Non-Accidental Injury to Children.* Dublin: Stationery Office.

Department of Health (1980a) *Non-Accidental Injury to Children. Guidelines on Procedures for the Identification, Investigation and Management of Non-Accidental Injury to Children.* Dublin: Department of Health.

Department of Health (1980b) *Task Force Report on Child Care Services,* Dublin: Stationery Office.

Department of Health (1983) *Non Accidental Injury to Children: Guidelines on Procedures for the Identification, Investigation and Management of Non-Accidental Injury to Children.* Dublin: Department of Health.

Department of Health (1984a) *Planning for the Future.* Dublin: Stationery Office.

Department of Health (1984b) *The Psychiatric Services: Planning for the Future.* Report on a Study Group on the Development of the Psychiatric Services. Dublin: Stationery Office.

Department of Health (1984c) *Towards a Full Life: Green Paper on Services for Disabled People.* Dublin: Stationery Office.

Department of Health (1986) *Health: The Wider Dimensions.* Dublin: Stationery Office.

Department of Health (1987) *Child Abuse Guidelines: Guidelines on Procedures for the Identification, Investigation and Management of Child Abuse.* Dublin: Stationery Office.

Department of Health (1990) *Health (Nursing Homes) Act 1990.* Dublin: Stationery Office.

Department of Health (1991) *Government Strategy for the Prevention of Drug Misuse.* Dublin: Stationery Office.

Department of Health (1992) *Green Paper on Mental Health.* Dublin: Stationery Office.

Department of Health (1993) *Survey of Children in Care of the Health Boards 1992.* Dublin: Stationery Office.

Department of Health (1994) *Shaping a Healthier Future: A Strategy for Effective Care in the 1990s.* Dublin: Stationery Office.

Department of Health (1995a) *Child Care (Placement of Children in Foster Care) Regulations 1995.* Dublin: Stationery Office.

Department of Health (1995b) *Developing a Policy for Women's Health.* Dublin: Stationery Office.

Department of Health (1995c) *Notification of Suspected Cases of Child Abuse Between the Health Boards and the Gardaí.* Dublin: Stationery Office.

Department of Health (1995d) *White Paper: A New Mental Health Act.* Dublin: Stationery Office.

Department of Health (1995e) *A Health Promotion Strategy: Making the Healthier Choice the Easier Choice.* Dublin: Stationery Office.

Department of Health (1996a) *Child Care (Placement of Children with Relatives) Regulations 1996.* Dublin: Stationery Office.

Department of Health (1996b) *Putting Children First Discussion Document on Mandatory Reporting.* Dublin: Stationery Office.

Department of Health (1996c) *National Alcohol Policy Ireland.* Dublin: Stationery Office.

Department of Health (1997a) *A Plan for Women's Health.* Dublin: Stationery Office.

Department of Health (1997b) *Child Care (Standards in Children's Residential Centres) Regulations 1996 and Guide to Good Practice in Children's Residential Centres.* Dublin: Stationery Office.

Department of Health (1998) *Report of the Task Force on Suicide.* Dublin: Stationery Office

Department of Health (1999) *Putting Children First Promoting and Protecting the Rights of Children.* Dublin: Stationery Office.

Department of Health (undated) *Services to Persons with Mental Handicap/Intellectual Disability: An Assessment of Need, 1997–2001.* Dublin: Stationery Office.

Department of Health and Children (1998) *Report of the Methadone Treatment Services Review Group,* Dublin: Stationery Office.

Department of Health and Children (1999) *Children First: National Guidelines for the Protection and Welfare of Children.* Dublin: Stationery Office.

Department of Health and Children (2000a) *The National Health Promotion Strategy 2000-2005.* Dublin: Stationery Office.

Department of Health and Children (2000b) *Our Children – Their Lives: National Children's Strategy* (Dublin: Stationery Office).

Department of Health and Children (2001a) Mental Health Act 2001. Dublin: Stationery Office.

Department of Health and Children (2001b) *Primary Care: A New Direction.* Dublin: Stationery Office.

Department of Health and Children (2001c) *Quality and Fairness: A Health System for You.* Dublin: The Stationery Office.

Department of Health and Children (2001d) *Report of the National Advisory Committee on Palliative Care.* Dublin: Stationery Office.

Department of Health and Children (2001e) *Youth Homeless Strategy: Report of the Forum on Youth Homelessness.* Dublin: Stationery Office.

Department of Health and Children (2001f) *Foster Care: A Child-Centred Partnership.* Dublin: Stationery Office.

Department of Health and Children (2002a) *Traveller Health National Strategy 2002–2005.* Dublin: Stationery Office.

Department of Health and Children (2002b) *Strategic Task Force on Alcohol Interim Report.* Dublin: Stationery Office.

Department of Health and Children (2002c) *Statistics.* Dublin: Stationery Office.

Department of Health and Children (2003a) *An Evaluation of 'Cancer Services in Ireland: A National Strategy 1996'.* Dublin: Stationery Office.

Department of Health and Children (2003b) *Health Service Reform Programme.* Dublin: Stationery Office.

Department of Industry and Commerce (1951), *Commission on Youth Unemployment,* Dublin: Stationery Office.

Department of Justice (1993) *A Proposal for a Structured Psychological Treatment Programme for Sex Offenders.* Dublin: Stationery Office.

Department of Justice (1994) *The Management of Offenders – A Five Year Plan.* Dublin: Stationery Office.

Department of Justice (1997a) *Tackling Crime.* Dublin: Stationery Office.

Department of Justice (1997b) *Report of an Expert Group: Towards an Independent Prisons Agency.* Dublin: Stationery Office.

Department of Justice, Equality and Law Reform (1998a) *The Law on Sexual Offences: A Discussion Paper*. Dublin: Stationery Office.

Department of Justice, Equality and Law Reform (1998b) *Strategy Statement 1998–2000 Community Security and Equality*. Dublin: Stationery Office.

Department of Justice, Equality and Law Reform (2000a) *First Progress Report of the Committee to Monitor and Coordinate the Implementation of the Recommendations of the Task Force on the Travelling Community*. Dublin: Stationery Office

Department of Justice, Equality and Law Reform (2000b) *Integration: A Two Way Process*. Dublin: Stationery Office.

Department of Justice, Equality and Law Reform (2003) *Strategy Statement 2003 – 2005 Community Security and Equality*. Dublin: Stationery Office.

Department of Labour (1983) *Shaping the Future: Towards a National Youth Policy*, A Discussion Document. Dublin: Stationery Office.

Department of Labour (1984) *National Youth Policy Committee Final Report* (Costello Report). Dublin: Stationery Office.

Department of Social and Family Affairs (2002a) *Statistical Information on Social Welfare Services*. Dublin: Stationery Office.

Department of Social and Family Affairs (2002b) *Study to Examine the Future Financing of Long-Term Care in Ireland*. Dublin: Stationery Office.

Department of Social, Community and Family Affairs (1997a) *Developing Active Welfare Policy: An Evaluation of the Back to Work Allowance Scheme*. Dublin: Stationery Office.

Department of Social, Community and Family Affairs (1997b) *Self-employed and the Long-term Unemployed: An Evaluation of the Area Allowance Enterprise Scheme*. Dublin: Stationery Office.

Department of Social, Community and Family Affairs (2001) *First Report of the Benchmarking and Indexation Group* (Dublin: Stationery Office).

Department of Social, Community and Family Affairs (2002) *Building an Inclusive Society: Review of the National Anti-Poverty Strategy under the Programme for Prosperity and Fairness*. Dublin: Stationery Office.

Department of Social Welfare (1997) *Sharing in Progress: National Anti-Poverty Strategy*. Dublin: Stationery Office.

Department of Social Welfare (yearly) *Statistical Information on Social Welfare Services*. Dublin: Stationery Office.

Department of the Taoiseach (1998) *Report of the Partnership 2000 Social Economy Working Group*. Dublin: Stationery Office.

Department of the Taoiseach (2001a) *National Action Plan Against Poverty and Social Exclusion, 2002–5*. Dublin: Stationery Office.

Department of the Taoiseach (2001b) *Principles of Quality Customer Service for Customers and Clients of the Public Service*. Dublin: Stationery Office.

Department of the Taoiseach (2002) *Building an Inclusive Society: National Anti-Poverty/Social Inclusion Strategy*. Dublin: Stationery Office.

Department of Tourism, Sport and Recreation (2001) *Building on Experience, National Drugs Strategy 2001–2008*, Dublin: Stationery Office

Devane, R. S. (1930) *Irish Ecclesiastical Record* 36 (5th Series, July–Dec.).

Devlin, M. (2002) 'A new impetus? The EU white paper on youth', *Irish Youth Work Scene*, Issue 35: 3–6. Dublin: NYF.

Devolution Commission (1996) *Interim Report.* Dublin: Stationery Office.

DICP (1994) *Benefit Take-up: Campaign Report.* Dublin: Dublin Inner City Partnerships.

Dooley, C. (2003) 'Youth work plan hit by cash shortage', *The Irish Times,* 6 Aug. 2003.

Downey, D. (1998) *New Realities in Irish Housing: A Study of Housing Affordability and the Economy.* Dublin: Consultancy and Research Unit for the Built Environment, DIT.

Downey, D. and I. Devilly (1999) 'Changing circumstances, latest consequences: new data on rents, conditions and attitudes in the private rented sector, 1998'. in Threshold, *Private Rented Housing: Issues and Options.* Dublin: Threshold.

Doyal, L. (1993) 'Human need and the moral right to optimal community care', pp. 276–86 in *Community Care: A Reader.* London: Macmillan/Open University

Doyle, A. (1999) 'Employment equality since accession to the European Union', pp. 114–38 in G. Kiely, A. O'Donnell, P. Kennedy, P. and S. Quin (eds), *Irish Social Policy in Context.* Dublin: UCD Press.

Doyle, P. (1988) *The God Squad.* Dublin: Raven Arts Press.

Drake, R. F. (1996) 'A critique of the role of the traditional charities', in L. Barton (ed.), *Disability and Society: Emerging Issues and Insights.* London: Longman.

Drudy, P. J. (1999) *Housing: A New Approach: Report of the Housing Commission.* Dublin: Labour Party.

Drudy, P. J. and M. Punch (2001) 'Housing and inequality in Ireland' in S. Cantillon, C. Corrigan, P. Kirby and J. O'Flynn (eds), *Rich and Poor: Perspectives on Tackling Inequality in Ireland.* Dublin: Oak Tree in association with the Combat Poverty Agency.

Drug Misuse Research Division (2003) *Trends in Treating Drug Misuse in the Republic of Ireland, 1996–2000.* Occasional Paper no, 9. Dublin: Health Research Board.

Dublin County Council Community Department (1987) *County Dublin Areas of Need.* Dublin: Dublin County Council.

Duffy, S. Q. and D. E. Farley (1995) 'Patterns of decline among inpatient procedures', *Public Health Reports* 110: 674–81.

Duggan, C. and M. Cosgrave (1994) *Participation Costs on Labour Market Provision for the Long-term Unemployed.* Limerick: PAUL Partnership.

Durkheim, E. (1964 [1895]) *The Rules of Sociological Method.* London: Collier Macmillan.

Duvell, F. and B. Jordan (2002) 'Immigration, asylum and welfare: the European context', *Critical Social Policy* 22 (3): 498–517

Eastern Health Board (1995) *Review of Adequacy of Child Care and Family Support Services 1994.* Dublin: Eastern Health Board.

Eastern Health Board (1996a) *Drug Services Review of 1995 and Development Plans for 1996.* Special Board Meeting. Dublin: Eastern Health Board.

Eastern Health Board (1996b) *Review of Adequacy of Child Care and Family Support Services 1995.* Dublin: Eastern Health Board.

Education Disadvantage Committee (2003) *Educational Disadvantage Forum: Report of Inaugural Meeting.* Dublin, Department of Education and Science.

Elwan, A. (1999) *Poverty and Disability: A Survey of the Literature.* Washington: World Bank.

Emerson, E. and C. Hatton (1994) *Moving Out: R-location from Hospital to Community.* London: HMSO.

Equality Authority (2003) *Annual Report 2002.* Dublin: Equality Authority.

Erikson, E. (1969) *Childhood and Society.* Harmondsworth: Penguin.

ESRI (1993) *The Role of the Structural Funds.* Dublin: ESRI.

ESRI (1997) *Medium-Term Review 1997–2003.* Dublin: ESRI.

Estes, C. L., S. Biggs and C. Phillipson (2003) *Social Theory, Social Policy and Ageing: A Critical Introduction* (Milton Keynes: Open University Press).

EU Commission (1993) *Growth Competitiveness and Employment.* Luxembourg: EU Publications.

EU Council (1996) *Background paper on long-term unemployment presented by Irish Presidency (11938/96).* Brussels: EU Council Secretariat.

EU Social Fund Evaluation Unit (1998) *ESF and the Long-term Unemployed.* Dublin: Department of Enterprise, Trade and Employment.

EU Social Fund Programme Evaluation Unit (1996) *Evaluation Report: Early School Leavers Provision.* Dublin: Department of Enterprise and Employment.

EU Study Group on Education and Training (1997) *Accomplishing Europe through Education and Training.* Brussels: European Commission.

EU White Paper on Education and Training (1996) *Teaching and Learning: Towards the Learning Society.* Brussels, European Commission.

European Commission (1998) *An Action Plan Against Racism.* Brussels: European Commission.

European Commission (2001) 'Communication from the Commission to the Council and the European Parliament on a Community immigration policy' COM/2000/0757 Brussels: EC.

European Commission (2003) *The Social Situation in the European Union.* Luxembourg: Office for Official Publications of the European Communities.

European Council (2003) 'Council Directive 2003/9/EC of 27 Jan. 2003, 'Laying down minimum standards for the reception of asylum seekers. Brussels: *Official Journal of the European Union.*

European Foundation for the Improvement of Living and Working Conditions (1987) *Locally Based Responses to Long-term Unemployment.* Dublin: EU Foundation.

European Monitoring Centre for Drugs and Drug Addiction (2003) *The State of the Drugs Problem in the European Union and Norway, Annual Report,* Luxembourg, EMCDDA.

European Race Bulletin (2000) *A Special Report on the UK and Ireland: The Dispersal of Xenophobia,* 33/34.

European Union (2001) *Housing Statistics in the European Union, 2001.* Finland: Ministry of the Environment.

Eurostat (2001) *Disability and Social Participation in Europe.* Luxembourg: Office for Official Publications of the European Communities.

Evans, D. (1996) 'The limits of health care', pp. 159–73 in D. Greaves and H. Upton (eds), *Philosophical Problems in Health Care.* Aldershot: Avebury.

Evans, P. B., D. Rueschemeyer, and T. Skocpol (1985) 'On the road towards a more adequate understanding of the state', in P. B. Evans, D. Rueschemeyer and T. Skocpol (eds), *Bringing the State Back In.* Cambridge: Cambridge University Press.

Expert Group (1997) *Towards an Independent Prison Agency.* Dublin: Stationery Office.

Expert Working Group on the Integration of Tax and Social Welfare Systems (1996) *Report.* Dublin: Stationery Office.

Fahey, T. (1995) *Health and Care Implications of Population Ageing in Ireland 1991–2011.* Dublin: National Council for the Elderly.

Fahey, T. (1998a) 'Housing and social exclusion', pp. 411–29 in S. Healy and B. Reynolds (eds), *Social Policy in Ireland: Principles, Practice and Problems.* Dublin: Oak Tree.

Fahey, T. (1998b) 'Population ageing, the elderly and health care', pp. 183–98 in A. L. Leahy and M. Wiley (eds), *The Irish Health System in the 21st Century*. Dublin: Oak Tree.

Fahey, T. (1999) (ed.), *Social Housing in Ireland: A Study of Success, Failure and Lessons Learned*. Dublin: Oak Tree Press in association with the Katherine Howard Foundation and the Combat Poverty Agency.

Fahey, T. and P. Murray (1994) *Health and Autonomy among the Over-65s in Ireland*. National Council for the Elderly (Report No. 39). Dublin: National Council for the Elderly.

Fahey, T., B. Nolan and B. Maitre (2004) *Housing, Poverty and Wealth in Ireland*. Dublin: Combat Poverty Agency and IPA.

Fahey, T. and D. Watson (1995) *An Analysis of Social Housing Need*. (General Research Series Paper no. 168) Dublin: ESRI.

Fahlberg, V. (1981) *Helping Children When They Must Move*, Practice Series 6. London: BAAF.

Fanning, B. (2002) *Racism and Social Change in the Republic of Ireland*. Manchester: Manchester University Press.

Fanning, B (2004) 'Asylum-seekers and migrant children in Ireland: racism, institutional neglect and social work', pp. 201–16 in D. Hayes and B. Humphries (eds), *Social Work, Immigration and Asylum*. London: Jessica Kingsley.

Fanning, B., A. Veale and D. O'Connor (2001) *Beyond the Pale: Asylum-seeking Children and Social Exclusion in Ireland*. Dublin: Irish Refugee Council

Farrell Grant Sparks(2002), *Final Evaluation of the Pilot Drug Court*, Dublin, Farrell Grant Sparks Consulting/Dr M. Farrell.

Farrell, M and E. Buning (1996) *Review of Drug Services in the Eastern Health Board Area*. Dublin: Eastern Health Board.

Faughnan, P. and P. Kelleher (1993) *The Voluntary Sector and the State: A Study of Organisations in One Region*. Dublin: CMRS.

Faughnan, P. and A. O'Donovan (2002) *A Changing Voluntary Sector: Working with New Minority Communities in Ireland*. Dublin: Social Science Research Centre, UCD.

Faughnan, P. and M. Woods (2000) *Lives on Hold: Seeking Asylum in Ireland*. Dublin: Social Science Research Centre, UCD.

Faughnan, P., N. Humphries and S. Whelan (2002) *Patching up the System: The Community Welfare Service and Asylum Seekers*. Dublin: Social Science Research Centre, UCD.

Featherstone, M. and M. Hepworth (1990) 'Images of aging', in J. Bond and P. Coleman (eds), *Aging and Society*. London: Sage.

Ferguson, H. (1993) 'Surviving Irish childhoods: child protection and the deaths of children in child abuse cases in Ireland since 1884', in H. Ferguson, R. Gilligan, and R. Torode (eds), *Surviving Childhood Adversity: Issues for Policy and Practice*. Dublin: Social Studies Press, TCD.

Ferguson, H. (1993/1994) 'Child abuse inquiries and the report of the kilkenny incest investigation: a critical analysis', *Administration* 41: 385–400

Ferguson, H. (1996) 'Protecting Irish children in time: child abuse as a social problem and the development of the child protections system in Ireland', in H. Ferguson and T. McNamara (eds), *Protecting Irish Children: Investigation, Protection and Welfare, Administration* 44 (2): 5–36.

Ferguson H. and P. Kenny (1991) *On Behalf of the Child: Child Welfare, Child Protection and the Child Care Act 1991*. Dublin: A & A Farmar.

Ferguson, H. and O'Reilly, M. (2001) *Keeping Children Safe.* Dublin: A & A Farmar

Finch, J. (1989) *Family Obligations and Social Change.* London: Polity.

Finch, J. and J. Mason (1993) *Negotiating Family Responsibilities.* London: Routledge.

Finn, M. (1992) *Survey of Housing Stock 1990.* Dublin: Environmental Research Unit, Department of the Environment.

Finneran, L. and M. Kelly (1996) *Labour Market Networks, Underclasses and Inequalities.* Dublin: UCD, Centre for Economic Research Working Paper 96/21.

First National Report of Ireland (1996) *Ireland: United Nations Convention on the Rights of the Child.* Dublin: Department of Foreign Affairs, Stationery Office.

Fitzgerald, E. and B. Ingoldsby (1999) *An Evaluation of the Employment Network and Whole-time Job Initiative* Dublin: Employment Network

Fitzgerald, E., B. Ingoldsby and F. Daly (2000) *Strategies for addressing long-term unemployment in Dublin – lessons from policy innovation* Dublin: Employment Pact.

Flanagan, N. and V. Richardson (1992) *Unmarried Mothers: A Social Profile.* Dublin: National Maternity Hospital/Social Science Research Centre, UCD.

Focus Ireland (1998) *Out on Their Own: Young People Leaving Care in Ireland.* Dublin: Focus Ireland.

Focus Ireland (2000) *Focussing on B&Bs: The Unacceptable Growth of Emergency B&B Placement in Dublin.* Dublin: Focus Ireland.

Focus Ireland and PACE (2002) *Crime and Homelessness 2002.* Dublin: Focus Ireland.

Focus Ireland, Simon Communities of Ireland, Society of St Vincent de Paul and Threshold (2002) *Housing Access for All? An Analysis of Housing Strategies and Homeless Action Plans.* Dublin.

Forde, W. (1995) *Growing Up in Ireland: The Development of Irish Youth Services.* Wexford: Cara Publications.

Forder, A. (1974) *Concepts in Social Administration: A Framework for Analysis.* London: Routledge & Kegan Paul.

Foucault, M. (1977) *Discipline and Punish: The Birth of the Prison.* London: Penguin

Fraser, M. (1996) *John Bull's Other Homes: State Housing and British Policy in Ireland, 1883–1922.* Liverpool: Liverpool University Press.

Fraser U. and C. Harvey (eds) (2003) *Sanctuary in Ireland: Perspectives on Asylum Law and Policy.* Dublin: IPA.

Fries, J. F. (1980) 'Aging, natural death and the compression of morbidity', *New England Journal of Medicine* 303 (3): 130–5.

Furlong, A. and F. Cartmel (1997) *Young People and Social Change.* Buckingham: Open University Press.

Fynes, B., T. Morrissey, W. K. Roche, B. J. Whelan and J. Williams (1997) *Flexible Working Lives: The Changing Nature of Working Time Arrangements in Ireland.* Dublin: Oak Tree.

Gallagher, P. (2001) *Report of the National Physical and Sensory Disability Database Development Committee.* Dublin: Health Research Board.

Gallagher, P. (2002) *Report of the National Physical and Sensory Disability Database Development Committee, 2001.* Dublin: Health Research Board.

An Garda Síochána, *Annual Reports.* Dublin: Stationery Office.

An Garda Síochána National Juvenile Office (1991) *Policy of An Garda Síochána in Respect of Juvenile Offenders and Guidelines for the Implementation of Procedures in Dealing with Juvenile Offenders.* Dublin: An Garda Síochána.

Gay and Lesbian Equality Network and Nexus Research Co-operative (1995) *Poverty: Lesbians and Gay Men: The Economic and Social Effects of Discrimination*. Dublin: Combat Poverty Agency.

Geddes, A (2000) 'Asylum seekers and welfare benefits in the UK', pp. 134–47 in M. Bommes and A. Geddes (eds), *Immigration and Welfare: Challenging the Borders of the Welfare State*. London: Routledge.

Geiran, V., M. McCarthy, M. Morahan and V. O'Connell (1999) *Young Offenders in Penal Custody*. Dublin: Brunswick Press

Gilligan, R. (1991) *Irish Child Care Services: Policy, Practice and Provision*. Dublin: IPA.

Gilligan, R. (1995) 'Family support and child welfare: realising the promise of the Child Care Act 1991', pp. 60–83 in H. Ferguson and P. Kenny (eds), *On Behalf of the Child: Child Welfare, Child Protection and the Child Care Act 1991*. Dublin: Farmar.

Gilligan, R. (1996) 'Irish child care services in the 1990s: the Child Care Act 1991 and other developments', pp. 56–74 in M. Hill and J. Aldgate (eds), *Child Welfare Services: Developments in Law, Policy, Practice and Research*. London: Jessica Kingsley.

Gillis, J. R. (1975) 'The evolution of juvenile delinquency in England 1890–1914', *Past and Present* 67: 97.

Goffman, E. (1961) *Asylums: Essays on the Social Situation of Mental Patients and Other Inmates*. New York: Doubleday.

Goode, D. A. (1989) 'Quality of life and quality of work time', pp. 337–49 in W. E. Kiernan and R. L. Schalock (eds), *Economics, Industry and Economy: A Look Ahead*. Baltimore: Paul H. Brookes.

Government of Ireland (1960) *The Problem of the Mentally Handicapped*. White Paper. Dublin: Stationery Office.

Government of Ireland (1985) *In Partnership with Youth: The National Youth Policy*. Dublin: Stationery Office.

Government of Ireland (1991a) *Child Care Act 1991*. Dublin: Stationery Office.

Government of Ireland (1991b) *Programme for Economic and Social Progress (PESP)*. Dublin: Stationery Office

Government of Ireland (1992) *Education for a Changing World, Government Green Paper*. Dublin: Stationery Office.

Government of Ireland (1995a) *Operational Programme for Integrated Local Urban and Rural Development* Dublin: Stationery Office.

Government of Ireland (1995b) *Charting Our Education Future*, White Paper on Education. Dublin: Stationery Office.

Government of Ireland (1996a) *Challenge and Opportunities Abroad*. White Paper on Foreign Policy. Dublin: Stationery Office.

Government of Ireland (1996b) *Refugee Act 1996*. Dublin: Stationery Office.

Government of Ireland (1996c) *Integrating Tax and Social Welfare: Expert Working Group Report*. Dublin: Stationery Office.

Government of Ireland (1996d) *Partnership 2000 for Inclusion, Employment and Competitiveness*. Dublin: Stationery Office.

Government of Ireland (1996e) *Working Group on a Courts Commission First Report*. Dublin: Stationery Office.

Government of Ireland (1996f) *White Paper on Science, Technology and Innovation* (1996). Dublin: Stationery Office.

Government of Ireland (1997) *Sharing in Progress: National Anti-Poverty Strategy*. Dublin: Stationery Office.

Government of Ireland (1998) *Treaty of Amsterdam White Paper*. Dublin: Stationery Office.

Government of Ireland (1999a) *Immigration Act 1999*. Dublin: Stationery Office.

Government of Ireland (1999b) *Expert Group on the Probation and Welfare Service Final Report*. Dublin: Stationery Office.

Government of Ireland (1999c) *National Steering Committee on Violence Against Women First Report*. Dublin: Stationery Office.

Government of Ireland (1999d) *Ready to Learn*. White Paper on Early Childhood Education. Dublin: Stationery Office.

Government of Ireland (2000a) *Ireland: National Development Plan 2000–2006*. Dublin: Stationery Office.

Government of Ireland (2000b) *Learning for Life*. White Paper on Adult Education. Dublin: Stationery Office.

Government of Ireland (2000c), *Illegal Immigrants (Trafficking) Act 2000*. Dublin: Stationery Office.

Government of Ireland (2000d) *Programme for Prosperity and Fairness*. Dublin: Stationery Office.

Government of Ireland (2001) *Benchmarking and Indexation Group – Final Report of the Benchmarking and Indexation Group*. Department of Social and Family Affairs.

Government of Ireland (2002a) *Building an Inclusive Society*. Dublin: Stationery Office.

Government of Ireland (2002b) *Basic Income: A Green Paper*. Dublin: Stationery Office.

Government of Ireland (2003a) *Sustaining Progress: Social Partnership Agreement 2003–2005*. Dublin: Stationery Office.

Government of Ireland (2003b), *Immigration Act 2003*. Dublin: Stationery Office.

Government of Ireland (2003c) *Social Welfare (Miscellaneous Provisions) Act 2003*. Dublin: Stationery Office.

Government of Ireland (2003d), *First Annual Report of the Inspector of Prisons and Places of Detention for the year 2002–2003*. Dublin: Stationery Office.

Greene, R. (1979) 'Legal aspects of non-accidental injury to children', *Administration* 27 (4): 460–74.

Guerin, D. (1999) *Housing Income Support in the Private Rented Sector: A Survey of Recipient of SWA Rent Supplement*. Dublin: Combat Poverty Agency

Guralnik, J. M. (1990) 'Prospects for the compression of morbidity', *Journal of Aging and Health* 3: 138–54.

Haase, T. (1996) *Local Development Strategies for Disadvantaged Areas: Evaluation of Global Grants*. Dublin: ADM.

Haber, C. (1983) *Beyond 60 – Five: The Dilemma of Old Age in America's Past*. Cambridge: Cambridge University Press.

Hannan, D. and S. Ó Riain (1993) *Pathways to Adulthood in Ireland*. Dublin: ESRI.

Hannan, D. and S. Shortall (1991) *The Quality of Their Education*. Dublin: ESRI.

Hannan, D. F., E. Smyth, J. McCullagh, R. O'Leary and D. McMahon (1996) *Coeducation and Gender Equality*. Dublin: Oak Tree.

Harbison, J. (2003) 'Poverty and disability: a Northern Ireland perspective' in S. Quin and B. Redmond (eds), *Disability and Social Policy in Ireland*. Dublin: UCD Press

Haynes, M. S. (1963) 'The supposedly golden age for the aged', *The Gerontologist* 3 (26): 26–35.

Hazan, H. (1994) *Old Age: Constructions and Deconstructions.* Cambridge: University Press.

Healy, J. and B. Reynolds (1998) *Surfing the Income Net.* Dublin: CORI.

Hendricks, J. and C. D. Hendricks (1977) *Aging in a Mass Society.* Cambridge: Winthrop.

Hensey, B. (1988) *The Health Services of Ireland.* Dublin: IPA.

Hickey, C. and D. Downey (2004) *Hungry for Change: Social Exclusion, Food Poverty and Homelessness in Dublin: A Pilot Research Study.* Dublin: Focus Ireland.

Hills, J. (1997) *The Future of Welfare.* York: Joseph Rowntree Foundation.

Hogg, J. (1995) 'Assessment methods and professional directions', pp. 219–35 in N. Malin (ed.), *Services for People with Learning Disabilities.* London: Routledge.

Honohan, P. (1992) 'The link between Irish and UK unemployment', *Quarterly Economic Commentary* Spring. Dublin: ESRI.

Horgan, G. (2004) 'Mothering in a disabled society', pp. 194–205 in P. Kennedy (ed), *Motherhood in Ireland: Creation and Context.* Dublin: Mercier.

Housing Unit (2001) *Managing in Partnership: Enabling Tenant Participation in Housing Estate Management.* Dublin: Department of the Environment and Local Government and the City and County Managers Association.

Housing Unit (2003) *Preventing and Combating Anti-Social Behaviour.* Dublin: Department of the Environment, Heritage and Local Government and the City and County Managers Association.

Hurley, L. (1992) *The Historical Development of Irish Youth Work*, Youth Work Research Series, no.1. Dublin: Irish Youth Work Centre.

Hurley, L. (1993) *A Study of Voluntary Youth Activity Within The National Youth Federation.* Dublin: Irish Youth Work Centre.

IFUT News (1997) Vol. xxiv. Dublin: Irish Federation of University Teachers.

Indecon (2000) *An Evaluation of the Back to Work Allowance and Area Enterprise Allowance Schemes.* Dublin: Department of Social Community and Family Affairs.

Inner City Organisations Network (1994) *Grasping the Future: An Action Plan for Dublin's North–East Inner City.* Dublin: Inner City Organisations Network.

Inquiry into the Operation of Madonna House (1996). *Report.* Dublin: Eastern Health Board

Inter-Departmental Committee on the Care of the Aged (1968) *Report.* Dublin: Stationery Office.

Inter-Departmental Committee on Issues Relating to Possible Transfer of Administration of Rent and Mortgage Interest Supplementation from Health Boards to Local Authorities (1999) *Administration of Rent and Mortgage Interest Assistance.* Dublin: Stationery Office.

Inter-Departmental Committee on the Reconstruction and Replacement of County Homes (1949). *Report.* Dublin: Stationery Office.

Irish Council of Churches (1972) *Drug Abuse: A Report to the Churches of Ireland.* Dublin: Irish Council of Churches.

Irish National Coordinating Committee for the European Year against Racism (1997) *The Framework Programme for the European Year against Racism 1997.* Dublin.

Irish National Coordinating Committee for the European Year against Racism (1998) *Equality Proofing and Racism: Proofing Government Policy, Provision and Procedures against Racism.* Dublin.

Irish National Organisation of the Unemployed (1997a) *Welfare to Work.* Dublin: INOU.

Irish National Organisation of the Unemployed (1997b) *Working for Work.* Dublin: INOU.

Irish Prison Service (2003a) *Annual Report 2003*. Dublin: Stationery Office.

Irish Prison Service (2003b) *Strategy Statement 2001–2003*. Dublin: Stationery Office.

Irish Traveller Movement (1991) *Traveller Accommodation and the Law*. Dublin: Irish Traveller Movement.

Irish Traveller Movement (1993) *Education and Travellers*. Dublin: Irish Traveller Movement

Irish Wheelchair Association (1994) *People First*. Dublin: IWA.

Jackson, A. (1998) *Smoking, Alcohol and Drug Use in Cork and Kerry*. Cork: Southern Health Board, Department of Public Health.

James, C. (1998) 'Women in prison: the Irish experience', unpublished PhD thesis, NUI Galway.

James, C. McCann (2004) 'Motherhood adjourned', pp. 218–27 in P. Kennedy (ed), *Motherhood in Ireland*. Dublin: Mercier.

Jenkinson, H. (1997) 'History of youth work', pp. 35–43 in P. Burgess (ed.), *Youth and Community Work*, Cork: UCC Centre for Adult and Continuing Education.

Jenkinson, H. (2000) 'Youth work in Ireland: the struggle for identity', *Irish Journal of Applied Social Studies* 2 (2): 106–24.

Johnson, Z., F. Howell and B. Molloy (1993) 'Community mothers programme: randomised controlled trial of non-professional intervention in parenting', *British Medical Journal* 306: 1449–52.

Joly, D. with C. Nettleton and H. Poulton (1992) *Refugees: Asylum in Europe?* London: Minority Rights Publications.

Kaim-Caudle, P. (1967) *Social Policy in the Irish Republic*. London: Routledge & Kegan Paul.

Kaplan, G. A. (1991) 'Epidemiologic observations on the compression of morbidity', *Journal of Aging and Health* 3: 155–71.

Kearney, D. (2003) Editorial: 'Act or inaction?' *Irish Youth Work Scene*. Dublin: NYF.

Kearns, K. (1994) *Dublin Tenement Life: An Oral History*. Dublin: Gill & Macmillan.

Kelleher, P. and C. Kelleher (1998) *Out on Their Own: Young People Leaving Care in Ireland*. Dublin: Focus Ireland.

Kellmer Pringle, M. (1974) *The Needs of Children* London: Hutchinson.

Kelly, F. (1988) *A Guide to Early Irish Law*. Dublin: Dublin Institute for Advanced Studies.

Kelly, M. C. (1994) 'Patients' perception of day case surgery', *Ulster Medical Journal* 63 (1): 27–31.

Kempe, H, and R. Helfer (1968) *The Battered Child*. Chicago: University of Chicago Press.

Kenna, P. and P. MacNella (2004) *Housing and Refugees: The Real Picture*. Dublin: Vincentian Refugee Centre.

Kennedy, F. (1975) *Public Social Expenditure in Ireland*. Dublin: ESRI.

Kennedy, P. (1984) 'The development of youth work services and policy in Ireland', unpublished MSocSc thesis, UCC.

Kennedy, P. (1987) 'The historical development of Irish youth policy', *Youth and Policy: The Journal of Critical Analysis* 21: 7–12.

Kennedy, P. (2002) *Maternity in Ireland: A Woman-Centred Perspective*. Dublin: Liffey Press.

Kenny, P. (1995) 'The Child Care Act 1991 and the social context of child protection', pp. 42–59 in H. Ferguson and P. Kenny (eds), *On Behalf of the Child: Child Welfare, Child Protection and the Child Care Act 1991*. Dublin: Farmar.

Keogh, F. (1997) *Illicit Drug Use and Related Criminal Activity in the Dublin Metropolitan Area*, Report No. 10/97. Dublin: Garda Research Unit.

Keynes, J. M. (1936) *The General Theory of Employment Interest and Money*. London: Macmillan.

Kiely, E. (1997) 'Theory and Values of Youth Work', pp. 44–54 in P. Burgess (ed.), *Youth and Community Work*. Cork: UCC Centre for Adult and Continuing Education.

Kilkenny Incest Investigation (1993) *Report*. Dublin: Stationery Office.

Kilmurray, A. and V. Richardson (1994) *Focus on Children: A Blueprint for Action*. Dublin/Belfast: Focus on Children.

Kugel, R. B. and W. Wolfensberger (eds) (1969) *Changing Patterns in Residential Services for the Mentally Handicapped*. Washington DC: President's Committee on Mental Retardation.

Labour Party (2001) *Curing Our Ills*. Dublin: Labour Party

Langford, S. (1999) 'The impact of the European Union on Irish social policy development in relation to social exclusion', pp. 90–113 in G. Kiely, A. O'Donnell, P. Kennedy and S. Quin (eds), *Irish Social Policy in Context*. Dublin: UCD Press.

Law Reform Commission (1990) *Report on Child Sexual Abuse* (LRC 32–1990). Dublin: Stationery Office.

Law Reform Commission (2003) *Law and the Elderly*. Dublin: Stationery Office.

Layard, R., S. Nickell and R. Jackman (1994) *The Unemployment Crisis*. Oxford: Oxford University Press.

Leddin, A. and B. M. Walsh (1995) *The Macroeconomy of Ireland*, 4th edn. Dublin: Gill & Macmillan.

Lennon L. (1998) *Under One Roof? A Report on the Future Options for the Organisation of Homeless Services in Dublin*. Dublin: Homeless Initiative.

Levy, R. J. (1989) 'Supporting the aged: the problem of family responsibility', pp. 245–80 in J. Eckelaar and D. Pearl (eds), *An Aging World: Dilemmas and Challenges for Law and Social Policy*. Oxford: Clarendon.

Liegeois, J. P. (1987) *Gypsies and Travellers*. Strasbourg: Council of Europe, Council for Cultural Cooperation.

Lockhart, B. (2002) 'Restorative justice', pp. 746–58 in P. O'Mahony (ed.), *Criminal Justice in Ireland*. Dublin: IPA.

Lonsdale, S. (1990) *Women and Disability*. London: Macmillan.

Lord Mayor's Commission on Housing (1993) *Report of the Lord Mayor's Commission on Housing*. Dublin: Dublin Corporation.

Loughran, H (1996), 'Interview with Fergus McCabe', *Irish Social Worker* 14 (3/4): 12–13.

Loughran, H (2001), Drug policy and drug courts, *Irish Social Worker* 19 (1): 12–14.

Lynch, K. (1989) *The Hidden Curriculum*. London: Falmer.

Lynch, K. (1998) 'The status of children and young persons: educational and related issues', pp. 321–53 in S. Healy and B. Reynolds (eds), *Social Policy in Ireland: Principles, Practice and Problems*. Dublin: Oak Tree.

Makrinioti, D. (1994) 'Conceptualization of childhood in a welfare state: a critical reappraisal', pp. 267–84 in J. Qvortrup, M. Bardy, G. Sgritta and H. Wintersberger (eds), *Childhood Matters: Social Theory, Practice and Politics*. Aldershot: Avebury.

Malin, N. (ed.), *Services for People with Learning Disability*. London: Routledge.

Malin, N., D. Race and G. Jones (eds) (1980) *Services for the Mentally Handicapped in Britain*. London: Croom Helm.

Mangan, I. (2003) *Older People in Long Stay Care*. Dublin: Irish Human Rights Commission.

Mansell, J and K. Ericsson (eds) (1996) *Deinstitutionalization and Community Living: Intellectual Disability Services in Britain, Scandinavia and the USA.* London: Chapman Hall.

Markson, E. (1997) 'Moral dilemmas', pp. 83–7 in C. L. Weiner and A. Strauss (eds), *Where Medicine Fails.* London: Transaction Publishers.

Marshall, T., (2000) *Racism and Immigration in Ireland: A Comparative Analysis.* Dublin: Department of Sociology, TCD.

Marshall, T. H. (1952) *Citizenship and Social Class.* Cambridge: Cambridge University Press.

Matheson, R. (1903) 'Housing of the people of Ireland during 1841–1901', *Journal of the Statistical and Social Inquiry Society of Ireland,* XI (LXXXIII) Nov.

McAleese, D. (1997) *Economics for Business.* Englewood Cliffs, NJ: Prentice Hall.

McCann, M., S. Ó Siocháin and J. Ruane (1994) *Irish Travellers: Culture and Ethnicity.* Belfast: Institute of Irish Studies, QUB.

McCann, N. and T. Ronayne (1992) *Experiences and Views of Education and Training among Unemployed in Ballymun.* Dublin: Ballymun Partnership/WRC.

McCarthy, P. (1998) *Market Economies: Trading in the Traveller Economy.* Dublin: Pavee Point.

McCarthy, P., S. Kennedy and C. Matthews (1996) *Focus on Residential Child Care in Ireland: 25 Years Since the Kennedy Report.* Dublin: Focus Ireland.

McCashin, A. (2000) *The Private Rented Sector in the 21st Century: Policy Choices.* Dublin: Threshold and St Pancras Housing Association.

McConkey, R. (1989) 'Our young lives: school leavers' impressions and those of their parents to life at home and their hopes for the future', pp. 11–40 in R. McConkey and C. Conliffe (eds), *The Person with Mental Handicap: Preparation for an Adult Life in the Community.* Dublin: St Michael's House.

McConkey, R and C. Conliffe (1989) *The Person with Mental Handicap: Preparation for an Adult Life in the Community.* Dublin: St Michael's House.

McCoy, S. and B. Whelan (1996) *Economic Status of School-leavers 1993–95: Results of School-leavers' Surveys.* Dublin: ESRI.

McCullough C. (1996) *Crime in Ireland: A Sociological Introduction.* Cork: Cork University Press.

McDonnell, O. (1997) 'Contesting concepts of care: the case of the home help service in Ireland', pp. 69–84 in A. Cleary and M. P. Treacy (eds), *The Sociology of Health and Illness in Ireland.* Dublin: UCD Press.

McDonnell, P. (2003) 'Education policy', pp. 28–44 in S. Quin and B. Redmond (eds), *Disability and Social Policy in Ireland.* Dublin: UCD Press.

McGee H. (2002) *SAVI Report, Sexual Abuse and Violence in Ireland.* Dublin: Liffey Press for Rape Crisis Centre.

McGettigan, D. (1994) 'The causes of unemployment: a review' in ESRI, *Economic Perspectives for the Medium Term.* Dublin: ESRI.

McGettrick, G. (2003) 'Access and independent living', pp. 68–82 in S. Quin and B. Redmond, B. (eds), *Disability and Social Policy in Ireland.* Dublin: UCD Press

McGovern, F. (1990) 'Vietnamese refugees in Ireland 1979–1989: a case study in resettlement and education'. Unpublished MEd thesis, TCD.

McIntyre, D. (1993) 'The stay safe programme', *Intercom,* June.

McKeown, K. (1991) *The North Inner City of Dublin – An Overview.* Dublin: Daughters of Charity.

McKeown, K., G. Fitzgerald and A. Deehan (1993) *The Merchants Quay Project: A Drug/H.I.V. Service in the Inner City of Dublin 1989–1992.* Dublin: Franciscan Friary, Merchants Quay.

McKeown, K., T. Haase and J. Pratschke (2001) *Springboard Promoting Family Well-Being Through Family Support Services.* Dublin: Stationery Office.

McKinsey & Co. Management Consultants (1968) *Towards Better Health Care – Management in the Health Board.*

McManus, R. (2002) *Dublin, 1910–1940: Shaping the City and Suburbs.* Dublin: Four Courts.

McSorley, C. (1997) *School Absenteeism in Clondalkin: Causes and Responses.* Dublin: Clondalkin Partnership.

Meghen, P. J. (1963) *Housing in Ireland.* Dublin: IPA.

Memery, C. and L. Kerrins (2000) *Estate Management and Anti-Social Behaviour in Dublin: A Study of the Impact of the Housing (Miscellaneous Provisions) Act 1997.* Dublin: Threshold.

Mental Health Commission (2002) *Annual Report.* Dublin: Mental Health Commission.

Merchants Quay Project (1998) *Annual Report 1997.* Dublin: Merchants Quay Project.

Milson, F. (1970) *Youth Work in the 1970s.* London: Routledge & Kegan Paul.

Mittler, P. and H. Mittler (eds) (2003) *Innovations in Family Support for People with Learning Disabilities.* Chorley: Lisieux Hall.

Molloy, S. (1998) *Accommodating Nomadism.* Belfast: Traveller Movement Northern Ireland.

Moore, G., P. McCarthy, P. MacNeela, L. MacGabhann, M. Philbin and D. Proudfoot (2004), *A Review of Harm Reduction Approaches in Ireland and Evidence from the International Literature.* Dublin: Stationery Office.

Moran, J. (1998) 'Interest groups and the making of public policy: the role of non-governmental organisations in the development of the refugee Act 1996', unpublished MA thesis, IPA.

Moran, R., M. O'Brien and P. Duff (1997) *Treated Drug Misuse in Ireland, National Report 1996.* Dublin: Health Research Board.

Morgan, M., B. Hickey, T. Kellaghan (1997) *International Adult Literacy Survey: Results for Ireland.* Dublin: Stationery Office.

Morris, J. (1991) *Pride against Prejudice: A Personal Politics of Disability.* London: Women's Press.

Muintir na Tíre (1943) *Official Handbook.*

Mulcahy, M. (1976) *Census of the Mentally Handicapped in the Republic of Ireland 1974: None-Residential.* Dublin: The Medico-Social Research Board.

Mullins, D. Rhodes, M. and A. Williamson (2003) *Non-Profit Housing Organisations in Ireland, North and South.* Belfast: Northern Ireland Housing Executive.

Mulvany, F. (2000) *Annual Report of the National Intellectual Database 1998/1999.* Dublin: Medico-Social Research Board.

Mulvany, F. (2001) *Annual Report of the National Intellectual Disability Database Committee, 2000.* Dublin: Health Research Board

Murphy, A. and B. M. Walsh (1996) 'The Incidence of the male non-employment in Ireland', *Economic and Social Review* 25: 467–90.

Murphy, J. (1993) 'A degree of waste: the economic benefits of educational expansion', *Oxford Review of Education* 19 (1): 9–31.

Murphy, M. (1996) 'From prevention to family support and beyond: promoting the welfare of Irish children', in H. Ferguson and T. McNamara (eds), *Protecting Irish Children, Administration* 44 (2): 73–101.

Murphy, P. (2002) 'Offender rehabilitation programmes for imprisoned sex offenders – grounds for optimism', pp. 705–25 in P. O'Mahony (ed), *Criminal Justice in Ireland*. Dublin: IPA.

Murphy, T. (1996) *Rethinking the War on Drugs in Ireland*. Cork: Cork University Press.

Murphy-Lawless, J. and P. Kennedy (2002) *The Maternity Care Needs of Refugee and Asylum Seeking Women*. Dublin: Northern Area Health Board.

Murray, K. and M. Norris (2002) *Profile of Households Accommodated by Dublin City Council: Analysis of Socio-Demographic Income and Spatial Patterns, 2001*. Dublin: Dublin City Council and the Housing Unit.

Na Fianna Handbook, n.d., n.p.

National Advisory Council on Drugs (2003), *An Overview of Cocaine Use in Ireland*. Dublin: Stationery Office.

National Crime Council (2002) *Tackling the Underlying Causes of Crime: A Partnership Approach*. Dublin: Stationery Office.

National Drugs Strategy Team (2002), *Review of the Local Drugs Task Forces, Report form the National Drugs Strategy Team*. Dublin.

National Education Convention (1994) *Report*. Dublin: Convention Secretariat.

National Intellectual Disability Database 1996 (1997) *Annual Report of the National Intellectual Disability Database Committee*. Dublin: Health Research Board.

National Qualifications Authority of Ireland (NQAI) (2003) *Outline National Framework of Qualifications*. Dublin: NQAI.

National Rehabilitation Board (1991) *Righting the History of Wrongs: A Rights Approach to the Issues arising out of Women's Experiences of Disability*. Dublin: Submission to the Commission on the Status of Women.

National Task Force on Medical Staffing (2003) *Report* (Hanly Report) Dublin: Stationery Office.

National Women's Council of Ireland (1996) *Victims of Sexual and Other Crimes of Violence Against Women and Children*. Dublin: National Women's Council.

NCO (2003) *First Progress Report on the National Children's Strategy*. Dublin: NCO.

NESC (1984) *The Criminal Justice System: Policy and Performance*. Report no. 77. Dublin: NESC.

NESC (1988) *A Review of Housing Policy*. Report no. 87 Dublin: NESC.

NESC (1993a) *A Strategy for Competitiveness, Growth and Employment*. Report no. 96. Dublin: NESC.

NESC (1993b) *The Association Between Economic Growth and Employment Growth in Ireland*. Report no. 94. Dublin: NESC.

NESC (1993c) *Education and Training Policies for Social and Economic Development*. Dublin: NESC.

NESC (1996) *Strategy into the 21st Century: Conclusions and Recommendations*. Report. Dublin: NESC.

NESC (1999) *Opportunities, Challenges and Capacities for Choice*. Report no. 105. Dublin: NESC.

NESC (2003) *An Investment in Quality: Services, Inclusion and Enterprise: Overview, Conclusions and Recommendations*. Report no. 110. Dublin: NESC.

NESC (2004) *Housing in Ireland: Performance and Policy*. Report no. 112. Dublin: NESC.

NESF (1994) *Ending Long-term Unemployment*. Report no. 4. Dublin: NESF.

NESF (1996a) *Jobs Potential of Work Sharing*. Report no. 9. Dublin: NESF.

NESF (1996b) *Long-term Unemployment Initiatives*. Opinion no. 3. Dublin: NESF.

NESF (1996c) *Equality Proofing Issues*. Report no. 10. Dublin: NESF.

NESF (1997a) *Early School Leavers and Long-term Unemployment*. Report no. 11. Dublin: NESF.

NESF (1997b) *Unemployment Statistics*. Report no. 13. Dublin: NESF.

NESF (1997c) *A Framework for Partnership: Enriching Strategic Consensus through Participation.* Dublin: NESF.

NESF (2000) *Social and Affordable Housing and Accommodation: Building the Future*. Report no. 18. Dublin: NESF.

NESF (2002a) *Early School Leavers*. Report no. 24. Dublin: NESF.

NESF (2002b) *Re-integration of Prisoners*. Report no. 22. Dublin: NESF.

NESF (2002c) *A Strategic Framework for Equality Issues*. Dublin: NESF.

NESF (2003) *The Policy Implications of Social Capital*. Report no. 28. Dublin: NESF.

Nic Giolla Choille, T. (1983) *Wexford Family Centre*. Dublin: ISPCC.

Nic Giolla Choille, T. (1984) *Cork Family Centre:* Dublin: ISPCC.

Nic Giolla Choille, T. (1985) *Darndale Family Centre*. Dublin: ISPCC.

Nirje, B. (1969) 'The normalisation principle and its human management implications', pp. 231–40 in R. B. Kugel and W. Wolfensberger (eds), *Changing Patterns in Residential Services for the Mentally Handicapped*. Washington DC: President's Committee on Mental Retardation.

NYC (1978) *A Policy on Youth Work Services*. Dublin: National Youth Council.

NYC (1980) *The Development of Youth Work Services*, Dublin: National Youth Council.

NYCI (1996) *Youth in Focus, a Comprehensive Overview of the National Youth Council of Ireland*, Dublin: National Youth Council of Ireland.

NYCI (2001) 'European White Paper is dangerous to the interests of 42.1% of the population', press release, 26 Nov.

NYCI (2002) 'Budget 2003: all stocking, no filler', press release, 4 Dec.

NYCI (2003a) 'Youth work – an introduction' http://www.youth.ie/work/start.html site visited: 9 June.

NYCI (2003b) 'Youth representatives give thumbs up to sustaining progress', press release, 21 Mar.

NYF (1995) *Irish Youth Work Scene*, Issue 13. Dublin: NYF.

NYF (1997) *Partnership and Youth: Report on the Linkages between Partnership Companies and Local Youth Services*, Dublin: NYF.

Ni Chiosan, B., (2001) 'Ireland and its European Refugees: The Case of the Kosovars', Paper to European Centres and Associations of Irish Studies Conference. Aarhus, Denmark.

Nolan, B. (1989) *Socio-Economic Mortality Differentials in Ireland*. ESRI Working Paper no. 13. Dublin: ESRI.

Nolan, B. (1991) *The Utilisation and Financing of Health Services in Ireland*. Dublin: ESRI.

Nolan, B. (1992) *Perinatal Mortality and Low Birth Weight by Age, Parity and Socio-Economic Basis*. ESRI Working Paper No 37. Dublin: ESRI.

Nolan, B. (2000) *Child Poverty In Ireland*. Dublin: Combat Poverty Agency and Oak Tree.

Nolan, B. (2003) 'Income inequality during Ireland's boom', *Studies* 92 (36): 132–43.

Nolan, B., T. Callan, C. T. Whelan and J. Williams (1994) *Poverty and Time: Perspectives on the Dynamics of Poverty*. General Research Series Paper 166. Dublin, ESRI.

Nolan, B. and C. Whelan (1999) *Loading the Dice? A Study of Cumulative Disadvantage.* Dublin: Oak Tree.

Nolan, B., C. T. Whelan and J. Williams (1998) *Where are Poor Households Found? The Spatial Distribution of Poverty and Deprivation in Ireland.* Dublin: Oak Tree.

Nolan, B and M. M. Wiley (2001) *Private Practice in Irish Public Hospitals.* Dublin: Oak Tree.

Nolan, C. (1987) *Under the Eye of the Clock.* London: Weidenfeld & Nicolson.

Norris, M. and C. O'Connell (2003) *Local Authority Housing Management Reform: Progress and Prospects.* Paper presented to the Irish Social Policy Association Annual Conference, 4–5 Sept. 2003, www.ispa.ie

Norton, D. (1994) *Economics for an Open Economy: Ireland.* Dublin: Oak Tree.

O'Brien, V. (1998) 'Relative foster care: practice implications arising from the relative and foster care regulations 1995'. Unpublished paper, Conference on Relative Foster Care, UCD, 6 June.

O'Brien, V. (2001) 'Family fostering: children's experiences of care by relatives', pp. 69–98 in A. Cleary, M. Nic Ghiolla Phádraig and S. Quin (eds), *Understanding Children*, vol. 2. Dublin: Oak Tree.

O'Connell, P. (1999) *Are They Working?* ESRI Working Paper, no. 105.

O'Connell, P. and F. McGinnity (1997) *Working Schemes? Active Labour Market Policy in the Republic of Ireland.* Aldershot: Aldgate.

O'Connor, J. (1995) *The Workhouses of Ireland.* Dublin: Anvil Books.

O'Connor, J. and H. Ruddle (1988) *Caring for the Elderly Part 2: The Caring Process: A Study of Carers at Home and in the Community.* Dublin: National Council for the Aged.

O'Connor, J., H. Ruddle and M. O'Gallagher (1989) *Sheltered Housing in Ireland: Its Role and Contribution in the Care of the Elderly.* Dublin: National Council for the Aged.

O'Connor, P. (1992) 'Child care policy: a provocative analysis and research agenda', *Administration* 40 (3).

O'Connor, P. (1998) 'Young women: just other young people', pp. 161–87 in P. O'Connor (ed.), *Emerging Voices: Women in Contemporary Irish Society.* Dublin: IPA.

O'Donnell, I. (1998) 'Crime, punishment and poverty', pp. 31–48 in I. Bacik and M. O'Connell (eds), *Crime and Poverty in Ireland.* Dublin: Sweet & Maxwell.

O'Donoghue, J. (2000) Speech by Minister for Justice, Equality and Law Reform at launch of *Integration: A Two Way Process.* Dublin.

O'Donovan, O. (1997) 'Contesting concepts of care: the case of the home help service in Ireland', pp. 69–84 in A. Cleary and M. P. Treacy (eds), *The Sociology of Health and Illness in Ireland.* Dublin: UCD Press.

O'Driscoll R. (1964) *The Young Guard of Eireann.* Dublin: Poblacht na hÉireann.

OECD (1965) *Policy Conference on Economic Growth and Investment in Education.* Paris: OECD.

OECD (1991) *Reviews of National Policies for Education: Ireland.* Paris: OECD.

OECD (1994) *The OECD Jobs Study.* Paris: OECD.

OECD (2003a) *Education at a Glance, 2003.* Paris: OECD.

OECD (2003b) *Economic Survey – Ireland.* Paris: OECD.

O'Farrell, F. (2000) *Citizenship and Public Service: Voluntary and Statutory Relationships in Irish Health Care.* Dublin: Adelaide Hospital Society.

Offe, C (1985) *Contradictions of the Welfare State.* London: Hutchinson.

Office for Social Inclusion (2003) *National Action Plan against Poverty and Social Exclusion 2003–2005*. Dublin: Department of Social and Family Affairs.

Office of the Ombudsman (2001) *Nursing Home Subventions*. Dublin: Office of the Ombudsman.

Office of the Tánaiste (1995a) *Interim Report of the Task Force on Long-Term Unemployment*. Dublin: Stationery Office.

Office of the Tánaiste (1995b) *Report of the Task Force on Long-term Unemployment*. Dublin: Stationery Office.

O'Hagan, J. (2000) *The Economy of Ireland: Policy and Performance of a Small European Country*, 8th edn. Dublin: Gill & Macmillan .

O'Hare, A and M. O'Brien (1992) *Treated Drug Misuse in the Greater Dublin Area, 1990*. Dublin: Health Research Board.

O'Hare, A. and M. O'Brien (1993) *Treated Drug Misuse in the Greater Dublin Area*. Dublin: Health Research Board.

O'Higgins, K. (1993) *Family Problems: Substitute Care Children in Care and Their Families*. Broadsheet Series no. 28. Dublin: ESRI.

O'Higgins, K. (1996) *Treated Drug Misuse in the Greater Dublin Area. A Review of Five Years 1990–1994*. Dublin: Health Research Board.

O'Higgins, K. and M. O'Brien (1994) *Treated Drug Misuse in the Greater Dublin Area: Report for 1992 and 1993*. Dublin: Health Research Board.

Oliver, M. (1989) 'The social model of disability: current reflections', in T. Jeffs and M. Smith (eds), *Social Work and Social Welfare Year Book One*. Milton Keynes: Open University Press.

Oliver, M. (1996) *Understanding Disability: From Theory to Practice*. London: Macmillan.

Oliver, M. and B. Barnes (1993) 'Discrimination, disability and welfare: from needs to rights', pp. 267–77 in J. Swain, V. Finkelstein, S. French and M. Oliver (eds), *Disabling Barriers: Enabling Environments*. London: Sage.

O'Loughlin, A. (2002) 'The "pocket money" issue: financial exploitation of older people: an Irish case study', *Irish Social Worker* 20 (1–2): 14–15.

O'Loughlin, A. and J. Duggan (1998) *Abuse, Mistreatment and Neglect of Older People in Ireland: An Exploratory Study*. Dublin: National Council on Aging and Older People.

O'Mahony, P. (1993) *Crime and Punishment in Ireland*. Dublin: Round Hall.

O'Mahony, P. (1996) *Criminal Chaos*. Dublin: Round Hall.

O'Mahony, P. (1998) 'Punishing poverty and personal adversity', pp. 49–67 in I. Bacik and H. O'Connell (eds), *Crime and Poverty in Ireland*. Dublin: Round Hall.

O'Mahony, P. (2002) *Criminal Justice in Ireland*. Dublin: IPA.

O'Mahony, P. (2003) 'Supporting asylum seekers', in U. Fraser and C. Harvey (eds), *Sanctuary in Ireland: Perspectives on Asylum Law* and Policy. Dublin: IPA.

O'Neill, J. (1997) *Tackling Disadvantage in Areas of High Unemployment*, Address to Irish Social Policy Association, 28 Oct. 1997. Dublin: Irish Social Policy Association.

O'Regan, C. (1998) *Report of a Survey of the Vietnamese and Bosnian Refugee Communities in Ireland*. Dublin: Refugee Agency/Department of Psychology, Eastern Health Board.

O'Reilly, T. (1986) 'The practice of policing in Ireland, *Studies* (Spring): 33–42.

Osborne, R. D. and H. Leith (2000) *Evaluation of the Targeted Initiative on Widening Access for Young People from Socio-economically Disadvantaged Backgrounds. Report to the Higher Education Authority*. Dublin: HEA.

O'Shea, D. (1992) 'Customer care in the public sector', *Administration* 40 (3): 234–47.

O'Shea, E. (2002) *Review of the Nursing Home Subvention Scheme*. Dublin: Stationery Office.

O'Shea, E. and C. Kelleher (2001) 'Health inequalities in Ireland' in S. Cantillon, C. Corrigan, P. Kirby and J. O'Flynn (eds), *Rich and Poor: Perspectives on Tackling Poverty in Ireland*. Dublin: Oak Tree in association with the Combat Poverty Agency.

O'Shea, E. and S. O' Reilly (1999) *An Action Plan for Dementia*. Dublin: National Council on Ageing and Older People.

O'Sullivan, D. (1992) 'Cultural strangers and educational change: the OECD report *Investment in Education and Irish Educational Policy*', *Journal of Educational Policy* 7: 445–69.

O'Sullivan, E. (1995) 'Section 5 of the Child Care Act 1991 and youth homelessness', pp. 84–104 in H. Ferguson and P. Kenny (eds), *On Behalf of the Child: Child Welfare, Child Protection and the Child Care Act 1991*. Dublin: Farmar.

O'Sullivan, E. (1996a) 'Adolescents leaving care or leaving home and child care provision in Ireland and the UK: a critical view', in M. Hill and J. Aldgate (eds), *Child Welfare Services: Developments in Law, Policy, Practice and Research*. London: Jessica Kingsley.

O'Sullivan, E. (1996b) *Homelessness and Social Policy in the Republic of Ireland*. Department of Social Studies Occasional Paper no. 5. Dublin: TCD.

O'Sullivan, E. (1998a) 'Juvenile justice and the regulation of the poor: restored to virtue, society and the God', pp. 68–91 in I. Bacik and M. O'Connell (eds), *Crime and Poverty in Ireland*. Dublin: Round Hall, Sweet & Maxwell.

O'Sullivan, E. (1998b) 'Homeless children: Ireland's failed response', *Simon Community Newsletter*, no. 246, June.

O'Sullivan, M. (1982) 'The Fostering Resource Group five years on', *Children First*, no. 2.

Owens, P. (1987) *Community Care and Severe Disability*. Occasional Papers in Social Administration. London: Bedford Square Press.

Papademetriou, D. (1996) *Coming Together or Pulling Apart? The European Union's Struggle with Immigration and Asylum*. Washington DC: Carnegie Endowment for International Peace.

Parker, G. (1993) 'Disability, caring and marriage: the experiences of younger couples when a partner is disabled after marriage', *British Journal of Social Work* 23: 565–80.

Parole Board (2002) *Annual Report*. Dublin: Parole Board.

Partnership 2000 Social Economy Working Group (1998). *Report*. Dublin: Department of the Taoiseach.

Pavee Point (1992) *DTEDG File: Irish Travellers: New Analysis and New Initiatives*. Dublin: Pavee Point.

Pavee Point (1995) *A Heritage Ahead: Cultural Action and Travellers* (1995) Dublin: Pavee Point.

Penketh, L. and Y. Ali (1997) 'Racism and social welfare', pp. 101–20 in M. Lavalette and A. Pratt (eds), *Social Policy: A Conceptual and Theoretical Introduction*. London: Sage.

Phillips, G. (2002) *An Empirical Study of the Intensive Probation Scheme in Cork*. Cork: Probation and Welfare Service.

Pierce, M. (2003a) *Minority Ethnic People with Disabilities in Ireland*. Dublin: Equality Authority.

Pierce, M. (2003b) 'Ethnicity and disability', pp. 113–28 in S. Quin and B. Redmond (eds), *Disability and Social Policy in Ireland*. Dublin: UCD Press.

Powell, W. F. (1992) *The Politics of Irish Social Policy 1600–1990*. New York: Edwin Mellon.

Power, A. (1993) *Hovels to High Rise: State Housing in Europe since 1850*. London: Routledge.

Power, A. (1997) *Estates on the Edge: The Social Construction of Mass Housing in Northern Europe.* London: Macmillan.

Pratt, J. (1987) 'Dilemmas of the alternative to custody concept: implications for New Zealand penal policy in the light of international evidence and experience' *Australia and New Zealand Journal of Criminology* 20: 22.

Primary Health Care for Travellers Project (1996) *Report* (1996) Dublin: Pavee Point.

Probation and Welfare Service *Reports* (1995, 1998). Dublin: Stationery Office.

Prospectus Report (2003) *Audit of the Structures and Functions in the Health System.* Dublin: Stationery Office.

Puntes-Markides (1992) 'Women and access to health care', *Social Science and Medicine* 35: 620–5.

Quin, S. (1995) 'Family, women and health', pp. 175–84 in I. Colgan McCarthy (ed.), *Irish Family Studies: Selected Papers.* Dublin: Family Studies Centre UCD.

Quin, S. (2003) 'Health Services and Disability', pp. 83–98 in S. Quin and B. Redmond (eds), *Disability and Social Policy in Ireland.* Dublin: UCD Press

Quin, S. and B. Redmond (eds) (2003) *Disability and Social Policy in Ireland.* Dublin: UCD Press.

Quinn, M. (2002) 'Youth crime prevention' in P. O'Mahony (ed), *Criminal Justice in Ireland.* Dublin: IPA.

Quinn, P. (1998) *Understanding Disability: A Lifespan Approach.* London: Sage.

Qureshi, H. (1996) 'Obligations and support within families', in A. Walker (ed.), *The New Generational Contract.* London: UCL Press.

Race, D. (1995) 'Historical development of service provision', pp. 46–78 in N. Malin, D. Race and G. Jones (eds), *Services for People with Learning Disabilities.* London: Routledge.

Raferty, M. and O'Sullivan, E. (1999) *Suffer the Little Children: The Inside Story of Ireland's Industrial Schools.* Dublin: New Island.

Reception and Integration Agency (2001) *The Office of the Reception and Integration Agency.* Dublin: Reception and Integration Agency

Redmond, B (1996) *Listening to Parents: The Aspirations, Expectations and Anxieties of Parents about Their Teenagers with Learning Disability.* Dublin: Family Studies Centre, UCD.

Redmond, B. and J. D'Arcy (2003) 'Ageing and disability', pp. 129–38 in S. Quin and B. Redmond (eds), *Disability and Social Policy in Ireland.* Dublin: UCD Press.

Redmond, B. and V. Richardson (2003) 'Just getting on with it: exploring the service needs of mothers who care for babies and young children with severe/profound and life-threatening intellectual disability', *JARID: Journal of Applied Research in Disability* 16 (3): 189–204.

Reeves, C. (1998) *Still Me.* London: HarperCollins.

Review Group on Health and Personal Social Services for People with Physical and Sensory Disabilities (1996) *Towards an Independent Future.* Dublin: Stationery Office.

Review Group on Mental Handicap Services (1991) *Needs and Abilities: A Policy for the Intellectually Disabled.* Dublin: Stationery Office.

Review Group on the Role of Supplementary Welfare Allowance in Relation to Housing. (1995) *Report to the Minister for Social Welfare.* Dublin: Stationery Office.

Reynolds, J. (1992). *Grangegorman: Psychiatric Care in Dublin since 1915.* Dublin: IPA.

Richardson, R. (1886) 'On the best means of saving youth when they leave school especially in large towns', *Irish Ecclesiastical Record* 158–60.

Richardson, V. (1985) *Whose Children?* Dublin: Family Studies Unit, UCD.

Roberts, S. and H. Bolderson (1999) 'Inside out: migrants' disentitlements to social security benefits in the EU', pp. 200–19 in J. Clasen (ed.), *Comparative Social Policy: Concepts, Theories and Methods.* Oxford: Blackwell.

Robins, J. (1980) *The Lost Children.* Dublin: IPA.

Robins, J. (1992) *From Rejection to Integration: A Centenary of Service by the Daughters of Charity to Persons with a Mental Handicap.* Dublin: Gill & Macmillan.

Robins, J. (1997) (ed.), *Reflections on Health, Commemorating Fifty Years of the Department of Health, 1947–1997.* Dublin: Stationery Office.

Robins, J. A. (1960) 'The Irish hospital: an outline of its origins and development', *Administration* 8 (2): 145–65.

Roche J. and S. Tucker (eds) (1997) *Youth in Society.* London: Sage.

Ronayne, T. (1991) *Life on the Dole: Experiences and Views of the Long-term Unemployed.* Dublin: Tallaght Centre for the Unemployed.

Ronayne, T. and M. Creedon (1992) *To Whose Benefit?* Dublin: Tallaght Centre for the Unemployed.

Ronayne, T. and E. Devereux (1993) *Labour Market Provision for the Unemployed: The Social Employment Scheme.* Limerick: PAUL Partnership.

Rothman D. (1984) *The Criminal Justice System: Policy and Performance.* Report no. 77 Dublin: NESC.

Roulstone, A. (1993) 'Access to new technology in the employment of disabled people', pp. 241–8 in J. Swain, V. Finkelstein , S. French and M. Oliver (eds), *Disabling Barriers: Enabling Environments.* London: Sage.

Ruddle, H. and J. O'Connor (1993) *Caring without Limits: Sufferers of Demential Alzheimer's Disease.* Dublin: Alzheimer Society of Ireland.

Ruddle, H., F. Donoghue and R. Mulvihill (1997) *The Years Ahead Report: A Review of the Implementation of Its Recommendations.* Dublin: National Council on Aging and Older People.

Ruddle, H., and Mulvihill, R. (1994) *Reaching Out: Charitable Giving and Volunteering in the Republic of Ireland.* Dublin: Policy Research Centre, National College of Industrial Relations.

Ruddle, H., and Mulvihill, R., (1999) *Reaching Out: Charitable Giving and Volunteering in the Republic of Ireland: The 1997/98 Survey.* Dublin: Policy Research Centre, National College of Industrial Relations.

Ryan, J and F. Thomas (1980) *The Politics of Mental Handicap.* London: Penguin.

Ryan, J and F. Thomas (1987) *The Politics of Mental Handicap*, rev. edn. London: Free Association Press.

Rynn, A. (1992) *Working with Perpetrators: What Are the Issues?* Dublin: Stationery Office.

Sabel, C. (1996) *Ireland: Local Partnerships and Social Innovation.* Paris: OECD.

Sales, R., (2002) 'The deserving and the undeserving? Refugees, asylum seekers and welfare in Britain' *Critical Social Policy* 22 (3) 456–78.

Schalock, R.H. (1989) *Quality of Life: Perspectives and Issues.* Washington DC: American Association on Mental Retardation.

Scott, P. (1995) *The Meanings of Mass Higher Education.* Buckingham: Open University.

Sexton, J. J. and P. O'Connell (1996) *Labour Market Studies: Ireland.* Luxembourg: European Communities.

Silke, D. (1994) *The Altadore Research Project: Older People's Attitudes to the Accommodation.* Dublin: TCD and Dublin Central Mission.

Simons, K. (1995) 'Empowerment and Advocacy', pp. 170-88 in N. Malin, D. Race and G. Jones (eds), *Services for People with Learning Disabilities.* London: Routledge.

Skilbeck, M. (2001) *The University Challenged: A Review of International Trends and Issues with Particular Reference to Ireland.* Dublin: HEA.

Smyth, P. (1998) 'Assertion of children's rights seen as essential', *The Irish Times*, 14 Jan.

Special Education Review Committee (1993) *Report.*. Dublin: Stationery Office.

Springhall, J (1977) *Youth, Empire and Society.* London: Croom Helm.

Steering Committee on the Future Development of Higher Education (1995) *Report.* Dublin: HEA.

STIAC (Science, Technology and Innovation Advisory Council) (1995) *Making Knowledge Work for Us.* Dublin: Stationery Office.

Streetwise National Coalition (1994) *News Sheet* No. 5. Dublin: Streetwise.

Streetwise National Coalition and Resident Managers Association (1991) *At What Cost?* Dublin: Focus Point.

Sunday Independent (2004) 'International crime gangs plying their evil trade here', 7 Mar.

Sweeney, P. (1998) *The Celtic Tiger: Ireland's Economic Miracle Explained.* Dublin: Oak Tree.

Tansey, P. (1998) *Ireland at Work: Economic Growth and the Labour Market 1987–97.* Dublin: Oak Tree.

Task Force (1996) *First Report of the Ministerial Task Force on Measures to Reduce the Demand for Drugs.* Dublin: Stationery Office.

Task Force (1997) *Second Report of the Ministerial Task Force on Measures to Reduce the Demand for Drugs.* Dublin: Stationery Office.

Taskforce on Autism (2001) *Educational Provision and Support for Persons with Autistic Spectrum Disorders.* Dublin: Stationery Office.

Task Force on Child Care Services (1980) *Final Report.* Dublin: Stationery Office.

Task Force on the Eastern Regional Health Authority (1997) *Interim Report* (June). Dublin: Department of Health.

Task Force on the Travelling Community (1995) *Report of the Task Force on the Travelling Community.* Dublin: Stationery Office.

Technical Working Group (1995) *Interim Report of the Steering Committee's Technical Working Group.* Dublin: HEA.

Thomas, C. (1993) 'De-constructing concepts of care', *Sociology* 27 (4): 649–69.

Thomas, K. (1976) 'Age and authority in early modern England', *Proceedings of the British Academy* 62: 205–48.

Thompson, N. (1997) 'Children, death and ageism', *Child and Family Social Work*, 2 (1): 59–65.

Thornley, D. (1967) 'The Blueshirts, from the years of the great test 1926–1939', in F. MacManus (ed.), *The Thomas Davis Lectures.* Cork: Mercier.

Threshold (1987) *Policy Consequences: A Study of the £5,000 Surrender Grant in the Dublin Housing Area.* Dublin: Threshold.

Threshold (1997) *As Safe as Houses? The Nature, Extent and Experience of Debt in the Irish Housing System.* Dublin: Threshold.

Tierney, M. (1978) *Modern Ireland Since 1850.* Dublin: Gill & Macmillan.

Tizard, J. (1960) 'Residential care of mentally handicapped children', *British Medical Journal* 1: 1041–3.

Tizard, J. (1964) *Community Services for the Mentally Handicapped.* London: Oxford University Press.

Tobias, J. J. (1967) *Crime and Industrial Society in the Nineteenth Century.* London: Batesford.

Tormey, B., (2003) *A Cure for the Crisis: Irish Healthcare in Context.* Dublin: Blackwater.

Tormey, W. P. (1992) 'Two-speed public and private medical practice in the Republic of Ireland', *Administration* 40 (4): 371–81.

Tovey, H. (1989) *Why Irish? Irish Identity and the Irish Language.* Dublin: Bord na Gaeilge.

Travelling People Review Body (1983) *Report of the Travelling People Review Body.* Dublin: Stationery Office.

Treacy, D. (1998) 'Time to choose between partitionism and partnership', *Irish Youth Work Scene* 22: 3–4.

Trent, J. W. (1994) *Inventing The Feeble Mind: A History of Mental Retardation in the United States.* California: University of California Press.

Tuairim (1966) *Some of Our Children: A Report on the Residential Care of the Deprived Child in Ireland.* London: Tuairim.

Tubridy, J. (1994) 'Social experiences of physical disability in Ireland', *National Rehabilitation Board Report,* Issue 6.

Tubridy, J. (1996) *Pegged Down: Experiences of People in Ireland with Significant Physical Disabilities.* Dublin: IPA.

Turley, G. and M. Maloney (1997) *Principles of Economics: An Irish Textbook.* Dublin: Gill & Macmillan.

Tussing, A. D. (1985) *Irish Medical Care Resources: An Economic Analysis,* ESRI Paper no 126. Dublin: ESRI.

Tutt, N. (1996) 'The search for justice: home and away', pp. 5–14 in *The Children's Bill 1996 : Issues and Perspectives.* Dublin: Children's Legal Centre.

Twigg, J. and A. Grand (1998) 'Contrasting legal conceptions of family obligation and financial reciprocity in the support of older people: France and England', *Aging and Society,* 18: 132–46.

UCD Services Industry Research Centre (1993) *Urban Development and Employment: Towards an Integrated Strategy.* Dublin: UCD.

Ungerson, C. (1995) 'Gender, cash and informal care: European perspectives and dilemmas', *Journal of Social Policy* 24 (1): 31–52.

UNHCR (2000) *The State of the World's Refugees.* Oxford: Clarendon.

UNICEF (2000) *A League Table of Child Poverty in Rich Nations.* New York: UNICEF.

Veale, A., L. Palaudaries and C. Gibbons (2003) *Separated Children Seeking Asylum in Ireland.* Dublin: Irish Refugee Council.

Virtue, Society and the God', pp. 68–91 in I. Bacik and M. O'Connell (eds), *Crime and Poverty in Ireland.* Dublin: Round Hall, Sweet & Maxwell.

Walker, A. (1993) 'Community care policy: from consensus to conflict', pp. 204–6 in J. Borna et al. (eds), *Community Care: A Reader.* Basingstoke: Macmillan.

Walsh, B. M. and A. Murphy (1997b) *Unemployment, Non-participation and Labour Market Slack among Irish Males.* Dublin: UCD Working Paper Series.

Walsh, D. and P. Sexton (1999) *An Empirical Study of Community Service Orders in Ireland for the Department of Justice, Equality & Law Reform.* Dublin: Stationery Office.

Walsh, P., M. Rafferty and C. Lynch (1991) 'The Open Road project: real jobs for people with mental handicap', *International Journal of Rehabilitation Research* 14: 151–61.

Walton, Lord (1995) 'Dilemmas of life and death: part 1', *Journal of the Royal Society of Medicine* 88: 311–15.

Ward, E. (1996) 'Ireland's refugee policies and the case of the Hungarians', *Irish Studies in International Affairs* 7: 131–41.

Ward, E. (1998) 'Ireland and refugees/asylum seekers: 1922–1996', pp. 41–8 in R. Lentin (ed.), *The Expanding Nation: Towards a Multi-Ethnic Ireland.* Dublin: Department of Sociology, TCD.

Ward, M. (1980) 'Marginality and militancy, Cumann na mBan', in A. Morgan and B. Purdie (eds), *Ireland, Divided Nation, Divided Class.* London: Ink Links.

Ward, P. (1997) *The Child Care Act 1991.* Dublin: Round Hall Sweet & Maxwell.

Ward, S. (1994) 'A basic income system for Ireland', in *Towards an Adequate Income For All.* Dublin: CORI.

Watson, D. and J. Williams (2003) *Irish National Survey of Housing Quality 2001–2002.* Dublin: ESRI and Department of the Environment, Heritage and Local Government.

Webb, A. and G. Wistow (1987) *Social Work, Social Care and Social Planning: The Personal Social Services since Seebohm.* London: Longman.

West, C. (1999) *The Cornel West Reader.* New York: Basic Civitas Books.

Westin, C. (1999) 'Regional analysis of refugee movements: origins and responses', pp. 24–45 in A. Ager (ed.), *Refugees: Perspectives on the Experience of Forced Migration.* London: Continuum.

Whelan C., S. Hannan and S. Creighton (1991) *Unemployment, Poverty and Psychological Distress.* Dublin, ESRI.

Whelan, B. J., R. Breen, T. Callan and B. Nolan (1992) *A Study of the Employment Possibilities of the Long-term Unemployed.* Dublin: ESRI (unpublished).

Whitehead, M. (1992) *The Health Divide: Inequalities in Health.* London: Penguin.

Whitfield, D. (1997) *Tackling the Tag: The Electronic Monitoring of Offenders.* London: Waterside Press.

WHO (1993) *Health for All by the Year 2000.* Geneva: WHO.

Whyte, J. (1980) *Church and State in Modern Ireland, 1923–1979.* Dublin: Gill & Macmillan.

Wiley, M. and B. Merriman (1996) *Women and Health Care in Ireland.* Dublin: Oak Tree.

Wiley, M. and R. B. Fetter (1990) *Measuring Activity and Costs in Irish Hospitals: A Study of Hospital Case Mix,* ESRI General Research Series no. 147. Dublin: ESRI.

Williams, F. (1999) 'Good-enough principles for welfare', *Journal of Social Policy* 28 (4): 667–87.

Williams, J. and S. Gorby. (2002) *Counted in 2002: the Report of the Assessment of Homelessness in Dublin.* Dublin: ESRI and the Homeless Agency.

Wolfensberger, W. (1972) *The Principle of Normalisation in Human Services.* Toronto: National Institute on Mental Retardation.

Wolfensberger, W. (1983) 'Social role valorisation: a proposed new term for the principle of normalization', *Mental Retardation* 21 (6): 234–9.

Wolfensberger, W. and L. Glenn (1975) *Program Analysis of Service Systems,* 3rd edn. Toronto: National Institute for Mental Retardation.

Woods, M. (1994) 'Drug using parents and their children: the experience of a voluntary/non-statutory project', *Irish Social Worker* 12 (2): 10.

Working Group on a Courts Commission (1998) *Fifth Report: Drug Courts.* Dublin: Stationery Office.

Working Group on Elder Abuse (2002) *Protecting Our Future* Dublin: Stationery Office.

Working Group on Inequalities in Health (1980) *The Black Report.* London: HMSO.

Working Party on Drug Abuse (1971) *Report.* Dublin: Stationery Office.

Working Party on Services for the Elderly (1988) *The Years Ahead: A Policy for the Elderly.* Dublin: Stationery Office.

Wren, Maev-Ann (2003) *Unhealthy State: Anatomy of a Sick Society.* Dublin: New Island.

Wyn, J. and R. White (1997) *Rethinking Youth.* Australia: Allen & Unwin.

Yeates, N. (1997) 'Gender, informal care and social welfare: the case of the carer's allowance', *Administration* 45 (2): 21–43.

Young, P., I. O'Donnell and E.Clare (2001) *Crime in Ireland.* Dublin: Stationery Office.

Index